D0085034

WOMEN IN POWER

Arts Insights showcases current research in the social sciences, humanities, and social work.

An initiative of McGill's Faculty of Arts, Arts Insights brings together research in the Social Sciences, Humanities, and Social Work. Reflective of the range of expertise and interests represented by the Faculty of Arts at McGill, Arts Insights seeks manuscripts that bring an interdisciplinary perspective to the discussion of ideas, issues, and debates that deepen and expand our understanding of human interaction, such as works dealing with society and change, or languages, literatures, and cultures and the relationships among them. Of particular interest are manuscripts that reflect the work of research collaborations involving McGill faculty and their colleagues in universities that are part of McGill's international affiliation network.

Arts Insights will publish two titles a year in English. The editors prefer original manuscripts but may consider the English-language translations of works that have already appeared in another language.

Series editors: Nathalie Cooke, Richard Schultz, Wendy Thomson

Projecting Canada
Government Policy and Documentary Film at the National Film Board
Zoe Druick

Beyond Wilderness
The Group of Seven, Canadian Identity, and Contemporary Art
Edited by John O'Brian and Peter White

Mordecai Richler
Leaving St Urbain
Reinhold Kramer

Women in Power
The Personalities and Leadership Styles of Indira Gandhi, Gold Meir, and Margaret Thatcher
Blema Steinberg

Women in Power

*The Personalities and Leadership Styles
of Indira Gandhi, Golda Meir,
and Margaret Thatcher*

BLEMA S. STEINBERG

McGill-Queen's University Press
Montreal & Kingston · London · Ithaca

© McGill-Queen's University Press 2008
ISBN 978-0-7735-3356-1

Legal deposit second quarter 2008
Bibliothèque nationale du Québec

Printed in Canada on acid-free paper that is 100% ancient forest free
(100% post-consumer recycled), processed chlorine free.
Reprinted 2008

McGill-Queen's University Press acknowledges the support of the Canada Council
for the Arts for our publishing program. We also acknowledge the financial support
of the Government of Canada through the Book Publishing Industry Development
Program (BPIDP) for our publishing activities.

Library and Archives Canada Cataloguing in Publication

Steinberg, Blema S.
    Women in power : the personalities and leadership styles of Indira
Gandhi, Golda Meir, and Margaret Thatcher / Blema S. Steinberg.

Includes bibliographical references and index.
ISBN 907-0-7735-3356-1

1. Gandhi, Indira, 1917–1984. 2. Meir, Golda, 1898–1978. 3. Thatcher, Margaret.
4. Leadership in women. 5. Personality and politics. 6. Leadership – Psychological
aspects. 7. Women prime ministers – Biography. I. Title.

D839.5.S72 2008   303.3'4082   C2007-906360-8

This book was typeset by Interscript in 10.5/13 Sabon.

To the memory of my late mother and father, Dorita Bacal Salomon and Moe George Salomon, whose life-long support and encouragement made it possible for me to become the woman I am,

and

To Margaret Thatcher and the memory of Indira Gandhi and Golda Meir, whose lives and careers have paved the way for other women to follow in their footsteps and become political leaders

Contents

Figures and Tables

Acknowledgments

This book has been nearly ten years in the making. Along the way my intellectual debts have been numerous. Foremost among them is the debt I owe Professor Aubrey Immelman, whose presentation at an annual meeting of the International Society for Political Psychology introduced me to the research of Theodore Millon and his role in broadening the scope of personality traits, based on the *Diagnostic and Statistical Manual of the American Psychiatric Association* (DSM–IV), to include normal as well as pathological variations. Immelman then developed a conceptual framework and methodology that permits an at-a-distance analysis of political personalities based on primary- and secondary-source materials. His approach provided the intellectual foundations for my study of the personality profiles of Indira Gandhi, Golda Meir, and Margaret Thatcher.

The research of professors Margaret Hermann and Juliet Kaarbo also stimulated me to think about leadership styles in prime-ministerial systems of government and suggested a way of categorizing that behaviour. Instrumental, too, were the editors of the journal of *Political Psychology* and their readers, who pushed me to think through the conceptual problems and the technical issues in my approach to the study of personality and leadership style.

My two doctoral research assistants, Spyridon Kotsovilis and Jeffrey Osweiler, not only performed the usual tasks of retrieving library materials, extracting, and coding but also served as colleagues in the development of various hypotheses as well as an instrument for measuring leadership styles. Each of them carefully read and critiqued every chapter with great care and forced me to clarify my ideas and improve the writing style. Curtis Fahey, my copy editor, once again did a superb job tightening the manuscript and pointing out factual omissions. Although I alone am responsible for this final version, there is no doubt that it is infinitely better as a result of his efforts. I also wish to thank Dianne

Tiefensee for her fine work on the index and Neda Hadjikhani for her invaluable help in proofreading the manuscript. At McGill-Queen's University Press, Philip Cercone, executive director and senior editor, was unfailing in his support and encouragement; Joan McGilvray, co-ordinating editor, and Ligy Alakkattussery, editorial assistant, were also very helpful in their respective roles. My deepest thanks go to all of them. Mircea Radita, my computer guru, not only quickly repaired the usual glitches but also repeatedly calmed an anxious author who was certain that "this time" a portion of the manuscript had been irretrievably lost.

I also wish to acknowledge the excellent assistance of a number of individuals who translated materials from Hebrew into English: Gad Elbaz, Dov Okunef, Janie Ben-Shach, and Dotan Shenhav.

Given the relative paucity of research materials available for the study of Golda Meir, as compared to Indira Gandhi and Margaret Thatcher, I was extremely fortunate to be able to interview many of Meir's former colleagues in the Labor Party and in the government. Many of these contacts were facilitated by Professor Shai Feldman, whom I met at a small dinner party hosted by the Canadian ambassador to Israel and his wife, Don and Jill Sinclair, and I am grateful for his help and their warm hospitality.

I offer my deepest appreciation to Shimshon Arad, Eytan Ben Tsur, the late Simcha Dinitz, Arie "Lova" Eliav, Michael Harish, Shlomo Hillel, Yitzhak Navon, Chaim Nivon, Ya'acov Nitzan, Shimon Peres, Viktor Shemtov, Gad Ya'akobi, Moshe Yegar, and Zvi Zamir for their willingness to be interviewed and to speak openly. Professors David Harmon and Meron (Ronnie) Medzini also provided helpful insights into Meir's character. In Israel, Chaim Zohar assisted in the research, and Professor Reuven Hazan of the Hebrew University in Jerusalem kindly took the time and interest to find another research assistant for me. As well, the Canadian chargé d'affaires, Henry Kolatacz, and his wife, Anne, Avi and Marty Pazner, and Amitai and Margalit Ziv entertained me in their homes. I thank them for their kindness and generosity.

For his unfailing love and support, I am grateful to my husband, Arnold, who cheerfully accepted my long hours in front of the computer, which extended even to evenings, weekends, and holidays. And to my children, Margot, Donna, and Adam, I now promise my full attention when you call, not the half-distracted voice of someone whose mind is otherwise engaged with "the book."

WOMEN IN POWER

Introduction

Over the past fifty years of political leadership around the globe, Indira Gandhi, Golda Meir, and Margaret Thatcher have emerged as giants among the most senior elected members of government. As historians begin selecting this period's important political figures, they will observe that each of these three women, whose lives and careers were rich and eventful, left an indelible stamp on her state's political, social, and economic development.

Currently, excellent biographies of all three women exist, filled with important insights about their early lives and their leadership. Few attempts have been made, however, to examine female prime ministers as a group of leaders who have acquired power and shared similar responsibilities; those studies that have explored female leaders in both presidential and prime ministerial systems have been mostly descriptive – biographical accounts with some attention paid to the role that gender played in their exercise of leadership.[1] This emphasis on individual biography at the expense of collective experience is not surprising, given that relatively few women have risen to positions of political leadership. In a cross-cultural comparison of world leaders, beginning in the 1970s, leaders were found to be "overwhelmingly male; less than .5% were women."[2] While these numbers have improved significantly since that time – close to eighty women have been elected as either president or prime minister since 1945[3] – male dominance continues in most areas of the world.

It is this gap in the literature – the lack of attention to the collective experience of women leaders – that this book addresses. Its main focus is the relationship between the personality profiles of Indira Gandhi, Golda Meir, and Margaret Thatcher and their respective leadership styles. Although personality profiling of interesting political figures, such as presidential candidates or terrorist leaders, does exist, there have been few systematic attempts, as yet, to explore the way in which leaders' personality profiles can affect and shape their leadership styles. Furthermore, this book's investigation of the role of three female leaders represents an effort to redress the predominant emphasis on male leaders in presidential systems.

But why Gandhi, Meir, and Thatcher? I chose to examine these three figures for a number of reasons, some less obvious than others. To begin, each woman had an extraordinary political career, often amidst political upheaval, crisis, and war, and their impact on their respective states was enormous. But they also lived interesting and, in some ways, comparable lives before attaining high office. The personality profile of each woman, forged in these early years, was distinctive and its effect on subsequent leadership behaviour deserves a thorough examination. From a comparative perspective, I selected these three women since they represented both the developed and developing worlds, old and newly created states, and large and small states. Apart from their gender, what is also common to all of them is that they operated within a system of parliamentary government, arguably more complex and dynamic, as well as volatile, than a presidential one. Many studies have examined the nature of prime ministerial leadership, but few have looked at female leadership in parliamentary systems of government through a comparative lens.

Beyond these points of convergence among these three women, I was also intrigued that all of them shared a much greater number of attributes than meets the eye. For example, their family composition: none of them had an older brother; Indira was an only child, Golda had an older and a younger sister, and Margaret had an older sister. In a previously published article, I showed the impact that the gender of siblings can exert on the career trajectory of women.[4] In the absence of an older male sibling, girls are more likely to receive encouragement at home to explore male-dominated realms of activity, including politics.

Although Indira's father, Jawaharlal Nehru, the first post-colonial prime minister of India, never explicitly groomed her for a political role, the death of his wife and the absence of any sons made Indira not only his hostess and travelling companion but increasingly his confidante during his tenure as prime minister. Given the Nehru connection, from that point on, a political future for Indira was at least a possibility.

Golda was the second daughter in a family of three girls. Her father was a largely unsuccessful breadwinner, who emigrated from Russia to Milwaukee, and her mother was a strong-willed, hard-driving woman who largely supported the family from the earnings of a small grocery store. Her older sister, Sheyna, whom she admired, provided something of a male role model; she was politically active in the Zionist movement, and Golda followed in her footsteps. Had Sheyna been a boy, he, like her father, might have tried to discourage Golda's political interests and activism as unsuitable pursuits for a young woman.

Margaret was also the second daughter, but in a family of two girls. Her father, Alfred Roberts, seems to have anointed her the "honorary" son, and, while her older sister and mother were left to read the novels that Roberts borrowed from the library for them, he urged Margaret to read non-fiction and science. He also attended lectures with Margaret and encouraged her interest in politics. As a member of the town council, and later mayor of Grantham, her father provided Margaret with a supportive role model as well as a conceptual framework for her thinking about economics.

Another interesting point of convergence among the subjects of my study is that none of them was considered to be intellectually gifted or particularly creative, though each was seen as hard-working and extremely competent. Indira Gandhi spent a couple of years at Oxford but was asked to leave after twice failing her Latin exam. Though Golda Meir was an excellent student who finished high school, she terminated her education after almost a year of teacher training in order to emigrate to Israel. She was never known either for the subtlety of her mind or for her appreciation of intellectual arguments. Margaret Thatcher was the best educated of the three women; she received a bachelor of science degree in chemistry and then went on to complete a law degree.

Another commonality among them is that all three women married well before they became prime minister, but with varying degrees of success. Indira Gandhi's husband, Feroze, resented her public role, given his own political aspirations, and was extremely competitive with her. Golda Meir's husband, Morris, also begrudged her eminent public presence because it involved her in a life away from him in an arena of activity – politics – in which he had little interest. Both women separated from, but never divorced, their husbands, and both were deeply saddened by their spouses' early deaths and their own failure to find happiness within their marriages. Margaret Thatcher's excellent marriage and her supportive husband stands in sharp contrast. Denis Thatcher was quite content to have Margaret pursue her own career interests while he remained largely out of the limelight, involved with his successful business interests and passion for golf.

Further, each of our female leaders had two children. Desperately lonely as a child, Indira Gandhi, perhaps not surprisingly, lavished a great deal of attention and concern on her sons, Rajiv and Sanjay. She would have loved to have had more children, but her husband was content with two. As a woman with few close friends and confidants, Indira came to rely, increasingly, on her children and to permit Sanjay, her youngest son – whose personality was most like that of her husband – to run roughshod over her and engage in ruinous financial adventures, corruption, and authoritarian behaviour. Indira's lenient treatment of Sanjay has been attributed, in part, to her unconscious guilt over the break-up of her marriage – guilt that Sanjay did not hesitate to exploit. The news of Sanjay's death in an airplane accident in June 1980 – he was piloting his own private plane at the time – was received across India, and particularly among some of Indira's supporters, with a clear sigh of relief. After his death, Rajiv, the older son, who was an airline pilot, was reluctantly cajoled into politics by his mother and succeeded her as prime minister after her assassination in 1984, only to meet a tragically similar fate in 1991.

Margaret Thatcher's children were twins, a son, Mark, and a daughter, Carol. Having had two children, she never evinced any desire for more. Thatcher was fortunate to have had a capable nanny who essentially raised the children until they attended boarding school. Carol developed into a responsible young woman and, after completing her law degree like Margaret, moved to Australia to escape her mother's long shadow. In sharp contrast, Thatcher's son Mark grew up to be a handsome, irresponsible young man who, like Gandhi's son Sanjay, used his mother's political connections to finance a series of unsuccessful business ventures. Interestingly, like Gandhi, Thatcher was never really able to discipline her son, who remained a source of considerable embarrassment for the family.

As a young woman, Golda Meir was a stay-at-home mother for her son, Menachem, and daughter, Sarah. To help clothe the children and pay for school fees, she took in washing from the school the children attended. Financially, more children were not an option. Later, her position with the Jewish Agency required her to travel abroad for months at a time, and, although she was torn between her motherly feelings and her sense of duty, her career won out. During her absence, the children were cared for by her mother, her sister Sheyna, and Golda's husband, Morris, who came from Tel Aviv every weekend to be with them. Sarah joined a kibbutz at a young age and Menachem became a professional musician – an accomplished cellist with the Israel philharmonic orchestra. Despite Golda's feelings of guilt about her maternal absences, neither child was cosseted by their mother. In fact, in one instance (on the eve of the Yom Kippur War) when the temptation presented itself for Golda to assuage the guilt by warning her daughter to leave her kibbutz, since she knew it to be in the path of an impending attack by the Egyptian army, she refused to indulge herself. Golda considered this to be privileged information, and, if the entire kibbutz could not be told, then neither could any members of her family.

Another interesting aspect of their lives is that, prior to their becoming prime minister, both Meir and Thatcher had significant careers in their respective parties and as members of their respective governments. Golda Meir held a number of important positions within the Labor Party and served as Israeli ambassador to the Soviet Union, minister of labour, and foreign minister before she became prime minister. Margaret Thatcher served in several shadow cabinet positions and as minister of education before she became government leader and then prime minister. Indira Gandhi's trajectory to the office of prime minister was a function, in part, of her dynastic inheritance; like so many other women leaders in South and Southeast Asia, she was a blood relative, in this case the daughter, of a deceased leader. As part of the cultural traditions of this region, being a relative – a wife, daughter, or even daughter-in-law of a former leader – provided an important access to power that offset any perceived disadvantages in being a woman.[5] Indira, moreover, witnessed her parents' leading role in the struggle for freedom against the British, and was exposed to politics as her father's hostess while he was the first prime minister of India. While she had been active as a member of the Congress Working Committee (CWC), and its parliamentary board, it was only after her father's death that Nehru's successor, Lal Bahadur Shastri, invited her to join the government; it was an expression of appreciation to the late Nehru for his previous political support. At that juncture, in 1964, Indira stood for a parliamentary seat in the upper house and was elected. Prime Minister Shastri's death two years later led to her selection as the leader of the governing party and then her election, in her own right, as prime minister.

None of our three women leaders was considered the most qualified candidate for the office of the prime minister by their colleagues at the time that each was elected leader of the party by their respective caucuses. Each emerged victorious as a result of political infighting. In the case of Gandhi, with the sudden death of Prime Minister Shastri, some members of the Congress Party, the "Syndicate," were determined to block the ascendancy of Morarji Desai. Indira was seen as the candidate most likely to defeat Desai and as someone whom they could then manipulate.

Another sudden death also catapulted Golda Meir into the prime minister's office. When Prime Minister Levi Eshkol suffered a fatal heart attack, a succession battle between Moshe Dayan and Yigal Allon loomed large. Meir, who by that time had retired from government, was persuaded to return as interim prime minister until elections could be held. But she chose to stay on and contest the elections as the leader of the Labor Party.

Thatcher's path to power was similar. After nine years as Conservative Party leader, Edward Heath faced considerable dissatisfaction within the Conservative caucus, but there were few challengers prepared to take him on. No one thought that Thatcher's chances of unseating Heath were promising. The entire shadow cabinet was behind him, but, in a vote of the caucus, he lost on a first ballot and chose to resign. Although four other Conservatives challenged Thatcher, she was elected by a convincing majority.

As their respective careers took off, it became abundantly clear that both Golda Meir and Margaret Thatcher were "conviction" politicians. Each had well-defined goals and possessed unshakeable convictions which they clung to tenaciously during the course of their years in the prime minister's office. For Meir, it was a particular definition of Israel's security which made it difficult for her to be responsive to Arab peace overtures. She had no patience for Palestinian nationalism and believed that a Palestinian state already existed, and that it was called Jordan. For Thatcher, her core beliefs centred on a free-market economy, a balanced budget, and the dangers of powerful trade unions. In contrast, Gandhi was a combination of pragmatist and opportunist. She possessed no fixed principles but moved from socialism to the advocacy of a free-market economy and then to populism – whatever seemed likely to keep India afloat economically, and herself in power.

As prime ministers, all three women enjoyed a reputation as strong-willed, tough, and resilient. They dominated their respective cabinets of male colleagues almost totally; their strength and determination led to each being described, at various times, as "the only man in a cabinet of women." Their ministers were careful how, when, and where they voiced their dissent; opposing viewpoints rarely received a sympathetic hearing. In the cases of Gandhi and Thatcher, membership in the cabinet became a function of loyalty to the prime minister, while ministers from the Labor Alignment in Meir's cabinet knew that she had a major role in rank-ordering the list of candidates for the Knesset and so were careful not to challenge her too openly.

Similarly, each of the three women faced a major war during their tenure in office; for Indira Gandhi, it was the India-Pakistan War in 1971; for Golda Meir, the 1973 Yom Kippur War; and for Margaret Thatcher, the Falkland Islands War in 1983. In the careers of both Gandhi and Thatcher, their respective wars were essential in strengthening and solidifying their hold on power. Gandhi's handling of the India-Pakistan War in 1971, which saw the creation of an independent state of Bangladesh out of former East Pakistan, revealed her patience, foresight, and diplomatic skills, earning her worldwide respect. Until the Falklands War, Thatcher faced almost certain defeat at the polls as a result of a floundering economy; however, her firm and resolute behaviour over the Argentinian invasion of the Falklands/Malvinas, coupled

with the success of the British Navy in the conflict, placed her in an unassailable position within the Conservative Party and the country.

Although Israel was ultimately able to defeat the Arab states in the
1973 Yom Kippur War, the battlefield losses and the government's
faulty strategic assumptions about the conditions under which Egypt
would attack led to widespread dissatisfaction with the Meir government. The formal state inquiry that followed exonerated Meir of any
wrongdoing in the period leading up to the 1973 war, but Labor Party
members and the public in general, shocked that Israel had come so
close to disaster, felt that it was time for a change of leadership. In this
instance, war weakened the prime minister rather than strengthening
her hold on power.

Another intriguing aspect about the subjects of this study is that none
of them can be considered feminists. Rather than viewing themselves in a
feminist mantle, they believed, instead, that their accomplishments were
based on hard work and thus saw no reason for actions to promote
women in politics. There were no women with full cabinet rank in either
Gandhi's or Meir's cabinet, and Thatcher had only one woman in a minor portfolio; women's issues, in general, were not part of their political
agenda. During Gandhi's time in office, the condition of the majority of
Indian women worsened, as reflected in literacy and employment rates
and the declining sex ratio as a result of the ongoing practice of killing
female infants.[6]

Thatcher's political agenda was also glaringly lacking in proposals
designed to advance the cause of women's rights in Britain. In fact,
Thatcher often enjoined women to stay at home, raise families, and assume traditional roles. She deplored the stridency of the feminists and
thought they had damaged the cause of women "by making us out to be
something we're not."[7] Golda Meir, similarly, was not a great admirer
of "the bra-burning" type of feminism, but she did think that the work
done by female labour activists in training young city-bred women for
life in the agricultural settlements throughout Palestine was exemplary.
In keeping with her general aversion to issues not directly related to the
struggle for Israel's security, however, she simply ignored issues of bias
or discrimination against women.[8]

Gender, however, can have a significant impact on leadership behaviour in two other ways. First, others – both allies and adversaries – may
perceive gender as salient and change their behaviour accordingly. Although she was Nehru's daughter, Indira Gandhi, to a large extent, owed
her selection as prime minister to her being female. As a woman, she was
initially assumed to be malleable, non-threatening, and without real ambition, content to serve as interim leader only. But, once in office, she
had to deal with male hostility directed at her gender. The disrespect she

experienced ran the gamut from despair over the presence of a woman leader to sexist overtones in the contempt expressed by her critics.[9] The fact that Indira Gandhi was a woman in the office of the prime minister seems to have made the president of Pakistan at that time, Yahya Khan, more bellicose and rigid than he might otherwise have been.[10]

Margaret Thatcher's political career was advanced because the Conservative Party felt that it needed a woman in government as part of its electoral appeal. But public opposition to her policies as education minister was frequently phrased in offensive sexist language. Once she became prime minister, Thatcher's total domination of her cabinet was aided by the inability of many of the men in it to deal with an assertive, bullying woman, especially one in a position of political superiority.[11]

Gender seems to have played a secondary role in shaping Meir's public career, aside from the mayoral election she lost because of explicit bias on the part of the religious parties. As prime minister, she does not seem to have experienced the direct effects of whatever gender bias that may have existed.[12] Support for her, as well as opposition to her, was based on her policies, not her gender.

The more common effects of female gender supposedly include the way in which female leaders develop a set of strategies and a repertoire of behaviours for dealing with both challenges and opportunities. It has been suggested that the dominant, assertive, competitive approach is a male style of leadership, whereas the female style is relationship-oriented.[13] I intend to question both ideas, for, as we shall see, the personality profiles of all three women leaders under examination score high in the dominant and assertive categories reflected in their exercise of power. It is an intriguing aspect of my findings that none of them was particularly concerned with exhibiting cooperative or empathic styles of leadership behaviour.

Yet it may well be that "to survive [women political leaders] must on the one hand make themselves like the stereotyped male – aggressive, competitive, ruthless, authoritarian – and on the other, continue to play the good woman role."[14] Indira Gandhi took great pains to stress that motherhood was the most important part of her life and that she scheduled her appointments to be available for Rajiv and Sanjay when they returned home from school. Gandhi also used gender imagery in a purposeful manner. She loved clothes, and her public appearances in beautifully coloured saris enhanced her appeal to the masses, as did her successful efforts to define herself as Mother India, the mother of her country. After the Bangladesh war, Mrs Gandhi was hailed as the Hindu goddess Durga and worshiped as the incarnation of *shakti*, images of female valour that she manipulated when needed.[15]

Throughout her own career, Margaret Thatcher used a variety of different approaches to her female gender as circumstances dictated. Early on, she assumed the public role of devoted housewife and mother, though in fact she spent little time at either task.[16] Later, she assumed the roles of mother to the nation, firm nanny, wartime dominatrix, and, still later, androgynous leader. She once remarked that she did not notice she was a woman: "I regard myself as the Prime Minister."[17] However, she also used her gender manipulatively, "sometimes relying on feminine wiles, sometimes as nanny, sometimes as bully, sometimes to coax, cajole and flatter, but always in a calculated manner."[18] Her femininity, in conjunction with her abrasive personality, enabled Thatcher to silence her opponents in the cabinet and to intimidate them in ways similar, they felt, to their nannies' treatment of them as children. At the same time, Thatcher used her feminine charms with great effect on a number of world leaders such as Ronald Reagan, whom she had under her spell. For example, she was successful in dissuading the American president from dealing away the U.S. nuclear arsenal in his conversations with the Soviet Union's Mikhail Gorbachev at the Reykjavik summit.

As a young woman separated from her husband, Golda had a number of intimate relationships with powerful figures in the Labor Party which may have helped her progress up the party ladder, although that was certainly not their express purpose. Unlike Thatcher and Gandhi, she never presented herself as a devoted housewife and mother; it is characteristic and telling that all her life she suffered from enormous guilt over the extent to which she left the care of her children to others. As prime minister, at the age of seventy-one, she was seen by the public as a grandmotherly figure, but it was not an image she deliberately manipulated for political advantage.

As important as the singular effects of gender are on leadership behaviour, they should not be overstated. Leadership style takes its shape and inspiration from a multiplicity of sources, among which the patterns of one's personality are the most consistent and crucial. Indeed, in the case of our three women leaders, the numerous aspects/patterns of the personalities developed through their earlier life experiences were carried into the prime ministerial office and translated into their particular leadership styles. Hence, it is to these personality patterns and linkages to leadership styles that the bulk of this study will be devoted.

In my examination of the personality profiles of Gandhi, Meir, and Thatcher, the following issues will be addressed. First, how can the personality of each of these women be systematically described – what type of personality profile can be constructed for each of them and what are its distinctive attributes? To assess the role of personality, I relied on

Theodore Millon's model of personality, the Millon Inventory of Diagnostic Criteria (MIDC). It is essentially an index that formally charts and scores twelve personality patterns across eight attribute domains. The MIDC personality inventory was used to code diagnostically relevant information based on a detailed extraction of material contained in major biographies and autobiographies of Gandhi, Meir, and Thatcher.[19]

Second, what explains the personality profiles of these three women from a psychological perspective? In short, how did they perceive their environment, and how did those perceptions shape their expressive behaviour, their interpersonal conduct, their cognitive style, their mood/temperament, and their self-image?

Third, what is the nature of the leadership style that each woman demonstrated during her years in office as prime minister? To assess leadership style, ten leadership style variables were chosen to measure leadership behaviour and materials from primary and secondary sources were extracted and coded.[20]

And, finally, what links can be postulated to exist between a leader's personality profile and her leadership style? In this study, a number of theoretical links were hypothesized to exist between particular personality patterns and leadership-style behaviours.[21]

The book is divided into three main parts. Within this framework, Part One examines Indira Gandhi; Part Two, Golda Meir; and Part Three, Margaret Thatcher. Chapters 1, 2, and 3 examine Indira Gandhi's life, her personality profile, and her leadership style; chapters 4, 5, and 6 explore the same issues for Golda Meir; and chapters 7, 8, and 9 provide a similar analysis for Margaret Thatcher. The purpose of the biographical chapters, 1, 4, and 7, is to provide the reader with a context in which the personality profile and the leadership style can then be examined. Some of the material that is used to illustrate both the personality dimensions of the profile and the leadership-style categories refers back to events mentioned in the biography but the treatment is different, that is, it applies highlights from the leader's life to a systematic framework to arrive at a methodologically justifiable portrait of her individual life – her personality and leadership and the relationship between them.

In the Conclusion, the links between the personality profiles and leadership styles of the three prime ministers are compared and contrasted, as well as the extent to which the initial hypotheses concerning the relationship between personality profiles and leadership style are supported by the empirical data. Ideally, knowledge of a leader's personality before she becomes prime minister should give us some tools to predict the likelihood of certain types of leadership behaviour and the absence of others. The extent to which this premise is true, as well as its implications for leadership selection, is addressed in this section.

   The book ends with an appendix, itself divided into four sections. In the first section, the concept of personality patterns and their measurement across a number of domains resulting in the creation of a personality profile are explored. The second section examines the concept of leadership style, the dimensions that have been selected to assess this behavior, and their measurement. Hypotheses concerning the expected relationships between various personality profiles and leadership styles are explored in the third section, while the last section explores the extent to which personality patterns are predictive of leadership style.

PART ONE

Indira Gandhi

Indira Gandhi: From Prime Minister's Daughter to Prime Minister

Loved and reviled during the course of her tenure as India's third prime minister (1966–77 and 1980–84), Indira Gandhi remains a continuing subject of interest and fascination, as witnessed by the continued emergence of new biographies. An opinion poll on who was the "best Prime Minister India has ever had," conducted by the *India Today* news magazine in September 2001, gave Gandhi 41 per cent of the vote, while her father, Jawaharlal Nehru, polled no more that 13 per cent.[1]

Born into India's most prominent political family on 19 November 1917, in the Anand Bhawan family home in Allahabad, Indira Nehru was an only child. Her family was extremely affluent, although she remembers little of this.[2] As a child, Indira was very attached to her mother, whom she saw as the unfair target of some hostility from the rest of the Nehru family because of her simplicity and deep religious feelings. The more sophisticated Nehru women, especially Jawaharlal Nehru's mother, Swarupani, and his sister, Nan (later Vijayalaksmi Pandit), mocked Kamala, whom they did not believe was good enough for Jawaharlal. Indira's father was quite stern in her early years, and a stickler for physical exercise and keeping fit. She had to run every day, and not just run, but run with style.[3] Indira's schooling was frequently interrupted, and she was primarily taught at home through her twelfth year. In a 1972 interview, she described a lonely, insecure childhood that had taught her to be self-reliant: "If you only knew what it did to me to have lived in that house where the police were bursting in to take everyone away! I certainly didn't have a happy and serene childhood. I was a thin, sickly, nervous little girl. And after the police came, I'd be left alone for weeks, months, to get along as best I could. I learned very soon to get along by myself."[4]

Indira became immersed in politics at an early age when in 1920 her father and mother decided to join Mohandâs (Mahatma) Gandhi and the "Quit India" movement and give up their luxurious lifestyle for *khadi* (hand spun and handwoven cloth) and simple Indian food. The program also included the boycott of titles, of government-owned, or aided, schools and colleges, of law courts, of legislatures, and of foreign goods, as well as resistance to unjust laws and a willingness to suffer imprisonment peacefully. Members of the Nehru family were among the first to be arrested; before Indira was thirteen, she saw her father convicted and sentenced to jail five times and her mother also spent considerable time in prison. Although prison-going was a matter of pride, Indira noted that "it was very disturbing to the rest of the family."[5] From an early age, she worried about the British, the police who confiscated Nehru property when her parents refused to pay fines, the disapproval of relatives who disliked her mother's encouragement of her father's political activities, and her paternal grandfather's work along the same lines. All of this caused Indira to become rather independent. "I felt that rather than relying on my parents, it was my business to protect them from all this as far as I could."[6] It also contributed to her becoming politically involved. Even as a youngster, Indira's games were primarily political. She would divide her dolls into rival teams of freedom-fighters and baton-wielding police and arrange a confrontation between the two. Needless to say, the freedom-fighters would always win. She would also climb on tables and deliver thundering speeches to the bemused servants of the household, repeating slogans she had picked up from her elders.[7]

Throughout Indira's childhood, her mother suffered from poor health, and a diagnosis of tuberculosis led Jawaharlal, accompanied by Indira, who was then nine years old, to take Kamala to Switzerland for treatment in 1926–27. Returning to Allahabad, Indira attended St Mary's Convent School, where her adolescent years were marked by her mother's deteriorating health and separation from her father because of his continuing imprisonment. In 1931 Kamala was also arrested; as president of the Allahabad Congress Committee, she had organized women to picket liquor stores and foreign cloth shops. Left out of Congress activities because of her age, Indira organized children into the Vanar Sena ("Monkey Army," from the Indian epic *Ramayana*), which served as Congress auxiliaries, bringing water to demonstrators, smuggling messages to Congress leaders, and spying on police stations.[8]

The death of her paternal grandfather, Motilal, on 6 February 1931 meant the disappearance of a protective presence for Indira, and, given the constant uncertainty of her family life, it became difficult for her to stay at Allahabad and study at St Mary's. She was sent to a residential and experimental school in Poona in the western Indian hills where she was utterly lonely and miserable. When her father was released from jail in 1933 and went to see her, she returned home with him. Indira then went to Santiniketan, an institution started and presided over by Rabindranath Tagore, a poet-philosopher and Nobel Laureate. Indira grew extremely fond of Santiniketan, but her happiness there was cut short when her mother's health worsened and doctors decreed that she should be taken to Switzerland. With Nehru in prison, the seventeen-year-old Indira immediately took over the responsibility of conveying her mother to the Swiss sanitarium. It was there, in February 1936, that Kamala Nehru died. Indira was grief-stricken; her mother's death at the age of thirty-six left an enormous void in her life.[9] Years later, when asked how she remembered her mother, Indira responded softly with half-closed eyes, "'I loved her deeply.'"[10]

Following this family tragedy, it was decided that Indira would continue her much interrupted education in England, rather than the United States, at the Badminton School near Bristol. Indira preferred England, because Feroze Gandhi, a young man whom she had known from the early days of the freedom struggle in Allahabad, and who had helped her look after Kamala during her last illness, was a student at the London School of Economics. After Badminton, Indira attended Somerville College, Oxford, where she read modern history. She loved the city of Oxford, but her heart was not in her studies. One winter she was taken ill with pleurisy and had to be sent to Switzerland to recuperate. By the time of her return journey to Oxford, the Second World War had begun, and, shortly afterwards, Indira announced her intention of leaving and returning home as soon as a passage could be secured. Feroze Gandhi, who had been courting Indira assiduously, decided to go back to India with her.[11]

Indira's stated reasons for leaving Somerville – that she believed formal education to be a waste of time, that she was in poor health, and, that, in any case, she wished to be with her father – appeared credible. They were fostered by the official profile of her issued after she became prime minister, as well as by numerous biographies published in later years. It was not until 1985 that the world learned that Indira had no choice. Having failed her Latin exam for the second time, she had been asked to leave the university.[12]

After Feroze and Indira returned from England, their closeness continued in their work for the Indian National Congress. At some point in 1941, Indira confessed to her father her intention to marry Feroze. Her father started, in the hesitant way that was typically his, to point out the pros and cons of such a marriage. In Feroze's favour was his long connection with the family and the care he had taken of Kamala, Nehru's wife, in Switzerland, his long attachment to Indira, and his dedication to the nationalist cause. But the factors opposing their relationship seemed much stronger. To begin with, Feroze was Parsi, not

Kashmiri Brahmin. Nehru, however, was less troubled by their religious differences than by the differences in their "backgrounds," which was a euphemism for class and wealth.[13]

Yet, in the face of the public outcry about their engagement and impending "mixed marriage," Nehru reversed himself and became supportive of the young couple, who were married on 26 March 1942 in Allahabad. But their honeymoon was destined to be short. The political ferment in the country and the mass civil-disobedience campaign ordered by the All India Congress Committee (AICC) on 7 August 1942 led to the arrest of the couple and their jailing. For decades, Indira had seen her father, grandfather, mother, grandmother, aunts, and others go to prison. Now this honour was hers. Two and a half decades later, as prime minister, she spoke of her arrest and imprisonment in 1942 as the "most dramatic incident" in her life. "'I had made up my mind that I had to go to prison. Without that ... something would have been incomplete.'"[14] Conditions in Indian jails were appalling, but there is no evidence to corroborate Indira's subsequent claim that she was considered "'so dangerous' as to be denied 'regular prison facilities.'"[15]

On her release from prison in May 1943, Indira moved into the Nehru family home at Anand Bhawan; she was joined by her husband after his prison release in August of that year. Feroze began to earn a living of sorts as an insurance agent and freelance journalist, and a year later, in August 1944, the first of their two sons, Rajiv, was born; their second son, Sanjay, would be born in December 1946.

With the end of the war, Nehru assumed the leadership of the interim government and appointed his son-in-law, Feroze, who needed a steady job, to the position of managing director of the *National Herald*, a Lucknow newspaper founded by Nehru. Indira moved to Lucknow with her husband and son but soon began commuting to Delhi with Rajiv to act as hostess and personal assistant for her father. She was unwell at the time and found the arrangement tiring, while Feroze became increasingly resentful of both her and his father-in-law. Temperamental differences between Feroze and Indira began to surface and accentuated the strain.[16]

On 15 August 1947 Jawaharlal Nehru became prime minister of the newly independent India. Nehru, Indira, and her sons moved to Teen Murti House in Delhi, leaving Feroze in Lucknow. According to Indira, the decision to help her father "wasn't really a choice,"[17] in the face of his awesome responsibilities and the developing violence of intercommunal conflict. Nehru's grief after Mahatma Gandhi's assassination on 30 January 1948 only increased Indira's sense of obligation to remain alongside her father. Marital difficulties (rumors of Feroze's "womanizing") also made it easier for her to resolve that her father's "needs – to organize the house and plan the menus and entertainment programs for all of the many guests – took precedence over everything else."[18]

Although Indira's life continued to be entirely subordinated to her father's, she found time to be extremely active in social welfare and cultural work. She established a school for destitute children in Delhi, presided over the Indian Council for Child Welfare, and was active in the women's section of Congress, establishing contact with the party rank and file. For the most part, however, Indira's role was largely apolitical, despite her position at the heart of the prime minister's house.[19]

Indira also found herself especially busy in the aftermath of independence with the hordes of people located in Hindu and Muslim refugee camps in Delhi. She spent eight to ten hours there every day doing relief work, bringing in cleaners, arranging for medical supplies and food rations, and listening to the refugees' grievances and requests. According to the Punjabi woman Subhadra Datta, who was in charge of the camps, Indira had the right temperament for relief work. She was fearless, decisive, and a good organizer. She also knew how to talk to people in distress. She was not emotional, but she was empathic and tough.[20]

When India's first general election was held, between October 1951 and May 1952, Congress Party workers urged Indira to stand for Parliament, but she declined on the grounds that her sons were too young. Another reason, likely the decisive one, was that Feroze was in the running for the constituency of Rae Bareilly, and Indira knew that her faltering marriage could not accommodate two political careers. Indira campaigned relentlessly both for her father and for her husband, and both men were elected. After winning his seat, Feroze moved from Lucknow to Delhi, having also been appointed managing director of the New Delhi edition of the *Indian Express*. He joined his wife and father-in-law in Teen Murti but quickly found the atmosphere of the prime minister's residence, where his wife was constantly at the beck and call of her father, stifling. Dom Moraes, one of Indira's biographers, writes that, at a reception, she was overheard by her father talking to some women. "'Don't talk nonsense,'" he snapped. Dom Moraes then asked, "'What did she do,'" and the wife of the Indian ambassador to Indonesia told him that "'she stopped talking.'" Her husband then added, "'In those days, she was like a small mouse that is with her father. Nehru's tone with her was often very peremptory and the answer was always a very meek, soft, 'Yes, Papu.'"[21]

In April 1953 Indira and her two children sailed to England for the coronation of Queen Elizabeth II, and from there she went on to the Soviet Union – her fist solo trip as the Indian prime minister's daughter. In October of 1954 Indira accompanied Nehru to China, but she complained to her close American friend, Dorothy Morton, that while she was working hard, she had not as yet found her métier.[22] In the next year, a succession of tours with Nehru followed, with visits to Indonesia, the United States and Canada, Scandinavia, Japan, the Soviet Union, Britain, and Europe. During their trip to the Soviet Union in 1955, Nehru was supposed to ask for Soviet financial and technical assistance for developing heavy industries, but, being inordinately proud, he seemed incapable of raising the subject. It was Indira, no less proud but more practical, who introduced the subject in their talks with Nikita Khrushchev and Nikolai Bulganin, which led to an agreement.[23] She also counselled patience to her father, who, having accepted the unproven hypothesis that it was the British who had destroyed Chou En Lai's decoy plane in Hong Kong en route to Indonesia, had proceeded to write out a stinging telegram to British Prime Minister Anthony Eden. As a result of Indira's suggestion that they wait for more solid evidence, Nehru cooled down and the telegram was never sent.

In 1956 Indira suddenly became a member of the Congress Working Committee, the highest policy-making body of the Congress Party. She had not sought membership; her inclusion in the CWC was the product of the efforts of Congress president U.N. Dhebar and Lal Bahadur Shastri. Many of her father's political colleagues perceived Indira as a conduit to the prime minister and as a potentially useful tool. The Congress "old guard" sought to establish her as someone with stature and position, but without any real substance. Although Indira was modest, self-effacing, and still unsure of herself, "she certainly did not see herself as a cipher," as the party elders would discover to their dismay.[24]

During this period, it was apparent to everyone in Delhi that relations between Feroze and Indira continued to be unhappy; although Indira would deny such rumours, she confided to her friend Dorothy Norman that all was not well with the marriage.[25] In September 1958 Feroze suffered his first heart attack – he had begun to drink and smoke heavily, and was considerably overweight. Indira, who was on her way to Bhutan with her father when Feroze was stricken, returned when she received the message of his illness, and proceeded to nurse him for several weeks. She, herself, then needed surgery to remove a kidney stone, and, in turn, Feroze looked after her with great tenderness. The couple then went on holiday with their children in the hopes of salvaging what was left of the marriage, but it was for naught. The breach between them continued to widen, and Feroze stopped going to the prime minister's house completely.[26] All the while, Indira's involvement in politics continued to grow.

In July 1959 the democratically elected Communist government of the state of Kerala was dismissed by Nehru, and the state was put under direct rule from Delhi. Feroze and others saw Indira's hand in this action; in April 1959, in her new role as Congress president, Indira had visited Kerala and launched a stinging attack against its Communist government, accusing it of being an agent of the Chinese. Kerala's Communists, for their part, accused her of bullying her father into taking this action.[27] But it was Nehru's trusted adviser, Krishna Menon, who had reported in September 1958, after a second tour of Kerala, that "sinister trends" were continuing to develop, and Nehru's own visit in June 1959 confirmed these fears. Nehru urged Kerala's chief minister, E.M.S. Namboodiripad, to call for free elections – arguing that these would test the opposition's claim that the government had lost all its popular support. But Namboodiripad refused and Nehru ordered the government's ouster.[28]

Feroze suffered a second heart attack a little less than a year later, on 7 September 1960, while attending a session of Parliament. Indira was in Kerala at the time, and she arrived at the hospital the following morning to witness his death three days before his forty-eighth birthday. She was grief-stricken and seemed totally shattered by the experience. Having believed that her father's needs were more urgent, she had given them greater priority. Perhaps she hoped, somewhat naively, that she might still be able later in life to mend her deteriorating relationship with her husband; now death had removed that possibility.[29]

By the beginning of 1961, Indira was back in active politics as a member of the CWC, the party's central body for disciplinary action. She was also a member of the Congress Central Election Committee for the 1962 general election, and in this capacity she campaigned strenuously for the party. As a member of the government's National Defence Council and chairman of the high-powered Central Citizens' Council, Gandhi also played a key role in leading the civilian war effort in the Sino-Indian border conflict, after the Chinese launched a massive punitive expedition against Indian forces on 20 October 1962, in the disputed Himalayan no-man's-land. She exhorted women to donate their jewelry and paid several visits to Himalayan forward areas in both Ladakh and the Northeast Frontier sectors, carrying donations of clothing and other necessities to the ill-equipped and frostbitten Indian army.[30]

In the following years, Indira's involvement in politics continued at the same pace, but in January 1964 Nehru's stroke, during the annual session of the Congress Party, signalled the inevitable changes that would later take place in the government. Despite his failing health, Nehru soldiered on until his death five months later, on 27 May 1964. During this latter period, Indira was his closest confidante and determined who should have access to her father.[31] At the time of Nehru's death, it was a foregone conclusion that the man to step into his shoes would be Lal Bahadur Shastri, a diminutive, highly respected individual with a long ministerial and party career behind him. His main virtue was that he was seen as a great conciliator. Indeed, the contrast between him and the other top contender for the job, Morarji Desai, could not have been more striking. Desai was a senior party leader and a seasoned administrator, but formidable resistance to him had built up because of his apparent authoritarianism, inflexibility, and intolerance.[32]

Opposition to this outspoken candidate had become solidified with the formation on October 1963 of the all powerful Syndicate – an exclusive caucus of state Congress bosses whose chief purpose was to keep Morarji Desai out of power.[33] Until about two years before Nehru's death, Desai had been regarded as his "natural successor." And no one believed this more fully than Desai himself – a fact that would be of critical importance in his dealings with Indira. From the time she became prime minister until the moment of her death, Desai, a single-minded and self-righteous man, opposed and harried her because of his firm belief that she had taken away the job which should, by right, have been his.[34]

As soon as the official mourning period for Nehru was over, Shastri was unanimously elected prime minister by the Congress parliamentary party. He invited Indira to join his cabinet, an offer that she reluctantly accepted, asking for a month's delay before being sworn in. She opted for a light portfolio, that of information and broadcasting, rather than foreign affairs, for which many thought she was more suited. Overall, Indira's relationship with Prime Minister Shastri demonstrates her ambivalence about wielding power. On the one hand, she preferred a relatively undemanding cabinet post, but, on the other, she expected to be treated as though she had a senior governmental position.

In August 1964 Indira Gandhi was elected for the first time to the Indian Parliament. For the previous twenty years, she had rejected serving as an elected representative either in a state legislature or in the national Parliament. It has been suggested that, although she adduced family responsibilities for this decision, the real reason lay in her preference for being an important voice in the ear of the prime minister rather than one of five hundred critics and debaters.[35] In any event, reluctant to face a strenuous election campaign so soon after her father's death, she had opted for a seat in the Rajya Sabha, the indirectly elected second chamber. Her performance in Parliament was, by all accounts, unimpressive, and she rarely spoke in that forum, or for that matter, in cabinet meetings.[36] Still, despite her lack of administrative experience, she received a passing grade, largely because she did not foster nepotism and never interfered with promotions in order to favour people – a welcome change from her predecessors.[37]

At the same time, Gandhi's overall dissatisfaction with her position in the cabinet led her to contemplate leaving the government and moving to

London with her sons. Prime Minister Shastri also had similar ideas; to remove this thorn in his side, he was planning to offer Gandhi the post of Indian high commissioner in London when he died suddenly on 2 January 1966, on his way to Tashkent. His death raised the question of the succession once again. No prior agreement on his successor existed, even within the Syndicate. The one thing its members and other Congress leaders were still agreed upon was that Desai had to be blocked.[38]

If not for the fact that Indira Gandhi, as Nehru's daughter, had the ultimate political pedigree, she could never have become India's third prime minister. Her parentage was an enormous asset in a country where heredity still commanded reverence. But she had other qualifications. She had a clean public face, the mass appeal of her father, and an image that spanned the entire country. While Uttar Pradesh, the largest and most populous of India's states, was her home state, she had a substantial following in other Hindi-speaking provinces; as well, she was popular in south India, owing to her support of regional languages and the reorganization of the state of Bombay along linguistic lines. As a consistent opponent of Hindu chauvinism, she provided the best guarantee for the security of Indian Muslims and other minorities. Other factors supporting her candidacy were that she was only forty-eight, had a modern and technology-oriented outlook, and had broad international contacts that could be valuable at a time when food and foreign exchange were in limited supply.[39]

Gandhi's ascendancy was also aided by the fatal flaws of her potential rivals – "Desai's authoritarianism, Nanda's obscurantism, and the limited, regional identity of [Congress President K.] Kamaraj and [Home Minister Y.B.] Chavan."[40] However, the most decisive factor in her favour was the decision of the Congress president to back her. Kamaraj's choice of Gandhi appears to have been dictated by two main considerations. First, "being a woman, Mrs. Gandhi, could be expected to be more pliable and dependent on the president than the other contenders. And secondly, she was the candidate most likely to defeat Morarji Desai – still the bête noire of Kamaraj and the Syndicate – in a contest."[41]

Indeed, in the vote of the Congress parliamentary party that followed on 19 January 1966, Gandhi easily defeated Desai by a comfortable majority of 355 votes to 169. On the surface, it was a remarkable development, but there was also a hidden agenda at work. While women were already represented in Congress committees, legislatures, and the central and state governments, their numbers were proportionately small, and their roles closely circumscribed in practice. Notwithstanding their acknowledged abilities, such women were not expected to provide strong and independent leadership. Their function, by and large, was to act as obedient and ornamental figureheads, following male cues. The elevation of a supposedly malleable woman to the office of the prime minister indicated the desire of her sponsors to neutralize the independent powers of that office, and manipulate it to their own advantage. Given Indira's youth and relative lack of governmental experience, her elders naturally expected her to bow to their superior wisdom, particularly in the case of party affairs.[42] Indira, in short order, would prove their lack of judgment.

Indira Gandhi's debut as prime minister was somewhat less than brilliant, for she seemed bewildered as to how to handle herself in office. Her performance in Parliament in the early months of her premiership, particularly during Question Period, was equally dismal. She was not very articulate and was unable to think on her feet. (Later, she would become a fluent, even fiery, debater.) Some Congress and opposition members continued to ridicule her, and a Socialist parliamentarian nicknamed her "the dumb doll," an epithet that would stick for several years. The Syndicate determined who would have which posts in the formation of her cabinet, and Indira found herself quite impotent in the face of their pressure. So, as a counterweight, she began to rely on a group of advisers, who had gathered around her during the Shastri era and whom the media dubbed the "kitchen cabinet." It had no fixed membership, expanding and contracting with Indira's moods and needs.[43]

In the two instances in which the prime minister was allowed to have her way, the results were salutary. Gandhi decided that only a linguistic reorganization could solve the Punjab problem, and she was supported by Kamaraj in this view. When communal rioting, instigated by the Hindu-revivalist Jan Sangh Party, erupted in several areas of the Punjab, even spreading to Delhi, the party leadership united behind Gandhi, and the government acted vigorously to restore law and order. Furthermore, Gandhi's flexibility in her handling of negotiations with the Naga rebels was a success and helped reduce tension and shatter Naga unity.[44]

In late March 1966 Gandhi visited the United States – her first foreign visit as prime minister. Although she insisted that the trip was a goodwill visit, and that she was not going with a begging bowl, the truth could not have been more different, since the economic realities facing India were grim. The United States had suspended aid to both India and Pakistan in 1965 at the time of the first India-Pakistan War, and it proceeded to stipulate stringent conditions before this aid would be restored. The World Bank and the International Monetary Fund both demanded that the rupee be devalued as a condition of assistance.[45]

President Lyndon Johnson received the Indian prime minister with great warmth. She promptly agreed to a substantial devaluation of the rupee, and she also accepted an American proposal to use the huge rupee funds the United States had accumulated in India, because of massive shipments of PL480 wheat, to set up an Indo-American Educational Foundation, modelled on the Ford Foundation. Both Nehru and Shastri, before her, had rejected this suggestion on the understandable grounds that it would give the United States undue and undesirable influence on higher education and research in India. Gandhi agreed, too, to shift the emphasis in Indian economic policy from the public to the private sector, and from multilateral aid to private foreign investment – decisions that would have momentous effects for India's trajectory in the twenty-first century. Granted, many of these decisions seemed unavoidable – the quid pro quo for food aid – but Gandhi, like her predecessors, could have said "no" and allowed India's economy to continue on a slow-growth trajectory. After her return to Delhi, there was a noticeable absence of Indian criticism of U.S. policies in Vietnam. In exchange, Johnson had promised India three and a half million tons of sorely needed food and $900 million dollars of additional aid. He also said that the United States would persuade the World Bank to be more responsive to Indian needs than it previously had been.[46] Back home in India, the reaction to what Gandhi had agreed to in her talks in Washington was extremely negative, both within her own party and without. She was charged with a "sell-out" over Vietnam as well as over economic policy. Important members of the Congress Party accused her of "deviating" from her father's policies. When, on 5 June 1966, Gandhi, guided by her chosen advisers, announced a 35 per cent devaluation of the rupee, the entire opposition, from the extreme left to the extreme right, condemned it unequivocally.[47]

Publicly, Gandhi defended devaluation as best she could, given her rudimentary knowledge of economics. Privately, she felt betrayed. Apart from the criticism, the discipline required to derive the expected advantage from devaluation was found to be lacking in both the government and the private sector. Moreover, the American promise of aid did not materialize; there was evidence that the Johnson administration was dragging its feet over dispatching the promised grain.[48]

All these developments would have a powerful and lasting effect on Gandhi and her style of leadership. Distrust and a deep sense of insecurity had been ingrained in her character since early childhood. Now these became more pre-eminent. She came to believe that she could "'trust no one'" because everyone, no matter how close or beholden to her, was "'capable of betraying her.'" These developments stimulated her need for greater control to avoid further betrayals, and Asoka Mehta and C. Subramanian, the principal advocates of devaluation, were the first to feel the cold blast of her distrust and disdain. In due course, they were eased out, a fate that others, too numerous to count, would meet in later years.[49]

At this time, Gandhi came to the conclusion that she had to destroy the Syndicate before it destroyed her. But she was realistic enough to realize that she would have to bide her time. She also concluded that, having been led up the garden path by the kitchen cabinet, attacked and vilified by the Syndicate, and disappointed by the United States and other aid givers, her political survival depended on a reversion to left-leaning policies and a revival of her mildly radical image. Some saw her policy switch as opportunist. One opposition MP lampooned her for "'behaving like a capitalist in Washington and a socialist in Moscow.'"[50]

In the years that followed, Gandhi was in better health than she had ever been. The sickly child had become a mature, robust woman with remarkable stamina. Tuberculosis had been beaten a decade earlier, and now she felt an unprecedented sense of well-being and vitality. During the 1967 election campaign, she put this energy to good use. As a campaigner, she was aware that her voice was squeaky, and that she was no great orator. Moreover, she lacked her father's breadth of vision and his philosophical outlook. She decided to overcome these deficits by concentrating on practical issues – people's daily problems – and trying to speak with as much poise as she could. Above all, her objective was to project her personality to as many of her countrymen as possible, and "to make them feel that no other leader cared for them half as much as she did."[51]

Word of her effectiveness as a campaigner spread – wherever she went, Gandhi drew large crowds and, on one occasion, was pelted with stones, but the sight of her wiping blood from her face with her sari, while continuing to speak, shamed her hecklers into silence and awed the crowd. Many years earlier, when she had campaigned in an area on her father's behalf, Indira had been pleasantly surprised to find that she could make the people listen to her; in 1967 she was elated to learn that her innate capacity was not only alive but seemed to be growing with each successive speech.[52]

For Gandhi, this campaign established an important fact of Indian politics. It demonstrated that, in the post-Nehru period, there were no nationally accepted political leaders except herself. Other senior Congress leaders, such as Kamaraj and Desai, received fewer invitations to campaign outside their home states, and when they did the crowds were noticeably smaller. They were identified either with particular regions of the country or with particular interest groups. Gandhi was the only person at the party's top level who, thanks in part to the tremendous advantage of her family background, was singularly free of the narrow, restrictive, personal, community, or language problems that beset her rivals in the Congress.[53]

The results of the 1967 general election confirmed Gandhi's assessment of her own strengths and others' weaknesses. Most members of the Syndicate not only lost their states to other parties but even failed to get themselves elected to Parliament or the state legislatures. The only two members of the Syndicate who survived the election were Sanjiva Reddy and S. Nijalingappa. Desai was elected to Parliament, but the Congress Party was defeated in Gujarat. A former chief minister, C.B. Gupta, who controlled the Congress machine in Uttar Pradesh and who had sided with Desai, was defeated. At the same time, the people of Uttar Pradesh voted for Gandhi and those of her supporters who were running for Parliament, as well as rejecting Gupta's nominees for the state legislatures.[54]

When the new Congress parliamentary party assembled after the elections to choose its leader formally, there was little doubt about the outcome. Gandhi's strength in the party was sufficient to rule out any effective challenge. Although Desai tried once again, he was forced to withdraw from the race and accept the post of deputy prime minister, without being allocated the home portfolio and without a single of his supporters receiving a cabinet post. She also excluded Sanjiva Reddy, a member of the Syndicate, by making him the speaker of the Lok Sabha, the lower house of Parliament.

Although Gandhi was more or less able to confront the Syndicate over the question of membership in her cabinet after the 1967 election, her first truly decisive battle with her political adversaries came over the choice of candidate for the presidency.[55] The presidential office had assumed new importance in the changed political situation. A substantial body of opinion in the opposition, and in the country at large, was articulating the position that the president should be no longer an ornamental figurehead but an active head of state who would hold the scales impartially between the Congress and other parties, especially in centre-state relations. He should also be expected to exercise his own discretion, if necessary, to prevent abuses of the constitution by the central government. Though the constitution in theory provided the president with extensive discretionary and emergency powers, during Nehru's tenure as prime minister, the convention had been firmly established that these powers could be exercised only on the advice of the prime minister. This continued to be the position of the Congress Party.[56]

The opposition parties had persuaded K. Subba Rao, then chief justice of India, to resign his office and accept their joint nomination for the presidential election. Rao was known to be a man of forceful and independent views, whom the central government would have difficulty controlling. The Congress leadership had two alternatives. It could either put up President Sarvepalli Radhakrishnan, whose national eminence made him an almost certain victor, for another term, or it could run Vice-President Zakir Husain, a Muslim. The issues involved in the

choice seriously divided the Congress leadership, with the prime minister and the Congress president on opposite sides.[57]

Kamaraj, the Congress president, believed that Radhakrishnan – a
Hindu, a South Indian, and a certain winner – should be given another
term, and that it would be folly for the Congress to risk defeat so soon
after its election reverses. Indira Gandhi was equally firm in her view
that Zakir Husain must be the Congress candidate. Her conviction was
based partly on strategic considerations, and partly on principle. With
non-Congress governments in several states and inner-party rivalry in
the Congress, she thought it imperative that she have a president whom
she could trust to do her bidding. Radhakrishnan's outspoken public
criticism of her government's performance in the previous year, and his
close contacts with Kamaraj, did not inspire such confidence. Husain,
an eminent scholar, was not noted for the independence of his views;
moreover, his position as a member of the minority community, as well
as the prime minister's nominee, would effectively bar him from playing
an independent political role. At the same time, the elevation of a Muslim to the country's highest office would emphasize at home and abroad
India's commitment to secularism.[58]

Kamaraj finally withdrew his opposition to Husain's candidacy, and
he was elected president. His impressive victory acted as a much-needed
shot in the arm for Congress, boosting the prestige of the party and especially that of the prime minister. Gandhi then decided that, for her to
play a decisive role in party affairs, she would need a stronger grip on
the party machinery. The key post of Congress president was due to fall
vacant at the end of 1967, when Kamaraj's term expired. Gandhi's
choice of candidate was G.L. Nanda, who shared her left-of-centre politics and posed no threat to her own position. The Congress right wing
sponsored S.D. Patil as a rival candidate.[59]

To deal with the impasse over the Congress presidency, Gandhi announced that she, herself, was willing to assume the post. By combining
the offices of prime minister and Congress president as her father had
done in 1951, she would have made her position unassailable. For that
very reason, the move was strongly and successfully resisted by other
Congress leaders. Gandhi was forced to accept Nijalingappa, a somewhat slow-witted conservative and one of the original members of the
Syndicate, as the choice of a party consensus. Nijalingappa made it
clear that the prime minister could not expect to meddle in party affairs.
During the course of the following year, Gandhi's opponents would
make increasingly overt attempts to discredit her, and challenge her
leadership, thus compelling her to rethink her position and seek new
sources of political support.[60]

Gandhi then decided to act against Desai. In a lightning strike, she divested him of the finance portfolio with the plea that, in view of his "strong reservations" on basic issues, it would be "unfair" to "burden him" with the responsibility of implementing the government's economic program. She then assumed the finance portfolio herself. Desai was taken totally by surprise; he rejected Gandhi's request for him to stay on as deputy prime minister without portfolio and resigned. Having seized the initiative, Gandhi did not give her adversaries time to recover from the shock of Desai's dismissal. She made another sensational populist move by nationalizing fourteen leading commercial banks by ordinance, bypassing Parliament, which was due to meet only twenty-four hours later. This was intended to underscore that nationalization was a "personal act" of the prime minister.[61]

The Syndicate was undoubtedly correct that this action was politically motivated and had little to do with economic reform. But their screams of outrage were drowned in the delirious welcome the public at large gave the nationalization ordinance. Low-paid government and private-sector employees, taxi and auto-rickshaw drivers, the educated unemployed, and others were so enthused that they danced in the streets with joy. And when the ordinance nationalizing the banks and the law to replace it were declared invalid by the Supreme Court, Gandhi again overcame the problem; she took over the management of the banks without disturbing their shareholders, and then completed the process of nationalization in a leisurely fashion by enacting a law that met the objections raised by the Supreme Court.[62]

In the days following the nationalization of banks, thousands of the capital's poor thronged to Gandhi's house daily to congratulate her and express their faith in her leadership by offering her bouquets of flowers and shouting for her victory. Wherever she went – and she travelled extensively throughout India – hundreds of thousands of middle-class and poor Indians would turn up to welcome her at every stop to hear her speak of her crusade against vested interests, and those who represented them in the party. Members of the Syndicate were pushed on the defensive; when they spoke of the importance of party discipline and bemoaned Gandhi's disregard of it, they appeared to be using the issue to browbeat her into submission and thereby maintain their hold on power. So successful was Gandhi in promoting herself and her policies, and denigrating the opposition, that the public seemed willing to forget that, in her first year as prime minister, she herself had rejected the proposal for bank nationalization, and that among her opponents were men like Kamaraj and Nijalingappa, both widely respected for their unquestioned honesty and integrity.[63]

Faced with the prospect of having to fight both the Syndicate and Desai, Gandhi increasingly felt the need to appeal to her natural constituency, the left, both within the Congress and without. She was also aware that the Congress Party was continuing to lose electoral support, not only among the young people but also among the party's traditional supporters – the Harijans, or former untouchables, religious minorities, and the poor in both urban and rural areas. The radical members of Congress insisted on a return to socialist programs and the removal of the "old discredited" leaders. The stage was thus set for Gandhi to give an ideological twist to her quarrel with the Syndicate. The death of President Zakir Husain, on 3 May 1969, provided the mise en scène.[64]

If past practice was to be followed, Vice-President V.V. Giri should have been adopted automatically as the Congress candidate for president. But neither faction within Congress wanted him. The Syndicate was determined to nominate one of its own members, Sanjiva Reddy, then speaker of Parliament. Gandhi also learned that the Syndicate's purpose in attempting to install Reddy in the presidential palace was to remove her from office and elect Desai instead. She tried to see if confrontation could be avoided, suggesting that Jagivan Ram, an untouchable,[65] be the Congress choice. But the Syndicate would not budge from its support of Reddy, who was chosen by a majority of Congress members.[66]

Presidential election results, announced on 20 August 1969, continued to underline the infighting in the Congress Party. V.V. Giri – not Reddy – won, but narrowly and with the help of various opposition groups such as the Communists, the Sikh party, the Akali Dal, and the regional DMK party of Tamil Nadu. Only a third of Congress MPs and a quarter of Congress MLAs voted for Giri.[67]

Throughout the autumn, "unity talks" and meetings were held between the warring Congress factions – the Syndicate old guard and Gandhi's followers. But it was to no avail. On 28 October the Congress President, Nijalingappa, wrote an open letter to Gandhi charging her with having created a "personality cult" that threatened the democratic working of Congress, and he concluded by chiding her for having made "'personal loyalty to you the test of loyalty to the Congress and the country.'"[68] "In October 1969, however, Nijalingappa's voice was considered a lonely reactionary rather than a prophetic one."[69] A few weeks later, the Syndicate held an inquisition; Indira Gandhi was tried in absentia and found guilty of indiscipline and defiance of party leadership. Seething with indignation and rage, Gandhi called a meeting of the cabinet which, with few exceptions, pledged its loyalty to her. Intense lobbying followed in order to ascertain who would hold onto the majority of the Congress. Gandhi won, and her Congress supporters took on the title Congress (R) and the Syndicate clique became Congress (O).[70]

The "Great Split" of Congress in 1969 marked a milestone in Gandhi's political development. As the New York *Times* commented, "'she ... proved herself a courageous, tough-minded politician, as well as an exceedingly skillful tactician – a prime minister in her own right, and not a transitional figure trading on her legacy as the daughter of Nehru.'"[71] The split also propelled Gandhi to consolidate her power. Within six months, she reshuffled her cabinet, removing Chavan, who had backed Reddy in the presidential struggle, and took over the home ministry herself.

But the implications of the "Great Split" were equally great for the Congress Party. It marked an abrupt end to the party's role, which had lasted for decades, as a coalition of groups ideologically stretched across a spectrum from extreme right to mild radicalism. Until that moment, opposition forces had often been contained within Congress; now they were pushed out. As well, this internal division marked the triumph of the parliamentary over the organizational wing of the party, which would rapidly atrophy. In order to prevent her position and authority from being seriously challenged again, Gandhi sought to control not merely the Indian president but also the cabinet, the president of Congress, the CWC, the Parliamentary Board, the Central Election Committee, and state leaders who had been loyal to the Syndicate.[72]

Under the counsel of her close advisers, Gandhi continued to implement a range of radical measures, the most dramatic and controversial of which was her proposed abolition of the privy purses and privileges that had been guaranteed to the 278 Indian princes at independence by the Indian constitution. All privy purses were tax-free. Gandhi engineered an amendment to rescind the privy purses and put it before Parliament in September 1970. While the amendment passed the lower house, it was defeated by one vote in the upper house. Gandhi then proceeded to have a presidential proclamation, issued by the obliging President V.V. Giri, to "derecognize" the princes, stripping them not only of their privileges and purses but also of their titles. Her actions were greeted with widespread public support.[73]

In response to the Supreme Court's invalidation of the proclamation abolishing the princes' privy purses, Gandhi, in need of popular endorsement, decided to call for national elections one year early, in February 1971. Soon after her announcement, a *Newsweek* reporter asked Indira what the issues were in the up-coming election. She answered without a pause: "'I am the issue.'"[74]

The results of the election were a Congress landslide and a tremendous mandate for Gandhi. Her Congress (R) won a two-thirds majority in the Lok Sabha: 325 out of 520 seats, which was seventy more than an undivided Congress had won in 1967. Indira was re-elected leader of the Congress parliamentary party uncontested on 17 March, and the old guard Congress (o) was virtually annihilated politically. Gandhi had become the most powerful Indian prime minister since independence. Indira, the woman – rather than Congress, the party – was the victor in 1971. Her leadership was indispensable to Congress; she was the only person in India "with a personal following transcending regional, communal and caste lines ... Her paramountcy derived from her enormous popular support, rather than the strength of the Congress party organization or state party bosses."[75]

Gandhi's power, although enormous in 1971, would grow exponentially, "leading to the virtual deification of the prime minister and winning her laurels, which even her father had failed to attain."[76] Such an apogee would be the result of her handling of the threat to India's security posed by its neighbour and old adversary, Pakistan. Following a coup against his predecessor, Ayub Khan, Yahya Khan had come to power in Islamabad in March 1969, after having promised free elections and the restoration of normal political institutions – including an uncontrolled press, abolished as far back as 1958. In December 1970 Sheikh Mujibur Rahman and his Awami League secured an absolute majority in the election of the Pakistan National Assembly capturing virtually every seat from East Pakistan on a program of maximum provincial autonomy, which verged on secession. Though the Bengalis of East Pakistan formed a majority of the country's total population, Pakistani politics had been dominated since independence by a small elite of politicians, bureaucrats, and generals from the western wing. Unwilling to come to terms with Bengali nationalism, and transfer power to the Awami League, Pakistan's military rulers refused to convene the newly elected assembly. The Awami League then launched a civil-disobedience movement; violence broke out, and, on 25 March 1971, the Pakistan army began a campaign of military repression on a vast scale. Hundreds of thousands of East Pakistani/Bengali refugees, bearing tales of hair-raising atrocities, began to stream across the eastern Indian border.[77] "In the organized burning of villages, destruction of crops, mass shooting of innocent people and the rape of tens of thousands of Bengali women, many Western reporters saw terror equaling, perhaps surpassing that which the Jews had suffered in Hitler's Germany."[78]

To those who had opposed the creation of Pakistan from the outset, the uprising came as a final indictment of the two-nation theory of Mohammed Ali Jinnah (the founder of Pakistan)[79] and as a heaven-sent opportunity for India to step in and smash Pakistan, once and for all. However, Gandhi was convinced that military intervention by India, at this stage, would not only amount to a flagrant breach of international law but would lend weight to Pakistani propaganda that the revolt was

a conspiracy by Hindu-dominated India. As well, the heads of the
Indian armed forces are believed to have advised against any military
action, until they had time to make adequate preparations.[80]

For the first few months of what became known as the Bangladesh
crisis, Gandhi repeatedly calmed her countrymen, including MPs who
were becoming increasingly critical of her government's inaction. She
gently told them that a "'wrong step or even a wrong word' would have
an 'effect different from the desired one.' This was the first indication of
the superb qualities of leadership Gandhi was to display throughout the
crisis and the resulting fourteen-day India-Pakistan war. She won admiration for the skill with which she wove together the military, political
and diplomatic strands of the Indian response to the crisis next door."[81]

Specifically, in refusing to make any warlike noises, while realizing
that war with Pakistan was becoming unavoidable, Gandhi gave primacy to the terrified refugees from East Pakistan whose numbers over
the months had grown to ten million. She appealed to the world community to help deal with the "'unbearable'" financial and other burdens the
refugee problem was imposing on India, by stopping "'Pakistan's brutal
repression'" so that the refugees could return home.[82] Her hope was that
international pressure would secure a peaceful settlement and that India
could avoid a war.[83]

But there was another strategic reason for not rushing into armed
conflict. The Indian chief-of-staff told Gandhi early on that it would be
foolhardy to become involved militarily until the rainy season had
ended. He was also worried about the threat of China coming to West
Pakistan's aid. If India could postpone hostilities until the winter, this
would make it difficult, if not impossible, for the Chinese army to tra-
verse the snowbound passes of the Himalayas.[84]

During a visit to Delhi on his way to China in early July 1971, Henry
Kissinger, President Richard Nixon's national security adviser, made it
clear to Gandhi that if India and Pakistan went to war over Bangladesh,
the United States would not be prepared to help India.[85] In light of this
development, India signed a "treaty of peace, friendship and cooperation" with the Soviet Union on 9 August 1971, accepting an offer
broached three years earlier by Leonid Brezhnev. During a visit to Moscow in September 1971, Gandhi received assurances of Soviet military
aid should India embark on a war with Pakistan over Bangladesh. At
the same time, in the hope of resolving the conflict peacefully, which
would allow the refugees to return to their homes, Gandhi, her close
personal adviser P.N. Haksar, and the Indian foreign secretary,
T.N. Kaul, embarked on a twenty-one-day tour of Europe and the United
States in an attempt to galvanize public opinion. They were listened to

sympathetically everywhere, except in the United States, where the conversations between Nixon and Gandhi were characterized by antipathy
and distrust – the product, in part, of the Indo-Soviet pact.[86]

Less than a month after Gandhi and Haksar returned from the United
States, on 3 December 1971, the Pakistani air force bombed nine Indian
air bases in the north and west, including those at Amritsar, Agra, and
Srinigar in Kashmir. With this air strike, Pakistan was named as the formal aggressor. But conflict between India and Pakistan had already become inevitable. Two weeks earlier, Indian forces had moved into
defensive positions on the Pakistan border and established operational
bases inside Pakistan in preparation for an assault on Dhaka scheduled
for 4 December 1971. When informed of the air strikes of 3 December,
Gandhi said to those who were with her, "'Thank God, they've attacked us.'" She had not wanted to be seen as the aggressor, although
she had approved plans for India's attack on Pakistan the next day.[87]

Two days later, on 6 December, Gandhi announced Indian diplomatic
recognition of independent Bangladesh and explained that combined
Indian and Bangladeshi forces were fighting the war in East Pakistan.
The war lasted only fourteen days; the Pakistani army, both outnum-
bered and under-equipped, surrendered unconditionally. After India's
victory in the Indo-Pakistan War, independence for Bangladesh, and the
signing of the Simla Accord – the peace agreement between India and
Pakistan – Gandhi's position in the summer of 1972 seemed unassailable. The journalist Kuldip Nayar, who had always been a fierce critic
of hers, conceded that she had "'won the war and appeared to have
also won the peace. She was the undisputed leader of the country; the
cynicism of the intellectuals had given way to admiration; the masses
were even more worshipful … She was hailed as the greatest leader India had ever had.'"[88]

From this pinnacle of power, fame, and popularity, Gandhi had nowhere to go but down, and her descent was swift. The summer of 1972
was extremely hot, and the monsoon rains failed, resulting in food scarcity all over the country. Inflation soared, the price of oil escalated, facto-
ries closed, and industrial unrest increased. During the years 1972 and
1973, there were more than 12,000 strikes in Bombay alone. Although
the weather was beyond Gandhi's control, the growing social turbulence
was not. "Her instinct was to impose order – to take charge without being fastidious about the means."[89] Partly as a result of her chaotic childhood, one of the things that Gandhi most feared was disorder; it made
her anxious and uncertain, and as she grew more powerful, she would interpret opposition to her government as a prelude to trouble and disarray
that had to be stamped out. Indira's policy of controlling the state governments by handpicking chief ministers became the rule rather than the

exception. "Unfriendly" state leaders were disposed of through recourse to "President's rule," under which states were run directly from Delhi. In addition, Indira began to suspend rather than dissolve state legislatures, in order to paralyse opposition to the Congress Party.[90]

At the centre, Gandhi surrounded herself with unswervingly loyal cabinet ministers. Cabinet meetings became forums to rubber-stamp – rather than formulate – policy. Party elections were a thing of the past. The Congress president and members of the CWC were all now nominated by Gandhi herself. But it was the extent of the corruption that was most dismaying to the Indian public. Corruption was not a new phenomenon; both the Nehru and Shastri governments had been tainted by it, but it was only under Gandhi that it became endemic to the workings of government at every level. "Power lay among Indira's chosen; they in turn acquired unprecedented amounts of patronage to dispense." Licences, permits, and clearances were required to establish every new business venture, to modify and expand existing ones, and to import equipment and spare parts. Foreign exchange was also regulated. Such measures gave bureaucrats and politicians enormous scope for exploitation.[91]

Worse, contributions to the Congress Party were collected in the untraceable and unaccountable form of cash that was delivered first to Gandhi's offices and then directly to her home. This was not an issue of personal corruption – that is, money flowing into numbered Swiss bank accounts – but rather a self-reinforcing, systemic by-product of Gandhi's centralization of power. Because she had dismantled the party structure and destroyed its organizational capacity, she could no longer rely upon the teams of dedicated regional and local party workers to canvass for and deliver votes. Instead, she communicated directly with the electorate, a strategy that required the expenditure of a huge amount of party funds to organize and transport crowds to rallies in the states that she would address.[92]

With the monsoon failing for the third year in a row in 1974, drought and food shortages continued, as did soaring inflation. Gandhi was forced to borrow from the International Monetary Fund with rigid conditions that involved curtailing government spending. The country was further crippled by more strikes and violence which led to police intervention. A nationwide railway strike was launched in May 1974. Invoking the Defence of India Rules, Gandhi declared the strike illegal and determined to break it at any cost, jailing between thirty and forty thousand railway workers. The imprisoned railway workers' families were thrown out of their government-owned houses and reduced to destitution. Gandhi managed to crush the strike after twenty days; many condemned the government's ruthless tactics, but those in the middle and upper classes praised Indira's actions.[93]

Then, on 12 June 1975, the Allahabad High Court of Justice ruled that Indira Gandhi was guilty of corruption and electoral malpractice during the 1971 general election campaign. Two offences were cited: that she had illegally used the services of a government official to "further her election prospects," and that she had used officials attached to the Uttar Pradesh state government to construct rostrums from which she addressed election rallies. While the charges against Gandhi were really too thin to justify unseating the head of government, the judge argued that the law was the law, and there was no special provision for the prime minister. This legal decision meant a mandatory penalty that would bar Indira Gandhi from holding – or contesting – any elective office for a period of six years.[94]

Indira's two sons and her close associates urged her not to resign. Publicly, Gandhi would say only that she would appeal Justice Jagmohan Lal Sinha's decision in the Supreme Court; privately, years later, she confided to writer Dom Moraes that there was never any question of her resigning. "'What could I have done except stay? ... You know the state that the country was in. What would have happened if there had been nobody to lead it? I was the only person who could, you know. It was my duty to the country to stay, even though I didn't want to.'[95] That assertion of indispensability was typical of Indira. In her mind, only she could run India."[96] Opposition parties insisted that Gandhi vacate her office at once, but she continued to argue that unless she was at the helm of the country, more chaos would ensue. At a huge public meeting in New Delhi on the evening of 25 June 1975, Jayaprakash Narayan and Morarji Desai both denounced her as "'moving toward dictatorship and fascism.'" Gandhi felt personally threatened, but, even more, she believed that if Narayan succeeded in ousting her, it would be a disaster for the country.[97] Later that evening, the president, at Gandhi's behest, and without cabinet consultation, signed a document proclaiming a State of Emergency. The government was authorized to impose media censorship, suspend court proceedings, and override the legislative and judicial branches of government, if necessary. By dawn the next day, Narayan, Desai, and 676 other opposition leaders had been arrested under the draconian Maintenance of Internal Security Act (MISA). As well, power to all major newspapers in New Delhi was cut off, thus imposing a news blackout on the capital.[98]

In Parliament – with most opposition members either behind bars or abstaining – Gandhi won an indefinite extension of the Emergency. She also forced through two unprecedented amendments to the constitution: one barred India's courts of law from hearing any challenges to the Emergency, and the other retroactively exonerated Indira Gandhi from any legal charges pending against her, as well as from "'all possible future charges of criminal actions while she was in high office.'" The amendments, themselves, were declared immune to Supreme Court review.[99] With regard to the arrests made after the declaration of the Emergency, Gandhi told Dom Moraes that "'there was a list of the main opposition leaders, which I approved'; the remainder of the arrests were left to the discretion of state governments and the police. The idea was to arrest anyone who was likely to exert a troublesome influence in the country or the area."[100] The number of arrests was extremely large; according to Amnesty International, 140,000 Indians were detained without trial in 1975–76.[101]

For the next twenty-one months – until she was defeated in an election that brought Narayan's Janata Party into power – Gandhi ruled India as a virtual dictatorship with surprisingly little opposition. There were no massive demonstrations against her outrageous acts – not even a ripple, and newspapers meekly followed the rigid censorship rules. In the initial months at least, the Emergency was also rather popular with the public at large. The return of normal and orderly life, after relentless disruption by strikes, protest marches, sit-ins, and clashes with the police, was applauded by most people. Government officials, senior and junior, unsure of what might happen to them otherwise, started arriving for work on time and taking fewer tea breaks.[102] Nonetheless, it is clear that Indira Gandhi had exaggerated the perils faced by India in mid-1975. The Commission on the Emergency, headed by former Supreme Court Justice J.C. Shah, reported in 1978:

> There is no evidence of any breakdown of law and order in any part of the country, nor of any apprehension in that behalf; the economic condition was well under control and had in no way deteriorated ... The public records of the times, secret, confidential or public and publications in newspapers, speak with unanimity that there was no unusual event or even a tendency in that direction to justify the imposition of emergency. There was no threat to the well-being of the nation from sources external or internal ... But Madame Gandhi, in her anxiety to continue in power, brought about instead a situation which directly contributed to her continuance in power and also generated forces which sacrificed the interests of many to serve the ambitions of a few. Thousands were detained and a series of totally illegal and unwarranted actions followed involving untold human misery and suffering.[103]

Gandhi's critics argued that she imposed the Emergency because she was "authoritarian by nature," fed up with dissent and vigorous opposition, and happy to have dictatorial powers. Others have argued that, although she behaved imperiously, the simple act of calling for fresh elections entirely on her own nineteen months later, and without being under pressure to do so, disproves this charge.[104] M.C. Carras notes that Gandhi's commitment to democracy was combined with a certain "ambivalence regarding the proper use of authority," which was further complicated by her conviction that her "personal worth was tied up with her desire to do great things for her country." She tended to identify herself with the nation completely, and therefore to look upon personal threats to herself as threats to India itself.[105] In this way of thinking, Gandhi was amply assisted by her son Sanjay, who had been a vehement proponent of the Emergency. Sanjay was totally without any political principles – he subsequently convinced his mother to postpone the general election twice, in February and November 1976, and those close to "the son" had no doubt that his plan was to keep on postponing them indefinitely. Despite his conservative political views, his emasculation of Indira's secretariat, and his corrupt and venal behaviour, Sanjay was the most trusted of all the people in Gandhi's life during this period. Over the years, Indira had become increasingly isolated emotionally, and Sanjay's enormous hold on her – she seemed frightened of him – may have derived from Indira's unconscious connection of Sanjay with Feroze, whom he resembled in character and temperament. Sanjay also played on his mother's guilt by accusing her of having caused his father's death by neglecting him.[106]

Fory Nehru, the wife of Indira's cousin B.K. Nehru, the Indian high commissioner in London, went to see Indira at the end of November 1976 and told her about what she had seen and heard about the excesses of the Emergency – the coercion used to force young men to submit to vasectomies as a way of controlling the birth rate, the brazen behaviour of the Sanjay loyalists, whose slum-clearance projects involved the destruction of thousands of the homes of the poor, the high-handedness of police officials, who extorted money from innocent citizens by threatening them with arrests under the Emergency's blanket powers, and so on. Instead of getting angry or even contradicting Fory, Indira held her head in her hand and three times repeated, "'Mein kya karoon' (what should I do?)."[107] Pupul Jayakar, a friend since childhood, described an exchange between Indira and the great sage J. Krishnamurthi, who met with Gandhi in December 1976. According to Jayakar, Indira wept and told Krishnamurthi that "she was 'riding a tiger' and did not know how to dismount. He did not give her any 'specific' advice but told her: 'Since you are more intelligent than the tiger, you will find a way.'"[108]

Gandhi's decision to hold a fresh general election, announced on 18 January 1977, was even more sudden and unexpected than the proclamation of the State of Emergency nineteen months earlier. No one was

more surprised than her political enemies; even her friends and supporters, few of whom had been taken into her confidence, were shocked.
She had defied Sanjay at last. Looking back, a decade after the event,
I. Malhotra observed that it was easy to see why Gandhi opted for elections, even though she risked the loss of power. "Evidently she wanted
to regain her credentials as a democratic leader, which she had lost. She
was also concerned about her 'place in history.' She did not want to be
known to future generations as the leader who destroyed democracy in
India, so lovingly nurtured by her own father."[109] Katherine Frank has
argued that, for Gandhi, the Emergency had been a means to an end –
to keep the country from falling into chaos. "For all her failings, and
despite her irrational belief that only she could lead and control the
country, on some level she remained committed to democracy. She was
guilty of hubris, but not megalomania."[110] Gandhi's decision to go to
the polls also had a narcissistic component: her memories of how people had reacted to her in the 1971 election campaign created a longing
in her to hear the applause of the multitudes once again. She wanted to
regain her ability to reach the people on an emotional level.[111]

In the early weeks of 1977, Gandhi campaigned vigorously. She visited
every one of the twenty-two states and spoke at 224 public meetings.
But, compared to past elections, the crowds who came to hear her were
smaller and, not infrequently, hostile. As the strength of the opposition
mounted, Sanjay urged his mother to cancel the election, but she refused.
The election results confirmed the electorate's dissatisfaction with
Gandhi and the Emergency. Narayan's Janata Party won 299 seats and
Congress only 153. Gandhi herself was humiliatingly defeated in her
constituency, as was her son Sanjay, who ran in a neighbouring riding.[112]

For the first time in her life, at the age of fifty-nine, Indira Gandhi
found herself without a job, an income, or a roof over her head. Out of
power, she lost her staff – secretaries, assistants, and domestic servants
– along with her government bungalow. Her nemesis, Morarji Desai,
was sworn in as the fourth – and first non-Congress – prime minister of
India, at the age of eighty-one. Nevertheless, after her appearances before the Shah Commission, which had decried her decision to declare a
State of Emergency, Gandhi found the energy to tour around the country. She observed that the Indian masses seemed to have forgiven her,
believing that, unlike the Janata Party, she cared about the poor. She
therefore decided, in November 1978, to stand in a by-election in a rural constituency and won by a large margin of 700,000 votes.[113]

But the Janata Party was not finished dealing with Gandhi. Its "hawkish majority" insisted that she should be expelled from Parliament and
imprisoned, until the prorogation of the house, for her refusal to apolo-
gize "for obstructing four officials" who were collecting information for

a parliamentary question on one of Sanjay's projects. This resolution was passed on the evening of 19 December 1978 after a heated debate: as a result, Gandhi went to jail for a week.[114]

Soon after, the Janata Party leadership was faced with a no-holds-barred power struggle between Desai, the prime minister, and Charan Singh, the home minister. Each accused the other of favouring family members through "dubious business deals." After President Reddy asked Singh to form a new government, which he failed to accomplish, the president dissolved parliament on 22 August 1979 and ordered an election in the first week of January 1980.[115]

In the meantime, as the 1980s began, India was threatening to disintegrate; political, sectarian, and ethnic upheavals rumbled in Assam, the Punjab, and Kashmir. Throughout the country, there was class and religious warfare; the upper castes turned on Harijans, Hindus on Muslims, Sikhs on Hindus, Hindus and Muslims on Christians, and members of the tribal communities. Frank has asserted that the fault lines in Indian society "were a direct product of Indira Gandhi's eleven-year tenure in office between 1966 and 1977," arguing that her centralization of power had severely undermined state and local autonomy and fuelled regional and communal discontent as a consequence. But, although Gandhi was the source of the crisis that India now faced, she was also perceived as the country's saviour. As she campaigned her way around the country in the closing weeks and days, travelling 40,000 miles and addressing up to twenty meetings a day, many people felt what she herself believed – that Indira was the only person who could hold India together.[116] The ballot boxes would confirm this sentiment.

Shortly after she was sworn in as prime minister for the fourth time on 14 January 1980, a Scandinavian journalist asked Gandhi how it felt to be India's leader again. She replied angrily, "'I have always been India's leader.'"[117] Nine days later, however, her mood would change to one of profound sorrow at the news of the sudden death of her son Sanjay, who had been trying out some acrobatic stunts in his new two-seat plane. For all her courage and composure, his death broke Indira's spirit.[118]

With Sanjay dead, Gandhi could have implemented fundamental changes in her government and shed her son's unsavoury legacy and associates. She might have won back the support of some of the intelligent men who had been her advisers in the past, like P.N. Haksar and Romesh Thapar, and those segments of the intelligentsia who were willing to forgive her for the "aberration" of the Emergency. But, in the years that followed until 1984, she made little attempt to do so. She charged that her intellectual critics were all under either American or Soviet influence, and she explained that she mistrusted the bureaucracy and let "'her own people' manage things because senior bureaucrats had never 'lifted a finger to help me. In the circumstances, am I to blame if I entrust sensitive jobs to men who may not be very bright but on whom I can rely?'"[119] Foremost among these people of "her own" was her remaining son, Rajiv, whom she finally persuaded to seek a seat in Parliament.

If some people expected the situation to improve with Gandhi's return to power, they would be disappointed. The situation throughout the country and in the political arena remained the same, if not worse. In general, the period from 1980 to 1984 continued to be characterized by persistent communal and caste killings, police misconduct, tribal insurgencies,[120] and, last but not least, political struggles within the Gandhi family – Sanjay's wife, Manetka, viewed herself, not Rajiv, as the logical heir apparent, and relations between her and Sonia, Rajiv's wife, and Indira became increasingly embittered and public.[121]

But it would be Gandhi's handling of the escalating conflict in the Punjab that proved her ultimate undoing. Its roots go back to 1966, after Indira first became prime minister, when she behaved in a way that her father had refused to consider. At that time, she acceded to the creation of a separate Punjabi-speaking state, and Haryana and Himachal Pradesh were carved out of the already mutilated Punjab which had been created at the 1947 Partition. The Sikhs represented a slim majority in the new Punjab – 56 per cent of the population; in the rest of India they comprised a mere 2 per cent of the population, while Hindus were 80 per cent. The Sikh religion, founded some five hundred years earlier, was an offshoot of Hinduism, and Sikhs in the Punjab had for the most part lived in harmony with their Hindu neighbours, intermarriage between the two groups being common.[122]

But certain issues concerning land distribution, access to rivers, and the capital city of Chandigarh, which the Punjab shared with Haryana, remained unresolved and a constant source of Sikh grievances; the Sikhs wanted sole possession of the state capital, the retention of Hindu Punjabi-speaking regions, and control over the river waters essential to agriculture in the state. In 1977 the Sikh majority in the Punjab became more assertive and their political party, the Akali Dal, defeated Congress in the elections. Although Indira was out of power, her son, Sanjay, with an eye to the future, sent some of his loyalists to the region to find a new Sikh holy man who could divide the Sikhs and break up the Akali Dal. Their choice, a demagogue named Jarnail Singh Bhindranwale, was a fundamentalist who welcomed their covert support, but it is inconceivable that Sanjay and his allies would have acted without Indira's approval.[123] In time, however, Bhindranwale and his followers would demand a sovereign Sikh state called "Khalistan" – an independent Punjab.

By 1981, Bhindranwale's supremacy in Sikh politics had become complete and unshakeable. He moved into the Golden Temple complex

in Amritsar – the holiest Sikh site – where, surrounded by his armed ac-
olytes, he held court and spewed venom against the government and
Hindus in general. Rioting and violence escalated in the Punjab during
the spring of 1983. Sewers outside the Golden Temple began to fill up
with bodies – victims of Bhindranwale's gang, which was located inside.
On the morning of 23 April, the Amritsar police chief, a Sikh named
A.S. Atwal, was shot dead leaving the temple after worship. He was one
of a number of prominent Sikhs killed because they did not support the
separatist goal of "Khalistan." The chief minister of the Punjab,
Darbara Singh, also a Sikh, begged Gandhi to allow him to send the police into the temple complex to arrest Bhindranwale and his guerrilla
army. But Indira temporized; she seemed to have lost any vestiges of her
old uncanny sense of timing and decisiveness.[124]

The mood in India was turning into one of deep despair. Some
blamed Gandhi for not making enough concessions to the Akalis, which
they thought would have weaned the majority of Sikhs away from the
influence of Bhindranwale and the terrorists; others denounced her for
doing nothing to curb the terrorists and for allowing them to use the
Golden Temple as a sanctuary. "She was indeed having the worst of
both worlds."[125]

On 5 October 1983, in an attempt to force Hindus to flee Punjab, terrorists stopped a bus and selectively killed six Hindu passengers. Next
morning, in response, Gandhi brought Punjab under direct central rule.
Far from improving, the situation in Punjab worsened, and in one night
in April 1984 terrorists burnt down no fewer than thirty-seven isolated
railway stations. Meanwhile, Bhindranwale, fearful of a government effort to enter the Golden Temple to arrest him, started to fortify the
building to make the operation difficult and costly.[126]

Operation Blue Star, which the Indian government launched on 6 June
1984 to capture Bhindranawale, was a disaster for Indian soldiers. Of
the over one thousand Indian troops sent into the Golden Temple, somewhere between three hundred and seven hundred are estimated to have
been killed, including nearly half the special forces that had led the raid.
At least one thousand civilian pilgrims were also killed. Bhindranawale
was finally killed, and his supporters routed, but at an enormous material, political, psychological, and symbolic cost – rumours of Indian desecration of the temple would abound.[127]

After the botched raid, Rajiv's Italian-born wife, Sonia, described how
"a shadow entered our lives."[128] Indira discussed the possibility of her
assassination with Rajiv and Sonia, and wrote out instructions for the
funeral. The defence minister tried to persuade the prime minister to
transfer her security from the police to the army, but was told not "even
to entertain this idea." She was the leader of a democratic not a military

government.[129] Nor would she countenance the removal of all Sikh security men from duty at her home. India, she insisted, "was secular." The Sikhs stayed. Even after Gandhi countermanded the order banning Sikh bodyguards, no one guessed there was an enemy within.[130] But they were terribly wrong. On 31 October 1984 Indira Gandhi was shot to death at point-blank range by her two Sikh bodyguards, who, faced with the rest of the security detail, dropped their guns. One of them said, "'I have done what I had to do. Now you do what you have to do.'"[131]

Five hours after being gunned down by men entrusted with protecting her life, and after her doctors had exhausted measures to revive her, Indira Gandhi was pronounced dead. Tragically, in the three days following her assassination, at least 3,000 Sikhs were slaughtered, more than 2,000 in Delhi alone. Over 50,000 Sikhs fled to Punjab and another 50,000 sought refuge in camps in Delhi.[132] Thirteen days following Indira's assassination, Rajiv Gandhi, who had become the new prime minister of India, would scatter his mother's ashes over her beloved Kashmiri Himalayas – her final resting place. Thus, a remarkable political career ended tragically and abruptly.

Indira Gandhi's legacy can best be described as an admixture of the "good, the bad and the ugly." Having flirted with socialism, she became a pragmatic politician who was prepared to allow capitalism to flourish with all its pluses and minuses. Like her father, she was able to give the masses the feeling that she cared about their welfare, thus enlisting millions of Indians in support of democratic institutions. But her populism was coupled with political impropriety. Although she professed to be concerned about corruption, under the influence of her son, Sanjay, kickbacks became a sine qua non for doing business in India – a situation that continues to have a negative impact on the Indian economy to this day. She reached her zenith with the defeat of enemies within and without – the Syndicate and then Pakistan in 1971; her nadir occurred, if not in 1984, certainly in 1975, when she declared a State of Emergency, jailed her political opponents, and silenced Parliament and the press. To her everlasting credit, however, she did repeal the State of Emergency nineteen months later and re-established civil liberties and the supremacy of Parliament. From that point on, democracy in India re-emerged on a stronger footing, and none of her successors has been tempted, thus far, to adopt authoritarian rule.

Mother India: The Personality Profile of Indira Gandhi

Gandhi's biographers have offered their readers a portrait of a woman with an extremely complex personality structure. As part of her personality profile, shyness and diffidence operated in conjunction with Ambitious, Contentious, and Dominant traits – a highly unusual combination of personality patterns. Moreover, unlike other political leaders analysed using this model, Indira Gandhi displayed a profile in which all ten of the personality patterns that have an adaptive or normal component (i.e., excluding the erratic and distrusting) were diagnostically significant (i.e., *present*, receiving scores of 5 or more). Each of these patterns was either *present* or *prominent* and the scores of four of them – the Ambitious, Reticent, Contentious, and Dominant – were high enough on the *prominent* gradation (scores of 10 to 23) to suggest minimal evidence for the *mildly dysfunctional* variant of the pattern (scores of 15 to 23).[1] Only the very disturbed patterns involving distrust and erratic qualities emerged as unimportant. The following analysis of the data for Indira Gandhi provides an MIDC profile, a diagnostic classification of that profile, and a clinical interpretation of significant MIDC scale elevations derived from the diagnostic procedure.

The MIDC profile yielded by the raw scores is displayed in Figure 1. Gandhi's most elevated patterns, with scores of 21, are Scale 2 (Ambitious) and Scale 7 (Reticent), followed by Scale 5B (Contentious) with a score of 20, Scale 1A (Dominant) with a score of 19, and Scale 8 (Retiring) with a score of 15. All these personality patterns fall within the uppermost range of the *prominent* category, offering minimal evidence of the *mildly dysfunctional* variant. Also in the *prominent* category are Scale 5A (Aggrieved) with a score of 14, and Scale 1B (Dauntless) and Scale 6 (Conscientious) with scores of 11. In the *present* range, with scores of 9 and 8 respectively, are Scale 4 (Accommodating) and Scale 3 (Outgoing). A score of 8 on Scale 9 is not diagnostically significant; the

Table 1
Personality scale scores for Indira Gandhi

Scale RT%	Personality Pattern	Raw	Ratio
1A	Dominant (Controlling)	19	12.8%
1B	Dauntless (Dissenting)	11	7.4
2	Ambitious (Asserting)	21	14.1
3	Outgoing (Extraverted)	8	5.4
4	Accommodating (Agreeable)	9	6.0
5A	Aggrieved (Yielding)	14	9.4
5B	Contentious (Complaining)	20	13.4
6	Conscientious (Conforming)	11	7.4
7	Reticent (Hesitating)	21	14.1
8	Retiring (Introverted)	15	10.1
	Scales 1–8	149	100.0
9	Distrusting	8	5.1
0	Erratic	0	0.0
	Full scale total	157	105.1

Note. For the basic scales 1–8, ratio scores are the raw scores for each scale expressed as a percentage of the sum of raw scores for Scales 1–8 only. For Scales 9 and 0, ratio scores are raw scores expressed as a percentage of the sum of raw scores for all ten MIDC scales (therefore, full-scale ratio totals exceed 100). Scale names in parentheses signify equivalent personality patterns in Millon, MIPS: *The Millon Index of Personality Styles Manual.*

MIDC manual specifies a clinical significance threshold of 20 for Scales 9 and 0, versus 5 for Scales 1–8.

The following subsections present and discuss, in order of their importance, research material relevant to the four most diagnostically significant patterns in Indira Gandhi's personality profile. A series of illustrations that best exemplify the patterns revealed in the data are provided in order to demonstrate, empirically, the salience of these patterns.

SCALE 2: THE AMBITIOUS PATTERN

As with all personality patterns, the Ambitious pattern occurs on a continuum ranging from normal to maladaptive. At the well-adjusted pole are situated the confident, poised, self-assured, ambitious, and persuasive personalities. Exaggerated Ambitious features occur inthose individuals characterized by arrogant behaviour, a sense of entitlement, and a lack of empathy for others. In its most deeply ingrained and inflexible form,

Figure 1
The personality profile of Indira Gandhi

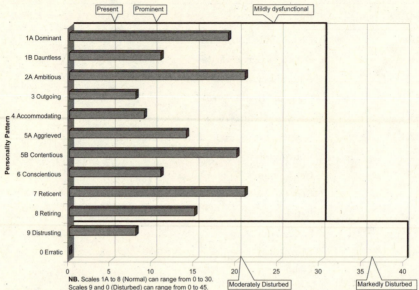

NB. Scales 1A to 8 (Normal) can range from 0 to 30.
Scales 9 and 0 (Disturbed) can range from 0 to 45.

the Ambitious pattern displays itself in an exploitative, manipulative style that is consistent with a clinical diagnosis of a narcissistic personality disorder.[2]

In Indira Gandhi's score of 21 on Scale 2 (Ambitious), the arrogant style is a more inflated variant of the Ambitious pattern, suggesting exaggerated features of the basic personality pattern with the potential for mild personality dysfunction. It is associated with self-promoting, pretentious, imperious, and unempathetic behaviour.[3]

Evidence of the confident, attention-getting, and narcissistic aspects of Indira Gandhi's personality can be found in the many accounts and narratives of her early life, as well as during her years in politics before she became India's prime minister. During her childhood, Indira's games primarily involved political themes. As noted in chapter 1, one of her pastimes involved dividing her dolls into teams of freedom-fighters and police and arranging a clash between the two; the team with which she identified, the freedom fighters, invariably won.[4] Similarly, on various occasions, she collected as many servants as she could and then stood up on a table and delivered speeches, "repeating disjointed phrases that she had picked up from the grownups' talk."[5]

At some point, her psychological involvement with the freedom-fighters was transformed into a more grandiose fantasy in which she was both a heroine and a martyr for the cause. An incident involving her younger aunt, Krishna, is quite telling. When she noticed Indira striking a rather curious pose and muttering to herself, Krishna asked what was going on – to which Indira solemnly replied that she was practising being Joan of Arc. "'I have just been reading about her,' she added, 'and some day I am going to lead my people to freedom as Joan of Arc did.'"[6] She told a biographer in 1967 that "'it was Joan's martyrdom that particularly attracted her; she died at the stake. This was the significant thing that I envisaged – an end like that for myself.'"[7] Indira would, in fact, die at the hands of two assassins, under circumstances that were at least suggestive of her vision of herself as a martyr.

Interestingly, Joan of Arc never appeared in Indira's correspondence or interviews during the years before she came to power, and she confessed to having no memory of the incident described by Krishna, and later confirmed by her father.[8] Whether or not the young Indira actually envisaged herself as Joan of Arc, however, it is clear that this theme became an important ingredient in her ambitious self-definition as an adult. Interviewed in 1972, after she was the prime minister, Gandhi claimed to have discovered Joan of Arc around the age of ten or twelve when she visited France. "I don't remember where I read about her, but I recall that she immediately took on a definite importance for me. I wanted to sacrifice my life for my country. It seems like foolishness and yet … what happens when we're children is engraved forever on our lives."[9]

Rebuffed as a member of the Congress Party because of her age, which was only twelve, Indira was infuriated and vowed that she would have an organization of her own instead.[10] Her thwarted sense of entitlement led to the creation of a children's group of freedom-fighters, the "Monkey Brigade," that acted as runners and assisted the Congress Party organization in its struggles with the British. At age eighteen, while a student at Badminton in England, Indira was asked in a sympathetic manner by the headmistress if she was unhappy so far away from home and friends. Indira retorted in a self-assured manner, "'I don't like being away from India at this time, but I must get to know the British to fight them.'"[11]

After the fall of Holland, Belgium, and Luxembourg in 1940, Indira confidently wrote her father from Les Frênes sanitorium in Switzerland, where she was recuperating from tuberculosis: "'[D]on't get agitated or worried about me … I shall be perfectly all right. A crisis is the one time when I do keep my head.'" Proof of her self-possession was the detailed plans she mailed to her father concerning what she would do if Switzerland became involved in the war, since she had been told that, in that contingency, all foreigners would have to leave.[12]

Even though Switzerland remained neutral, Indira became restless. Against medical advice, she announced to the head of Les Frênes that she was leaving. She boarded a bus in Geneva which drove through

France to the Spanish border and then on to Barcelona. From there, she caught a plane to Lisbon, only to find herself stranded for nearly two months waiting for a flight to England. Once in England, she determined to marry Feroze, to whom she had been secretly engaged for four years. Ever since she had been a patient at Les Frênes, Indira was repeatedly advised not to have children – advice that only made her even more determined to marry.[13] Shortly before her marriage, she was again advised that, as a tubercular, she ought not to have children. "When her doctor's diet for putting on weight did not work, she sa[id] 'I ignored all the doctors' instructions and made out a regimen for myself. I succeeded.' As she said many years later, 'I always wanted to have children – if it had been up to me, I would have had eleven. It was my husband who only wanted two.'"[14] Indira's confidence in her own judgment, whether it took the form of a decision to marry, to organize a diet plan, or to have children, was indisputable. This trait would continue manifesting itself later in her life.

By the mid-1950s, Indira's two sons were in boarding school and her marriage to Feroze was effectively over. She felt that it was time for her to establish herself in her own right – while realizing that, as long as her father was alive, she would have to devote her work and her life to his. It had come to a point where Indira clearly wanted to be more than Nehru's hostess. She complained to her father's secretary, M.O. Mathai, that Nehru would never discuss political issues at meals. And she told a number of people that she wished her father would confide in her more. While Nehru had long made a habit of sending Indira out on fact-finding tours, he did not seek advice from her, or even discuss problems or issues in any depth with her. Despite his awareness of his daughter's knowledge and reliability, Nehru turned to others, such as Desai and Kamaraj, for serious analysis; he saw Indira as an assistant rather than a confidante or an adviser, and "Indira was becoming increasingly dissatisfied with this subordinate role."[15]

Having decided in 1956 to become a member of the Congress Working Committee, Indira was faced with a choice. Membership on the CWC was possible in two ways: either by direct appointment by the Congress president, or by election by the party members. "Significantly, [Indira] insisted upon being elected. She wanted both a mandate and a power base."[16] Here was hard evidence that her political ambitions were beginning to take shape. In the next two years, she rose further to become a member of the Parliamentary Board, a governing council similar in function to an Eastern European Communist Party politburo.

After her father's death in 1964, as we have seen, Congress Party officials decided that Lal Bahadur Shastri would succeed him, and he was unanimously elected as Nehru's successor by the Congress parliamentary committee. As for Indira's own ambitions, Welles Hangen, a journalist, wrote that "no public figure in India disclaim[ed] political ambition so insistently, and none [wa]s more disbelieved."[17] For some political reporters, this was an accurate description of the situation then, and remained true of Indira throughout her political career.[18] There is, however, no indication that Nehru would have favoured her succession. The limit of his ambition for her was reported to be that Indira would be a minister in Shastri's cabinet and thus an "instrument of continuity." The very thought of dynastic succession in a parliamentary democracy such as India was repugnant to Nehru.[19]

Shastri's decision to appoint Indira to the cabinet stemmed in part from his desire to express his gratitude to her father, whose support of his candidacy had helped him attain the office of the prime minister, and in part from his belief that her presence would lend the government strength. But Shastri did not want a potential rival, and thus he excluded Indira from the making of policy or participating in the cabinet's major committees. Indira began to voice her resentment and reveal the depth of her feelings over being "slighted" and "ignored" by the new prime minister. Her sense of entitlement – an exaggerated, more narcissistic variant of the Ambitious pattern – became more apparent. "Indira asked the journalist Inder Malhotra if he had seen ... 'that Shastri had appointed Swaran Singh as Foreign Minister, a position held by Nehru ... ' When [he] said that [he] had, she burst out: 'Should he not have consulted me and Krishnamachari? I do not want that job. But surely I should have been consulted.'"[20] Overall, Indira's relationship with Shastri demonstrates her ambivalence about wielding power. On the one hand, she preferred a relatively undemanding cabinet post, but, on the other, she expected to be treated as though she had a senior governmental position.

That Indira's ambition and self-confidence continued to grow is amply illustrated in the following incidents. Early in 1965 a major crisis occurred in southern India. Under the terms of the Indian constitution, Hindi was scheduled to become the sole official language of the country that year – a prospect that was of increasing concern to non-Hindi speaking states, even when Nehru was alive. Nehru's previous promise that Hindi would never be forced on unwilling people, and that English would continue to be an "associate official language" for as long as non-Hindi states wanted it, had calmed their fears. Unfortunately, some of Shastri's ministers had created an impression of Hindi zealotry, and people in non-Hindi speaking south India demanded assurances of Nehru's pledges in the form of a constitutional amendment. When Shastri claimed that this would cause unrest in the Hindi-speaking states, an eruption of violence took place in the southern state of Tamil Nadu.

Both Shastri and Kamaraj, the leader of Tamil Nadu, stayed in Delhi waiting for calm to be restored.[21]

In contrast, Indira took the first available plane to Madras, rushed to the centre of the trouble, and helped bring the situation under control. Later, when Malhotra mentioned the accusation levelled by the prime minister that she had exceeded her responsibilities by flying to Tamil Nadu without his express instructions, she flared up. "'She said that she did not look upon herself as a 'mere minister of information and broadcasting,' but as one of the leaders of the country. 'Do you think this government can survive if I resign today? I am telling you it won't. Yes, I have jumped over the Prime Minister's head and I would do it again whenever the need arises.'"[22] Indira's behaviour clearly underlined her sense of self-importance and of being special, a characteristic of the most exaggerated features of the Ambitious personality.

At the same time, Indira recognized that while Shastri wanted her in the cabinet, he did not want her in a position of power. And so, "in order to assert herself and emphasize her considerable experience in foreign affairs (experience which, in comparison to her, both Shastri and Swaran Singh lacked), Indira went from London on to Belgrade and met Tito and then on to Moscow where she conferred with the new Soviet Premier, Alexei Kosygin."[23]

A crisis in Kashmir in August 1965 also provided Indira with a platform to launch herself. Arriving in Srinagar for a holiday, she learned that Pakistani troops, disguised as civilian volunteers, were poised to capture Srinagar and foment a pro-Pakistan uprising in Kashmir. Indira was urged to take the next flight back to Delhi. She not only refused but chose to fly to the front when hostilities broke out. The press hailed her, and the troops were enthused by her presence among them. It was this occasion that prompted the back-handed compliment that she was the "only man in a cabinet of old women."[24] But her ambition to be recognized and valued would be thwarted once again. Back in Delhi, Indira prepared a short report on how to fight the war with Pakistan and presented it at a meeting of the cabinet's Emergency Committee. In her words, "Shastri took the paper from me, held it gingerly, as one would a dead rat by its tail, and asked: '*Is ka kaya karein* (What should we do with it?).'" "Dharma Vira, the cabinet secretary, she added, said that the paper should be given to him, and as Indira told Malhotra, 'this was the last I ever heard of it.'"[25]

Although Shastri had been upstaged by Gandhi once again, as in Madras, the effects were not lasting. The defeat of the Pakistan army made Shastri a hero overnight. Indira was "furious" that her contribution to the war effort had not brought her the glory and the attention she craved. Her inner circle – consisting of Dinesh Singh, minister of state for foreign affairs; Ashoka Mehta, deputy chairman of the

Planning Commission; Inder Gujral, who knew her through his brother, the artist, Satish Gujral, who had painted her portrait; and the journalist Romesh Thapar – continued to feed her hostility to Shastri and to foster her political ambitions. Gandhi's anger with Shastri was returned in kind. The prime minister had enough of her "'meddling'" and was planning to offer her the post of high commissioner to Britain. However, he held back on the offer until it was too late – his death on 11 January 1966 meant another succession in less than twenty months.[26]

The Syndicate of party bosses and other Congress leaders were united once again in their determination to block Moraji Desai from the office of prime minister. Even though Indira's performance as information and broadcasting minister had been lacklustre, and that as a parliamentarian extremely poor, the general election was only thirteen months away and the first to be held in the absence of the dominating figure of Nehru. That clinched the issue of the next prime minister in favour of Indira. Of all the Congress leaders, she alone had something of her father's charisma and mass appeal as well as popularity among Muslims, Harijans, and other minorities. She also projected another winning quality that surprised her supporters – modesty. Desai staked his claim in a strident manner, while Indira maintained a low profile and dignified silence. When pressed, she said she would be "'guided by the wishes of the Congress and its President Kamaraj.' Her stance was popular in a society that valued renunciation, but it was clearly a pose. At the time of her father's death, she might have been uninterested in become prime minister. But the intervening Shastri interlude had changed things. She now wanted the job and was more or less convinced that it was hers."[27]

Publicly, she kept up the facade of being a reluctant prime minister, even after she had been duly elected. But the truth was exactly the opposite. During the succession drama, writing to her son Rajiv in England, she quoted some lines from one of Robert Frost's poems that more accurately reflected her drive and ambition: "To be king is within the situation / and within me."[28]

Indira's early political life trajectory demonstrates how, fuelled by arrogance and a sense of entitlement, she had managed to circumvent the Syndicate and create widespread public support; the reward for her ambition was the office of the prime minister, which she would occupy for fifteen years, making her the longest-serving Indian prime minister.

SCALE 7: THE RETICENT PATTERN

At the well-functioning pole of the Reticent pattern one finds the circumspect personalities. These individuals, who score from 5 to 9, are generally cautious in their outlook. Exaggerated Reticent features occur in insecure, inhibited personalities. In its most deeply ingrained, inflexible form, the

Reticent pattern displays itself in withdrawn behaviour patterns that are consistent with a clinical diagnosis of avoidant personality disorder.

Gandhi's elevation of 21 on Scale 7 (Reticent) parallels her elevation on Scale 2 (Ambitious). The Insecure style is a more inflated variant of the Reticent pattern, suggesting exaggerated features of the basic personality pattern with the potential for mild personality dysfunction. It is associated with guarded, insecure, wary, and apprehensive behaviour.[29]

Like the self-confident dimensions of Gandhi's personality, her reticent behaviour can be observed from the time she was a child. Indira was only four years old when, in 1921, she watched the court proceedings as her grandfather, Motilal Nehru, and her father, Jawaharlal, were sentenced to six months' rigorous imprisonment, each for their part in the non-violent nationalist struggle against the British that Mahatma Gandhi had unleashed. Jail-going by the family elders, including her beloved mother, Kamala, became a regular occurrence. For Indira, this was an enormous wrench, and even when her parents returned from prison, the agony continued because of the uncertainty of when they might again be arrested.[30]

Nor were her parents always available even when they were home. From an early age, Indira was forced to contend with the demands of the nationalist movement, and the huge crowds converging on her home, which deprived her of her parents' attention. In that situation, Indira had little choice but to keep her problems to herself and not expect much help. "Every night after supper she had to walk along a dark corridor to reach her room, where she had to climb a stool to switch on the light. She was scared but never told her parents or anyone else. Her lifelong refusal to share her fears with others was thus deep rooted."[31] Indira's reticence and emotional aloofness were, in part, the products of a self-reliance that both parents instilled in her and that enabled her to survive the multiple separations from them.[32]

Another factor contributing to Indira's reticence was her solitariness. She grew up in a household with no other children, and, apart from kindergarten in Delhi, she was not sent to school until 1924, when her grandfather decided to enrol her in St Cecilia's, a private school with mostly British pupils that was run by three British women. She was shy and tongue-tied in the midst of the other girls and acutely aware of her skinniness. She also felt like a freak as the only student at the school who wore *khadi* clothes. On top of everything else, she was frightened of the British-sergeant major who taught the girls drill and cracked a whip to keep them in line.[33]

When Nehru learned of Indira's attendance at St Cecilia's, he was furious, since it violated the principles of the Congress boycott of all things foreign. Indira was withdrawn from St Cecilia's and taught by

Indian tutors at home for the next two years. Then, in the aftermath of Indira's mother's delivery of a premature baby boy who died, Kamala was diagnosed with tuberculosis and hospitalized, leaving Indira even more alone and sad, for she was deeply attached to her mother.[34]

Kamala failed to improve and the decision was made for the family to take her to Switzerland and the Alps for treatment. Indira briefly attended an international school nearby that she liked; however, in the summer of 1926, the Nehrus enrolled her in a school that was four hours from Geneva in Chesières, where there would be no "coddling and arguing" and there would be more suitable companions for her.[35] She did not tell her parents that she was unhappy at Chesières, a family-run school headed by a huge man and his equally repellent wife, who treated their handful of students like servants. In the face of Kamala's illness, Indira did not feel she had the right to complain. Instead, she took on a nurturing role, becoming the mother to her sickly "child," thus inverting the usual parent-child relationship. Her father encouraged her to be independent, and she somehow felt that he, as well as her mother, were vulnerable and needed her protection.[36]

All prominent Gandhi biographers strongly emphasize the issue of her shyness: "The young Indira, who was emotionally close to her mother, suffered from the same curse of shyness throughout childhood and adolescence."[37] "'At school, she was a quiet, shy, modest girl who liked to keep in the background,'" one of her contemporaries commented.[38] Fellow students would say, "'There goes Nehru,'" when they saw her "'gliding through the quad with her notebooks ... a wand-thin, remote figure in beautiful saris ... unknowable ... Not unfriendly; simply apart.'"[39]

Developments in the Nehru household further exacerbated this trait. In 1931 Kamala and Jawaharlal recognized that they both might again be sent to jail and that Motilal's death that February meant there was no one to care for Indira. The decision was made to send her away to an Indian boarding school in Poona, nine hundred miles from home. Once there, "she was hesitant of confiding in anyone, she felt terribly lonely, she missed her parents intensely and, as she admitted later, was all bottled up, too proud to show it, and when she wanted to cry in that school ... she would draw up the bedclothes to smother her sobs at night, or stand behind a tree quietly and stoically and let the tears trickle down her face."[40]

Shy, reticent individuals, like Indira, are characterized by their anguished temperament. "They have learned to be watchful and to guard against the ridicule and contempt they expect from others. They [are] exquisitely sensitive to signs that portend censure and derision."[41] To ward off the rejection they feel is inevitable, they are reluctant to express their feelings too openly and thus they appear as reticent and lonely – afraid to reach out to others. What seems to have saved Indira from utter emotional devastation was the awareness that her intense loneliness and sadness was the result of a profound and stirring cause – Indian independence.[42]

Indira's loneliness and fear of rejection were not alleviated by her relationship with her father. Although Nehru took a keen interest in his daughter's academic progress, and her physical fitness, their relationship did not blossom into warmth. Her unresponsiveness during her adolescence troubled her father, and, when she was fifteen, he wrote to his sister, Mme Vijaya Lakshmi ("Nan") Pandit, from his jail barrack in Dehra Dun, that he had been writing to "Indu" regularly and that it was a very one-sided correspondence, evoking almost no response. When hasty letters to him did come, they contained excuses, and no reference at all to his letters or the questions he had asked nor any acknowledgment of the books he had sent for her birthday and on other occasions. Nehru was puzzled at her behaviour and thought it might be the product of a growing selfishness. He suggested to his sister that a course of field or factory work might bring her down from the clouds.[43]

It never seemed to have occurred to Nehru that his insistence on imposing upon Indira his views of suitable reading material, diet, health practices, and so on would lead her to rebel. And rebel she did, in the only way that a reticent, cautious child could. Rather than angry, open confrontation with her father, Indira engaged in a pattern of avoidance. Perhaps at this stage in her life, an overt challenge to her father, whom she also loved and idealized, was simply not possible, given her shy, apprehensive nature. That would come later, when the stakes were higher – involving the man she wished to marry.

Accepted at Somerville College, Oxford, in 1935, for studies commencing in October 1936, Indira arrived on a cold, rainy afternoon "'feeling terribly nervous and agitated.'"[44] She was nearly two years older than the other members of the class of 1937 and the only one from a famous family. During her stay at Oxford, "she only spoke once on a platform – at the India League in London at Krishna Menon's insistence – and it was a fiasco. She froze with nervousness, and, when she finally opened her mouth to speak and uttered an intelligible sound, someone in the audience yelled, 'She doesn't speak, she squeaks.'"[45]

After Kamala's death, on 28 February 1936, when Indira was eighteen, Nehru began a passionate affair with a young Indian woman. "When Indira realized that she would now have to share Nehru's affection, she retreated."[46] It would be easy enough for Indira, once she entered politics, to respond angrily to public acclaim for Shastri, rather than her; but it was quite a different matter, as an eighteen year old, to express her rage openly at her father for his choice of another woman in his life. About Shastri, she cared little; her father, she idolized. Rather than try to compete for Nehru' attention, his shy, apprehensive daughter, who feared his scorn and derision, withdrew into a lonely shell. That pattern of withdrawal, in situations where she feared the potential for rejection, would continue. "Even at forty-two, as a married woman and president of the Congress party, she [wa]s described as retiring and ill at ease in social settings."[47]

As a young adult, "[Indira's] anxiety was rarely expressed; on the contrary she appears to have dealt with it by withdrawing further from emotional contacts, even with her parents."[48] Reticence and withdrawal are the emotional responses of individuals who are exquisitely sensitive to the opinions of others. Ensconced in a sanatorium in Switzerland, in the middle of December 1939, for treatment of pleurisy, "Indira kept her distance from the other patients, in part because a *Life* magazine article by John Gunther on 'Nehru of India,' which included family photographs, had been circulating around the sanatorium and it made her feel self-conscious."[49] Indira seems to have feared that the responses of the people who read the article would be negative, and she would become an object of derision.

An incident on Indira's way back to India from Switzerland serves to illustrate this point further. The long journey, which took her first from Switzerland to Portugal, then on to England before she left, with Feroze, for India, had to be broken by a week's halt at the South African port of Durban, where Nehru's name was already well known. Understandably, the Durban Indian community arranged a formal reception in Indira's honour. "Indira accepted [the invitation] but strictly on the condition that she would not be asked to speak, not even to thank the hosts. She was evidently haunted by the memory of a previous evening ... when, suddenly asked by Krishna Menon to speak, she found herself paralyzed and the words had stuck in her throat."[50]

The reticent trait is discernible during her early political career as well. When U.N. Dhebar, the Congress president, decided to retire in January 1959, before the end of his second term, the other party leaders pressed Indira to succeed him. Her immediate, instinctive response was that "'I couldn't manage it. I did not have doubts. I was absolutely certain that I wouldn't be able to handle it.'"[51] Indira then said she felt she must consult her father. G.B. Pant, the union home minister, who was well aware of Nehru's reluctance to promote his daughter, replied: "'It has nothing to do with your father. It is for you to decide.'"[52] Indira, nevertheless, proceeded to seek out her father's opinion. She later learned that Pant had already spoken to her father and that Nehru had tried to dissuade Pant from encouraging Indira.[53] But, to Indira, Nehru merely said, "'It must be your decision. I am not going to enter into it.'"[54] She sensed, however, that he did not want her to accept the post.[55]

Notwithstanding Nehru's cool response, Pant and Dhebar persisted. Pant, argued, "'It's not a question of your decision. We have decided and you have to do it. This is your duty.'"[56]After a good deal of pressure from both of them, Indira acquiesced and agreed reluctantly to become Congress president. She had second thoughts almost immediately.[57] She telephoned Pant to say, "'No Pantji, I have thought about it, I can't do it.'"[58] He then proceeded to tell Indira that the newspapers had already been informed. The following day a series of editorials and columns appeared in the national papers arguing that Indira couldn't handle the job.[59] Indira continued to insist to Dhebar that "'I simply cannot do it. It is not fair to me or the organization.'"[60] Dhebar and Pant asked Indira if she was willing to let the press "'get away with what they are saying.'"[61] Indira realized she would be humiliated if she refused. She agreed to accept the post with an unenthusiastic "'all right.'"[62]

When Shastri asked her to join his cabinet, she accepted reluctantly but asked for a month's delay, and opted for the minor portfolio of information and broadcasting. She accepted Shastri's offer partly from a sense of duty, to carry on her father's work, and partly because she needed a job. Nehru had never made any provision for his daughter's future, and a place in Shastri's cabinet provided her with both a salary and a roof over her head in the form of a government bungalow.[63]

Paradoxically, it was precisely the Reticent dimension of Indira's personality that later made her so attractive as the choice to succeed Prime Minister Shastri following his death in 1966, after only nineteen months in office. The Congress Party felt it needed a period of reconstruction to rebuild its declining reputation. "Indira Gandhi had what mattered greatly to the group of leaders who masterminded her rise – a reticence that made her apparently content to stay in the background of events." She had largely eschewed controversy or ambition, and her subdued public manner seemed to guarantee respect for the principle of collective leadership and control by the Syndicate of party bosses. As between her and Morarji Desai, the other leading candidate, she looked colourless and manageable – a much safer choice. Indira knew that she needed the support of the party bosses, who did not so much favour her as oppose Desai. She tactfully refrained from canvassing for votes or formally declaring her candidacy, and said she would abide by Congress President Kamaraj's wishes. "Her reticence was noted and approved."[64] Some of Indira's reticence was undoubtedly manufactured for the occasion – as noted in the previous section, she was clearly ambitious – but, at the same time, there was clearly a shy and awkward dimension to her personality that did not fail to impress her supporters.

SCALE 5B: THE CONTENTIOUS PATTERN

At the normal, well-adjusted pole of the Contentious pattern are to be found the cynical, headstrong, resolute personalities. Exaggerated Contentious features occur in complaining, irksome, oppositional personalities. In its most deeply ingrained, inflexible form, the Contentious pattern displays itself in caustic, contrary, negativistic behaviour patterns that are consistent with a clinical diagnosis of negativistic or passive-aggressive personality disorder.

An elevation of 20 on Scale 5A (Contentious) in Indira Gandhi's profile was the third most important dimension in her personality profile. The Oppositional style is an inflated variant of the Contentious pattern which is associated with complaining, irritable, discontented, resistant, and contrary or ambivalent behaviour.[65]

The passive-aggressive behaviour exhibited by Indira Gandhi was an expression of the conflict between her reticence, on the one hand, and her ambition and assertiveness, on the other. "Rather than attacking preemptively to ward off anticipated threats, she more often withdrew into herself, for both the cultural environment, and her own psychological and physical needs precluded a spontaneous expression of aggressive feelings. However she ... confessed to a stubborn streak as a child, and stubbornness is a passive way of expressing aggression."[66] Like Woodrow Wilson and Winston Churchill, Indira's repressed defiance and hostility to her father was reflected in a pattern of persistent weakness in her schoolwork.[67]

This is evident at every stage of Indira Gandhi's education. Having been removed from St Cecilia's, as part of the Congress boycott of all things foreign, Indira was then – after being tutored at home for two years – sent to St Mary's in Allahabad. It, too, was a Western school, but in protest she wore Indian homespun clothes which immediately announced her radical politics and singled her out from her classmates. "She had little to say about her studies, except that they 'seemed so remote from the life we had at home that I just wasn't in the mood to take in anything ... It seemed that what they were trying to teach me had nothing to do with life.'"[68] Even when Indira expressed a positive attitude towards reading, writing to her father that she had read a great many books from the Anand Bhawan library, and asking him to recommend more, Nehru remained dissatisfied. In an unposted letter, he chided her for not telling him what books she had read, and then went on to lecture her to the effect that those who read too many books quickly can be suspected of not reading them properly at all. Indira's reading had clearly become a contentious subject. "Nehru wanted to control her intellectual development. Indira wanted freedom to read what she liked including fairy tales when she was little and romantic novels as she got older." For Nehru, this was a shocking waste of time; he urged his daughter to read H.G. Wells and books about Garibaldi. Later he would send her his own books for her edification. Sometimes Indira read them – with little understanding, as she confessed later – sometimes she resisted. "She clearly resented the pressure on her to read a certain kind of worthy book, and when she complied and did read what was urged on her but could not understand it, she felt slow and inadequate."[69] This, in turn, built up her resentment and served to widen the gulf between daughter and father.

Later, in 1934, Indira attended Santiniketan, which, as she would subsequently say, "'removed [me] from an atmosphere of intense political living. I had never been in a quiet place before ... I had always been in crowds ... And this was ... partly the reason for the considerable bitterness in me ... I built up a lot of hatred and bitterness inside me.'"[70] Having acknowledged the angry, bitter feelings that seem to have found expression in her passive-aggressive behaviour, she went on to write that "'I think it was really at Santiniketan that I washed it out.'"[71]

In November 1935 Indira went back to school, in Bex, Switzerland. Predictably, after travelling and living on her own in Germany any Switzerland, she found school life irksome. "There was scarcely any free time to write letters, read or take solitary walks. And she resented what she considered wasted hours spent at compulsory singing, drawing, sewing and needlework classes."[72] Likewise, at Oxford, she found the work gruelling: a full schedule of lectures and tutorials in the four areas she was reading for her pass moderations exam. "'They work us like slaves,'" Indira protested to her father in mid-October of her first year, but several weeks later she reported that "'she was settling down now & find it easier to spend a whole morning solidly working.'"[73] Although she performed well enough in her tutorials, she failed her first attempt at her exams in December. Since nearly everyone else had passed on the first attempt, this failure left her feeling depressed, and she wrote to Nehru complaining: "'The thrill of Oxford has worn off I am afraid, and Oxford life, as it really is, is not a very attractive spectacle.'"[74]

During the summer of 1938, Indira collapsed with a severe attack of pleurisy – the lung disease that Kamala had suffered from. She took a term off to recuperate, but early in October 1939, two weeks before she was due back at Oxford, Indira came down once again with pleurisy and was advised to go to a sanatorium in Switzerland as soon as she was well enough to leave the hospital.[75] Ensconced at Les Frênes tuberculosis sanatorium, she was told that she would need to stay for seven months. A family friend, Lady Maharaj Singh, who visited Indira, told her that the medical director thought she should stay at Les Frênes for another year and then spend another two years in the mountains of India. At that juncture, unhappy, bored, and discouraged by her lack of progress, Indira began plotting to leave Les Frênes against medical advice if necessary.[76] She suggested to Nehru that her illness was largely psychosomatic. "'I think my fatigue and insomnia are due most to the state of my nerves.'"[77] And she attributed the state of her nerves to her "'wretched months'" at Les Frênes and the insufferable dullness of "'the little gossiping group of Les Frênes patients whose main topics of conversation are: food & the strangers who pass by on the road below.'"[78] Finally, in October 1940, Indira informed Dr Auguste Rollier that she was leaving.

Even those events that can be considered positive in an individual's life, such as marrying a loved one, will often be experienced and interpreted within the context of the individual's personality. Thus, Indira's marriage to Feroze Gandhi, in 1942, did not alter her personality profile; more specifically, the Contentious aspects of her character continued to receive expression. After India attained its independence from Britain on 14 August 1947, Indira was living with her husband Feroze and her children in Lucknow, which she found "'dreary' and 'narrow minded.' Above all, she hated provincial politics. 'What a peculiar deadness there is in our provincial towns,' she wrote to Nehru in December. 'What makes the atmosphere sickening is the corruption and the slackness, the smugness of some and the malice of others. Life here has nothing to offer.'"[79] Her complaints about Lucknow were a displacement, in part, of her general sense of isolation, compounded by her knowledge that "Feroze was still involved with other women."[80]

Indira felt pressured to help her father, the first prime minister, with his enormous responsibilities, and the task of attending to his official and personal needs at home fell progressively on her shoulders.[81] Having become official hostess for her father, "she was also, like Kamala, very proud and like her, possibly silently resentful that her abilities were not always recognized."[82] A friend, who came to know her when she was living with her father at the official residence, observed that "'even then the aunts looked down on her as socially inept.' Gandhi confided to this friend that 'all would have been well if she had been willing to be made into a carbon copy of them.' Buried in some of her 'half-sentences' according to the friend, was the complaint that her father 'should have protected her from the aunts.'"[83]

Not surprisingly, the Contentious trait manifested itself in Indira's official political life as well. On 2 February 1959 Indira was formally elected president of the Indian National Congress. Because her predecessor had resigned mid-term, she was elected for the remaining eleven months only, although she would be eligible for re-election. But just ten months into her presidency, she decided that she did not want to serve another two-year term: "'The routine part of the work takes too much time and is too confining. I have felt like a bird in a too-small cage.'"[84] In this complaint, we can also feel a sense of frustrated ambition; Indira is a bird that longs to try her wings; instead, she is cooped up in a cage that is too small an arena for her perceived abilities.

Shortly before Nehru's death on 17 May 1964, she again wrote to her friend Dorothy Norman about her resentment of the shackles of duty and responsibility that she felt. "'My need for privacy and anonymity has been growing steadily these last three years until now I feel I cannot ignore it without risking some kind of self-annihilation.' She also stated that 'the desire to be out of India and the malice, jealousies, and envy with which one is surrounded is now overwhelming. Also the fact that there isn't one single person to whom one can talk or ask advice.'"[85] In this letter, there is evidence not only of Indira's Contentious trait but also of her Reticent one – her desire to withdraw from public life to avoid the feeling of being rejected.

With her subsequent decision to join Prime Minister Shastri's government, Indira's contentiousness found a new outlet – the prime minister himself. Although she had rejected suggestions by a small but growing number of supporters that she succeed her father, she expressed strong resentment when Shastri failed to consult her on his choice of foreign minister.[86] By 1966, Shastri had "started ignoring Indira and other senior colleagues even more openly than before, and running the government with the help of a few trusted officials. Indira was furious. During this period I used to see her frequently and she never missed an opportunity to emphasize that she was being treated shabbily. Once or twice she even talked of resigning though, in my view, not very seriously."[87]

The above episode again demonstrates the conflicting patterns in Indira's personality profile. Not only is the contentiousness evident, but so is the struggle between her reticence and her ambition. Her reticence is expressed in her inability to choose to succeed her father, but, at the same time, the Ambitious trait is present in the sense of entitlement – her right to be treated as though she were special by the prime minister. This leaves her feeling angry and frustrated, which finds expression in her litany of complaints.

SCALE 1A: THE DOMINANT PATTERN

At the normal end of the Dominant pattern are the assertive, tough, outspoken, and strong-willed personalities. Exaggerated Dominant features occur in controlling, forceful, and overbearing individuals. In its most deeply ingrained, inflexible form, the Dominant pattern displays itself in aggressive, domineering and belligerent behaviour that is consistent with a clinical diagnosis of sadistic personality disorder.[88]

The above description is consistent both with Indira's score of 19 on the Dominant pattern (Scale 1A) – she was tough, assertive, controlling, and overbearing, and enjoyed wielding power – and with the clinical impressions of Indira Gandhi drawn from the literature. Consider, for example, the following incident early in Indira's life. One day after their initial arrest, for implied disloyalty to Great Britain, Motilal Nehru and his son Jawaharlal were sentenced to six months' imprisonment and a fine of 500 rupees each. In accordance with the policy of civil disobedience, they refused to pay the fine, but the result of this refusal was the steady stripping of Anand Bhawan of its valuable carpets and furniture by the police. When the four-year-old Indira saw the police snatching away the things she knew belonged to her "Mommy and Papu and Dadu, she went like a fury after them, particularly the police inspectors, and cried and stamped her feet, while the others looked on grimly and then tried to pull her away." Indira would later recollect that "'I protested to the police indicating my strong displeasure in every way I could, and once nearly chopped off an officer's thumb with a bread slicing gadget.'"[89]

Told by her elders that at age twelve she could not be a member of the Congress Party, Indira reacted angrily and formed the "Monkey Brigade." Modelled on the legendary monkey army that helped Lord Rama, the hero of the epic *Ramayana*, to conquer Sri Lanka, Indira's brigade acted as an auxiliary of the Congress Party and performed a variety of tasks, such as writing notices, addressing envelopes, putting up posters, and getting messages past unsuspecting policemen.[90] "'I did that in a fit of temper,'" Indira Gandhi proudly recalled many years later. "'I was twelve years old at the time and I wanted to be a member of the Congress Party – but they turned me down. They said I would have to be eighteen or twenty-one or something like that. I was exceedingly angry and I said 'I'll have an organization of my own.'"[91]

Indira's assertiveness also manifested itself in her relationship with her family. As was the practice, Kamala and Jawaharlal had an arranged marriage in which two very different people were joined together. Kamala was the daughter of a wealthy Kashmiri family that was very traditional and Indian in its outlook. "'[She] was an unsophisticated, quiet person, while the Nehru family was very sophisticated. She was very Indian, they were very Western, and she was made to feel that she was not 'in,' a member of the family recalled.'"[92] Both her sister-in-law, Vijaya Lakshmi, and mother-in-law, Swarup Rani, made no effort to conceal the fact that they considered Kamala gauche and plebeian. Vijaya Lakshmi, in fact, seemed to take a sadistic pleasure in embarrassing Kamala over her lack of familiarity with Western norms of social etiquette. She would offer friends and visitors gleeful accounts of how Kamala had employed the wrong piece of cutlery at the dining table or had failed to find the proper expression during a conversation. She also carried tales against Kamala to her father and brother. If Jawaharlal did not give much credence to Vijaya Lakshmi's stories, he also did not rebuke her for doing so, nor did he do anything to check his mother's overbearing behaviour.[93] None of this was lost on Indira, who suffered from her mother's rejection by the Nehru family. As she said, "'We were very close to each other and when I thought she was being wronged I fought for her and quarreled with people.'"[94] Indira's antipathy to her Aunt Vijaya Lakshmi was also exacerbated by the treatment she received at her hands. Vijaya Lakshmi regarded Indira as a gangling, awkward girl and made no secret of her disdain for her.[95]

Gandhi's desire for power and control manifested itself not only verbally, but also in her refusal to speak. When she became an adolescent, she learned how to assert herself by refusing to respond – verbally or in letters – to others, including her father, an action she knew would induce a sense of impotence in them. During a stay at Bhowali with her mother, who was confined to her sanatorium bed for treatment of her tuberculosis, Indira was able to make one visit to Nehru at Almora Jail. They quarreled, but about what is not clear, and "Indira threatened not to come back [to see him] for six months, then fell silent, turned her back, and left."[96]

During the time that Indira was studying at Oxford, Nehru wrote in March 1937 to say that he planned to come to Europe in early summer and that he had been invited for a weekend at the country home of Lord Lothian, who was a great admirer of his and had favourably reviewed Nehru's autobiography. Lothian, however, was a prominent member of the "Cliveden set," which supported Neville Chamberlain's policy of appeasement. In late April, Indira wrote to Nehru about his trip to England, in which she pointed out that the Cliveden set was commonly known as "'Hitler's friends in Britain.' 'Your staying with him would amount to the same as if you spend a weekend with Hitler himself or with Mussolini.'" She argued that it would create a terrifically bad impression on all people in England who were even slightly left-wing and who sympathized with India and the Congress. She then asked him to reconsider and change his mind.[97]

This was the first recorded episode of Indira blatantly disagreeing with her father and attempting to influence his behaviour. It was not well received.[98] Nehru replied that he knew all about Lord Lothian's pro-fascist and pro-Hitler activities and acknowledged their danger. But, he wrote, he had decided to accept the invitation, and then he proceeded to put Indira in her place by pointing out to her his international status and his acquaintance with international affairs. "'I have to judge what I should do and should not do.'"[99] Indira, however, held her ground. She acknowledged that "'of course you are the only person who can decide what is the best thing to do. I was only stating my own opinion on the matter. And I am afraid it is still unchanged ... I shall hate being away from you for even a couple of days but I don't think I could bear to stay with Lothian.'"[100] She then proceeded to write a polite note to Lord Lothian declining his invitation.[101]

Prior to the outbreak of the Second World War, Nehru, worried about Indira's health and concerned about the coming conflict, was reluctant to allow her to return to England. "But, again, Indira was adamant. This time she defied and overruled Nehru. In April 1939, she went to Bombay and set sail for Europe on the SS Strathaird."[102] Later, when Indira encountered resistance from her father with regard to her marriage to Feroze Gandhi, "she told him that her mind was made up and that was that. She even threatened to stop talking to him."[103] Even Mahatma Gandhi did not escape her combativeness. "Gandhi suggested that (she and Feroze) ... remain celibate after marriage; Indira ... turned his suggestion down flat, saying 'you can tell a couple not to get married ... but when they are married, to ask them to live a life of celibacy makes no sense. It can result only in bitterness and unhappiness.'"[104]

The Dominant part of her personality was especially evident in the political arena. In her new role as Congress president, Indira visited Kerala in April 1959. A Communist government elected two years later had created significant unrest by introducing a bill to subject parochial schools to state controls and accountability. Mass agitation was launched to unseat the government. Nehru refused to intervene on the grounds that the government had been duly elected. Indira told a journalist that her father had spoken as prime minister. "As Congress president, I intend to fight them and throw them out."[105]

At Indira's urging, Nehru visited Kerala on 22 June 1959 and saw for himself the atmosphere of group hatred. When Kerala's chief minister, Namboodiripod, rejected his call for fresh elections that would test the opposition's claim that the government had lost all popular support, Nehru, on 31 July 1959, ordered the dismissal of the Communist government. This was the first time in independent India's history that a state government had been dissolved, and it created a dangerous precedent.[106]

With hindsight, Indira's critics view the dismissal of the Kerala government as prophetic: the first display of her "ruthlessness," her authoritarian tendencies, and her indifference to democratic norms. Indira clearly supported – and may have expedited – her father's dismissal of Kerala's government, but she did not orchestrate it.[107] Yet, as one of her biographers, Katherine Frank, underlines, "what is significant about Indira's response to the unrest in Kerala is that it touched a raw nerve in her – her fear of disorder and loss of control. It was Indira's overreaction to political instability – rather than an innate authoritarianism – that marks Kerala as a revealing episode in her political development. Indira did not share Nehru's faith that democratic institutions would survive unstable circumstances. In the face of conflict and instability, her instinct was to choose order above democracy."[108]

Gandhi's decision to step down from the party presidency after only one term has been attributed in part to her desire to spend more time with her children; a more convincing explanation seems to be that she had discovered, to her great disappointment, that her father still held the real power as prime minister. She had to go to him, either to uphold the position of a state Congress party, as in Kerala, or to overrule a state party boss. "For a proud, self-willed person like Indira," K. Bhatia writes, "that must have been galling."[109] If she could not control, she would not play the game of politics.

When language riots broke out in Madras in March 1965, Shastri decided to wait out the crisis. Indira, however, immediately hopped on a plane to Madras where she gave assurances to the protesters against Hindi and helped restore peace. Shastri was extremely annoyed at the way she had "'jumped over his head.'"[110] The Dominant side of Indira's personality was again evident when, as we have seen, she decided to assert herself by going on a foreign tour, as Congress president, that took her to London, Belgrade, and Moscow. There can be little doubt that "her duties as Congress President appear to have given Mrs. Gandhi increasing self-confidence, and the shy and retiring young hostess of Teen Murti was developing rapidly into an assertive and imperious woman who could no longer be dismissed or ignored with impunity."[111] Nor was her husband exempt from her forceful personality and her angry moods. "As Congress President, she had occasion gently to admonish her husband, though without naming him for his outspoken criticism of the party to which she belonged. Now, however, she was fed up – and furious."[112] The occasion for her anger was Feroze's criticism of her handling of the Kerala crisis.

The tough and unsentimental aspects of her Dominant style were also in evidence in her relationship with her father's political associates. "When serious allegations of corruption were made against Matthai [the prime minister's principal private secretary] and publicised, by her husband, Feroze, among others, Indira, with sound political sense, did not hesitate to dissociate herself from him, and is believed to have persuaded her father to relieve him of his duties. It was a practical and unemotional approach which would be characteristic of her future political relationships and which contrasted strongly with her father's more sentimental and easy-going nature."[113]

UNDERSTANDING INDIRA GANDHI'S PERSONALITY PROFILE

The findings presented in this chapter present an interesting and intriguing picture. Unlike other political leaders who have been profiled using this model, only Indira Gandhi displays a personality profile in which the scores of four of her patterns, the Ambitious, Reticent, Contentious, and Dominant, are sufficiently high to be indicative of somewhat maladaptive personality patterns. Such findings are not that surprising given the assessment of her many biographers that she was an extraordinarily complex character. As Z. Masani observes: "Ambition and diffidence, assertiveness and reticence had been inseparably interwoven in her character ever since the days when a painfully shy and introverted school-girl had dreamt of leading her people like Joan of Arc. While one part of her personality sought fulfilment in political leadership, the other craved the greater intimacy, peace and security of private life."[114]

Thus it was that Gandhi's expressive behaviour, interpersonal conduct, cognitive style, moods, and self-image lacked consistency and varied enormously over the course of her life, as measured prior to her becoming prime minister. The larger question is how her multifaceted personality profile can be explained.

The biographical facts around her life until her ascent to the prime minister's office indicate, unmistakably, that the Reticent and Retiring aspects of her personality developed early. As Gandhi discussed her childhood, the most common adjectives she used to describe it were "lonely and insecure." As a very young child, Indira was indulged by her grandfather; however, his death, her mother's illness, and her father and mother's frequent imprisonment meant that Indira grew up a lonely, solitary child largely in the company of servants. A constant awareness that those whom she loved and depended upon could disappear at any moment meant that she could rely only on herself. Nor could her extended family be counted upon to fill the gap. Her father's sister thought her ugly and stupid and was overheard to say so. This was a particularly scarring experience and, as a result, she made little effort to evoke affection if it was not spontaneously forthcoming. "Her aloofness, a means of overcoming the anxieties of her unstable and insecure childhood, was necessitated by the absence (and hence unreliability) of those who might have eased those anxieties."[115] Indira's diffidence was also exacerbated by the absence of any continuity in her schooling, which became hostage to Indian politics and her parents' frequent absences from home.

Another dimension of Indira's personality, Ambition, can also be traced to parental influences. Exposed to a highly politicized environment – both her parents spent time in jail – Indira identified with both their struggle to end British rule and their conviction that they could make it happen. As a child, her heroine was the liberator of France, Joan of Arc, and at the age of twelve she created her own children's group to help the Indian National Congress. She found her studies irrelevant, since they seemed to have so little bearing on the task of ridding India of the British which was her parents' major preoccupation. However, unlike Margaret Thatcher, whose father encouraged her interest in politics and stimulated her ambition, Jawaharlal Nehru seemed to believe that democracy and dynastic rule were bad companions and he never encouraged his daughter's political ambitions. In 1938 Indira finally joined the Indian National Congress Party and subsequently became its president in 1959, notwithstanding her father's less than enthusiastic endorsement of the idea. Paradoxically, Indira's ambition may have been fuelled by her desire to show her father that she was capable of political leadership.

With her mother's death, her father increasingly relied upon his daughter to act as his hostess, especially after he became India's first prime minister. Although she was never his confidante, Indira began to feel as though she should be and that her political ideas were often better than the advice he received from some of his colleagues. A growing sense of self-confidence occasionally bordering on arrogance went hand in hand with her new role as hostess for her father.

An intriguing aspect of Indira's personality profile is the strong presence of both Reticence and Ambition, for these two traits are not usually present together at high levels in a personality profile. Large amounts of shyness and diffidence appear to be logically incompatible with confidence, arrogance, and a sense of entitlement. But the dual traits of Reticence and Ambition that coexisted in Indira's psyche can be understood as follows. "Her loneliness, lack of an even tenor of life and her vision of the great tasks expected of her appear to have developed in her a feeling of great vulnerability and inadequacy, goading her to develop a dual defensive mechanism. On the one hand, despite her painful shyness, she strove to excel in whatever she had to do. On the other, she enveloped herself in impenetrable reserve. She was unable to confide her thought and emotions to anyone except a very few, and she guarded her privacy most zealously."[116]

Indira possessed not only Reticent and Ambitious traits but also Contentious ones. Her father, who observed her moody, fretful nature, her recalcitrance, and her obstinance, wondered what was wrong with his daughter. The answer lay in his relationship to her. Indira's Contentious personality traits can be explained in part by her deep disappointment with her father. She was pained by the way in which he allowed his family to treat her beloved mother, who was less sophisticated and educated. Unlike Margaret Roberts (Thatcher), who idealized her father and disdained her mother, Indira adored her mother and was critical of her father. Intellectually, she accepted her parents' going to prison as a necessary component of the freedom struggle; emotionally, she clearly felt abandoned. Nehru's letters to his young daughter in which he chided her for her despondency and gave her well-meaning but insensitive advice on every subject from health issues to suitable reading materials was not what she wanted to hear. As a young child, she swallowed her disappointment by becoming uncommunicative and refusing to respond to her father's letters. As well, her infrequent visits to him in prison once resulted in her threatening not to return. Indira's self-image, that of being misunderstood and unappreciated, stemmed from her father's attempt to mould her into an intellectual – something she was not. She felt demeaned not only by him but also by the rest of the family for her lack of social graces.

Ample evidence also exists of Indira's Dominant traits both in the private and public realms. As a young child, Indira was inhibited in her assertiveness by ambivalence, her love for her father, and her rage at his "choosing" to go to prison. However, as a young woman, she was able to express her strong will by defying her father more openly and choosing a husband whose social standing was inferior to hers; it also provided a way for her, unconsciously, to vindicate and uphold her mother's denigrated position in the family.

Moreover, having been treated as something of an intellectual dullard by her father, Indira responded by becoming more authoritative and even dogmatic in her views. Ambition and Dominance would propel her, albeit unconsciously, to try to prove that whatever her father had accomplished for India, she could do better.

These four strong personality traits persisted well into Indira's prime ministerial years. Her first years as prime minister were marked by great inner uncertainty and consequently by indecision and vacillation in her leadership. Most people were not surprised; indeed, it confirmed the general impression that she was inherently a weak, reticent, and retiring person thrust to the centre of power by the memory of her father and the divisions among the Congress politicians who survived him. This dimension of her personality seems to have been reinforced by the existing political configuration that pitted Gandhi against the Congress Party bosses. Faced with a hostile environment, Indira, instinctively, withdrew emotionally. The 1967 elections, in which the Congress lost in eight of the seventeen states, was, according to Bhatia, a turning point in Gandhi's political career.[117] Through her extensive campaigning, she found that she could reach the masses effectively and that they responded to her much more positively than to any of her rivals within the Congress Party. Buoyed by the recognition of her potential power, the Ambitious, Dominant, and Contentious patterns in her personality profile received far greater expression as she prepared for the overt struggle for power within the Congress Party in 1969.

Successful in her struggle to control Congress by 1970, Indira Gandhi was transformed into a politician whose ambition, dominance, and contentiousness were to be far more in evidence than the shy, aloof dimensions of her personality. To rephrase Lord Acton, power "suppresses" and absolute power "suppresses" absolutely. The acquisition of power, and the sense of accomplishment it engendered, seem to have resulted in a significant diminution in the expression of the Reticent dimensions of Gandhi's personality profile and permitted a greater expression of the Ambitious, Dominant, and Contentious traits. Nowhere was this to be more in evidence than in her decision to declare a State of Emergency in 1975, which effectively suspended civil liberties, the functioning of Parliament, and the freedom of the press.

An examination of the overall influence of the Ambitious, Reticent, Contentious, and Dominant dimensions of Gandhi's personality patterns suggests that she can be best understood as both a "compensatory narcissist" and, to a lesser extent, an "abrasive negativist." A highly Ambitious personality pattern, combined with substantial Reticent and Contentious features, is characteristic of the compensating variant of the narcissistic personality. The early experiences of compensating narcissists reveal that all have suffered "wounds" early in life. Rather than collapse under the weight of inferiority and completely retreat from public view, the compensating narcissist develops an illusion of superiority. Life thus becomes a search to fulfil aspirations of status, recognition, and prestige.[118]

When one explores the impact of the Contentious-Dominant pattern – the "abrasive negativist" – one sees individuals who are caught in conflicts between their own agenda and a loyalty to others, and who, as a result, are overtly and intentionally contentious and quarrelsome. Such individuals, in fact, feel so torn by conflict that every request or expectation feels like a major burden, an opportunity to incur contempt. Past experience has shown them that even their most conscientious performances are likely to be evaluated with disappointment and derision.[119]

To understand the impact that Indira Gandhi's personality patterns had on the Indian body politic, we now turn to a study of her leadership style.

3

Indira Gandhi's Leadership Style

This chapter analyses the empirical evidence of Gandhi's leadership style during her tumultuous years as India's prime minister. Cluster A explores Gandhi's motivation, her task orientation, and her personal investment in performing her duties as prime minister; Cluster B examines her management style, both with her cabinet and in the realm of information gathering; and Cluster C studies Gandhi's interpersonal relations with members of the civil service, her personal staff, the caucus, the extra-parliamentary party, the opposition, the media, and the public.[1] (See Table 2.)

CLUSTER A: INDIVIDUAL STYLE

Motivation

In the area of motivation, the four factors that shaped Indira Gandhi's political choices – *power, pragmatism, ideology,* and *personal validation* – were explored in order of significance to her leadership style.

POWER

Of all the components that motivated Indira Gandhi in her policy choices, the goal of maintaining and amassing power and control loomed as the most important, accounting for 44.4 per cent (143) of the relevant biographical items extracted and coded. Throughout her career as prime minister, a focus on power loomed large in Indira's calculations.

From the time that Gandhi became prime minister, in 1966, the opposition – as well as the more liberal members of the Congress Party – tried to get her to lift the Emergency that Nehru had imposed during the war with China in 1962, given that the situation had become stable. The chief ministers of various states, however, were reluctant to part

Table 2
Leadership-style categories: Indira Gandhi
Total number of items (relevant passages/extracts collected and assessed): 1,275

CLUSTER A: Individual Style	
I. MOTIVATION (total evidence in this category: 322)	
a Pragmatism (138)	42.8%
b Personal Validation (25)	7.7%
c Ideology (24)	7.4%
d Power (143)	44.4%
II. TASK ORIENTATION (total evidence in this category: 82)	
a Process (7)	8.6%
b Goal (75)	91.4%
III. INVESTMENT IN JOB PERFORMANCE (total evidence in this category: 64)	
a Circumscribed (6)	9.4%
b Tireless (58)	90.6%

CLUSTER B: Managerial Style	
IV. CABINET MANAGEMENT STRATEGY (total evidence in this category: 88)	
a Uninvolved (0)	0.0%
b Consensus Builder (1)	1.1%
c Arbitrator (3)	3.4%
d Advocate (Authoritative/Peremptory) (84)	95.5%
V. INFORMATION MANAGEMENT STRATEGY (total evidence in this category: 120)	
1. Degree of involvement (35)	
a Low (5)	14.3%
b High (30)	85.7%
2. Sources (85)	
a Ministerial (11)	13%
b Independent (74)	87%

CLUSTER C: Interpersonal Style	
VI. RELATIONS WITH PERSONNEL (total evidence in this category: 129)	
1. Degree of Involvement (29)	
a Low (1)	3.5%
b High (28)	96.5%
2. Type of Involvement (100)	
a Collegial/Solicitous – (Egalitarian) (11)	11%
b Polite/Formal (6)	6%

Table 2
Leadership-style categories: Indira Gandhi (*Continued*)
Total number of items (relevant passages/extracts collected and assessed): 1,275

c *Attention-seeking/Seductive* (16)	16%
d *Demanding/Domineering* (39)	39%
e *Manipulative/ Exploitative* (28)	28%

VII. RELATIONS WITH THE PARTY (total evidence in this category: 172)

1. Caucus (59)

a *Uninvolved* (2)	3.4%
b *Cooperative/Harmonious* (5)	8.5%
c *Competitive/Oppositional* (31)	52.5%
d *Controlling/Overbearing* (21)	35.6%

2. Extra-Parliamentary Party Organization (113)

a *Uninvolved* (4)	3.5%
b *Cooperative/Harmonious* (13)	11.5%
c *Competitive/Oppositional* (70)	62.0%
d *Controlling/Overbearing* (26)	23.0%

VIII. RELATIONS WITH OPPOSITION PARTIES (total evidence in this category: 94)

a *Uninvolved* (3)	3.2%
b *Cooperative/Harmonious* (8)	8.5%
c *Competitive/Oppositional* (36)	38.3%
d *Controlling/Overbearing* (47)	50.0%

IX.   RELATIONS WITH THE MEDIA (total evidence in this category: 89)

a *Open* (44)	49.4%
b *Closed* (45)	50.6%

X.   RELATIONS WITH THE PUBLIC (total evidence in this category: 105)

a *Active* (105)	100%
b *Passive* (0)	0%

with the sweeping powers that they had acquired during the Emergency. "Indira herself was reluctant to do away with it: Why should any politician cede away her power? Some civil libertarians saw in her reluctance early signs of the fondness for authoritarianism that Indira would exhibit later in her career."[2]

On 3 May 1969 the Indian President, Zakir Husain, who had been Gandhi's choice to succeed Sarvepalli Radhakrishnan in 1967, died suddenly. As we have seen, Gandhi's enemies in Congress wanted the speaker of Parliament, Sanjiva Reddy, to be the next president. Gandhi knew that Reddy as president could remove her from office and install

Desai as prime minister.[3] She was advised by P.N. Haksar, her principal
official adviser, that the best way to vanquish the Syndicate would be
to convert the struggle for personal power into an ideological one.[4]
Gandhi acted on his suggestion, at once, by dismissing Moharji Desai as
finance minister, assuming his portfolio, and nationalizing the banks,
thus strengthening her leftist image.[5] But there could be no mistaking
her real purpose, which was to maintain herself in power.

On 12 November 1969 the Syndicate bosses expelled Gandhi from
the Congress Party and the party was instructed to elect a new leader
who would be the new prime minister as well. Only 65 Congress parliamentarians went along with the Syndicate; 226 voted for Gandhi. However, the vote meant she had lost her majority in the 525-seat Lok
Sabha. She refused to be intimidated and formed her own Congress
Party, which became known as Congress (R), in opposition to the Syndicate's Congress (O). Of the 705 delegates to the emergency session of
the All India Congress Committee, 446 voted with Gandhi.[6] In this new
reincarnation, "Indira had become something ruthless and new. She had
astonished people ... with her capacity for a fight to the finish, even to
bringing the eighty-four-year-old party of liberation to rupture. She had
made use of realpolitik, suiting the action to the moment's need, undeterred by any backlog of sentiment or ethics. Her own emergence from
an image of extreme withdrawal and reserve was now complete."[7]

But she did not stop there. In order to prevent her position and authority being jeopardized again, Gandhi sought to control not merely
the Indian president but also the cabinet, the president of Congress, the
Congress Working Committee, the Parliamentary Board, and the Central Election Committee. To extend her control to the states beyond
New Delhi, over the next few years, she tactically "eased out" state
leaders who had failed to support her against the Syndicate, including,
in time, the chief ministers of Rajasthan, Andhra Pradesh, Madhya
Pradesh, and Maharashtra. She then replaced them with her own people by "nominating" candidates for chief minister who were then ratified in office by the dominant Congress legislative party.[8]

In the general election that took place in March 1971, Gandhi won a
two-thirds majority in Parliament and was thus now in a position to get
any legislation she wanted passed. She was indisputably the most powerful politician in India and probably the most powerful woman in the
world. "Her power gradually shaped her outlook – no dissent would be
allowed, no criticism tolerated. Everything, everyone, was judged on
the single overarching criterion of loyalty to Indira – that, and how useful they were to sustain Indira's own power."[9]

The ultimate litmus test of her drive for power and control came
in 1975. When she was found guilty of election fraud, she decided that

remaining in office, but not being allowed to vote until her appeal was settled, which could be many months, would reduce her to the lamest of lame-duck prime ministers. The opposition was determined to oust her from office, and she responded by declaring a State of Emergency. As a result of the challenges posed by J.P. Narayan, the Socialist leader, and Morarji Desai, the Congress stalwart, "Indira was convinced that India would self-destruct if she relinquished power."[10]

Hence, once the State of Emergency was implemented in June 1975, foremost among the "urgent and important government business was a series of bills introduced to amend the constitution. The primary purpose of these amendments was to make the Emergency and Indira invulnerable to the judiciary ... Indira also strengthened her new regime by eliminating the remaining opposition in the states. She used the President's rule to dismiss the non-Congress government that had just come to power in Gujarat, and did the same in Tamil Nadu, which had been under the regional DMK Party. Although much of the opposition was in jail, Indira increasingly resorted to ordinances to shortcut parliamentary delays. She would wait for parliament to recess and then instruct the president to act."[11]

Even after Gandhi ended the State of Emergency in 1977, called for new elections, and was roundly defeated, only to return to office in 1980, her desire for power did not diminish. Not content with the vast punitive and preventive powers in its legal armoury, her 1980 government sought even more power. A national-security ordinance was issued that year and soon converted into a parliamentary act. It authorized detention without trial for up to twelve months to prevent acts prejudicial to the security of the state, the maintenance of public order, and the delivery of essential supplies and services. An Essential Services Maintenance Act banning strikes in key public utilities and providing for summary trials of strikers followed.[12] She proceeded to use the fears of an increased level of caste, language, religious, and regional conflicts, and the elites' demands for a stronger and more forceful central government, to her advantage. "Prime Minister Indira Gandhi capitalized on these fears ... She believed in strong central government, and the concentration of power in party and government in her hands."[13]

Indeed, Gandhi played high-stakes politics with the domestic conflicts in the Punjab and Kashmir as a way of increasing her power. In Punjab, in the late months of 1981 and 1982, she played the "Hindu card" by secretly supporting a Sikh demagogue and fundamentalist, Jarnail Singh Bhindranwale, as a way of splitting the Sikh community and weakening the Akali Dal Party, which had defeated Congress in the 1977 election. Her policy was also designed to increase her strength among the Hindu majority in the rest of the country.[14]

Her quest for power would spill over to the international stage. In Sri Lanka, Gandhi's government appeared to facilitate the same sort of secessionist movement that it was fighting in the Punjab and Kashmir. By covertly supporting the Tamil Tigers, Gandhi may have wanted to placate the huge Tamil population in south India. As well, she may have wanted to dampen down Tamil separatism by backing extremists in order to split the Tamil population and maintain the status quo.[15]

In each of these cases, Punjab, Kashmir, and Sri Lanka, Gandhi's efforts to maintain or enhance her power led to disastrous results; her interference succeeded only in making secessionist efforts more powerful than they otherwise might have been. Her insatiable motivation for political dominance thus exhibited all the classic elements of ancient tragedy: a heroine blinded by her quest is ultimately destroyed by her own (un)doings.

PRAGMATISM

While the acquisition of power was an important element in Indira Gandhi's motivations, the evidence suggests that pragmatism, or flexibility, especially as affairs of state were concerned, was only marginally less significant to her political calculus, accounting for 42.8 per cent (138) of the biographical data extracted.

Just before she became prime minister, Gandhi was interviewed for the BBC program "Panorama." One pointed question was whether her "pronounced left-wing views" would affect relations with the United States. Her answer revealed her pragmatic streak. "'I don't see the world divided into left and right. I think most of us are in the center, and in a country like India where the basic problem is one of poverty and of trying to convince the average man that we are on his side, you have to be more or less in the center and try to keep as many people with you as possible.'"[16]

Characteristic of her pragmatism is the following example. Faced with a grim food situation during her first months in office, which made the need for American aid desperately necessary, Gandhi was forced to follow the economic policies of the former prime minister, Shastri, that she had denounced only a few months earlier as an "unacceptable departure" from the course charted by her father. Her leftist image had contributed to her rise to the top. Now it became a thing of the past. She abandoned the socialist rhetoric that she was so fond of as Congress president. "Pragmatism" became her new watchword.[17]

Increasingly, Gandhi came to realize that, if the measures needed to revitalize the Indian economy turned out to be those advocated by the United States, she was not going to shy away from them merely so as not to invite a cry from the left. It was consistent with her practical approach that, wherever controls were productive, they should be enforced, but wherever unnecessary, they should be discarded.[18] Whatever would eradicate poverty, she favoured; the merit of a particular economic measure or political act had to be weighed against that fundamental goal, not decided a priori on the basis of a particular ideological perspective. Hence, in an early interview with Anthony J. Lucas of the New York *Times* on 27 March 1966, Gandhi exclaimed: "'How can anybody who is the head of a nation afford not be a pragmatist? You have to be pragmatic, you have to be practical, every day.' Mrs. Gandhi, in any case, was fitted neither ideologically nor temperamentally for the role of a revolutionary leader. She was, above all, a pragmatist and a gradualist."[19]

For many years, commentators would argue that Gandhi's leftist policies were "'largely a defensive strategy born out of pragmatism ... [she] realized that she would lose ground to leftist forces unless [she] moved to the left ... so she often made use of left slogans to discredit the opposition and to contain her enemies within the party by representing the party conflict as a fight between forces of progress and reaction.'"[20] But, while socialist slogans were freely used to win mass support, Gandhi was quick to reassure the rich that she stood for peaceful and gradual change.[21] "It would take Indians some years to discover that everything Indira did was dictated by a keen instinct for self-preservation, and that every position she took, whether radical or rightist, was always flexible."[22]

For example, witness Gandhi's ambiguous election manifesto for the 1971 general election, which called for the "'advance of socialism ... [while giving] scope to the private sector to play its proper role in the economy.'" The future, she maintained, held something for everybody – a message that, as one of her biographers later put it, demonstrated her ability to "ride both horses, convincing the rich and the poor that she would protect each from the other."[23] She displayed the same ability during the 1972 economic crisis, when the need for foreign aid, especially a standby credit from the International Monetary Fund, required the abandonment of radical policies and reversion to economic liberalization and concessions to foreign investors. When radicals protested against this "retreat from socialism," Gandhi took a pragmatic decision to appease the left by imposing a ceiling on urban land ownership.[24]

Gandhi's pragmatism also surfaced in her dealings with Pakistan. If she had a tendency to be a hardliner in her dealings with her neighbour before she became prime minister, once in office, she showed patience and reserve. She also kept "'the door open,'" as she said, for talks with China.[25] And on the issue of Punjabi Suba, an ostensibly Punjabi-speaking but actually Sikh-majority state, she made a practical decision to accept the Sikh demand for reorganizing Punjab in such a way as to exclude

Hindi-speaking areas and leave the Sikhs in a majority in the smaller Punjab while the residual Hindi speakers would have their own state of Haryana.[26] In the aftermath of the second Indo-Pakistan War in 1971, which India won, Gandhi put aside her innate dislike and mistrust of Prime Minister Ali Bhutto of Pakistan, choosing not to humiliate him; instead, she signed a peace agreement with Pakistan at Simla, in which both sides agreed that they would undertake not to resort to force, or threaten to use force in Kashmir, and would settle the issue only on a bilateral basis.[27]

Finally, in her dealings with the superpowers, Gandhi was careful to balance India's economic and political interests through a carefully calibrated set of relationships. This meant enhanced political relations with the Soviet Union, which became the chief supplier of military hardware for India, and increased reliance on the United States for economic and technical assistance.[28]

IDEOLOGY

Notwithstanding a general and traditional (by way of her political and family ties to the Congress Party and Nehru respectively) commitment to socialism, Indira Gandhi was a decidedly non-ideological leader. Only 7.4 per cent (24) of the total 330 biographical extractions on motivation reveal ideology as a reason for her policy choices. "Throughout her life she defied labels of any kind and recoiled from rigorous definitions of political concepts. Her commitment to socialism never rested on intellectual grounds; there is no evidence, for example, that she ever systematically studied socialist thought. There was thus a certain superficiality in her socialist outlook."[29]

At the beginning of her term as prime minister in 1966, Gandhi did not see herself as doctrinaire, preferring instead to call herself a pragmatist. However, in a revealing conversation with some editors, she said that she believed in socialism, "'but not in a dogmatic way.'" She then revealed the fuzzy nature of her concept of socialism. "'I believe in the people's right to a better life – not only materially but also mentally and spiritually. I have been lucky to have had a rich life of the mind, and it hurts me to see people steeped in such poverty that they are rendered incapable of appreciating culture and the arts. I would like conditions to be created where all the people would be able to enjoy and appreciate these finer values of life.'"[30]

In another interview that she gave in March 1966, Gandhi ruminated, "'Yes I suppose you could call me a socialist, but you have to understand what we mean by that term. Socialism like democracy, covers such a wide range. It covers what is happening in Sweden, the Soviet Union, and China. We used the word because it came closest to what

we wanted to do here – which is to eradicate poverty. You can call it socialism; but if by using that word we arouse controversy, I don't see
why we should use it. I don't believe in words at all.'"[31]

Characteristically, for three years (1966–69), Gandhi steered clear of
any open alignment with the party's competing groups and factions.
Then she announced to the country and the party, in July 1969, that she
stood with the Congress left and against the party's conservative leadership. For the first time in her career, she had staked her political future
on an ideological issue.[32] But the precise motives for her intensified leftist stance were far from clear and her words were often contradictory.
"She espoused radical change, but also took pains to assure the proper-
tied classes that reforms would not threaten their interests."[33] This quo-
tation illustrates the ambivalent and tenuous nature of Gandhi's
commitment to ideology as a motivating factor for her behaviour.

PERSONAL VALIDATION

There is limited evidence that Gandhi was motivated by the need for
personal validation. Only 7.7 per cent (25) of the biographical data on
this subject refer to this dimension. Still, it played an interesting part in
her overall motivation, as the following examples illustrate.

On 12 November 1969 the split within the Congress Party became final when the Syndicate formally expelled Gandhi from the Indian National Congress, on the grounds that she had rebelled against the
official working committee by sponsoring a rival one. However, a meeting of the All India Congress Committee in Delhi, on 22 November, vin-
dicated Gandhi's claim that a majority of the party was behind her. In
her address to the AICC, after tracing her family's and her own long involvement with the Congress, she spoke of her expulsion from the
party. Her voice broke and tears rolled down her cheeks. For a moment,
it seemed as though she would be unable to continue her speech. But
she recovered quickly and asserted amid much applause: "'Nobody can
throw me out of the Congress.'"[34] "'It is not a legal question, nor one
of passing a resolution to pronounce an expulsion order. It is a question
of the very fibre of one's heart and being.'"[35] Gandhi's need for personal validation was clearly evident.

According to one biographer, "the real danger to India lurking within
Indira Gandhi's psyche in the late sixties was not ruthlessness or hypoc-
risy – the gestural radicalism or sham populism her critics invariably accused her of – but, rather, her growing belief that only she could lead
the country."[36] This belief was strengthened after she was found guilty
of electoral malpractice on 12 June 1975, a decision that meant a mandatory penalty barring her from holding – or contesting – any elective
office for a period of six years. Initially, Gandhi felt that she had no

choice but to resign; however, her sons and one of her daughters-in-law, Sonia, convinced her that chaos would ensue if she took that path. Years later, she confided to Dom Moraes that there was never any question of resignation, saying, as we have seen, that "'it was my duty to the country to stay, though I didn't want to.'"[37] "That assertion of indispensability was typical of Indira. In her mind, only she could run India. By now, she had come to believe a phrase that the Congress President Dev Kanta Barooah, had coined: 'Indira is India; India is Indira.'"[38]

Many significant decisions in Gandhi's life, such as her marriage to Feroze and the split in the Congress Party, seem to have been prompted by a need for self-validation, particularly when her will, dignity, or beliefs were somehow under attack. From that perspective, one can understand "the emergency decision [as] a defensive reaction against threats to her self-esteem, resolve, and her vision of India."[39]

In November 1976 Gandhi postponed the general election for a second time, at the urging of her son Sanjay. According to P.N. Dhar, she was "uncomfortable about the second postponement on the grounds that it suggested that she was afraid to face the people. When he [Dhar] again urged Indira to go ahead with the elections she became nostalgic about the way people reacted to her in the 1971 election campaign, and she longed to hear again the applause of the multitudes."[40]

It is even suggested that Gandhi's decision to "return to democracy" in 1977 seems to have signalled her need to be respected by others. Although her earlier imposition of a State of Emergency did bolster her sense of self in the short run, in time "the decision created an inner conflict regarding her self-image. Holding elections may have been a way for her to restore her damaged self-esteem which in the past had been linked with her championing of democracy."[41]

Task Orientation

Prime Ministers can be divided into two groups: those primarily interested in *process* – consensus building and respecting the hierarchy of relations within the cabinet – and those more *goal*-oriented, who focus, instead, more on ends and their implementation. The empirical evidence indicates that Indira Gandhi was overwhelmingly concerned about *goal* implementation and rather little with the question of *process*. Of the 82 codings on this dimension, 91.4 per cent focused on *goal*, rather than *process*, implementation.

GOAL IMPLEMENTATION

As if to underline how sharply goal-focused she was, Gandhi observed about herself: "'I am always direct ... I never spend my time in preliminaries ... And I have no time for flowery things. Not that I don't believe in them, but I think that first I should get the job done, then sit and talk. So I say: Hurry up, get to the point.'"[42]

This tendency increased with her successive administrations. In her first term in office, Gandhi made the "green revolution" – which referred to the provision of state subsidies and credit, electrical power, water, fertilizers, and hybrid seeds to farmers – a key government priority.[43] Later, during the economic crisis of 1966, Gandhi, by deciding on devaluation, revealed that she could, when necessary, take an unpopular decision. By swiftly imposing that decision on her reluctant colleagues, she also demonstrated her political sagacity and skill.[44] Then came the fourth five-year plan, the goal of which, Gandhi said, shortly after its inception in 1969, was to enable India "'to stand on our feet as soon as possible and not take a very large amount of foreign aid.'"[45]

Similarly, the 1975 Emergency, from its start, was touted as a program of national regeneration. To achieve this, Gandhi announced a twenty-point economic plan that included initiatives making bonded labour illegal, cancelling all debts owed by the rural poor to money lenders, limiting land ownership among the wealthy, cracking down on smugglers and tax evaders, providing income tax relief to the middle classes, and controlling the price of essential commodities.

Gandhi also demonstrated that she was strongly goal-oriented in the foreign-policy arena. As early as June 1971, she had decided that India would have no choice but to go to war with Pakistan over Bangladesh; according to General Sam Manekshaw, she had issued orders in April 1971 to prepare for war with Pakistan.[46] Following India's overwhelming victory in the Bangladesh war, there was no doubt that Gandhi wanted – and actively worked for – India to emerge as a strong regional military-political-economic power.[47] To make India self-reliant in nuclear technology was another important element in her foreign policy and "she always acted in pursuit of [that goal]." At the same time, she emphatically maintained that her nuclear policy was entirely peaceful and that she did not want India to acquire nuclear weapons.[48]

PROCESS IMPLEMENTATION
The contradictions inherent in Indira Gandhi's philosophy of democratic socialism occasionally yielded a gradualist strategy of change. When coping with conflict during her early years in government, she laboured to absorb opposing segments of a discordant situation, opting, intellectually, for the "definite maybe" of the middle-of-the-roader.[49] Later, the overwhelming structural difficulties of enacting change sometimes forced Gandhi to move incrementally. In an interview with one of her biographers, she declared:

"'We believe in the educational system being changed. Everybody says so. And yet, it isn't really possible to do it, except in slow, small steps, because it affects so many millions of people whose lives would be disrupted.'"[50]

Investment in Job Performance

Indira Gandhi was heavily involved in her role as prime minister. Of the 64 relevant biographical items, 90.6 per cent showed a *strong* investment in her job performance and only 9.4 per cent a *weak* investment. Illustrative of her strong investment in her job as prime minister are the following examples.

Gandhi's first hundred days in power were characterized by a vigorous attempt at shaping events at home. She showed a verve in office that had been missing when she became minister of information and broadcasting. Infected with a sense of urgency, she told the National Press Club in Washington: "'Time is not with India, but against it. With the increase in population we have to run to stand still.'"[51]

During the 1967 election campaign, a protester struck Gandhi with a stone, breaking her nose; however, she continued to campaign across the country with her nose, and top half of her face, swathed in white bandages that made her, she joked, look like a white-masked version of Batman.[52] "She traveled from one end of the country to the other [during the 1967 election campaign] like a hurricane."[53] In a three-day tour of Mysore State, she covered six districts, travelled six hundred miles, and made twenty-two public speeches.[54]

Gandhi demonstrated the same intense involvement during the 1971 election tour. From mid-January 1971 until polling began on 5 March, she was almost continuously on the move. According to the record kept by her staff, she covered 30,000 miles by air and 3,000 by road and rail, addressing 409 election meetings with a total attendance of 20 million people. Throughout these weeks, she was reported to have kept up an eighteen-hour working day, with four or five hours for sleep and rest, and not to have cancelled a single meeting because of illness or fatigue.[55]

As her biographers remark, "politics had taken over Indira's life; she had very little time for her family, friends, for reading or any other activities unrelated to her sixteen-hour, or longer, working day ... It was a work-driven life, with no time for reflection, personal or idle conversation or relaxation."[56] During the sixty-three-day campaign in 1979, she travelled 45,000 miles, visited 384 constituencies, and addressed more than 1,500 rallies.[57] Even during her final tenure, between 1980 and late 1984, Gandhi went overseas no fewer than eighteen times, visiting nearly forty countries,[58] a truly remarkable investment of energy in her duties.

CLUSTER B: MANAGERIAL STYLE

Cabinet-Management Strategy

Indira Gandhi demonstrated a cabinet-management strategy that was characterized by a strong *advocacy* role. She would tolerate only those ministers who were demonstrably loyal to her. In just three instances is there evidence of her acting as an *arbitrator* between different groups within the cabinet, and in only one instance did she try to build *consensus* within the cabinet. Of the 88 biographical items that were extracted on this issue, 84 or 95.5 per cent were coded as *advocate*.

ADVOCATE
During the initial six months that Gandhi was prime minister, her capacity for independent thinking and forceful action was somewhat tempered by her need to maintain the support of the Congress "old guard." At a cabinet meeting she called on 5 June 1966, she raised the issue of the necessity for devaluation of the Indian rupee and then sat back and listened to the various arguments pro and con. At last, she said simply, "'If we don't devalue, we don't get aid.'"[59] Indicative of her intended management style, Gandhi made her decision, and the cabinet followed suit.

In early 1969 the *Indian Express* commented editorially on the uneasy relationship within the cabinet. "'Collective Cabinet responsibility is the cornerstone of our Constitution. Lapses from the principle account for much of the misunderstandings and controversies generated in recent weeks.'" Gandhi was perceived as not doing enough to maintain relations with the members of the cabinet's old guard, resulting in a virtual halt in "effective consultation and discussion."[60]

Typical was her finance minister's demotion later that same year. When Moharji Desai heard about Gandhi's decision to nationalize the banks, he thundered: "'As long as I am finance minister, this cannot be implemented. If the prime minister wants to do it, she will have to change her finance minister.' This was exactly what Gandhi proceeded to do. 'You are quite welcome to stay on as deputy prime minister, however,' she told Desai, after first telling him that he had been relieved of his prestigious finance portfolio."[61]

Especially after the Congress Party split in November 1969, "cabinet members, party presidents, and various chief ministers would get their jobs and stay in them entirely on the basis of their loyalty to Indira." She would also periodically reshuffle her cabinet so as to keep any possible rivals off balance.[62] It made another cabinet minister, Dr Ram Manohar Lohia, say admiringly, "Mohre jamane mein bohut tez hai [She's adept at placing her pawns]."[63]

Gandhi's disdain for her cabinet associates grew increasingly blatant in the 1970s. After the unconditional surrender by Pakistan on 16 December 1971, ending the Indo-Pakistan War, Gandhi was strongly advised by her principal private secretary, P.N. Haksar, who served from 1966 to 1973, and General Manekshaw to announce a unilateral cease-fire, so as not to humiliate and damage West Pakistan any further. The disgruntled defence minister, Jagivan Ram, whom Gandhi had largely ignored throughout the whole crisis, dealing directly with General Manekshaw and the army, was silenced. The cabinet, at her behest, endorsed the idea of restraint, and Gandhi announced an immediate cease-fire on the western front.[64]

When, in August 1971, Gandhi decided to sign a twenty-year Treaty of Peace, Friendship and Cooperation with the Soviet Union, "the manner in which the Indo-Soviet Treaty was negotiated ... was characteristic of Indira's political style. The negotiations were conducted in Moscow in complete secrecy. The political affairs committee of the cabinet was not taken into confidence, until the draft had been finalized, and the cabinet, as a whole, was not informed till the morning of the day on which the documents were signed."[65]

Not content simply with a strong advocacy role within the cabinet, Gandhi moved further to weaken the cabinet's role in its entirety. Under the leadership of Haksar, the prime minister's secretariat became "an all-powerful body which eclipsed not only the cabinet secretariat, but also the cabinet, the individual ministries, and departments."[66] As Gandhi's power grew, ministers, anxious to ingratiate themselves with her, started "passing the buck to the boss" through the prime minister's secretariat, instead of discharging their own assigned responsibilities.[67]

Further evidence of the diminution in the cabinet's relevance occurred in 1974, when India detonated an underground nuclear device to great public acclaim. This "peaceful nuclear experiment" had been kept a closely guarded secret. Not even Gandhi's cabinet knew; they were not informed until four hours after the explosion that India had become the sixth nuclear power in the world.[68]

Even on a matter as important as the declaration of a State of Emergency, the cabinet's role was reduced to that of an endorsing body. On 26 June 1975 Gandhi met with her cabinet at 6 A.M. and, as the eight ministers filed into the room (the other nine were not in Delhi), they were each given a copy of the Emergency proclamation order and a list of the prominent members of the opposition who had been arrested. The news of the Emergency had not been leaked, and most of those present were dumbstruck, both by the fact of the Emergency and by the long list of detainees. Though the cabinet meeting had ostensibly been called to approve the Emergency, no vote was taken. This was not unusual: votes were not taken in cabinet meetings, because that would have made it possible for the prime minister to be overruled by her ministers. Instead, a "consensus" was reached and the Emergency proclamation "approved." No discussion, however nominal and perfunctory, preceded this approval. Not only did "no one say no" to the Emergency, there was no real discussion of why this extreme measure had been taken in the dead of night. The cabinet meeting to ratify the Emergency was over in less than half an hour.[69]

One of her biographers later asked Gandhi: "'I have read that you did not consult the cabinet in taking the emergency decision [of 1975 to impose Emergency Rule]. Is this true and how do you explain this?' Indira replied: 'It is a fact. I did not consult the cabinet but it was ratified by the cabinet immediately thereafter. But that is not the only instance when this is done. The Cabinet is never consulted on the budget. The same is true regarding the devaluation of the rupee in 1969. The PM is not bound to put everything before the Cabinet.'"[70] She was backed in this assertion by a close adviser, an eminent lawyer and chief minister of the state of West Bengal, S.S. Ray, whom she asked, prior to her declaration of a State of Emergency, whether she could take such an important decision without referring it to the cabinet. Ray later testified that he advised her that cabinet rules allowed her to submit the matter to the cabinet simply for ratification. Prior consent was not deemed necessary.[71]

After the State of Emergency had been in place for eighteen months, Gandhi decided to call new elections for March 1977. Again, the cabinet, the chief ministers, the home minister, and even the president were not informed of her decision, and they were all as shocked by it, as were the Indian people as a whole.[72]

Gandhi's successful return to power in January 1980, after her 1977 electoral defeat, did not mean a meaningful restoration of power to the cabinet. In the six months before his death, on 23 June 1980, in a plane crash, Gandhi's son Sanjay had entrenched himself in power, becoming the general secretary of the AICC just eighteen days before his death. His mother had already given her son free rein over her administration: it was Sanjay who ordered bureaucratic transfers and who oversaw business licences.[73] All in all, the power he wielded was greater than that of any cabinet minister.

By 1982, Gandhi's supremacy was undisputed. But this in no way diminished her innate sense of insecurity. Her own position might be invulnerable, but she worried that some of her ambitious followers, biding their time, might try to block her elder son Rajiv's succession when the time came. To prevent this development, she had formed a cabinet of "yes" men content to do her bidding and to speak only when spoken to.[74] But even this was not enough to alleviate her anxiety. "To keep everyone on tenterhooks and not to let anyone build up a power-base for himself was the [other] obvious answer to her problem. She re-shuffled her cabinet at least once every three months."[75] Thus, it would be safe to argue that, during her tenure as PM, Gandhi's cabinet was gradually reduced to a quasi-ceremonial role of "rubber-stampers" con-trolled by an increasingly powerful yet perennially insecure leader.

Information-Management Strategy

DEGREE OF INVOLVEMENT
Indira Gandhi demonstrated a high degree of involvement in the search for and analysis of policy-relevant data. Of the thirty-five biographical extractions on this topic, 85.7 per cent were coded as *high* and the re-mainder as *low*.

High
During her first year in office, based on the information provided by her advisers, Gandhi devalued the rupee by 57 per cent. When this measure did not obtain the intended results, she became increasingly suspicious of accepting advice too easily – and also wary of the motives of those who offered it. From that point on, she tried to be more involved in the search for relevant information on which to base her policies.[76]

Characteristically, scarcely six months after the Congress split in No-vember 1969, Gandhi divided the Intelligence Bureau (IB) into two, leaving the original bureau in charge of internal intelligence and counter-espionage and entrusting external intelligence to the newly formed research and analysis wing, RAW. She then brought the IB, RAW, and Revenue Intelligence – until then a part of the finance ministry – under the prime minister's direct control.[77]

During the 1971 East Pakistan/Bangladesh War, Gandhi was kept in-formed of every move of the Indian troops, who were fighting alongside Bangladeshi forces.[78] Throughout the course of the war, she chose to ig-nore the advice of her defence minister, Jagivan Ram, relying instead on the information provided by the military chiefs.[79]

Low
Indira Gandhi was less involved in the search for and analysis of policy relevant data early in her career as prime minister. She then relied heav-ily on Dinesh Singh, whom she had appointed as minister of state in her first cabinet. She assigned him a wide variety of functions and it was clear that he had enormous freedom of action.[80]

By 1969, she had substituted her reliance on Singh with a growing dependence on P.N. Haksar, who had become the head of the prime

minister's secretariat and main policy formulator. She trusted his intelligence and judgment implicitly and depended on him for her understanding of policy-relevant information. However, his influence lasted
only until 1973, when Gandhi chose not to renew his appointment. After that, she relied on P.N. Dhar and her own family circle, while continuing, herself, to play a greater role in the analysis of information.[81]

Sources of Information

Gandhi strongly preferred to draw upon a variety of sources for her information, rather than relying solely on her cabinet or the civil service.
Of the 85 relevant items dealing with this issue, 87 per cent demonstrated her preference to search for and rely upon *independent* information outside this circle, while 13 per cent showed her relying on
institutional sources such as her cabinet or the senior civil service.

INDEPENDENT
During the economic crisis of 1973–74, Gandhi's anti-inflationary program was not a product of cabinet or civil service initiatives but was
based on a book by a well-known Indian economist, V.K.R.V. Rao. His
entire analysis was framed in free-market terms of supply and demand,
as were his policy suggestions. Inflation was to be controlled by holding
down spending in the public and private sectors and by curbing deficit
financing by the government. Gandhi accepted the Rao approach to
"socialist planning," veering to the right in her decision in 1974 to
undo the nationalization of the wholesale trade in food grains, in effect
since the previous year.[82]

Gandhi's "outsourcing" of information gathering would sometimes
take place when she wanted a denial of existing information. For a long
time, she refused to give any credence to the reports of forced and brutal
sterilizations that took place under Sanjay's direction during the Emergency. She would ask "her people" to look into these reports, and then
be reassured when they told her they were unsubstantiated rumours.[83]

Gandhi's reliance on non-cabinet or civil sources of information intensified with the Emergency's weakening of the cabinet and the
strengthening of the prime minister's office and the apparatus it controlled. For example, in November 1976, she again postponed the general election – this time for a full twelve months. Both this and the
earlier postponement announced the previous February would prove to
be strategic mistakes. But Sanjay, who had no formal role in government, had convinced his mother to postpone the elections, not once but
twice.[84] When Gandhi finally opted for elections to take place in
March 1977, "probably she hoped – or was encouraged to hope by her

intelligence agencies and craven advisers – that she could restore democracy and yet remain in power by winning the election."[85] It was not to be.

As Gandhi's drive for power and her insecurity about her political future entered its final phase, outside influences on her decision making intensified. In the run-up to the January 1980 general election, Dhirendra Brahmachari, a handsome, forceful swami who had been Gandhi's yoga teacher for twenty years, persuaded her to agree to "counter rituals" – various rites and mantras that he performed to annul the harmful forces unleashed by those who, he claimed, were seeking her destruction. Gandhi not only gave credence to Bramachari's occult prognostications, she also heeded his political advice.[86]

Even at the end of her life, Gandhi was ignoring advice from informed civil servants in favour of other independent sources of information. An object lesson occurred in 1984, when she asked for advice, on the Akali Dal problem in Punjab, from Subhadra Joshi. Joshi, who had worked with her during the Partition riots in Delhi, was a Punjabi herself and a politician with vast experience of communal conflict. She tried to persuade Gandhi that there were still ways in which a peaceful settlement might be reached. But Gandhi did not heed Joshi's advice. Instead, she continued to be guided by her inexperienced and far from diplomatic oldest son, Rajiv, and her Kashmiri advisers, Arun Nehru and Arun Singh.[87]

MINISTERS/CIVIL SERVANTS

As with her level of involvement in information gathering, Gandhi's reliance on her ministers and members of the civil service occurred more frequently in her early years in office. An illustration of this was her decision to make Dinesh Singh a minister of state in her first cabinet. From the early months of her term as prime minister, she relied on him heavily. A presidential order was issued to the effect that the prime minister assigned to him "such functions as she may," and she was accused in Parliament of making Dinesh Singh "'a virtual de facto Prime Minister.'"[88] Also, it was on the recommendations of P.N. Haksar, a senior civil servant and the head of the prime minister's secretariat, that Gandhi implemented a range of radical measures in 1970, the most dramatic and controversial of which was her proposed abolition of the privy purses and privileges, which had been guaranteed to the Indian princes at independence by the Indian constitution.[89]

Gandhi's early reliance on ministers and civil servants, however, was not a matter of choice but rather reflected her insecurity and inexperience. A highly suspicious woman, who only became more so, her distinct preference, as noted above, was for information and analysis from individuals whose loyalties were only to her, and not to their careers in government. Thus, as her power and insecurity grew, her reliance on institutional channels of information waned in favour of independent sources whom she thought more loyal and reliable.

CLUSTER C: INTERPERSONAL STYLE

Relations with Senior Civil Servants and Personal Staff

Indira Gandhi's dealings with her aides, advisers, and members of other branches of government were coded for the degree of involvement and the type of behaviour exhibited. In general, there were few references in the literature to her degree of involvement; only 29 items were extracted and, of these, 96.5 per cent were coded as *high* and 3.5 per cent as *low*.

DEGREE OF INVOLVEMENT

High

As prime minister, Indira started to rely on a group of advisers, quickly dubbed the "kitchen cabinet" by the media, that had gathered around her during the Shastri era. Prominent in this group was Dinesh Singh, with whom she spent so much time that he was soon romantically linked with her – a speculation that he did not discourage.[90] According to the journalist Kuldip Nayar, until 1967, "'every important paper received by Mrs. Gandhi, or sent by her, was routed through Dinesh Singh.'"[91]

When Gandhi summoned her confidant, S.S. Ray, the chief minister of West Bengal in June 1975, to talk about the chaos she felt was enveloping the country, she spent two hours with him discussing what she should do in this situation. He left to consider her constitutional position and returned for further conversations with her that led to her decision to impose a State of Emergency.[92]

Low

Some biographers have remarked that Gandhi's high level of involvement with ministers and bureaucrats was very selective. Her inability to communicate effectively with people at an intermediate level, where most political relationships operate, meant that she often failed to inspire trust and confidence in associates who did not know her well. Nor were they reassured by her inclination to make decisions in isolation.[93] Consequently, she did become involved with personnel, but only those whom she perceived as deserving of her intimacy. Notwithstanding advice to the contrary, she refused to dismiss Sikh members of her personal guard after the Golden Temple debacle, a decision that would prove fatal.

TYPE OF INVOLVEMENT

There were many more extractions for the type of involvement; of the 100 extractions, 11 per cent were coded as *collegial/egalitarian,* 6 per cent as *polite/formal,* 16 per cent as *attention-seeking/seductive,* 39 per cent as *demanding/domineering,* and 28 per cent as *manipulative/exploitative.* Characteristic of Gandhi's behaviour with personnel are the following examples.

Demanding/domineering

After being appointed foreign minister by Gandhi in 1969, Dinesh Singh was then unceremoniously dropped by her. "This was a familiar pattern of behaviour for Indira: People who got too big for their breeches would be taught a lesson or two. She never liked people to publicly flaunt their good standing with her."[94]

In the aftermath of the split in the Congress, Indira had an opportunity to start afresh. She was still the prime minister of the country, no longer beholden to the party bosses. From that point on, cabinet members, party presidents, and various chief ministers would get their jobs and stay in them entirely on the basis of their loyalty to her. She would also periodically reshuffle her cabinet so as to keep any possible rivals off balance. From 1969 to 1977, the Congress had five presidents, the turnover designed, apparently, to prevent institutional consolidation of power by any potential challenger.[95]

Gandhi's relations with the Supreme Court were also controlling. In response to the court's ruling, in the spring of 1973, on the government's constitutional amendments of 1971, she chose to bypass the three most senior judges, who had voted to limit Parliament's power to reform the constitution, in the selection of an individual to succeed the retiring chief justice, thereby ignoring previous practice. Instead of appointing one of these three men, she instructed the president to name another member of the court who had supported the government's actions.[96]

Illustrative of Gandhi's domineering tendencies when dealing with personnel and members of other government branches is the following testimony of her own principal secretary, reported by Manohan Singh. Singh, the chairman of a flourishing engineering company, had been involved in the negotiations between the Indian government and the Sikhs in Punjab in the three years before Gandhi's death in 1984. He told one of her biographers of a conversation he had with Dr P.C. Alexander, Gandhi's principal private secretary and her key adviser on the Punjab. "'The PM never listens – either she demands an explanation, or she gives you a lecture,' Singh quoted Alexander as saying."[97]

Another example involves a meeting of the National Development Council, consisting of the Planning Commission and all state chief ministers in Delhi, early in 1984, under Gandhi's chairmanship. Gandhi

refused to allow the chief minister of Andhra to read a statement deploring the ousting of their colleague Farooq Abdullah. When told that,
if he persisted, his statement would still not go on record, he and the
other non-Congress chief ministers staged a walkout. Gandhi then ordered the non-elected officials from non-Congress states also to leave
the meeting. These individuals were not involved in any political dispute; thus, they had chosen to stay on, even after the walkout by their
political bosses.[98]

Manipulative/exploitative

As demanding as she was, Gandhi could be exploitative as well. Following the "Great Split" in the Congress Party in 1969, she decided to extend her control to the states beyond New Delhi. Over the next few
years, she arranged for a number of state leaders who had failed to support her against the Syndicate to be tactically "eased out" of office. The
new chief ministers were individuals who would never have been elected
in an unfettered vote in their respective parliamentary caucuses. Hand-
picked chief ministers, who were then ratified by the legislature in states
ruled by Indira's Congress Party, became an established pattern.[99]

In general, ministerial selections appeared to be based on two criteria:
loyalty to the prime minister and their absence of a personal power
base. Gandhi picked a succession of incompetent men to head state administrations and her increasingly authoritarian style transformed the
system of centre-state relations from one of political bargaining to one
akin to feudal tutelage.[100]

Not even her closest personnel would be immune from her manipulative tactics. Her most trusted adviser, P.N. Haksar, earned her ire by telling her that her son Sanjay's behaviour had become a liability to her,
and that granting him a lucrative government contract would make her
vulnerable to criticism. Despite the massive contribution Haksar had
made to her prime ministership, from 1967 to 1973, Gandhi jettisoned
him without explicitly telling him that she had done so. Instead of automatically renewing Haksar's contract, she just allowed it to expire.[101]

On 25 June 1975 Gandhi and S.S. Ray, the chief minister of West
Bengal, went to visit the president of India, Fakhruddin Ali Ahmed.
Gandhi told the president about her plans for a state of emergency, and
Ray hinted that, since Indira had promoted Ahmed's candidacy for the
presidency, it would be appropriate if he went along with the prime
minister's request for the president's signature on the document imposing the emergency. Ahmed quickly acceded.[102]

Gandhi manipulated not only the president but her own ministers as
well. On 23 April 1983, when militants entrenched inside the Golden
Temple shot and killed the most senior police officer in Amritsar, the

Punjabi chief minister urged the Indian government to enter the temple and round up the terrorists. Gandhi hesitated and the government's failure to act at this juncture spread panic in Punjab and increased the popularity of the terrorists. Indira's home minister, P.C. Sethi, articulating government policy, repeatedly assured the Sikhs and Parliament that the government would not send police or paramilitary forces into the shrine. However, increasing unrest and deaths led Gandhi to change her mind and plan to enter the Temple to round up the provocateurs. Sethi was then sidelined and given little to do in the making or implementing of Punjab policy. When questioned by one of her biographers about this bizarre state of affairs, Gandhi badmouthed one of her most loyal colleagues: "'You know that the home minister is usually either drunk or doped or both.'" She was then reminded that it was she alone who had appointed him and given him the most crucial portfolio.[103]

Attention-getting/seductive

Another intriguing element in the mix of Gandhi's interpersonal behaviour with staff and other officials was her feminine charm, which she employed considerably more than the other two subjects of this study to advance her political goals. Golda Meir may have exhibited that aspect of herself with her lovers, while Margaret Thatcher clearly enjoyed flirting with some of her key aides, but neither woman included it quite so deliberately in her dealings with foreign and domestic audiences. For instance, Gandhi's dignity and bearing helped to win her a sympathetic hearing from Western politicians when she visited abroad during 1966, though opposition MPs criticized her for having "'projected a personal image abroad.'" As on previous foreign tours, Gandhi's personal charm and so-called "feminine mystique" figured prominently in the press coverage she received. She was especially attentive to the importance of being elegant and well groomed whenever she appeared in public. According to one reporter, when she arrived in London she made "'a dashing appearance out of the plane in a most unusual ankle-long yellow cape.'"[104] In the same vein, Masani reports the view of "Mrs. Gandhi's critics," who "say she is cold-blooded, calculating and fickle in her relationships, turning on her charm when it is expedient."[105] Both in public and private, Masani notes, "she remain[ed] a very 'feminine' woman, not only in her appearance but in her social manners and behaviour. She [wa]s aware of her feminine appeal and charm and ma[d]e no attempt to suppress it."[106]

Collegial/egalitarian

Gandhi actively sought to establish a good collegial relationship with her staff. For example, preparations for and conduct of the 1971 Indo-Pakistani War were characterized by mutual trust and respect between Gandhi and the leaders of the military. The results were an excellent coordination of military and political actions. This cooperation was the product of Gandhi's efforts to establish close personal rapport with the armed forces, from the officer corps down to the ranks. She chatted easily with the ordinary soldiers, demonstrating an informal and maternal manner that presented a marked contrast with the severity of their elitist officers.[107]

Gandhi could also display personal attention, great sympathy, and understanding for those around her. During the 1977 electoral campaign, she took the opportunity to reassure party workers that she had no intention of deviating from her father's policies. In the face of the vilification she was receiving from the opposition, she urged her campaign workers to face the voters unitedly and boldly.[108]

Polite/formal

A final element of Gandhi's interpersonal behaviour with staff was her politeness and formality. Addressing large crowds, she was just as warm as when she was with her family and close friends. It was with groups in the middle – especially officials or groups of politicians – that she would appear cautious, restrained, and on guard.[109]

Her reserve and strong sense of etiquette would manifest itself even in the face of India's enemies. Notwithstanding Pakistani President Bhutto's abusive outburst against Gandhi, she did not allow it to deflect from her diplomatic objectives. She maintained a dignified silence on his comments and in their face-to-face meetings to negotiate the end of the Indo-Pakistani War in June 1971, treating him coolly but with politeness.[110]

RELATIONS WITH THE PARTY

Parliamentary Caucus

Gandhi's relationship with the party caucus was overwhelmingly *competitive/oppositional* from 1966 to 1970. From 1970 on, it became *manipulative/exploitative* as power gradually shifted from the cabinet to the prime minister's secretariat and, later, to the prime minister's house next door.[111] The party caucus and the cabinet increasingly assumed a rubber-stamp function and the cabinet no longer operated as a centre of policy making. Of the 59 items that were coded in this category, 62 per cent were *competitive/oppositional*, 23 per cent were *manipulative/exploitative*, 8.5 per cent were *cooperative/harmonious*, and 3.4 per cent were *uninvolved*.

COMPETITIVE/OPPOSITIONAL
Gandhi's *competitive* streak became evident early on. By 1967, the friendship that she had established with various chief state ministers,

especially those in the south, was in jeopardy as a result of the issue of
India's national language. Gandhi and Morarji Desai strongly disagreed
over the replacement of English by Hindi as the national language. Under the Indian constitution, Hindi was to have become the official national language by 1965. Riots in that year, however, led to a
postponement of the implementation of that provision. In 1967 the
government then came forward with a constitutional amendment that
seemed to satisfy the non-Hindi speaking states. Desai thought Gandhi's
concession was an act of weakness, not flexibility, and that Hindi
should be the national language. For her part, Gandhi suspected that
Desai was trying to undermine her electoral support in Uttar Pradesh –
the largest of the Hindi-speaking states – where there had been pro-
Hindi agitation. Desai held that Gandhi's stance was meant to weaken
the position of the leader of the Uttar Pradesh Congress party,
C.P. Gupta, who had been a strong supporter of Desai's campaign to
become prime minister of India.[112]

Throughout 1969, the continuing enmity between Gandhi and Desai
was reflected in the ever-deepening fissure in the Congress Party between its radical and conservative wings.[113] Following the split in the
party in 1969, and the virtual eclipse of the Congress organization (O),
at the hands of the electorate, Parliament became the nearly exclusive
power preserve of the Congress reformers led by Gandhi.

Having successfully achieved two impressive coups at her opponents'
expense, the defeat of the Syndicate's candidate for president of Congress, and the nationalization of the banks, Gandhi, according to her biographers, might have been expected to rest on her laurels. "Success,
however, appears to have encouraged her to consolidate her position
still further" and "she was unwilling to make peace with the Syndicate
except on terms that left her supremacy unchallenged."[114] This competition continued well into the 1970s and beyond.

In the middle of the 1977 election campaign, Jagjivan Ram, the powerful Harijan minister of irrigation and agriculture, resigned from the
cabinet, defected from Congress, and founded a new party which immediately joined the fold of the opposition Janata Party. At a press conference, he called upon his fellow Congress members to join him in his
move to end the "'totalitarian and authoritarian trends ... in the nation's politics.'"[115]

MANIPULATIVE/EXPLOITATIVE
Increasingly, Gandhi became more *manipulative* in her dealings with
the party's Syndicate. In part, her behaviour was a response to the Syndicate's own devious tactics. For example, the choice of president of India in 1967 was important both to the Syndicate and to her. The

president could, on the advice of the prime minister, dissolve Parliament
and order fresh elections. This would give Gandhi a tremendous hold
on Congress parliamentarians, particularly given that she would become extremely adept at "massaging the president into signing virtually
whatever ordinance she wanted."[116] The battle for the presidency
reached its peak when the Syndicate approached the right-wing Jan
Sangh and Swatantra parties to support Neelam Sanjiva Reddy, the
speaker of the Lok Sabha and, until the 1967 general election, a member of Gandhi's cabinet. After that election, Reddy had been "unceremoniously dumped" by her. The choice of Reddy by the Congress
Parliamentary Board infuriated Gandhi, who supported the candidacy
of Jagjivan Ram, an untouchable, and she denounced the Congress
leaders for the breach of an important principle – secularism.[117]

On coming out of the meeting of the board, Gandhi made no attempt
to appear calm and imperturbable. At a hurriedly summoned press conference, she declared that the party bosses would have to face the consequences of their action. She then added that their decision to "'force' a
presidential candidate that she disliked on her was really an 'assault on
her views and attitudes and ... social and foreign policies.'"[118] Journalists who had attended the press conference speculated that she was
about to strike at Y.B. Chavan, her home minister, for his disloyalty in
backing Reddy. However, she seems to have realized that any action
against Chavan would smack of a personal vendetta and detract from
the ideological crusade she claimed to be leading. She decided, therefore, to act against her finance minister, Morarji Desai. She divested
him of the finance portfolio on the grounds that, in view of his "'strong
reservations on basic issues, it would be unfair to burden him'" with
the responsibility of implementing the economic program – the nationalization of the banks – with which he so profoundly disagreed.[119]

In an exchange of letters during this period with C.B. Gupta, the chief
minister of Uttar Pradesh, Gandhi said that some party leaders were
"conspiring" against her. Although she did not name Desai explicitly,
he was convinced that her reference was clearly to him. He accused her
of paranoia. "Indeed, whenever it suited her during her long career,
Indira leveled charges of conspiracy against colleagues – as a way of
getting rid of them politically from her circle."[120]

There certainly was a grain of truth in the above statement about
Gandhi. But the relationship between her and the party caucus was not
just a one-way flow. The party was also capable of hostility towards its
leader. In June 1974 forty Congress MPs had met at the residence of
Mohan Dharia, a junior minister whom Gandhi had dismissed for his
condemnation of "police brutality" against followers of Jayaprakash
Narayan and for his declaration that she should negotiate with

Narayan's Jayaprakesh [JP] movement. The consensus at the meeting was that efforts should be renewed to persuade Gandhi to seek a settlement with the JP. The meeting was held in great secrecy, but when Gandhi was informed about what had transpired, she began to feel as though she were facing a conspiracy within her own ranks.[121]

When Gandhi announced the State of Emergency on 26 June 1975, she justified it on the ground that it was, paradoxically, the only way to safeguard and preserve Indian democracy against a variety of enemies such as the "fascist" JP movement, backed, she maintained, by a "foreign" hand. What she did not publicly acknowledge was that she also had enemies within – dissidents in her own Congress Party. At least fifty Congress members on the left had defected to J.P. Narayan and his movement, and, on the right, another sixty or seventy, who deplored her socialist stance, wanted to replace her with Jagjivan Ram, the minister of irrigation and agriculture.[122]

COOPERATIVE/HARMONIOUS
In her initial period in office, Gandhi sought to establish a rapport with parliamentarians outside the formal workings of the upper and lower houses of Parliament. Her cooperative behaviour during that time can best be assessed as tactical. For her own party members, there were meetings of the Congress Parliamentary Board or the Congress parliamentary party.[123] She also behaved in an accommodating fashion when she needed the caucus to support her in 1967 in her bid to become prime minister once again.[124]

Thereafter, glimpses of cooperative behaviour would occasionally surface, but, again, they must be judged against a background of political calculation and expediency. The success of Jayaprakash Narayan's political movement, in opposition to Congress, led to a substantial number of Congress MPs adopting a less deferential attitude towards Gandhi. Many of them esteemed Narayan highly and felt that, instead of confronting him, Gandhi should try to be more conciliatory. Some of them suggested that to her. Under their pressure, she agreed to meet him at the prime minister's house, in November 1974, but the meeting ended acrimoniously,[125] suggesting that Gandhi's cooperative stance was politically motivated.

UNINVOLVED
Although Gandhi's father had loved Parliament and shown it enormous respect, using it both as a sounding board and as a forum for educating the country in democracy and egalitarianism, she developed a tremendous disdain for Parliament, partly because of the way the members had treated her in the first difficult months of her prime ministership.

She started absenting herself, even from important debates, and later, in the years of her supremacy, treated Parliament with scant respect. During the Emergency, she reduced this august body to a mere rubber-stamp,[126] and nothing changed in this regard during her final tenure as prime minister.

Extra-Parliamentary Party Organization

Gandhi's relations with the party organization largely paralleled those with the party caucus. Of the 113 items coded on this topic, 62 per cent were *competitive/oppositional* and 23 per cent were *overbearing/manipulative*, for a total of 85 per cent. She behaved *cooperatively* towards the party organization 11.5 per cent of the time and was *uninvolved* only 3.5 per cent of the time.

COMPETITIVE/OPPOSITIONAL
Indicative of Gandhi's confrontational behaviour are the following examples from her 1967 conflict with the party, leading to its schism in 1969. In the run-up to the February 1967 general election, the Congress Party was in the midst of selecting candidates for the elections. Naturally, Gandhi was anxious that as many of her allies as possible received nominations to run. But the Syndicate was determined "to put the squeeze on her." Knowing that she and Krishna Menon were once again close politically, the party bosses turned down Menon's request for a ticket from Bombay. Gandhi was appalled, but there was little she could do.[127]

In marked contrast to the formation of her first cabinet, in 1967, when she had consulted closely with the Syndicate, after the general election Gandhi kept her own counsel. The organizational leadership of the Congress was not consulted, and even Kamaraj was shown the list only a short while before it was due to be submitted to the president.[128]

Throughout the autumn of 1969, unity talks and meetings were held between the warring Congress factions – the Syndicate old guard and Gandhi's followers – without success. On 28 October the Congress President, Nijalingappa, wrote an open letter to Indira charging Gandhi with having created a "personality" cult that put the future of Congress at risk and confused loyalty to her with loyalty to the Congress and the country.[129] Privately, Nijalingappa scoffed in his diary at what he considered Gandhi's arrogance and obstinacy. "'During the course of our talks,' he wrote in exasperation, 'for the second time she asserted, "I'm the Prime Minister of India."'"[130] Nijalingappa clearly resented the demand of the leader of the parliamentary wing of the majority party, that is, the prime minister, to determine policy without the input of the leader of the organizational wing. What was surprising was that the old

Congress leadership had calculated so badly. They had hoped to get a puppet; instead, they got a woman who, if the occasion demanded, was prepared to manipulate the strings just as well as they did.[131]

Finally, the Congress Party stalwarts had their fill of Gandhi and expelled her from the party in November 1969. But the prime minister of India was determined not to take such action lying down. After tracing her family's and her own long involvement with the Congress, Gandhi spoke of her expulsion from the party. "She ... asserted amid much applause: 'Nobody can throw me out of the Congress.'"[132]

In the post-1969 period, there was no doubt that Gandhi had emerged much the stronger from the Congress conflict and split. "'The "dumb doll" had been suddenly transformed into a confident, assertive and dominant leader to whom the appellation "ruthless" had also begun to be attached.'"[133] "Crucial to Gandhi's thinking seemed to be the belief that, by eliminating the party bosses, she would be doing more than getting rid of what she perceived to be their malevolent influence. She would be asserting the primacy of the Congress Party's parliamentary wing. It had been traditional for the party leaders – who were not necessarily members of Parliament – to dictate party policy to legislators at the centre as well as in the states. As long as the parliamentary leader of the ruling party – meaning the prime minister – was in consonance with the Congress bosses, the overall arrangement worked just fine. But when the disputes between Indira and the Syndicate began, the whole question of party supremacy in legislative matters came dramatically to the fore."[134]

The struggle was to continue well into the 1970s, and, in many ways, party unity under Gandhi never recovered after the trauma, even in periods when party solidarity was essential. By June 1975, when she was most in need of a strong party to back her, Congress members were divided on ideological issues and over whether to stand with their leader to confront the JP movement and other opposition parties. After the court ruling that year that she had been guilty of corruption and malpractice during the 1971 election, it was widely rumoured that some colleagues were advising her to resign. Others pressed her to stay on. Clearly, the party was divided.[135]

MANIPULATIVE/EXPLOITATIVE
Another avenue for dealing with the party organization was for Gandhi to manipulate and exploit it. In October 1969 the president of the Congress Party, Nijalingappa, as part of the struggle between the Syndicate and Gandhi's supporters, dropped two of her close associates from the working committee of the party. Calling the manoeuvre shabby, she sacked several junior ministers sympathetic to the Syndicate.[136]

"It was Indira's desire to have a homogenous, closely knit party organization functioning as a 'liaison' between the government and the public, playing an interpretative role, preparing the masses and creating the right climate for any sociological, political or legislative reform planned by the government, in fact, a party which, having enunciated policy, plays an active part in helping government to execute it. This, the old Congress [dominated by Syndicate members] would not do."[137]

But the Congress split changed all that, with the conservative faction expelling Gandhi from the party in November 1969 and her own faction affirming their confidence in her leadership.[138] The 1971 general election featured a campaign by the Congress Party that she ran almost exclusively. Since there was no party machine worth the name, and hardly any leader to question her, Gandhi was the sole selector of the candidates and, virtually, the sole campaigner.[139] By 1972, Congress's organizational party structure had fallen into complete decay. Party elections became a thing of the past. The Congress president and members of the cwc were all now nominated by the prime minister herself.[140]

By 1974, Gandhi controlled the organizational wing of the Congress Party – including the Congress president, Dev Kanta Barooah, and most of the states' chief ministers. With Fakhruddin Ali Ahmed, a loyal, malleable, seventy-year-old Muslim as president, her position was virtually unassailable. This was neatly summed up by the telling slogan, already quoted, "'Indira is India, India is Indira.'"[141] The process of emasculating the party organization was accelerated by Gandhi's own preference to establish her unshakeable supremacy in the ruling party and to cut down to size anyone in her ranks who could even remotely become a rival centre of power. Having seen the role that chief ministers in the states had played in the making of the prime minister, she wanted to make sure that, in the future, the prime minister alone would make or unmake chief ministers.[142] This trend would continue after the Emergency and beyond.

In response to the debate as to why Gandhi decided to call the elections in March 1977, one of her biographers wrote: "The element of risk seemed small as far as a Congress win was concerned for it had held the stage without competition ... During that period [of the Emergency] Mrs. Gandhi had disciplined the dissidents in her party through arrest or the threat of arrest."[143]

Several of the chief ministers whom Gandhi had allowed Sanjay to hand-pick just before his death in 1980 turned out, in a matter of months, to be major embarrassments. She found it necessary to fire, amidst derision from the press and the public, the chief minister in Rajasthan, because his government's incompetence and corrupt ways had become too much even by the prevailing permissive standards.[144]

COOPERATIVE/HARMONIOUS

As in relations with her caucus, Gandhi tried, early in her tenure, to be cooperative with the organizational wing of the party since she could not yet afford to confront it. As already recounted, in the struggle to control the presidency of India, in 1967 the Syndicate's preferred candidate was Sanjeeva Reddy, the speaker of the Lok Sabha, while Gandhi's was V.V. Giri, the incumbent vice-president of India. There was no agreement between them, and Gandhi suggested a compromise by putting forth Jagjivan Ram, who, as a Harijan leader, could be considered an appropriate choice in what was then being celebrated as Mahatma Gandhi's centenary year. She also suggested postponement of the decision, so that the matter could be sorted out with less bitterness later.[145] In fact, "right until the moment she was outvoted at the Bangalore meeting of the parliamentary board, [Gandhi] tried hard to find a meeting ground with the syndicate. Contrary to the reputation for being incorrigibly combative and confrontational that she was soon to acquire, she seemed genuinely reluctant to reach the parting of the ways with the syndicate and thus bring about a split in the Congress."[146]

Relations with Opposition Parties

It is hardly surprising, given the nature of the competitive and manipulative relationships that existed between Gandhi and both her caucus and the Congress Party organization, that the same type of behaviour characterized her relations with the various opposition parties. Of the 94 relevant items that were coded on this subject, 50 per cent were *manipulative/exploitative*, 38.3 per cent were *competitive/oppositional*, 8.5 per cent were *cooperative*, and 3 per cent were *uninvolved*.

MANIPULATIVE/EXPLOITATIVE

By the summer of 1972, India was facing growing inflation and a rise in the price of oil. Government cuts in expenditures only fuelled the industrial unrest that had begun to spread through the country. In the face of growing social turbulence, Indira's instinct was to try and impose order. Her policy of controlling the state governments by hand-picking chief ministers now became the rule. "Unfriendly" state leaders were disposed of through recourse of "president's rule," under which states were run directly from Delhi. In addition, Indira began to suspend, rather than dissolve, state legislatures, in order to paralyse opposition to the Congress Party in the states.[147]

In a similar fashion, although Gandhi initially balked at dissolving the state assembly of Gujarat since Congress held a two-thirds majority there, faced with widespread unrest and anger at the corruption in government, she imposed president's rule on Gujarat on 9 February 1974.[148] She also faced serious unrest in Bihar, when the socialist trade-union leader, Georges Fernandes, launched a nationwide railway strike in May. Gandhi declared the strike illegal and was determined to break it at any cost. Fernandes and other labour leaders were arrested on 1 May, and in the next few days over 20,000 railway workers were detained and jailed; their numbers would rise to something between thirty and forty thousand. The jailed railway workers' families were thrown out of their government-owned houses and reduced to destitution.[149]

The most illuminating case of Indira's mode of behaviour towards the opposition occurred as part of the Emergency. Among the actions that Indira took beginning on 26 June 1975 were orders to the police in Delhi and elsewhere in India to arrest many members of the political opposition. At the top of the list, of the thousands apprehended, were Nayaran and Desai.[150] Twenty-six anti-Congress political organizations were banned, including the Hindu extremist RSS on the right and the Communist Party Marxist, as well as the underground Naxalite Marxist-Leninist branch of the Communist Party, on the left.[151]

During this period, Gandhi gave an interview to one of her biographers in which she tried to justify her treatment of the opposition political leaders as follows: "'As for the arrests, the top political leaders were given due consideration. They were not imprisoned; they were quartered in houses.'"[152] She also told the journalist Dom Moraes, "'As regards the arrests after we declared emergency, there was a list of the main Opposition leaders, which I approved. The rest of the arrests were left to the discretion of state governments and the police: The idea was to arrest anyone who was likely to exert a troublesome influence in the country or the area.'"[153]

Fernandes was one of Gandhi's few critics who escaped the first wave of arrests in June 1975. Going underground, he led a sabotage operation in which railway lines were blown up and bombs set off in Bihar, Bombay, and Karnataka. Gandhi was convinced that Fernandes and his followers were plotting to assassinate her. When the police could not track him down, they arrested and tortured his brother Lawrence. Eventually, in June 1976, Fernandes was caught in Calcutta and jailed.[154] As we have seen, according to Amnesty International, 140,000 Indians were detained without trial in 1975–76, as against just under half that number put into jail by the British during the "Quit India" movement in 1942 in the entire subcontinent.[155]

Overall, during the nineteen months of the Emergency, the opposition was severely handicapped by being out of the public gaze, with no chance to make its views heard, while the government, with its monopolistic control of the media as well as public meetings and demonstrations, was able to keep up a steady barrage of accusations and condemnations in extreme language against it.[156]

Gandhi also strengthened her new regime during the Emergency by eliminating the remaining opposition in the states. She used president's rule to dismiss the non-Congress government that had just come to power one year earlier in Gujarat, and she did the same in Tamil Nadu, which had been under the regional DMK Party.[157]

Gandhi's heavy-handedness against the opposition continued even after her return to power in 1980. On the heels of the general election that year, she issued a national-security ordinance, later converted into a parliamentary act, which authorized detention without trial for up to twelve months to prevent acts prejudicial to the security of the state, and an essential-services act banned strikes in key public utilities. A countrywide trade-union strike against these two measures in 1981 was crushed; 23,000 activists were arrested but were released after the strike was over.[158]

Gandhi proceeded to extend this pattern of relations to the state level. State elections in Kashmir on 5 June 1983 resulted in a Congress win in the Hindu-dominated Jammu region, but it was overwhelmingly defeated by the National Conference Party in Kashmir. Having failed to control the election, Congress tried to discredit it. As soon as the results were known, Gandhi and Congress made loud and inaccurate accusations that it had been rigged.[159]

Faced with increasing violence in the Punjab in the early 1980s, a number of people had tried to persuade Gandhi to negotiate with the dissidents there. She had repeatedly withdrawn from negotiations in the past because she thought it politically expedient not to reach a settlement. Yet the task of flushing out Bhindranwale and his terrorist accomplices from the Golden Temple turned out to be much tougher than originally expected. The quality of the fortifications, the quantity of arms, the terrorists' control of commanding heights, and the strength of the resistance all came as a surprise. Casualties were heavy and Sikhs all over the world were outraged as never before.[160]

After the Golden Temple debacle on 6 June, Gandhi should have proceeded with caution in Kashmir. Instead, she pushed ahead in July 1984 with her plan to topple the Kashmiri chief minister, Farooq Abdullah. She claimed that Farooq had been colluding with Kashmiri dissidents and had condoned Pakistani aid to the secessionist movement.[161]

Clearly, Gandhi's style was becoming more blatantly manipulative, almost to the point of recklessness. But her behaviour, especially her intransigence in Punjab, proved to be a serious mistake that ultimately led to her assassination and provoked widespread violence. It may have been an expression of her belief in her own invincibility after her re-election in 1980. Alternatively, it may have been a function of the ongoing grief she continued to feel after Sanjay's death, triggering in her a sense of resignation, or even unconscious anticipation of her untimely end.

COMPETITIVE/OPPOSITIONAL

Gandhi's competition with the opposition was legendary throughout her career as prime minister. During the 1967 election campaign, she rebutted accusations concerning her government's failings and, when provoked or bullied, fought back with impressive vigour. For instance, in Jaipur, the opposition, whose candidate was the dowager queen, aroused Gandhi's ire when they attempted to disrupt her meeting. She launched into a blistering attack on the entire princely system, asking her audience to "'go and ask the Maharajas how many wells they had dug for the poor in their states when they had ruled them?'"[162] She also talked about the "negativism" of opposition alliances or the "one party" – that is, the Communists – who, according to her, seemed to want to participate in the democratic process only to destroy it from within.[163] She charged the Communists with spreading dissension through their emphasis, in their election manifesto, on the differences in pay and facilities between ordinary soldiers and the officers. Gandhi was proud of her army, she stated, and any attempt to create a rift would be "dangerous."[164]

The 1971 general election turned into a referendum on Gandhi's leadership. The "grand alliance" of her opponents coined the slogan "Indira Hatao" (Remove Indira). In an inspired response, the prime minister declared that she was not opposed to any individual and was interested only in freeing her people from the scourge of poverty; her battle cry would be "Garibi Hatao" (Remove Poverty). The impact on the country was instant and electric, especially among the poor – the vast majority of the population who thought that "they had found their redeemer."[165]

Gandhi's *competitive* spirit frequently served to unite her disparate opponents against her. For example, appalled at how much had gone wrong in India in the 1970s, Jayaprakash Narayan, who had retired from politics shortly after independence, decided to re-enter the political world. Because of his moral stature, he was able to unify Gandhi's assorted opponents on both the left and the right. With the exception of the Communist Party of India, opposition forces rallied to his JP movement and his call for a "total revolution" to bring down Gandhi's government.[166]

Unable to ignore Narayan, Gandhi reluctantly agreed to meet with him in November 1974.[167] Instead of a reconciliation, the result was an explosive confrontation. She accused him of being backed and financed by the United States through the Central Intelligence Agency (CIA). He said that she wanted to establish a Soviet-backed dictatorship.[168] Four months later, on 6 March 1975, Narayan led a five-mile-long march through Delhi to Parliament where he presented a charter of demands to the speaker of the Lok Sahba. At a rally that followed, he openly called for Gandhi's resignation.[169]

Even the Communist Party of India, a habitual supporter of Gandhi even during the Emergency, turned intensely hostile to her in 1982, in an attempt, perhaps, to efface the memory of their earlier support of her actions. She hit back by describing the Communists as a bunch of "'opportunists' who had joined with 'reactionaries' and 'communalists' against her."[170]

The same combativeness would be exhibited in Gandhi's dealings with officials from the Indian states. In the state elections held in January 1983, a movie actor by the name of Nandamuri Taraka Rama Rao – popularly known as NTR – and his party, the recently formed Telegu Desam, defeated the Congress Party in Andhra Pradesh, winning nearly 150 seats in the 295-member assembly. NTR became the chief minister. In July 1984 the chief ministers of the various states met with Indira to discuss economic issues, and NTR read out a statement deploring the dismissal, earlier that month, of Chief Minister Farooq Abdullah of Kashmir. Gandhi ruled his statement out of order and asked that it be removed from the record. In response, NTR and other non-Congress chief ministers walked out of the chamber. Indira then ordered all non-Congress officials – who were not chief ministers and who had stayed on in the room as they were supposed to do – to leave as well.[171]

COOPERATIVE/HARMONIOUS
Gandhi's display of *cooperation*, during the first years in office as prime minister, likely stemmed from the dual imperative of her father's legacy of political accommodation and the need to behave with political expediency. She continued Shastri's practice of gathering together opposition leaders in Parliament for informal meetings on current issues.[172] In addition, she made a special effort to establish cordial relationships with various state chief ministers, including ones belonging to opposition parties.[173] With her gradual consolidation of power, however, that spirit would resurface only rarely and for brief periods, such as during the war between India and Pakistan. Gandhi was in Calcutta when that war broke out, and she flew back to Delhi immediately, conferred with her cabinet, and secured the support of the opposition leaders for her plans.[174]

UNINVOLVED
Only at the very beginning and end of her career did Gandhi display elements of apathy and indifference towards the opposition, although for diametrically opposed reasons. For example, her unpropitious performance in Parliament in 1966, leading to her nickname "the dumb doll," prompted her to avoid contact with the parliamentary opposition. She started to skip sessions and once called Parliament a "zoo."[175]

As early as January 1984, Gandhi's government had reconciled itself to the inevitability of military action in the Punjab against Bhindranwale, who was holed up in the Golden Temple with his fighters. Repeatedly, the journalist Malhotra asked Gandhi why she was not meeting the opposition leaders, individually and collectively, to win over as many of them as possible in favour of the grave action she was planning to take. She argued that, as a seasoned observer of the political scene, he should know that it would be a useless exercise. "'They hate me so much that they don't even care for the national interest.' She then went on to insist, 'You should know that if I invite them, they won't even come.'"[176]

Relations with the Media

Gandhi's relations with the media vacillated between being *accessible, informative*, and *friendly* to being *inaccessible, uninformative*, and *unfriendly*. Of the 89 relevant items that were extracted on this topic, 50.6 per cent were coded as *closed (inaccessible)* and 49.4 per cent as *open (accessible)*. A majority of the items coded as *open* occurred prior to the imposition of Emergency Rule, while the vast majority of items coded as *closed* took place afterwards.

OPEN/ACCESSIBLE/FRIENDLY
Illustrative of the *open* and *accessible* dimensions of Gandhi's behaviour are the following examples.

On her flight to Madras in January 1967 to launch the Congress election campaign in the southern states, the prime minister relaxed and talked to the correspondents accompanying her, and was filmed by a West German television unit.[177]

During the discussions on the cabinet appointments in 1967, Gandhi took time to brief the press directly either by meeting the correspondents one by one, for a minute or two, or by seeing them together.[178]

As prime minister in the pre-Emergency period, "[Gandhi] felt wonderful being on the international stage in her own right ... Her name raced across the front pages of newspapers all over the world, and foreign television reporters clamored for interviews with her. By now, she was starting to become more comfortable with the news media."[179]

Soon after her announcement, on 27 December 1970, that she intended to go to the people to seek a fresh mandate for her government, a *Newsweek* reporter asked Gandhi what the issues were in the up-coming election. She answered without a pause: "'I am the issue.'"[180]

During the crisis in the Punjab, in 1984, she gave Andrew Niel, the editor of the London *Sunday Times,* a lengthy interview in which "'she showed no strain or anxiety.'"[181] In the same vein, on her return from

Ladakh in 1984, "Indira called in half a dozen editors of Delhi newspapers, including me, for one of the 'group briefings' she liked to hold."[182]

CLOSED/INACCESSIBLE/UNFRIENDLY

At the same time, Gandhi could be equally *closed* and *inaccessible* in her relations with the media. In sharp contrast to her father, she was ill at ease with the press and always gave the impression of having to suffer through media sessions. Nehru, whose relations with the press were confident and cordial, met the capital's press corps once a month. Gandhi held her third news conference in three years on 1 January 1969.

Assessing Gandhi's relations with the press, Frank Moraes, one of India's most respected editors, was puzzled by her inhibitions since the press treated her with kid gloves and were less harsh in their judgments then they had been with Nehru. Moraes recalled, "Nehru talked a great deal in an interview. You started him off, and off he went. She is not forthcoming. She's rather like a convent schoolgirl, tongue-tied. Nehru didn't care what the newspapers said about him. With her, if there's an article, editorial or cartoon she doesn't like, one of her entourage lets her disapproval be known."[183] Individuals, like Gandhi, who have both strong Reticent and Retiring personality traits, are characterized by being easily discomfited; they are painfully self-conscious and prone to feelings of rejection.

On 25 June 1975, the day that Gandhi declared a State of Emergency, preparations had been made for a massive censorship of the media, beginning with a cut-off in the electricity supply to the Delhi newspapers so that these papers would not appear the next morning. "Indira endorsed censorship, while letting Sanjay [her younger son] and Dhawan [her private secretary] work out the mechanics of imposing it."[184]

The following day, Gandhi's old friend, Mohammed Yunus, told the minister of information and broadcasting, Inder K. Gujral, to close down the BBC office in Delhi and arrest its correspondent, Mark Tully, because the BBC had broadcast news that Jagjivan Ram and Swaran Singh had been placed under house arrest. When he got off the phone, the minister sent for the monitoring report of the BBC and learned that it had not, in fact, broadcast that Ram or Singh were under house arrest. He communicated this information to Gandhi, but that same evening she told him, in person, that she was relieving him of his portfolio because the information ministry needed "'a different and firmer handling in the circumstances.'"[185] Left unstated was her determination to have a media that would be controlled by the government and her perception that Gujral would be unwilling to "play ball."

Interviewed by Carras, Gandhi painstakingly tried to justify this imposition of censorship in 1975. "'Originally I think, we had to have some kind of control. Then my view was that censorship should be

lifted. And I advocated what I had advocated for all the years before –
that we should evolve some kind of code of conduct which they themselves could work. Somehow it just didn't work ... And, of course, the
press had been very much against us. Now it is one thing to be against
us and not to support the government and to express views against the
government. But deliberately to guide the opposition movement in the
way they were doing at that moment was very harmful.'"[186]

Censorship was, in fact, a key feature of the Emergency. The press council – an independent body – was abolished. The government banned "publication of objectionable matter" and issued strict press guidelines that only
"positive" information and news should be stressed. In its efforts to control
the media even further, more than forty foreign correspondents were asked
to leave India, their accreditation withdrawn on the flimsiest of pretexts.
Among those forced out were British and American journalists – from the
Guardian, the Baltimore *Sun*, and the Washington *Post* – as well as Mark
Tully of the BBC, who had been covering India for years.[187]

Gandhi's hostility to the press continued even after the State of Emergency ended with her call for general elections in January 1977, and her
subsequent defeat at the ballot box. Returned to power in 1980, she
still retained a "siege mentality." In 1983 she criticized the press, which,
she complained, "'acted as the opposition rather than discharging its le-
gitimate functions.' She knew very well that the Indian press, like India,
was extremely diverse and reflected a wide variety of shades of opinion.
But, in denouncing it, she treated it as a malign monolith."[188]

Relations with the Public

Unlike her ambivalent relations with the media, in her relations with
the public, Indira Gandhi's leadership style was extremely *open*. The Indian crowds seemed to energize her; her shyness melted away and she
felt a special bond with the masses, who loved the combination of her
aristocratic background and her simple down-to-earth manner. She appeared to derive some symbolic legitimacy from the crowd's adulation,
which may have reinforced her belief that she had an inherent right to
lead India, as Joan of Arc had led France. Of the 105 relevant items that
were extracted on this topic, virtually all of them demonstrated an *open*
style, as illustrated by the following examples.

OPEN
On Christmas Day 1966, Gandhi made a highly significant statement to
the press. Referring to Kamaraj and Desai – both of whom, though not
yet allies, wanted her out – she said: "'Here is a question of whom the
party wants and whom the people want. My position among the people
is uncontested.' This was perhaps the first blatant indication of Indira's

key strategy in the years to come. She was asserting a direct, personal relationship with the electorate which bypassed the party organization, its rules and its norms."[189]

In the face of the hostility emanating from the opposition and certain Congress members after she became prime minister in 1966, Gandhi decided to spend some time out of Delhi and see for herself what was happening around the country. She wanted to become a hands-on manager, she told her associates, and there was no better way to do this than to meet with people at the grass-roots level.[190]

During her first election campaign in January and February 1967, she was similarly hands-on, travelling more than 35,000 miles as she crisscrossed India with extraordinary energy. She adopted her father's style of going right into a crowd to speak to people. As her reputation for being a good campaigner spread, she was deluged with invitations from state party organizations. Quickly acquiring a feisty style that was appreciated by the crowds, largely the peasantry, she used metaphors from everyday life which they could easily understand.[191]

"Throughout her political career Indira Gandhi was always on the move. There was scarcely a week during which she was not out of Delhi. She always regarded these journeys as her conduit to the Indian masses ... [She] frequently made the point that only by being with the masses could you understand the masses – and the masses were not in Delhi."[192]

As a politician, her confidence was such that, even though she had written a prepared speech, "'when I saw the audience I just tore it all up and said what I like instead. It is natural and from the heart that way. I always size up an audience the minute I see it. It is not difficult really, for I grew up in crowds. I like crowds.'"[193]

"Her approach and her language were populist; she spoke in the regional language; she wore her sari as the local women did and ate their food with her fingers. But at the same time, Indira appeared lofty and awesome, copiously garlanded, immaculate in a sea of whirling dust as her prime ministerial car roared to a halt before a huge crowd. It was an unbeatable combination."[194]

Especially during election campaigns, Gandhi seemed to come alive among an equally electrified crowd. For example, between early January and the elections in early March 1970, she covered over 30,000 miles by air and 3,000 by road and rail. She addressed 410 election meetings attended by 20 million people, many of whom had trekked miles to see and hear her. Describing this marathon campaign and her popular appeal, which surpassed even Nehru's in his heyday, to an interviewer, she said: "'It was exhilarating ... a sort of movement – a people's movement. It is true that I like being with the people. I shed my fatigue when I am with them ... I don't see the people as a mass, I see them as so many individuals ... Each person really feels that I am communicating with him.'"[195]

On the eve of the Indo-Pakistan War 1972, Gandhi further enhanced her popular appeal by visiting refugee camps and military outposts. She spoke to ordinary soldiers and to the sick and wounded in the camps. Her presence and words of encouragement – widely reported with photographs in the press – buoyed India's armed forces, the refugees, and the country at large.[196]

Even during the Emergency, despite heightened fears of a coup or an assassination attempt, Gandhi seemed remarkably cavalier about her own security. To the dismay of her bodyguards, she would habitually plunge into crowds. She was determined to remain close to the masses and "'would allow nothing to sever that connection.'"[197] Even after she lost the 1977 election, and her lawyers were fighting in the courts to have the election fraud charges against her dismissed, "she took the battle to the streets of India to win back the affection of the people."[198]

In her last and most arduous election campaign, in late 1979, Gandhi travelled 45,000 miles, visited 384 constituencies, and addressed more than 1,500 rallies. An estimated 90 million people – or one in every four of the Indian electorate throughout the country – saw and heard her.[199]

One of her biographers notes that "she has been known to interrupt a heavy schedule to comfort and console someone in distress. On such occasions, she is capable of great tenderness and self-effacement, listening attentively and sympathetically to other people's personal problems."[200] Overall, "Indira's empathy with the Indian people, especially the poor, the deprived and the downtrodden, had to be seen to be believed. Millions, from one end of the country to the other, would squat on bare earth to listen to her speak from high rostrums, bewitching them even when most of what she said was above their heads. Or they would line the roads for hours under scorching sun or pouring rain, to catch a glimpse of her."[201]

THE RELATIONSHIP BETWEEN PERSONALITY PROFILE AND LEADERSHIP STYLE

As with the period before she became prime minister, Gandhi's tenure as a prime minister of India reveals a fascinating and complex portrait of leadership. The empirical investigation and analysis of Gandhi's leadership behaviour in ten selected categories demonstrates that, in nine of the ten, leadership-style patterns strongly matched our theoretical expectations for the Ambitious, Dominant, and Contentious personality patterns.[202] Indira Gandhi emerged as someone who was motivated primarily by *power* and *pragmatism*, who was strongly *goal*-oriented, who was *tireless* in the exercise of her job, who was an *advocate* within her cabinet, and who largely sought information from *independent* sources.

As well, the type of involvement she exhibited with personnel, the caucus, the party organization, and the opposition, which was largely *competitive* and *controlling*, fit expectations for those ranking high on the
Ambitious, Dominant, and Contentious scales.[203] Her openness in her
dealings with the public also matched the theoretical expectations for
these three personality types.[204]

The one area in which our theoretical expectations were not borne
out concerned the media. Rather than demonstrating a *closed* (inaccessible and unfriendly) stance vis-à-vis the media – which all of Gandhi's
most important personality patterns, the Ambitious, the Dominant, the
Reticent, and the Contentious, would theoretically have predicted[205] –
her leadership behaviour in this area revealed an almost equal division
between an *open* and *closed* style. These results can be explained, primarily, by the political situation in which Gandhi found herself. Empirically, Gandhi was far more open to the media prior to the declaration
of a State of Emergency in 1975, and increasingly closed from 1972 on.
From 1966 to 1972, she was trying to acquire and consolidate her
power in the struggle with the Congress Party bosses. In this situation,
media coverage both domestically and externally was viewed as a plus.
From 1975 to 1977, after having declared a State of Emergency, Gandhi
was fighting to hold onto power and suppressed the media, which she
regarded as undermining her efforts. After her defeat at the polls in
1977, she returned to power in 1980 but remained closed and inaccessible to the media, which she viewed as irredeemably hostile to her.

But personality patterns can also explain the oscillation between her
open and *closed* behaviour with the media. Both Ambitious and Dominant traits are theoretically linked to openness with the media, while
Reticent and Contentious traits are associated with a closed stance.
Given the presence of all four major traits at high levels in Gandhi's personality profile, it could logically follow that the evidence would be
split, as in fact it was.

Apart from this one area, what is interesting is how little impact the
Reticent and Retiring patterns in Indira Gandhi's personality profile
seem to have had on the remainder of her leadership style. One explanation may be that, since these personality patterns accounted for only
37 per cent of the five patterns that were ranked at 15 or more, the
other 63 per cent that were reflected in the Dominant, Ambitious, and
Contentious patterns simply overwhelmed the impact of the Reticent
and Retiring dimensions.

A second possible explanation for the minimal impact of the Reticent
and Retiring personality patterns in Indira's personality profile may be
related to the nature of her profile. All of the materials on personality
patterns that were coded were extracted from biographical accounts of

her childhood, adolescence, and young adulthood and until the time she was appointed as prime minister. Still, the majority of the extractions that demonstrated her Reticent and Retiring personality patterns were overwhelmingly drawn from her childhood and early adolescence. If personality is consolidated only in late adolescence, the inclusion of data reflecting the Reticent and Retiring patterns, in her childhood and early adolescence in equal weight, may have skewed the results, producing a pattern that could not provide a meaningful link to her leadership behaviour as prime minister.

A third possible explanation involves the impact of role responsiveness. Although Indira Gandhi demonstrated some Reticent and Retiring personality traits when she assumed the office of the prime minister, the demands of the job and the initial hostility she encountered from the Congress elite – the Syndicate – seem to have galvanized the Ambitious and Dominant dimensions of her personality into action and allowed the suppression of the Retiring and Reticent elements of her profile. This, in turn, enabled her to appeal over the head of the Syndicate and establish a strongly personal and very effective relationship with the masses which boosted her self-esteem and fuelled the Ambitious and Dominant aspects of her personality.

It should be noted that these three explanations are not mutually exclusive; it could well be that all three were involved, in varying degrees, in producing the unexpected outcome just described. Of far greater significance, however, is the overall strength of the relationship between Indira Gandhi's personality patterns and her leadership style. In nine out of ten categories, and fifteen out of sixteen items, theoretical expectations of the links between personality patterns and leadership style were met. This strong empirical evidence suggests that the study of a leader's personality profile may be an important technique for assessing leadership style.

PART TWO

Golda Meir

4

Golda Meir: From Immigrants' Daughter to Prime Minister

Golda Mabovitch (Meir) was born in Kiev, Russia, in May 1898. She was one of eight children, of whom only three daughters survived: Sheyna, the eldest, Golda, and a younger sister, Zipporah, later called Clara. The four sons and one daughter who were born in the nine-year interval between the births of Sheyna and Golda died in infancy.[1] The birth of a strong and healthy girl, named Golda, broke that pattern.

The first eight years of Golda's life were spent in Kiev and Pinsk, during difficult and turbulent times, when anti-Semitism raged and the Czarist order was beginning to crumble. Golda's own memories of the period consisted mainly of physical threats, the fear of pogroms, economic insecurity, and discrimination. "That gay, heart-warming, charming shtetl on whose roofs' fiddlers eternally play sentimental music, has almost nothing to do with anything I remember."[2] What she did recall, very vividly, was the potential violence from Gentile neighbours; the mounted Cossack patrols; the fact that her father, a skilled carpenter, who was barely able to support his family, was cheated out of a lucrative contract, the result of overt discrimination; and the involvement of her older sister in clandestine political-discussion groups. When she was six years old, her father emigrated to the United States, leaving the family behind. Two years later, he sent for his wife, Bluma, and three daughters, Sheyna, Golda, and Zipporah (Clara) to join him in Milwaukee, Wisconsin.[3]

In Milwaukee, the family struggled to survive despite the joint efforts of both parents. Her father continued to work as a carpenter, and her mother provided a steady income by running a small grocery store with Golda as an unwilling clerk before and after school. Despite arriving late for school on numerous occasions as a result of her work in the store, Golda quickly established herself as an excellent student in elementary school, which stimulated her desire to continue her education at the secondary level. Her interests were further cultivated when

Sheyna permitted her to tag along to attend informal meetings of a group of young Russian emigrés who vigorously debated politics, revolution, Zionism, and philosophy.[4]

Golda's first political success occurred at the age of ten when she became the main organizer and keynote speaker of a benefit show to raise money for her classmates who could not afford the nominal charge for textbooks. Even at this early stage in her life, one could see the beginnings of a pattern that would be repeated many times: identification of a wrong that needed to be rectified; a focus on fund-raising; diligent organizing and persuasion that included convincing the owner of a hall into renting it on the promise of payment after the event; and the ad-lib delivery of major appeals for funds.[5]

Conflicts with her parents came into a sharp focus when Golda finished elementary school. Golda was passionate in her desire to attend high school, while her parents were convinced that further education was not only unnecessary but probably dangerous to a young woman's marital prospects. Her mother also wanted Golda to help out full time in the store, a prospect that Golda disliked intensely. In her desire to continue her schooling, Golda was probably influenced by her older sister's political interests and activities, which had led Sheyna to break with her parents and move out, as well as by her own academic success. This led Golda to see possibilities for herself beyond her particular circumstances and the traditional roles of most young women of her generation. Notwithstanding the battles that ensued, Golda decided to enrol in high school and get a part-time job to assure her economic independence.[6]

With the fights and arguments between Golda and her parents continuing over her studies, the situation at home became unbearable. A miserable Golda decided, unbeknownst to her parents, to accept an invitation from her older sister and her husband, an unskilled labourer, to come to Denver, Colorado. At that time, Sheyna was recuperating from a serious bout of tuberculosis. Golda slipped out of the house without telling her parents, only mailing them a postcard as to where she had gone. In Denver, Golda began school but then quarrelled with her older sister and moved out. At the age of fifteen, she was living on her own, working, and delighted with her independence. She also became an increasingly active member of a group of young Jewish intellectuals. As a result of these discussions, Golda decided that the Labor Zionist movement, a blend of utopian socialist ideals and fervent commitment to a Jewish state in Palestine, was her philosophical and emotional home, and she made a personal commitment to work and live in Palestine.[7]

When Mrs Mabovitch discovered that Golda was not living with Sheyna but on her own, she was so horrified that she insisted Golda return to Milwaukee, promising her she could go on to high school and then on to the normal school to become a teacher. Golda gladly accepted; in Denver she had to work full time to support herself and was making no progress towards an education. Back at home, Golda finished high school and started teacher training. At the same time, she continued to correspond with Morris Meyerson, whom she had met at one of the meetings of the Labor Zionist movement in Denver. Morris was reticent and profoundly disinterested in politics. But Golda was drawn to him by what she conceived to be his superior erudition, his interest in art and music, and what she called his "'beautiful soul.'"[8]

During their courtship, Morris and Golda struggled with their different ideals and plans for the future. Morris definitely did not want to go to Palestine. He wrote to her, protesting: "'The idea of Palestine or any other territory for the Jews is, to me, ridiculous. Racial persecution does not exist because some nations have no territories but because nations exist at all.'"[9] But Golda was adamant. She had even dropped her teacher-training program to become a full-time worker for the Labor Zionists. Her job was to build up membership in existing Labor Zionist chapters, start new chapters, raise money to send to Palestine, and prepare people to emigrate there following the end of the First World War. She would not marry Morris, she told him, unless he agreed to emigrate with her to Palestine as soon as the war was over and they could afford to go. Recognizing that Golda and Palestine were inextricably linked, Morris capitulated, and in 1917 they were married.[10]

However, rather than subsiding over the years, the differences between Golda and Morris became increasingly pronounced, leading to their eventual separation eleven years later. Golda loved to have people around her, to attend meetings and participate in discussions and arguments. Morris was more introverted, preferring to spend time at concerts or in art galleries. A quiet man whose tastes were for solitude and privacy, he was the direct antithesis to his wife, for whom ideas were not intellectual contemplation but a springboard for action.[11]

Golda's work for the Labor Zionist movement required her to travel from city to city, which meant leaving Morris for weeks and sometimes months at a time. At the first American Jewish Congress in Philadelphia in 1918, where Zionists and non-Zionists gathered to discuss the impact of the 1917 Balfour Declaration's promise of a Jewish homeland in Palestine, Golda was a delegate. Even at the young age of twenty, her ability to speak with passion and without prepared notes impressed many at the congress.[12]

The first twenty years of Golda's life established the themes and directions that would colour the next sixty. She felt little attachment to the Russia of her childhood and had come to regard the United States as a way station en route to Palestine. In her mind, the logic was as simple as it was elegant: "To be Jewish is to be a Zionist and to be a Zionist is to participate in the creation of the Jewish state in Palestine."[13] It was that sense of identity and purpose that gave meaning and direction to her life and career, and, to that end, she was prepared to sacrifice a great deal – her physical health and emotional comfort, as well as that of her husband and children.

Golda's involvement in the Zionist movement honed her political skills and gave her an arena in which to use them when she and Morris arrived in Palestine – then administered by Britain under a League of Nations mandate – in 1921. She established a reputation as an effective speaker before medium- to large-sized groups and as a persuasive advocate in more intimate settings. Her success was the product of the depth and sincerity of her convictions, her straightforward, powerfully simple and logical presentation, and her ability to speak extemporaneously. She also demonstrated her talent for directing and organizing other people. More important, she was prepared to work very, very hard, taking for granted that public needs had priority over private wishes.[14] Reflecting on the earliest days of her marriage, when she was travelling extensively, Golda wrote, "Whenever I was out of town, I wrote long letters to him [Morris], but they tended to be more about the meeting I had just addressed, or the one I was about to address, the situation in Palestine, or the movement, than about us or our relationship."[15] The priority that Golda attached to the public sphere would remain a constant for the rest of her life.

The twelve years between Golda's arrival in Palestine in 1921 and her accession to a position in the emerging Zionist political elite can be seen as laying the foundation for her life ahead. The centrality of Jewish and Zionist identity to her self-definition and self-assessment justified the hardships and trials of that period. Notwithstanding the heat and ugliness of Tel Aviv in July 1921 – a few streets of unattractive buildings, empty lots of discarded rubbish, and acres and acres of sand and dusty ground – and the difficulties the newcomers had in finding sufficient food and shelter in the first few days, Golda noted: "There were all kinds of compensations for these small hardships, like walking down the street on our first Friday in Tel Aviv and feeling that life could hold no greater joy for me than to be where I was – in the only all Jewish town in the world – only here could Jews be masters, not victims of their fate. So it was not surprising ... I was profoundly happy."[16]

It was at Golda's insistence that she and Morris joined a collective farming community, a kibbutz. After a few months of waiting, they were accepted grudgingly at the kibbutz of Merhavia. Although the kibbutz members had serious reservations about the "soft, pampered Americans," this farm settlement, founded in 1909, sorely needed new strength.

The land yielded few crops, swamps around it still needed to be drained, and the terrible hardships of working there had defeated a number of pioneers who had lost heart and left or fallen ill with malaria.[17]

The members of the kibbutz remained suspicious of the commitment of the new arrivals, even after Golda had eagerly demonstrated her ability to work as hard as anyone without ever asking for special favours. However, her total embrace of communal and collective life, and her obvious pleasure in living with people "who debated everything so thoroughly and with such intensity and who took social problems seriously,"[18] won her growing acceptance. But no matter how much she enjoyed the discussions and the debates, Golda demonstrated a penchant that would remain throughout her public career, that of seeing something that should be done and doing it, without much regard for the ideological niceties.[19]

The emphasis on equality in the kibbutz encouraged women to tackle the hard work in the fields and led many to see work in the communal kitchen as an atavistic throwback that was synonymous with gender inequality. But, for Golda, who believed passionately in equality, kitchen work and the quality of the communal meals were not ideological issues. To her, there were only simple practical questions: Why shouldn't even simple food be properly cooked? Why was it more virtuous to drink tea out of chipped and rusted mugs rather than clean glasses? Why shouldn't the herring be peeled and why not a "tablecloth" for Friday night suppers?[20] And so, in the face of objections from some of the other women, she reorganized the kitchen. That style of leadership – directive and problem-oriented – would be a hallmark of her life in politics and in leadership positions.

In 1922 Golda was sent by the kibbutz to take a special course in the care and raising of poultry; Merhavia's chicken coops became so successful that poultry farmers around the area came to learn. Golda was elected to the settlement's "steering" committee, which was responsible for setting overall policy – a great honour for a relative newcomer. Later that same year, she was also elected a delegate to the newly formed council of the Histadrut, another accolade.[21] At Degania, "mother of the kibbutzim," where the Histadrut convention took place, Golda met many of the major personalities of the Jewish labour movement in Palestine, returning to Merhavia excited and stimulated by their speeches.

But the kibbutz experience also brought to a head the conflict between the public and private dimensions of Golda's life. She gladly accepted and even savoured the back-breaking labour as her contribution to creating the Jewish homeland: "I enjoyed everything about the kibbutz – whether it was working in the chicken coops, learning the mysteries of kneading dough for bread in the little shack we used as a bakery, or sharing a midnight snack with the boys coming back from guard duty, and staying on in the kitchen for hours to hear their stories. After a very short time I felt completely at home as though I had never lived anywhere else ... In the main I felt absolutely fulfilled."[22] The problem was her husband, Morris. It was just those aspects of communal life that pleased Golda the most – the camaraderie, the shared communal existence, and the involvement of everyone in all aspects of kibbutz life – that Morris regarded as impossible barriers to happiness. He suffered deeply from the lack of privacy and from what he felt to be the intellectual limitations of their way of life. No one in Merhavia, at that time, was interested in talking about the kinds of things that mattered to him – books, music, and paintings. Nor did it help that Morris found the work on the kibbutz almost unbearably tedious, and, since he was not very robust, he was frequently ill with malaria.[23]

Golda, who wanted a baby, had to face the fact that Morris was completely opposed to the collective child-rearing methods of the kibbutz, preferring that he and his wife bring up their children as they saw fit, without the scrutiny of a committee and eventually the entire kibbutz. His persistent opposition to having a child at all unless they left Merhavia, coupled with the deterioration in his health, forced his wife to accede to his wishes.[24]

Hence, the ensuing period between 1923 and 1928 was extremely difficult for the Myersons. Golda and her husband, like most of the other Jewish immigrants, were poor, and life in Palestine was arduous. After a few weeks in Tel Aviv, Morris and Golda were offered jobs at the Jerusalem offfice of Solel Boneh (an unofficial public works department) and they both jumped at the chance to move to Jerusalem. In the autumn of 1923, Golda gave birth to a son, Menachem, and the family was forced to live on Morris's wages, which were sometimes paid in credit slips that no one wanted to accept in lieu of money. When a daughter, Sarah, was born in the spring of 1926, Golda did the laundry for Menachem's entire nursery school in exchange for school fees. It was not the work Golda minded – in Merhavia she had worked much harder – but the irresistible thought that there she had been part of a "dynamic society whose success mattered to me more than anything else in the world. In Jerusalem I was a sort of prisoner, sentenced – as are millions of women by circumstances beyond their control – to battling over bills ... trying to keep shoes from falling apart ... worrying whenever a child coughed or ran a fever that our inadequate diet and inability to keep the apartment warm in winter might be permanently damaging their health."[25] At least, the hard life of the kibbutz had a larger political meaning; poverty in Jerusalem was a strictly private affair and this left Golda filled with "a bitter resentment against my lot in life."[26]

In 1928 Golda accepted an invitation to become the secretary of the Women's Labor Council of the Histadrut.[27] This Histadrut position was to be pivotal in her public and personal life. It gave her an entrée to the political elite; from that point on, she would play an increasingly significant role in the emergence of the state of Israel and the politics of the Labor Party. But it also affected her private life. Golda's position with the Women's Labor Council meant moving from Jerusalem to Tel Aviv, with her two children, as well as substantial travel throughout the Yishuv (Jewish settlements in Palestine) and abroad to the United States. Morris chose to remain in Jerusalem, visiting Tel Aviv in the early years only on weekends. While he remained close to his children, the emotional distance between husband and wife grew and their separation became final ten years later, although they never divorced.[28]

From 1928 on, Golda was emotionally and romantically involved with a number of men in the Labor Zionist movement. These relationships were a product both of her passionate nature and her enthusiasm for the company of intelligent and gifted men. The first, Zalman Rubashov, known as Shazar, was nine years older than Golda and a member of the Histadrut executive committee. He was a scholar and editor of the daily newspaper *Davaar*. They soon became, in Golda's words, "'very good friends.'"[29] However, by 1934, it was clear that he would never divorce his wife and they gradually drifted apart.[30] Golda also developed an intimate relationship with David Remez, who sponsored her for various jobs and then became her closest confidant and lover. "I was no nun," admitted Golda.[31] Remez and Golda did not live together, but Remez spent more time with her than he did at his own home. Their relationship was discreetly concealed with work. But in their letters, when one of them travelled, they expressed their love frankly and openly.

When Golda was forty-one, she became intrigued with Zalman Aranne, secretary of the Labor Council, a year younger than her and very handsome, who adored her and had the capacity to make her laugh. Golda was torn between her deep affection for Remez and the intense love of Aranne.[32] Then, in 1939, at the age of forty-eight, she began a romantic relationship with a new man. David Remez seemed to be abroad more than usual, and her work no longer permitted her to accompany him often, while her intimacy with Zalman Aranne was more sporadic. Unlike Golda's other lovers, Ya'acov Hasan disagreed violently with her on political issues. Hasan was one of the founders of Mapam, a party far to the left that had split from the traditional Labor Party, Mapai. Mapai wanted a state for the Jews; Mapam wanted a bi-national state with the Arabs. Mapai felt closely linked with the United States; Mapam regarded Soviet Russia as "a second homeland." Despite their political differences,

Golda clearly was smitten by this big broad-shouldered man and acknowledged to a close companion that she loved him the most "'as a man.'"[33]

As intense as her relationships were, they did not interfere with Golda's work and travels. Throughout the 1930s, she visited Britain and the United States on numerous occasions on behalf of the Women's Labor Council. Her job was to build up the Pioneer Women organization – a sister to the Women's Labor Council – that would be responsible for committing money to Jewish Palestine, as well as training and sending young people as immigrants. The goal was to build membership and add new chapters to the Pioneer Women by stimulating interest in all the special women's activities in Palestine, such as day nurseries and work on kibbutzim. Although Golda's audiences in the United States in the early 1930s were small, membership and chapters gradually did grow, and her effectiveness as a fund-raiser began to be noticed.[34]

When important visitors came to Palestine, such as Zionist delegates, heads of labour organizations, or wealthy philanthropists, Golda was responsible for taking them around and showing them the progress made by the Histadrut, and what still needed doing on the farms and in the towns. She also served as chairman of the board of directors of the Workers' Sick Fund, supervising the working conditions of Histadrut members employed on building British army camps all over Palestine, running a variety of other labour negotiations,[35] and, above all, trying to help solve what was becoming a massive unemployment problem.[36]

Golda's own son, Menachem, thought it was "an awesome assemblage of tasks for anyone: no wonder my mother's health, though not yet actually poor, began to show signs of wear and tear. There were even twenty-four hour stretches – rare to be sure, but they did happen – when she was flat on her back with an excruciating migraine headache, prone, pale, and exhausted on the couch, cold compresses on her head, impatiently waiting to recharge her batteries."[37]

Undeterred by fatigue, Golda marched on with her duties and deepening political involvement. In 1935 she was elected to the Secretariat, the very inner circle of the Histadrut, and became active in the formation of the Mapai political party. And, in 1937, she was given the responsibility for the formation of a Jewish maritime service. At that time, the Jews in Palestine had no sailors and no ports, and the British would not allow them to start a merchant marine or a navy. Once again, Golda went back to the United States asking for money to build a harbour at Tel Aviv that would be independent of both the British and the Arabs.[38]

With the onset of the Second World War, at the invitation of the British authorities, Golda became a member of the War Economic Advisory Council, on which she functioned as an adviser on a range of problems, such as food rationing and allocation of materials. She simultaneously led a most effective campaign to recruit Jewish youth into the British army or navy, while, as a member of the Histadrut executive, she participated in plans for the rescue of Hitler's victims, in defiance of the British. During 1944, Golda received twofold national attention as a feisty and defiant witness in a British trial against two young Jews accused of smuggling stolen British arms to the Haganah (the official military wing of the Jewish Agency)[39] and as one of the few members of the political elite who was neither arrested nor forced into hiding by the British crackdown in 1946.[40]

Evidence of her growing political importance was Golda's appointment in 1946 as acting head of the political bureau of the Jewish Agency in Jerusalem. In that capacity, she was immediately responsible for all the Yishuv's military actions. She had the definitive say on numerous policy matters, and Haganah commanders consulted with her on all operations having political ramifications – and almost everything did. At the same time, she was also the Yishuv's representative in the increasingly bitter political negotiations with the local British authorities over the settlement of the new immigrants arriving from Europe, many of whom were survivors of the Nazi concentration camps.[41]

By 1947, it had become quite clear to the British that, as long as they stayed in Palestine, the country would be an armed camp and they, as the permanent warders of a small, poorly armed but powerfully motivated force, would be engaged in a life-and-death struggle against them. In February, British Foreign Minister Ernest Bevin referred the Palestine problem to the United Nations. The United Nations created a Special Committee on Palestine (UNSCOP) composed of eleven representatives of the world community. Golda testified before this committee, and a few months later a report was drawn up that led the way to the decisive 29 November 1947 partition of Palestine into a Jewish state, an Arab state, and an international zone comprising Jerusalem and its environs. For neither Arabs nor Jews was this an ideal arrangement; the land allotted to Jews – an allocation that was too much in Arab eyes – was one-eighth the area envisioned in the Balfour Declaration, and it was so fragmented that Jews and Arabs would both be required to pass through each other's territory in order to get from one of their own enclaves to another. But Golda, who had so fiercely opposed the Peel Partition scheme a decade earlier, was now happy, like almost everyone in the Yishuv, to have something, however small, as a Jewish state.[42]

Attacks by local bands of Arabs began on 30 November 1947, and by February 1948 some 15,000 irregulars, equipped and armed by the Arab states, were entrenched in the heart of Palestine, busily engaging the whole region in open warfare. Arab states had massed their armies on the border of Palestine, deferring the actual invasion until 15 May 1948, the end of the mandate, to avoid embarrassing Great Britain.[43] In light of these ominous developments, it became clear that, if the Jews in Palestine were to protect their land, they would need the funds to buy sufficient arms. But the treasurer of the Jewish Agency returned from the United States, in January, with a pessimistic report that no more than five to seven million dollars could be raised from American Jewry. If this held true, the army would be unable to provide adequate security, and the Jewish state most certainly would be overrun. Golda volunteered to undertake a fund-raising mission in the United States and the party executive agreed that she should leave at once.[44]

Previous appeals to foreign Jewish communities had been couched in terms of hundreds of thousands of dollars to be donated in the course of a year; now Golda would ask for many millions to be donated immediately. It was a continuation of what she had been doing for several years, but at a much larger order of magnitude. In six weeks of non-stop touring and talking, she raised an astonishing $50 million. Some years later, David Ben-Gurion remarked: "Someday when history will be written, it will be said that there was a Jewish woman who got the money which made the state possible."[45]

Earlier, in November 1947, just prior to the passage of the partition resolution, the Jewish Agency had also chosen Golda to be their secret emissary to King Abdullah of Transjordan. Abdullah, by no means secure on his throne, had little to gain from war with Israel when the British left, and the Israelis were certainly willing to explore any avenue to remove the well-armed and well-trained Arab legion from the military equation. The result was two almost surreal sessions; during their first meeting at a Jewish home in Naharayim, on the border of Jordan, Abdullah assured Golda that he would not join in any attack on the Jews. If the United Nations decided on partition, he would annex the Arab part to his kingdom. He promised friendship and assured her that he would gladly accept partition. Golda, however, was troubled by his question as to what would be the attitude of the Jews to a proposal to include a Jewish state in Abdullah's kingdom. When her response was strongly negative, he dropped the subject.[46]

Shortly before Golda's second attempt to contact Abdullah personally, an emissary from Jordan arrived to enquire whether the Jews were prepared to cede Abdullah a part of the territory assigned to them by the partition resolution. A concession would raise his prestige in the Arab world, for he would then possess more territory than what was originally set aside for the Arabs by the United Nations. The emissary was told that the proposal was unacceptable and that the Jews neither could nor would yield any territory from their tiny state. He was also told that the boundaries determined by the United Nations would be valid only if peace was established. In the event of war, the Jews would fight for whatever they could get.[47]

Notwithstanding this unpromising exchange, it was thought advisable to make a final effort to prevent hostilities with Jordan. In the first week of May 1948, a second interview between Golda and the king was arranged. This time Abdullah refused to go to Naharayim. News of their previous meeting had been leaked, and Abdullah insisted on taking extraordinary security measures. He suggested that Golda, dressed as an Arab woman, come to Amman. Prime Minister Ben-Gurion agreed, and she and a travelling companion, an Oriental Jew born in Jaffa, acted as her interpreter. During the course of the ride, which took several hours, the car was stopped for identification ten times without incident. Golda's ultimate destination was not the palace but the home of a wealthy friend of Abdullah's.[48]

In the course of the hour-long interview, Golda recalled the king's promise of November. Abdullah made no attempt to deny his pledge not to attack the Jews, but he added that the situation had changed. He hoped that war could be avoided, provided that the Jews did not declare a state and stopped immigration for several years. He would take over Palestine unpartitioned, merge it with Jordan after a one-year interval, and give the Jewish community representation in Parliament.[49] Golda quietly declared that a Jewish state was not negotiable and regretted that his majesty seemed to have opted for war. On the way back to Jewish Palestine, they could see where the Iraqi forces were already massing. The Arab chauffeur, frightened by the number of checkpoints they would have to pass, let his passengers out in the hills, two miles before the border. It was 3:00 A.M. and a good half-hour's walk. This time, if a guard were to intercept them, their cover would be blown. Decent Arab women did not go sauntering through the hills in the middle of the night. Fortunately, they were met by a Haganah scout who had been on the lookout for them.[50]

In view of her loyalty to Ben-Gurion, and his praise for her fund-raising activities in the United States, Golda had every reason to expect that she would be a part of the future multi-party provisional government of Israel. Ben-Gurion had argued for her inclusion primarily on the grounds that she was a woman, not because of her intrinsic abilities. In a speech to Mapai on 3 March 1948, he stated: "'It is necessary to have at least one woman in the provisional government. First of all, because she is suitable for such a position. Nevertheless, this is not enough. There are plenty of other party members who are suitable ... It is not acceptable that half of the Yishuv, half of the Jewish people [women] will not find representation in the first government we are trying to establish in the

land of Israel.' Ben-Gurion then went on to observe that women had
made their mark in many important fields and that everyone owed gratitude to their own mothers. 'I say a woman in a Jewish government is a
flag for the entire east ... a woman in a Jewish government is a political
flag for the entire Arab world ... and we have the woman that is suitable
for this, even were she not a woman ... It will be a great privilege, I believe[,] to have a woman coming from our party.'"[51]

Given Golda's dislike of being viewed as a spokesman for women,
rather than as an accomplished politician in her own right, one can only
imagine her dismay at the way in which Ben-Gurion presented her candidacy to Mapai for her inclusion on the party's list. On 6 March 1948
Mapai announced its list of four people who would form part of the
government. Golda was not among them. She "was deeply insulted.
The entire affair was not mentioned in her book, nor in Marie Syrkin's
biography of her. Meyerson said nothing in public with respect to the
matter and bore her pain in silence."[52]

Golda then returned to the United States as a member of the Jewish
delegation to the United Nations, in order to make certain that supplies
arrived for the Yishuv through the UN. The situation into which she had
been placed was not to her liking. She found it difficult to function as
number two or three in a delegation that lacked specific responsibilities,
or a clear mission, and she returned to Tel Aviv only to be hospitalized
in April 1948 with a suspected heart attack. The stress over the years,
and particularly the previous weeks, had taken its toll. After a few days
of rest, she went back to work. Ben-Gurion wanted her to return to Jerusalem to be head of the Yishuv in that area. She felt it was a temporary and insignificant posting and believed that the crucial decisions
would be made in Tel Aviv.[53]

Notwithstanding these rebuffs, Golda remained an important political figure in Mapai and in Israel. She was one of two hundred people invited to participate in the signing of the proclamation of the State of
Israel on 14 May 1948. She was deeply moved by the signing, later re-
calling: "'All I remember from signing the declaration is that I cried in
front of everybody. I couldn't even wipe off the tears.' When asked
'why are you crying so much Golda?' she replied, 'Because my heart
breaks when I think of all those who were supposed to be here and are
not. I answered but could not stop crying.'"[54]

No sooner had her signature dried on the declaration of independence
than Golda travelled to the United States to raise more funds to cope with
the five invading Arab armies that had already crossed the borders of the
new state. This time she raised an even more incredible $75 million.

Appointed ambassador to Moscow two days before her scheduled departure from the United States, Golda was in a car accident and suffered

a broken leg. The leg healed, but phlebitis and a number of blood clots developed. Given the enormous pressure placed upon her to arrive in Moscow as soon as possible to take up her post, lest the Soviets be angry at the delay, she left New York for Israel before complete recovery. Her failure to heed medical advice resulted in chronic suffering and an operation several years later.[55]

Golda served as the Israeli ambassador in Moscow for seven months. This was a period largely of failure and frustration. She was unsuccessful in promoting or advancing anything that was expected from her. It was truly "mission impossible" and no one blamed her for the failure. Other than Moscow, she did not visit any other city, including the city of her birth, Kiev.[56] The one area in which she had an impact was in her relations with Russian Jewry. Although there were three million Russian Jews in the country, the assumption was that the large majority were completely assimilated. Golda's second visit to a Moscow synagogue on Rosh Hashonah brought out a crowd of approximately 50,000 people, when normal synagogue attendance for this holiday was about two thousand. When she appeared, she was immediately engulfed by the crowd which was overjoyed to see her. The spontaneous mass outpouring was touching and indisputable evidence that a sense of Jewishness had not been extinguished in the Soviet Union. Some years later, when Soviet Jews were finally allowed to emigrate, they would provide a significant number of new citizens for the state of Israel.[57]

On 20 April 1949 Golda returned to Israel; she became a member of Parliament during the first elections in 1949 and began a seven-year tenure as minister of labour and housing. Three major factors underlay her selection for this portfolio: it was the portfolio she requested, having rejected an offer to become deputy prime minister; her previous career in the Histadrut meant that she was familiar with both the issues and the key players; and the developing pattern of relations between Israel and the USSR did not require a high-profile ambassador. Golda's first major challenge was the construction of housing and infrastructure for the hundreds of thousands of Jews from Europe and elsewhere in the Middle East who were flocking to Israel only to live in tents. She was ideally suited to the challenge of designing and building cheap simple housing that would allow the new immigrants to leave the transit camps. When the costs quickly grew far too large to be accommodated by the national budget, she again travelled abroad to solicit funds and sell Israeli bonds.[58]

For the first time, Golda was a candidate in a contested election in 1955. Mapai was anxious to have a Labor mayor of Tel Aviv, and Prime Minister Ben-Gurion decided that Golda was the only candidate who had a chance. She ran for mayor under duress but failed to be elected;

two representatives of religious parties on the town council voted against her because of her gender. Twenty years later, Golda offered a rather matter-of-fact account of the incident in her autobiography, even noting that it was fortunate for her because she could then stay in the Labor Ministry. At the same time, she acknowledged that she was "enraged by the fact that the religious bloc had managed – at the last minute – to exploit the fact that I was a woman, as if the women of Israel hadn't done their full share – and more – in the building of the Jewish state."[59]

Early in 1956, Ben-Gurion reshuffled his cabinet to remove Moshe Sharett from the foreign ministry and replaced him with Golda. As a condition of membership in the cabinet, Ben-Gurion insisted that Golda give up the surname of Meyerson and take on a Hebrew name – Meir.

A major area of disagreement between Ben-Gurion and Sharett had been the question of Israeli retaliation for *fedayeen* (Arab commando group) activities which had begun in 1955. Both agreed the *fedayeen* raids had to end but differed sharply as to method. Sharett wanted to use diplomatic means to pressure the great powers, who in turn would coerce the Arab states to stop aiding and abetting the infiltrators. He felt that Israeli retaliation would result only in a storm of international criticism. Ben-Gurion was far less concerned about international public opinion and believed strongly that the government of Israel had a paramount responsibility to protect its citizens; the rift between the two men led to Ben-Gurion's insistence that Meir take the foreign ministry position.[60] Ben-Gurion considered her, alone among his associates, tough enough to confront the crisis.[61] Like Ben-Gurion, she was an activist on security matters and totally approved his policy. She was also devoted to him heart and soul and often used to say, "If Ben-Gurion asks me to jump from the fifth floor, I'll do it right away."[62]

But Meir never felt fully comfortable with foreign office officials. Her closest personal relationships were with some of her political contemporaries in the labour movement. She considered the diplomatic professionals to be too polished, excessively inclined to understand diverse points of view, and afflicted with analytical and intellectual traits that made communication and understanding between them difficult. In contrast, Meir's own talent lay in the simplification of issues; the very word "analysis" provoked her to irritability. When officials analysed the contradictory waves of influence that flowed into decision making, she tended to interrupt them with an abrupt request for the main point.[63]

Then, in July 1956, Nasser nationalized the Suez Canal, blockaded the Gulf of Aqaba to Israeli shipping, and signed a military pact with Syria to unite their high commands (on 24 October of that year, the pact was expanded to include Jordan). These developments convinced the government of Israel that war was inevitable. The foreign and defence ministries began to plan a secret campaign, in which Meir was actively involved, to seize the initiative.[64] The French offered Israel arms and began making their own secret plans for a joint Anglo-French assault on the Suez Canal. The Sinai campaign began on 29 October and ended on 5 November. Israeli forces crossed and captured the whole of the Gaza strip and the Sinai peninsula, destroying a third of the Egyptian army in the process.[65]

Although Israelis supported their government's actions, in Britain, indignation at the use of force ran high, and the United States took the side of Egypt. The matter was brought to the United Nations, and the United States and the Soviet Union applied great pressure to obtain the withdrawal of British and French forces from the canal. On 8 November 1957 Israel was also forced to agree to the withdrawal of its forces, but with the proviso that agreements had to be reached to ensure Israel's security against acts of belligerency by land or sea.[66]

From the time Meir arrived in Washington in December 1956 to head the Israeli delegation to the UN, she was cast in a fighting role. As she saw it, the issues were clear-cut: Israel had the moral right to defend itself against Egyptian infiltrators based in Gaza and against the blockade of its shipping through the Gulf of Aqaba. A passionate and compelling speaker, she lessened some of the initial hostility of the delegates to Israel's initiative, persuading them of the country's need for assurances that a defeated Egypt would no longer interfere with its shipping. Convincing her listeners that the Gaza strip should not be re-established as a base for aggression would prove more difficult. During that period, Meir was in constant negotiations with Secretary of State John Foster Dulles and members of his department. American patience with Israel's refusal to withdraw grew increasingly thin, as had that of Britain and France, but Meir refused to be intimidated. Finally, after prolonged private negotiations that lasted until March 1957, a compromise formula was hammered out for the imminent withdrawal of remaining Israeli forces based on American support for certain "assumptions": UN responsibility in the Gaza strip, and UN protection of the right of free and innocent passage for Israeli shipping in the Gulf of Aqaba and the Strait of Tiran.[67]

The post-conflict problem of the Arab refugees was one of the major political questions that Meir had to face at the United Nations. The territorial partitions and upheavals of the post-colonial world had resulted in vast movements of peoples. A population transfer of 15 million refugees had taken place between India and Pakistan; West Germany resettled 9 million refugees from East Germany; 400,000 Karelians in Finland were absorbed by the Finns. However, the Arab states refused to permit the integration of the Palestinian refugees, approximately 500,000 of whom had originally fled Israel in 1948 and who were being maintained by the United Nations Relief and Works Agency (UNRWA) in refugee camps. Arab spokesmen in the General Assembly called for the return of one million Arabs to Israel, which already had an Arab minority of 250,000, consisting of 100,000 Arabs who had not left the country, along with their children, and refugees who had returned immediately after the armistice under special arrangements for the reunion of families.[68]

The Arab states made no secret of their purpose in blocking every constructive proposal for the resettlement and rehabilitation of the Arab refugees. "'Any discussion aimed at a solution of the Palestine problem which will not be based on ensuring the refugees' right to annihilate Israel will be regarded as a desecration of the Arab people and an act of treason,'" read a resolution adopted by a conference of refugees in 1957, and official pronouncements from Cairo, Beirut, Bagdad, Amman, and Saudi Arabia reiterated this thesis with unflagging insistence.[69]

Some liberals sympathetic to the plight of the displaced Arabs urged the Jewish state to respect the desire of refugees to come home. Meir pointed out that Arab strategy called not for repatriation but for reinvasion by a hostile fifth column that was openly pledged to Israel's destruction. "'This is an army,'" she declared, and refused to consider the subject further. Instead, she contrasted the continued exploitation of Arab refugees as tragic pawns in the Arab fight against Israel with the Jewish state's acceptance of 500,000 Oriental Jews from the Arab countries into Israel.[70]

Cut off from normal contact with its neighbours and unable to rely solely on remote and not always reliable friends in Europe and the United States, Israel increasingly attempted to seek acceptance from Asian countries. It enjoyed warm relations with Burma, but, by and large, the combination of Muslim solidarity and Russian-Chinese Communist influence served to nullify Israel's efforts, as its exclusion from the 1954 Bandung Conference of Asian and African states confirmed.[71]

Israel began looking to Africa to break out of its diplomatic isolation. Initial contacts had been established, in the early 1950s, by representatives of the Histadrut who met respective members of indigenous labour movements at international conferences. Since African trade-union leaders were also closely involved in the nationalist movements of their countries, these encounters resulted in a greater understanding of Israel's political aims. Into these relations, Meir introduced a new element: instead of seeking out Africans in order to discuss the question of Arab refugees, or the status of Jerusalem, her prime objective became one of practical assistance to the developing states. Israeli engineers, teachers, and sanitation experts went to cities and villages in Africa, and Africans who wanted to study cooperative farming or road construction came to

Israel. Precisely because Israel had been obliged to discover solutions to social and economic problems under conditions of hardship and scarcity, it was a more useful model than a rich, powerful country with unlimited resources.[72]

Meir's great strength – that people believed her – stood her in good stead on her African journeys. She was convinced that it was Israel's duty to assist struggling young states; it was *halutziut* (pioneering) on an international scale. The fledgling statesmen she encountered were politically astute: they knew exactly how advantageous their friendly relations might prove to Israel, but in Meir they also perceived how genuine was the friendship Israel offered. For the next nine years, she travelled extensively in Africa, visiting Liberia, Ghana, Nigeria, the Ivory Coast, and the former French Cameroons. Only two African states, Somalia and Mauritania, failed to establish diplomatic relations with Israel upon gaining their independence. In addition to offers of technical assistance, Meir also brought her no-nonsense, practical, and unassuming personal style to her hosts. She charmed African leaders. "'You are like a mother to us,' one of them touchingly said to her in a public greeting at a dinner; another quipped, 'you should change the name of your ministry to the friendly ministry.' When a sophisticated auditor commented later, 'How corny,' Meir silenced him. 'No,' she said, 'seed corn.'"[73]

During her tenure as foreign minister, Meir continued to strengthen Israel's ties with France, while finding time to address thousands in Buenos Aires and Mexico City. Israel's capture of Adolf Eichmann in Argentina, and his trial in Jerusalem, brought Meir once again to the floor of the United Nations Security Council to justify this violation of Argentina's laws. She spoke with diplomatic restraint as she explained why Israeli agents had not killed Eichmann quietly; in trying Eichmann, she argued, Israel was seeking a moral examination of the social forces that had made Eichmann possible.[74]

But her successes on the international scene did not translate into a free hand at home. After the Knesset elections of 3 November 1959 in which Mapai increased its majority to forty-seven seats, Meir complained bitterly to Ben-Gurion that she felt he still had no faith in her authority. "Golda's grievances were well-founded. She was foreign minister more for show than substance." France had been removed from her jurisdiction; she played no part in relations with Germany; and, in her work with England and Italy, she constantly collided with Defense Ministry emissaries. "Ben-Gurion personally initiated and conducted all important contacts with the United States, and Golda did no more than follow his instructions."[75] At no stage did the prime minister relinquish the direction of foreign policy, nor was he likely to have done so whoever his foreign minister might have been. And, as long as he was at the helm, Ben-Gurion's central role in the shaping of policy was not seriously challenged. In the Defense Ministry, a group of younger Mapai members, such as Moshe Dayan and Shimon Peres, occasionally attempted to conduct delicate negotiations that were properly the responsibility of the Foreign Ministry. But Meir dug in her heels and the practice soon came to an end.[76]

In 1963 Ben-Gurion retired, nominating Levi Eshkol as his successor. From his kibbutz in Sde Boker, he obsessed about the Lavon affair[77] and attacked the juridical authority of the committee which had decided that Lavon had been made to resign in 1955 on the basis of forged evidence. At a Mapai convention in 1965, the conflict between the followers of Ben-Gurion and those of Eshkol erupted into the open. Meir found the conflict precipitated by Ben-Gurion painful – particularly his allegations that Eshkol was a liar and that the government was not only incompetent but corrupt in its unwillingness to reopen the Lavon affair. Meir told Ben-Gurion that "if he [Eshkol] is a liar we are all liars, we are all corrupt."[78] She would not offer up Eshkol as a sacrifice to placate the former prime minister. In an angry confrontation with him, she reminded Ben-Gurion that he had chosen Eshkol as his successor. Eshkol was the same wise temperate man to whom he had recently entrusted the reins of power. She deplored Ben-Gurion's efforts to pull down the man he had helped to elevate, as well as his creation of a splinter Labor party, called Rafi.[79]

For the next two years, Meir continued to serve as foreign minister under Eshkol. When Ben-Gurion's faction received only ten seats in the 1965 elections of the 120-member Knesset, Eshkol was able to form a government with a firm majority. It was assumed that Meir, having campaigned against Ben-Gurion, would remain in office. But her active life and frequent travels were taking a toll on her health and stamina; as well, she had been secretly diagnosed with lymphoma (cancer of the lymph nodes). She felt she was missing the joys of time spent with her grandchildren and in quiet reflection, and she decided to retire from the cabinet completely, even though she was offered a post as deputy minister.[80]

Within a few months, however, Meir succumbed to the blandishments of delegations of Mapai luminaries that she was the only personality strong enough to steer the party through the coming negotiations with other dissident left-of-centre factions, notably Achdut Ha Avodah, Mapam, and, the most recent departure, Rafi. She became head of the Mapai party, charged with rebuilding the Labor coalition. As in her selection in 1949 as the minister of labour and housing, Meir's availability for this new post was premised on three factors. First, her absence from day-to-day political life (she was, however, still a member of the Knesset) meant she was not tied to any of the personalized factions that had formed around several powerful individuals jockeying for position in the cabinet. Second, her political philosophy was a rather uncomplicated embrace of the basic principles of socialist Zionism; she showed little interest in the nuances of philosophy and ideological distinctions that exerted a centrifugal force among the parties in the coalition. And, finally, as she had repeatedly demonstrated, she could mount extremely persuasive appeals for cooperation and action.[81]

For the next two years, all of Meir's formidable toughness and political skills would be bent on achieving Labor unity without debilitating compromises. As party chairperson, but without a cabinet portfolio, she played a relatively modest role in discussions and planning, during early 1967, concerning the growing Arab threat. In response to both Nasser's decision to close the Gulf of Aqaba and the Strait of Tiran to Israeli shipping – despite international guarantees of the right of free passage – and United Nations Secretary General U Thant's decision to honour the Egyptian demand for the removal of the UN Emergency Force (UNEF) from Sharm el-Sheikh, Foreign Minister Abba Eban thought that a swift diplomatic tour of the Western capitals was warranted to see if diplomacy could achieve some results. One Israeli minister suggested that Meir be sent, since she was regarded as tougher and less likely to be swayed by American pressure not to run the blockade. When the affronted Eban threatened to resign on the spot unless he was the envoy, the cabinet dropped all objections, and he flew to Paris, London, and then to Washington.[82]

Although Meir was not directly involved in the critical decisions surrounding the Six-Day War of June 1967, or the protracted negotiations at the United Nations, in Washington, and elsewhere in its aftermath, she clearly supported the decision to initiate military action once it appeared to Israel that war was inevitable. She also endorsed Israel's decision to retain control of the West Bank, Gaza, and the Golan Heights – land that was captured from their Arab protagonists during the course of the war – pending formal negotiations with Jordan, Syria, and Egypt.[83]

By early 1968, Meir had completed the task of forging a workable political coalition, the Labor Alignment, and celebrating her seventieth birthday. As she observed, "It is not a sin to be seventy but it is also no joke."[84] She retired once again and meant it – or so she thought. Her retirement lasted slightly more than a year. Prime Minister Eshkol was known to be in poor health, having previously suffered a heart attack. A few months before his death in February 1969, Finance Minister Pinchas Sapir invited Foreign Minister Eban for an intimate talk, in which he told Eban that Eshkol's physicians were pessimistic about his ability to survive another heart attack. Since there would have to be an election in 1969, they should have a plan for maintaining continuity of leadership in the event of the prime minister being incapacitated. Sapir said he thought Meir might accept the task, but that such willingness would depend on the agreement of all members of the cabinet to retain their present functions. That would enable the cabinet to remain intact with only a change at the top. Eban agreed, given his belief, which he had earlier expressed to British Prime Minister Harold Wilson, that a race between Defense Minister Moshe Dayan and Deputy Prime Minister Yigal Allon, the two putative contenders, was a "non-starter" in view of the risks that it posed for party unity.[85]

Most observers agreed that Dayan and Allon were the leading candidates to succeed Eshkol. But Dayan had never persuaded people like Sapir, who was probably the most powerful figure in the Labor Party, that he could be a leader of the party, particularly since he had left it earlier with Ben-Gurion and Peres to form a rival Labor party, Rafi. As for Allon, he also had two strikes against him. Until the merger of the party – Meir's great success – Allon, like Dayan, had been a member not of Mapai but of Achdut Ha Avodah. He was considered a man of integrity, but Sapir felt he did not have the ability to be a national leader. Most important, Sapir was determined to keep Dayan out of the prime minister's office; he was concerned that, in a pitched battle between Dayan and Allon, the former might win. Hence, the choice of Meir, who would forestall the battle between Dayan and Allon. Moreover, she was seen as an extremely tough negotiator – someone who would not make too many concessions to the Arab states.[86]

After Eshkol suffered a fatal heart attack in February 1969, Allon himself beseeched Meir, for the sake of the party so recently unified and the country, to perform this last service and take over as interim prime minister until scheduled elections in October 1969. Meir, claiming to be extremely undecided, insisted on discussing the matter with her son and daughter and their spouses. According to her, they were all agreed that she really had no choice but to say yes.[87] Like Gandhi, Meir portrayed herself as the reluctant candidate, disavowing any ambition of her own.

Golda Mabovitch Meir became prime minister on 7 March 1969, having been selected by the Central Committee of the Labor Party by a vote of 287 in favour and none opposed; forty-five former members of Rafi, who wanted Dayan, abstained. On 17 March, the Knesset gave Meir and her new national-unity cabinet an overwhelming vote of confidence. Only twelve votes were cast in opposition; Ben-Gurion abstained, still angry over Meir's stand on the Lavon affair. The election of an interim prime minister averted a showdown between the chief contenders – Allon and Dayan – and postponed the confrontation until the fall election. That consideration was probably crucial in securing her government almost unanimous approval.[88] But, just as the Congress

Party chose Indira Gandhi as interim prime minister to avoid a succession struggle between the chief contenders – only to see her grow into a powerful and confident prime minister – the Labor Alignment also miscalculated; Golda Meir found the role of prime minister to her liking and decided not to step down before the next election.

An issue that Meir had to confront, as have all her successors, was that of the territories occupied as a result of Israel's victories in the Six Day War. Like her predecessor, Eshkol, Meir did not think that "Israel's territorial structure was its only important attribute." "She was not a romantic territorialist. The maintenance of Israel's Jewish and democratic character appealed to her more than anything else."[89] In a luncheon talk to a group of Hebrew journalists, shortly after taking office, she declared, "I rebel against someone saying there's no peace because we haven't decided on our map." In her view, the dispute with the Arabs was "over the very fact that we're alive, and it doesn't matter what territory we live in." On the other hand, she rejected annexing occupied land, "because I want a Jewish state ... without me having to count the Jewish and non-Jewish population every morning, for fear the figures have changed."[90] As for the Israeli settlement in Hebron, Kiryat Arba, she had written that Jews should have the right to live there, even if, at some point, Hebron was returned to Jordan. Under her leadership, Israel enunciated in clear terms a willingness to accept the principle of withdrawal to secure, recognized, and agreed-upon boundaries. She and her closest cabinet colleagues also promised that, at some appropriate time in the future, "'a most sizeable part of the West Bank would revert to [King Hussein of Jordan].'"[91] But Meir was more inclined to articulate this principle than to "risk" putting it into practice, since she was resolved not to be sold short on Israeli security.[92] Hence, she endorsed Allon's formula of maintaining a "security frontier" on the Jordan River. This position left her government with some flexibility; it had the option either of returning or, as seemed increasingly likely, of continuing to control most of the West Bank via Jewish settlements in the Jordan valley, in the Hebron area, in the Gaza strip, in the northern Sinai peninsula, and on the Golan Heights, a policy that she quietly encouraged.[93]

In March 1969, Egypt and Syria initiated what came to be called the "War of Attrition"; it was characterized by low-level, protracted, and deadly armed clashes between Israeli and Egyptian air and ground forces at the Suez Canal, and between Israeli and Syrian forces in the Golan that lasted until August 1970. Egypt's declared intention was to change the adverse military and territorial status that it had inherited from the 1967 war. The level of casualties and destruction during the War of Attrition was far heavier than in the wars of 1956 and 1967, and the duration was far longer. By December 1969, Meir's cabinet decided to respond to Nasser's constant bombardment of Israel's position east of the canal by bombing well into the heart of Egypt. The Soviet Union protested the Israeli raids and threatened to intensify the supply of its arms to Egypt.[94]

Responding to the escalating conflict, the United States tried to mediate. In a speech on 9 December 1969, American Secretary of State William Rogers offered his plan for a negotiated and comprehensive Arab-Israeli settlement. It outlined a "package settlement," which consisted of an end to the state of war between Egypt and Israel, the establishment of secure borders and demilitarized zones, a just settlement of the refugee problem, and withdrawal of Israeli armed forces from Egyptian territory occupied in the June 1967 war. The problem of Jerusalem would be settled by having both Israel and Jordan share in the city's governance. The Meir government, which had not been consulted beforehand, felt that the plan was being forced upon it. Nor did it like the plan's contents – it was determined not to return to the pre-June 1967 borders, which could be only precariously defended. The government also objected to the large number of proposed negotiating partners. And, finally, neither the government of Israel nor that of Egypt had any confidence or trust in Rogers as a mediator. The Israeli government rejected the proposal within forty-eight hours.[95]

Some members of the Israeli cabinet (Abba Eban, the foreign minister, and Moshe Shapira, minister of the interior) thought that Soviet threats to increase military assistance to Egypt meant that Israel would soon find itself in an escalating global crisis, and that an unconditional and unilateral Israeli cease-fire and a halt in bombing raids for forty-eight or seventy-two hours might begin a process of negotiation to end the War of Attrition. Meir, however, strenuously objected to any cease-fire, fearing that, if Egypt were to agree to a freeze in the fighting, there would be no guarantee as to its being honoured. Moreover, she was concerned that Nasser could use a cease-fire to rebuild his damaged military.[96]

In fact, in response to the increased range of Israeli bombings, the Egyptian leader appealed to the Soviet Union in January 1970 for help. Leonid Brezhnev, fearful that Nasser might resign and thereby make way for an American-dominated Egypt, finally agreed to the dispatch of Soviet anti-aircraft missiles with accompanying personnel to carry out the training and disposition of the new anti-missile force. In April 1970 Israel shot down six Egyptian aircraft flown by Soviet pilots. However, once the new Soviet anti-aircraft missiles were fully deployed in mid-June, losses of Israeli planes and air crews increased. On 24 June another Rogers initiative was launched, tying it to a cease-fire in the War of Attrition. Specifically, the United States proposed the following: first, that Israel accept a stand-still cease-fire on the Egyptian front for a period of three months – during which time neither Egypt nor Israel would be permitted to bring missiles or artillery closer to the front than before; second, that Israel, Egypt, and Jordan each issue a statement that they accepted the UN Security Council's Resolution 242, and specifically that resolution's call for "withdrawal from occupied territories"; and third, that Israel would undertake negotiations with Egypt and Jordan as the cease-fire came into force.[97]

Meir's immediate, intuitive reply was an indignant negative. But increasing Israeli losses, combined with promises by President Richard Nixon to reinforce American economic and military aid and not to require any Israeli withdrawal from the occupied territories until a satisfactory peace treaty had been concluded, led to an Israeli decision to agree to a cease-fire.[98] Nasser also accepted the cease-fire, but he did so deceptively, as Meir had feared, using the ninety-day halt in fighting, which came into effect on 7 August 1970, to construct shelters and move Soviet-made missiles close to the Suez Canal. Nasser accepted the second Rogers initiative because he saw it as an opportunity to halt his devastating military losses and, if possible, stall U.S. delivery of more Phantom jets to Israel. Unable to force Egypt to remove the missiles that it had illegally installed, the United States proceeded to provide Israel with additional Phantom aircraft.[99]

After Nasser's sudden death, his successor, Anwar Sadat, sent a cable to Israel, in December 1970 via the Americans, suggesting that he would consider making an agreement with the Israelis if they withdrew from all of Sinai. Sadat's thinking posited some form of phased Israeli withdrawal in exchange for something far less than a peace treaty – a military agreement. Similarly, Moshe Dayan approached Meir with the idea of a unilateral, but partial, withdrawal from Sinai. He felt that, if Egypt agreed to rebuild the canal cities and open the canal itself, which had been closed since the June 1967 war, this would be the best assurance that Egypt's intentions were not to launch another war. In his calculations, he took into account the fact that, if Egypt violated Israel's expectations, the latter would be able to take care of the situation. But, in her trademark fashion, Meir refused to countenance Dayan's idea: "We retreat one inch from the canal … [we] will in no time land at the international border."[100] She would remain firmly convinced that the destruction of the state of Israel remained the principal goal of the Arab states, and that their interest in negotiations was merely a gradual means to achieve that end.

After the War of Attrition and the acceptance of the American cease-fire, Israel seemed to be safe both from war and from the fear of becoming a source of tension for its American ally. That may explain, in part, the negative response to two new initiatives coming from Anwar Sadat in February 1971 on the heels of the end of the second ninety-day cease-fire. His first proposal, similar to the earlier Dayan initiative, called for an interim agreement based on the need to open the Suez Canal. As part of the second initiative, Sadat was prepared to recognize Israel if a full Israeli withdrawal from all the occupied territories, including East Jerusalem, took place, with the first step being withdrawal from the canal to the strategic Gidi and Mitla passes in Sinai. Meir did not take positive action on Sadat's initiatives in large measure because its contents contained "the Arabs' maximal positions."[101] The Israeli cabinet was also cool to his idea, questioning the logic of Israel agreeing to any withdrawal short of a comprehensive peace with Egypt.[102]

But, even before Sadat's plan could be fully explored, it was frustrated by an independent initiative of UN envoy Gunnar Jarring, who presented Israel and Egypt with a proposal for a comprehensive peace settlement. Jarring suggested that Egypt should give Israel a list of assurances on peace, recognition, and the end of the state of war, while Israel should give Egypt an undertaking on the withdrawal of its forces to the pre-5 June 1967 demarcation lines. Gaza would be restored to Arab rule.[103]

Egypt accepted the proposal – the same one that Israel had offered earlier to Egypt on 19 June 1967 – and the United States then exercised strong pressure on Israel to accept it. During discussions in the Israeli cabinet, it was agreed that Sadat's readiness to talk for the first time about a "peace agreement" with Israel should be applauded, but Meir added that the terms of the peace agreement, including its territorial demands, had to be negotiated between the parties. At the same time, she expressed a willingness to withdraw to secure and recognized boundaries that would be agreed upon in the negotiating process. Eban and Allon were opposed, however, to the addition of a statement that Israel "will not withdraw to the 4 June 1967 lines," feeling that the point could be made in the course of negotiations. Meir worried that Israel could become the target of Egyptian "salami tactics" and preferred to spell out the bottom line in advance. Critics of her government have suggested that the sentence in the Israeli reply that rejected the 4 June 1967 borders spelled the failure of the Jarring mission and the loss of an opportunity for peace. But her supporters have countered that, if Sadat had been truly ready for a settlement at that stage, the wording of the Israeli reply to Jarring would not have induced him to abandon the effort.[104]

At its meeting on 22 March 1971, the Israeli cabinet accepted the principle of a partial Israeli withdrawal in return for something less than full peace. The devil, however, was in the details; Meir was totally opposed to the acceptance of even a token Egyptian police force on the Israeli-occupied East Bank of the canal that the Egyptian government insisted upon. Moreover, she wanted to retain portions of the Sinai and keep Jerusalem and the Golan Heights under Israeli jurisdiction and control. For Israel, a non-belligerent relationship with Egypt, without the trappings of full peace and normalization, was insufficient compensation for the return of all of Sinai. Israel wanted peace treaties, not armistice agreements. The Egyptian leader twice repeated his offer in the next eighteen months, but Meir remained unimpressed by the overtures, and rejected them. It is a tragic irony that Israel was obliged to accept a much less favourable interim arrangement after the 1973 war.[105] An atmosphere of deadlock ensued which would continue until October 1973, when the Egyptians overturned the status quo with the crossing of the Suez Canal.

Throughout 1971 and 1972, Meir did not take Sadat's peace overtures seriously, because she knew that U.S. Secretary of State Henry Kissinger was not interested in putting either his time or his influence behind an Egyptian-Israeli negotiating effort. Indeed, since the status quo was not sufficiently troublesome to warrant changing it, there was no reason for Washington or Israel to have forced a new diplomatic initiative. "There was no real or perceived strategic threat to Israel because of its occupation of the territories including Sinai."[106] At a meeting with President Nixon on 1 March 1973, Meir insisted that a stalemate was safe, because the Arabs had no military option. Since she considered Israel militarily impregnable, there was no need for change. In this opinion, she was joined by Generals Ariel Sharon and Yitzhak Rabin and Defense Minister Moshe Dayan.[107] None of them considered the possibility of a war for limited strategic objectives – to unfreeze the status quo – rather than to inflict an overwhelming military defeat on Israel.

At the same time, perturbed about the results of the U.S.-Soviet summit in May 1972, in which the Middle East was effectively "put on ice," the Egyptian leader told Rumanian President Nicolae Ceausecu that he was prepared to meet with a senior Israeli. This message, when reported to Meir personally by Ceausecu, elicited the reply: "This is the best news I have heard for many years."[108] But she took no action. "All her instincts told her not to trust Sadat."[109]

As for Palestinian demands for the return of pre-war territory, Meir continued to be extremely dismissive. Her position on this subject had been clearly articulated after the Six Day War, when she asked rhetorically, "These Palestinians, who are they?"[110] In her view, the Palestine of the Balfour Declaration had included territory on both sides of the Jordan. In 1922, as the controlling power, Britain had taken more than two-thirds of the "promised land" to set up the state of Jordan; then, in 1948, Jordan seized the West Bank from what remained of Palestine. From her perspective, Arabs who had fled from villages in Israel to Jordan or the West Bank had lost no homeland. They had moved to another part of what had recently been called Palestine. "'Why,' she asked, turning Pan-Arabic doctrine on its head, 'cannot Arabs who were one people in 1922 live as one people now? Israel has absorbed a larger number of Jews from Arab countries than the number of Arabs who left Israel, though the difference between Jews from the caves of Libya and those from Western Europe is infinitely greater than that between an Arab from Jaffa and one in Nablus or Amman.'"[111]

Thorny as this issue may have been and would become, despite Meir's dismissive attitude, it paled before what lay ahead in the immediate future. Unhappy with the military deadlock, but faced with Israeli air superiority and Israeli fortifications along the Suez Canal – the Bar-Lev line – the Egyptians had developed a plan to outflank the Israeli positions by launching an amphibious assault. Sadat was feeling both domestic and international Arab pressure, after having declared each of the two previous years to be "the year of decision" in which Egypt was to have removed the Israeli presence from Egyptian soil. Israel had mobilized in May 1973, in response to the threat of an Arab attack, but Israeli intelligence was right when it discounted data suggesting that military conflict was imminent. Intelligence assessments in September, however, misinterpreted evidence, this time dismissing the signs of political and military preparations for a major, and imminent, offensive. Notwithstanding a continued Syrian reinforcement of troops on the Golan Heights along the Israeli border, Israeli intelligence officials interpreted it as being the reflexive result of Syrian fears of an Israeli attack.[112]

On 25 September, a secret meeting was held between Jordan's King Hussein and the Israeli prime minister. Exactly what Meir learned at that meeting remains a matter of conjecture. Lou Kadar, the personal assistant who accompanied her, had the distinct impression that Hussein, after taking an hour to come to the point, made it quite clear that the Syrians were in a "pre-jump-off position for war and that the Egyptians would cooperate."[113] In contrast, Mordechai Gazit, the director general of the prime minister's office, who also attended the meeting, asserted that "Hussein did not tell us nor did we hear from any other source that a Syrian-Egyptian co-ordinated attack was forthcoming."[114]

When Meir met with Dayan, Allon, and Yisrael Galili (a minister without portfolio on whom she often relied for advice), as well as the commander of the air force, the chief of staff, and the head of Military Intelligence Research, on 3 October, the military evaluation was that Israel faced no danger of a joint Syrian-Egyptian military assault, and that it was unlikely that Syria would attack alone. The build-up and movement of Egyptian forces in the south was interpreted as the kind of manoeuvres generally held at that time of year. On Friday, 5 October, Meir was informed that the families of the Russian advisers in Syria were packing up and leaving in a hurry. It reminded her of what had happened prior to the Six Day War, leaving her feeling very uneasy, despite reassurances from the minister of defence, the chief of staff, and the head of intelligence that sufficient reinforcements were being sent to the fronts to carry out any holding operation that might be required.[115] Early the following morning, Meir was told that an attack would take place at 6:00 P.M. later that day.[116] Egypt had chosen that day to launch its offensive because it knew that Israelis would be unprepared. It was Yom Kippur, the Day of Atonement, the holiest day in the Jewish calendar, with most Israelis observing the holiday and many spending the day in synagogue.

At a hurriedly summoned meeting of her advisers, at 8:00 A.M., it was clear that Dayan and the chief of staff, David Elazar, were in disagreement about the appropriate Israeli response. Elazar was in favour of a pre-emptive strike and recommended the mobilization of the entire air force and four army divisions. Dayan, on the other hand, wanted to call up the air force and only two divisions, arguing, that, if there was a full mobilization before a shot was fired, the world would call Israel the aggressor. Meir agreed with Dayan that Israel should not take any pre-emptive action, and with Elazar that there should, nonetheless, be a full mobilization.[117] On the issue of pre-emption, the prime minister told those in attendance, "'Look, this war is only beginning now. We do not know how long it will take, we don't know if we will be in dire need of ammunition and so on. And if I know the world, if we begin, no one will give us a pin; they will say, 'How did you know that they [the Arabs] would have attacked?'"[118]

The ministers who had been summoned from around the country to meet at 12:30 were stunned by what they heard. They had not been informed previously of the Arab build-up on the borders. Furthermore, they had been told for years that, even in a worse-case scenario, the Israel Defense Forces (IDF) would have at least forty-eight hours to call up the reserves before war broke out. Now they were being told that a two-front war was less than six hours away, with the army still not mobilized.[119]

During the course of the meeting, Meir was informed that the shooting had started; the war had begun at 2:00 P.M., four hours earlier than expected.[120] For as long as she lived, she would regret that she had not listened to her intuition and "the warnings of my own heart" and ordered a full-scale call-up earlier.[121]

During the first few hours of the war, the Bar-Lev Line, too lightly manned, began to crumble under the Egyptian assault; the Israeli tank force suffered huge losses and dozens of Israeli aircraft were brought down by new missiles of unexpected accuracy. By nightfall, Egyptian helicopters carrying commando troops had seized strategic points east of the canal, and boats and bridges had begun to ferry 70,000 Egyptian troops and 1,000 tanks across the water. In the north 40,000 Syrians with 800 tanks had driven deep into the Golan Heights.[122]

These developments caused Dayan to fall apart emotionally. Profoundly depressed, he was fearful that Israel would be left without sufficient arms to defend itself, and he did not believe that a counter-attack was possible. His words had a deep effect on the prime minister. She heard them "in horror," she would write, and the thought of suicide crossed her mind. When she stepped outside her office to confer with Lou Kadar, she was despairing, telling her that "Dayan is speaking of surrender."[123] Moments later, she said, "Get Simcha," the Israeli ambassador in Washington, who was directed to put pressure on the American administration for arms.[124]

Despite a heroic defence by the Israeli forces, the situation remained critical, and the tide of battle did not turn until a massive American resupply program took effect. Seymour Hersh, the American investigative journalist, makes a persuasive case that Meir secretly threatened Henry Kissinger, through her emissary, Simcha Dinitz, to use Israel's nuclear arsenal against the Arab states unless American arms arrived quickly. This "blackmail" effort convinced Kissinger that he had to change course and could no longer stall on Israeli demands.[125] Having sustained enormous losses in the first ten days of the war, by 19 October, Israel was able to drive the Egyptian armies back across the canal and establish an Israeli bridgehead on its west bank, only sixty miles from Cairo. Equally, the Syrians had been pushed back and Israel was once again in control of the Golan Heights. Concerned about their clients' losses, the Soviet Union demanded a cease-fire, and Israel came under pressure from Kissinger to agree to one. Although Meir would have liked the cease-fire to have been postponed for a few more days so that the defeat of the Egyptian and Syrian armies would have been even more conclusive, American and Soviet pressure finally produced a cease-fire under the supervision of a UN force.[126]

The Yom Kippur War was the pivotal event in Meir's career as prime minister, for, as much as any soldier fallen in battle, she herself was one of its casualties. The cost of Israel's victory in that war was far higher than in any of the country's previous wars. Over 6,000 troops had been killed or wounded in eighteen days of fighting, and on the Syrian front the toll would continue to mount for some days. Economic losses were only beginning to register.[127] It was in the aftermath of this sombre "triumph" that voting took place for the eighth Knesset. When the election results became known on 31 December, 1973, Labor had won only 51 of the 120 seats. It lost six seats partly as a result of the defection of a new party founded by Shulamit Aloni that was critical of the increasing presence of

Israel in the territories and of Meir's concessions to the religious parties. A member of the Labor Party, Aloni had been excluded from the list of Labor candidates on the grounds that her appearance on the list would irritate Meir. Indeed, it could be said that "Golda Meir had many great qualities, but these did not include tolerance of diversity."[128]

Amidst this charged post-war, post-election atmosphere, Meir set about the difficult task of trying to form a new coalition government. She felt "dead tired" from the physical and psychological effects of the previous months and the struggle within her own party and her potential coalition partners.[129] Dayan announced that he would not join her new cabinet, and his threat was widely interpreted as an effort to influence the party platform by threatening a parliamentary crisis. The National Religious Party also announced it would not join unless the composition of the cabinet was broadened to include the Likud Party. By early March 1974, Meir was able to constitute an administration; however, it could count on the support of only fifty-eight supporters, so that it had to rely on abstentions in order to survive. Meir still insisted on excluding Aloni and her three Knesset members from the list. After reading out a list of potential ministers, Meir then proposed one other "minor" change. She suggested that a new prime minister be found.[130]

Ministers and party leaders trooped to Meir's house in Jerusalem to urge her to stay in office. Crucial negotiations with Syria were still ongoing, and until an agreement with Syria was signed, the Yom Kippur War would not be officially over and the danger still existed that violence might again erupt. Although deeply wounded at the barrage of criticism directed against her, Dayan, and Galili, on the grounds that the three of them – without consulting others – had presumed to make crucial decisions that had led to the outbreak of the war, Meir agreed to stay on.[131]

What proved to be the last of Meir's cabinets experienced the shortest lifespan in Israel's history. Its tenure was undermined by a commission, chaired by Supreme Court Justice Shimon Agranat, that had been established shortly after the war to determine responsibility for the government's palpable unpreparedness for the Arab offensive. Issued in early April 1974, the commission's report completely exonerated Meir but offered a serious indictment of the Military Intelligence Service, of the Sinai field commanders, and even of the chief of staff for their sluggish reaction to advance warnings of a possible enemy offensive. Where the commission refused to speculate was in the murky area of Defense Minister Dayan's personal responsibility for Israel's early battlefield setbacks.[132]

On this last point, Israeli public opinion was much less equivocal and an explosion of outrage greeted the report. It seemed unconscionable that career officers were being punished while Dayan, the self-proclaimed architect of Israel's military supremacy, was being absolved.

To argue, as the Agranat Commission did, that the minister of defence was not obliged to adopt additional precautionary measures, other than those recommended to him by the general staff, seemed ludicrous.[133]

With the Knesset and her own party in turmoil, and the country still mourning its dead, Meir decided, irrevocably, to resign. This time she put her resignation into effect without waiting for counter-pressures. In accordance with the Israeli constitutional system, she remained as interim prime minister for several weeks until a new coalition government could be cobbled together. During this period, the disengagement agreements with Syria were finalized. As Meir described it, "and then I myself went home, this time for good."[134]

The remaining four years of Meir's life were exceedingly unhappy. She lived with sadness over the number of Israeli deaths that had occurred on her watch, and for which she largely blamed herself for not ordering a full mobilization of Israeli forces sooner. As well, she became increasingly embittered by the "revisionist" interpretations of the onset of the Yom Kippur War, and particularly the willingness of many younger Israeli scholars to fault her refusal to be more open to negotiations with President Sadat of Egypt. But she never lost her conviction about the correctness of her views, and continued to believe, until the end, that the Arab world would never truly accept the right of Israel to live in peace within secure and recognized frontiers.

As is true of both Indira Gandhi and Margaret Thatcher, Golda Meir's legacy is mixed. On the one hand, she is lauded for her role in helping to build the state of Israel, in establishing good relations with many African states, in providing for housing for Israel's thousands of immigrants, and for her strength and stability during the Yom Kippur War. On the other hand, she is castigated for encouraging the settlements in the West Bank, for denying the existence of the Palestinians, for failing to pursue various offers of negotiations with Egypt, and for allowing a situation to develop in which the Third Temple came close to being lost.

Golda Meir's strengths and weaknesses as a leader are evident in the biographical facts set out above. A full and clear understanding of these strengths and weaknesses, however, can be achieved only through an analysis of her personality profile, as the next chapter will demonstrate.

5

The Jewish Grandmother:
The Personality Profile of Golda Meir

Though she was widely perceived in the foreign press as a genial, grandmotherly figure, Golda Meir's personality is more properly characterized as evincing a strong mixture of Dominant/Controlling traits in conjunction with a Contentious/Complaining pattern. Unlike Indira Gandhi, whose personality profile revealed four patterns that scored at levels of 19 or more, Golda Meir had only one score that reached 18, the Dominant pattern (Scale 1A). Her other scores, in descending order of magnitude, were 17 on the Contentious pattern (Scale 5B), 12 on the Conscientious pattern (Scale 6), 12 on the Aggrieved pattern (Scale 5A), and 11 on the Dauntless pattern (Scale 1B). The remainder of her personality patterns scored at 9 or less. (See Table 3.) The analysis of the data for Golda Meir presented in this chapter includes an MIDC profile, a diagnostic classification of the subject, and a clinical interpretation of significant MIDC scale elevations derived from the diagnostic procedure.

The MIDC profile yielded by the raw scores is displayed in Figure 2.[1] Although all of these scale elevations fall within the *prominent* (10–23) range, only two of them, the Dominant (Scale 1A) and the Contentious (Scale 5B), approach the *mildly dysfunctional* level. The remaining five of the ten basic scales (Scales 1–8) did not reach a level of *prominence* (10 to 23) and were thus considered insignificant for psycho-diagnostic purposes.

In the section that follows, each of these five most prominent personality patterns are examined, in order of their importance, alongside the facts and features of Golda Meir's biographical record. Read together, the enduring aspects of Meir's personality as coded begin to take on a more concrete form. Biographical and autobiographical materials collected from thorough research serves to demonstrate, empirically, the importance and significance of these patterns in the creation of Meir's personality profile.

Table 3
Personality scale scores for Golda Meir

Scale RT%	Personality Pattern	Raw	Ratio
1A	Dominant (Controlling)	18	18%
1B	Dauntless (Aggrandizing)	11	11%
2	Ambitious (Asserting)	9	9%
3	Outgoing (Extraverted)	5	5%
4	Accommodating (Agreeable)	7	7%
5A	Aggrieved (Yielding)	12	12%
5B	Contentious (Complaining)	17	17%
6	Conscientious (Conforming)	12	12%
7	Reticent (Hesitating)	6	6%
8	Retiring (Introverted)	1	1%
	Scales 1–8	98	100%
9	Distrusting	12	12%
0	Erratic	0	0%
	Full scale total	110	112%

Note. For the basic scales 1–8, ratio scores are the raw scores for each scale expressed as a percentage of the sum of raw scores for Scales 1–8 only. For Scales 9 and 0, ratio scores are raw scores expressed as a percentage of the sum of raw scores for all ten MIDC scales (therefore, full-scale ratio totals exceed 100). Scale names in parentheses signify equivalent personality patterns in Millon, MIPS: *The Millon Index of Personality Styles.*

Figure 2
The personality profile of Golda Meir

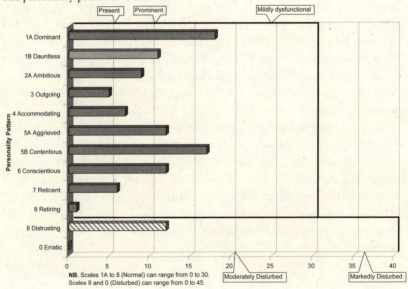

NB. Scales 1A to 8 (Normal) can range from 0 to 30.
Scales 9 and 0 (Disturbed) can range from 0 to 45.

SCALE IA: THE DOMINANT PATTERN

Assertive, tough, outspoken, and strong-willed are the descriptive terms used to describe individuals in the normal range (scores of 5 to 9) of the Dominant pattern. Exaggerated Dominant features (scores of 10 to 23) are present in controlling, forceful, and overbearing individuals such as Golda Meir. Meir's elevation of 18 on Scale IA (Dominant) is an in-flated variant of the Dominant pattern known as the Controlling style, suggesting exaggerated features of the basic personality pattern with the potential for a mild personality dysfunction. It is associated with force-ful, overbearing, intimidating, and abrasive behaviour.[2] Controlling in-dividuals, though often somewhat disagreeable, tend to be emotionally stable and conscientious.

Golda Meir's assertive and tough-minded personal style can be observed from the time she was a young child in Russia. Following an incident in which a number of Jews were killed, the community in Pinsk mourned. Every adult Jew fasted in the synagogue. Children were naturally exempt, but Golda, not yet five years old, insisted on joining the fast. If Sheyna and her mother could fast, so could she. As the day wore on, the family begged her to eat something, but "the stubborn child refused until the elders re-turned from the synagogue."[3] Indeed, her sister Sheyna recalled that one of Golda's predominant personality traits was her stubbornness.[4] Golda's own memories also attest to her strong-willed, overbearing character. As she described her relations with her older sister: "Sometimes, when Sheyna and I got into a fight and I lost my temper, I used to threaten to tell Maxim, the big, red-faced policeman in our neighborhood, all about her political activities."[5]

In the United States, Golda's Dominant personality trait continued to manifest itself prominently. The early questioning of parental and sis-terly authority is an exemplary case. After finishing primary school, Golda was determined to go to high school, notwithstanding the strenu-ous objections of both her parents, who hoped that she would marry as soon as possible and continue to work – perhaps as a secretary. "As Sheyna had done before me, I tried to explain in every way I knew to change my parents' mind. In tears, I explained that nowadays an educa-tion was important, even for a married woman, and argued that in any case I had no intention whatsoever of getting married for a very long time. Besides, I sobbed, I would rather die than spend my life – or even part of it – hunched over a typewriter in some dingy office."[6]

Defiantly, Golda enrolled at North Division High School in the fall of 1912. She worked afternoons and weekends at a variety of jobs, includ-ing teaching English to immigrants at ten cents an hour.[7] As the argu-ments between Golda and her parents, on the subject of her continuing school, escalated, Golda began writing to her sister Sheyna, who was married and living in Denver. "In my secret letters to Denver, I wrote in detail about the continuing fights over school that were making my life at home almost intolerable and were leading me to decide to become independent as soon as possible."[8]

The pressure on Golda to stop studying and get married continued to mount. But it was an offer from Sheyna and her husband that led Golda to take action. "I can't imagine that I would have agreed under any circumstances to stop studying and marry the probably much-maligned Mr. Goodstein [a man twice her age whom her mother was pushing on Golda]; but Sheyna and Shamai's offer [to come to live and study in Denver] was like a lifeline, and I grabbed at it."[9]

However, Golda had not chafed under her parents' authority only to see it replaced by that of a bossy older sister who wanted her to observe a curfew and keep her closely informed about her friendships. She decided to move out. "I marched out of the apartment in the black skirt and white blouse I had been wearing all day without taking anything else with me, not even a night gown. If I was leaving Sheyna's home and authority, I was not entitled, I thought, to keep anything that Sheyna or Shamai had bought for me. I closed the door behind me, and that, I thought, was that; I was on my own at last."[10] When Golda made up her mind, Sheyna said of her sister, "she carries out her decision."[11]

As Golda became increasingly involved in the Zionist movement, her strong will and determination became more evident. Even marriage to Morris would be contingent on his willingness to live in Palestine. "I knew that even if he [Morris] agreed to come [to Palestine] we would still have to wait for a year or two – until we raised enough money for the fare, among other things, but it was imperative that before we got married, Morris should know that I was determined to live there. I didn't present the situation to him as an ultimatum, but I did make my position clear."[12] Morris knew that he would lose Golda if he refused, so he agreed to her demand. It would take them until 1921 to save enough money to buy passage to Palestine along with a small group of American Jews.

Golda's assertiveness and leadership potential were on display on the voyage to Palestine. The trip itself was extraordinarily difficult; there were fights among the crew members, inadequate food supplies, and the loss of all the luggage. But, displaying equal amounts of leadership and stubbornness, Golda was undeterred; there would be no waiting for the baggage in Brindisi, Italy, and no turning back. She announced, "'I am going,'" and walked up the ship's gangplank. The others watched her go and meekly followed suit.[13] Then, as Golda recalled, "I suggested to my companions [fellow Americans and pioneer emigrants bound for Israel] that we give up our 'luxurious' cabins and join the Lithuanians on deck. No one was very keen about the idea, particularly since deck passengers were not entitled to any hot meals and by now we were all looking forward to some decent food. But I pressed the point; I argued that, in fact, it was our duty as potential pioneers ourselves to start sharing the life of our fellow-Zionists."[14]

Once in Israel and looking to join a kibbutz, Golda found that the members did not see her and her husband as particularly desirable candidates, but, typically, as someone with a strong Dominant trait, she fought her way in. "The group ... couldn't imagine that an 'American' girl either could or would do the extremely tough physical work that was required ... I felt as though I were back with the Lithuanians again, having to prove that even though I lived in the States, I was still perfectly capable of doing a hard day's work. I argued that no one had the right to make such assumptions and that it was only fair to give us a chance to show what we could do."[15] "I was determined to prove that I was at least as rugged as any of the other women in the settlement and that I could carry out whatever mission was assigned to me."[16]

Further events only accentuated Golda's Dominant/Controlling personality pattern. With the outbreak of the Second World War, the Jews in the Yishuv were forced to address the problems of Jews both in Europe and in Palestine. During the Israel's Workers Party conference on 9 April 1940, Golda made it clear that she was opposed to theoretical debates and strongly urged her fellow members to focus on concrete problems, "'above all the need to take action in America, to obtain the moral and financial support of the Jewish communities there.'"[17]

Four years later, Golda's rise within the party was reflected in her appointment, along with Levi Eshkol, as a member of the party's secretariat. One of the other members, Aharon Beker, described the impact of her domineering behaviour. He depicted how one evening Eshkol came to his apartment and poured out his heart. "Golda intervenes in everything," he said. "It is impossible to know who is responsible for what. I do not wish to make an issue out of this, but who will be the secretary?" When the decision was made that Eshkol would be appointed secretary of the party, Golda was distinctly unenthusiastic; she did not believe that he was sufficiently assertive or firm.[18]

In the aftermath of the war, Britain strongly opposed the efforts of Jewish survivors of the European concentration camps to reach Palestine. When it intercepted boatloads of refugees, members of the Yishuv, in retaliation, bombed most bridges connecting Palestine to its neighbours. Britain responded by jailing most of the Jewish leaders in the Yishuv and putting them in Latrun (a British-run fortress near Jerusalem). Only Golda was allowed to remain free. The British may have hesitated to arrest a woman, or thought she was more moderate, or it may have been that the British governor, who had met with Golda a few times and had been impressed by her, decided to spare her the "privilege" of being arrested.[19]

As the only major leader not in jail, Golda was appointed acting head of the political bureau of the Jewish Agency in Jerusalem. In that capacity she was immediately responsible for all the Yishuv's military actions. Under her leadership, the political bureau adopted a policy of non-cooperation towards the British authorities. When two members expressed an objection to this decision, an infuriated Golda argued that a refusal to cooperate with the British mandate government was the only way for the Yishuv to express its anger at British policy. She became aggressive and abrasive, demonstrating the strength of the Dominant dimension in her personality, and implied that those who opposed that policy had personal and financial reasons for their actions.[20]

During the War of Independence in 1948, the leaders of the new state of Israel found themselves hopelessly short of funds to buy weapons to deal with the Arab onslaught. It was agreed that someone needed to go to the United States and address the various Jewish communities about the desperate straits in which Israel found itself. At first, Ben-Gurion decided that he should be the one to make the trip. Golda disagreed strongly and pressed her case. "'But no one can take your place here,' I argued [to Ben-Gurion], 'while I may be able to do what you can do in the United States.' 'No, I need you here.'" He was adamant, but Golda refused to be put off. "'Then let's put it to a vote,' I said. He looked at me for a second, then nodded. The vote was in favour of my going."[21]

When Golda was told that she would be appointed as Israel's ambassador to the Soviet Union, she protested strongly. First, she argued that she did not speak either Russian or French, and then she asserted that, not being a diplomat by nature, she could not go around and around issues but had to be direct and say what was on her mind.[22]

As minister of labour and housing from 1949 to 1956, Golda's forceful response to her colleagues on the issue of new housing for immigrants revealed her strong-willed nature. "But there had to be priorities, and for me, at least, housing and jobs for the immigrants headed the list. Not all of my colleagues agreed with me. A barrage of experts explained to me in detail, with charts and graphs, why a housing programme of the kind I envisaged was not a good idea. It would only lead to inflation, they said ... But I couldn't accept or support any recommendation that didn't deal with the absorption of immigrants, first and foremost, from the human point of view."[23]

Many of the immigrants who had been placed in crowded transit camps were unemployed. To prevent a growing economic gap between them and the existing population, an emergency economic regime was established. In a speech in the Knesset, Golda, who tended to see everything in black and white, argued that only one choice was possible between "'either a budget cut in immigration, or a budget cut in food and clothing. After all, this is all that is being demanded from us, a little less irresponsibility so we do not waste the asset for which our loved ones died. They died for greater immigration, not for wealth.'"[24]

As is typical in the Dominant/Controlling personality, Golda was extremely outspoken. During the debates in the Knesset about the high levels of unemployment, her spokesmen decided to include quotations from the fathers of the Labor Party in order to make her words stronger. She refused, arguing: "'This is not for me. You think that anyone will believe me? Do you think that these quotations will impress anybody? It's not me. I am not known as a scholar. Please get me the facts and the numbers.'"[25] On another occasion, she commented, "Whenever I read or hear about the Arabs whom we allegedly dealt with so brutally, my blood boils. In April in 1948, I myself stood on a beach in Haifa for hours and literally beseeched the Arabs of that city not to leave."[26] Similarly, when Golda decided to run for the position of mayor of Tel Aviv in 1955, she was denounced by the religious right on the grounds that she was a woman. She was furious and did not conceal her anger. "To have objected to my being mayor of Tel Aviv because I was a woman was a political tactic for which I had great contempt, and I said so without mincing words."[27]

The more involved Meir became in the field of politics, the more her Dominant personality pattern expressed itself. Notwithstanding her strong ideological stance, as foreign minister, she never removed anyone from her ministry because they failed to share her ideas and opinions. However, her facial expression, her obvious lack of patience, or, sometimes, her interruption of other people in mid-sentence revealed the level of her disapproval. Since promotion in the Foreign Ministry was based, at least in part, in not challenging the minister, especially in public, most officials went to great lengths not to express any new radical ideas.[28] There were some officials, however, who treated Meir with a lack of respect for her refusal to read long memos and for her disinterest in reading books, articles, and policy papers. Over time, she "rewarded" them with appointments to remote and insignificant states.[29]

M. Medzini, one of her biographers, notes that Meir was stubborn and dogmatic. Lacking an ability for original and creative thinking, she filled the void by defending the ideas she did have with great conviction. She believed in the correctness of her views and refused to change them, showing the inflexible, stubborn, and tough sides of her character. And, in her dealings with people, she could be intimidating and abrasive.[30]

David Ben-Gurion, Israel's first prime minister, described Meir as a "woman with narrow horizons." Her assertive, strong-willed, and blunt style, coupled with her strong beliefs that she defended vigorously, all of which are characteristic of the Dominant personality, led her to be referred to as "the only man in the Ben-Gurion government."[31] The same designation was applied to both Indira Gandhi and Margaret Thatcher. Shimon Peres, defence minister, acting prime minister, prime minister, and subsequently president, also described "Meir as a powerful personality." But he saw her as someone "who, in her eyes, wasn't given a chance. She was motivated not so much by the desire for power, but for the self-expression of views she held as incontrovertible truths."[32]

As foreign minister, Meir travelled widely in an effort to establish closer relations with black Africa – a way of leapfrogging the cordon sanitaire that the Arab states were trying to impose on Israel. She encountered a number of African leaders who were disappointed with Israel's willingness to maintain strong relations with French President Charles de Gaulle, given his treatment of French colonial possessions in Africa. Meir was brutally frank with her audience: "I do not share your [African leaders] hatred of de Gaulle, but let me tell you the truth – whether you like it or not. If de Gaulle were the devil himself, I would regard it as the duty of my government to buy arms from the only source available to us. And now let me ask you a question. If you were in that position, what would you do?"[33]

While travelling in southern Africa, Meir again revealed her assertive personality in the exercise of her convictions. "I heard a police officer [at the Rhodesian border] say, 'Whites only.' 'In that case,' I said, 'I'm sorry, but I won't be able to enter Southern Rhodesia [present-day Zimbabwe] either.' There was great consternation, and the Rhodesians tried very hard to get me to leave the bus, but I wouldn't hear of it. 'I have no intention of being separated from my friends,' I repeated. The whole busload of us traveled back to Lusaka, where Kaunda received me as though I were Joan of Arc rather than just a woman who couldn't and wouldn't tolerate discrimination in any form."[34]

Many of Meir's colleagues who worked with her before she became prime minister also found her to be strong-willed and domineering. In the view of Abba Eban, "since Golda was a tough character with a domineering streak, the temptation for senior officials to adapt their advice to her prejudices was strong. While she was foreign minister, habits of consultation in the ministry were few."[35] Some also faulted her for her dogmatism and intense convictions. "What made people so negative about Golda was her certitude. She knew everything. She was once asked by one of her colleagues to put herself in Nasser's shoes. Her response was 'I won't.'"[36] Meir's Controlling nature was also reflected in a rigid, principled stance. "What Golda lacked was flexibility, i.e., the ability to say for tactical reasons something she did not believe. She could have said we are ready to explore the issue rather than utter a loud resounding no. Some of the crises with the United States and the United Nations could have been avoided had she not been so direct and blunt. She was very rigid on tactics."[37]

Nor did students who did not share her views find her dogmatism easy to deal with. During the time that Michael Harish was a student and headed the students organization at Hebrew University, the Lavon affair was a hot topic. Harish described himself as having felt at ease when meeting with Ben Gurion, but meeting Golda was another matter. He was far more anxious, since "she could be extremely tough if you were weak on the facts, or if you had an opinion that differed from hers."[38]

For Abba Eban, who worked under Meir in the Foreign Ministry, Golda's dominating personality was also reflected in her cognitive style. "Golda's talent lay in the simplification of issues." Eban then contrasted her cognitive style with that of the foreign-policy specialists, who were "conscious of the intrinsic complexity of international relations. They perceive the multiple elements that go into most decisions and policies. They react with resignation to the idea that Israel's vital interests are not all that vital to non-Israelis."[39] In contrast, Meir refused to give serious consideration to the various competing pressures that affected the making of foreign policy both in Israel and in other states. For her, defending Israel's vital interests, as she defined them, was all that mattered. A member of the Israeli diplomatic corps who served under Meir at the United Nations also observed that "there was little that was nuanced about her thinking. Hers was very much a black and white orientation. She was not a conceptual thinker. She relied on her guts. She would ask, 'is he with us or against us?'"[40]

Simcha Dinitz, one of Meir's political advisers and later ambassador to the United States, concurred that "Golda entertained strong convictions. She believed she possessed an inner truth. On certain issues, she simply could not be swayed. She demonstrated little interest in being liked or approved, she believed in remaining steadfast to the truth as she saw it. This trait made it difficult for her to change her mind."[41] Eban also noted that "when Golda assumed the office of prime minister, Sapir told colleagues 'that she would be content to hold office for a year and then pass the burden to younger hands'; [it] was sheer illusion. Her defiant personality certainly gave the nation's military and political struggle a strong dimension."[42] Moshe Dayan also observed that "she [Golda] [was] a courageous, stubborn and determined woman,"[43] while Prime Minister Eshkol had the same qualities in mind when he referred to her as the "Klafte."[44]

Although she was a firm supporter of her friends, she could be vengeful and combative towards her enemies. As an example of her vengefulness, former Israeli president Yitzhak Navon described her treatment of Ben-Gurion. In the beginning, he said, "'her relationship with B.G. was like a love affair. She admired him totally and whole-heartedly. He was a mentor to her.'" Then problems began after she became foreign minister. She bitterly resented that Peres, as defence minister, dealt directly with the French before the 1956 Suez campaign, leaving her "out of the loop" even though she was the foreign minister. With the growing strength of a younger generation of political leaders, such as Peres, Dayan, and Allon, "'Golda and her cronies, Sapir, etc., felt betrayed by Ben-Gurion's support and encouragement of these people. When Ben-Gurion decided that he wanted to reopen the Lavon affair under an independent judicial inquiry, Golda didn't trust his motives; she thought that B.G. was fighting to reopen the case in order to get the old guard out of the party.'"[45]

In 1965, at the annual Labor Party convention, with more than three thousand people in attendance, Moshe Sharett arrived in a wheelchair and spoke against Ben-Gurion. Meir leaned down and kissed him. Since it was at Ben-Gurion's insistence that Meir had earlier replaced Sharett as foreign minister, "he [Ben-Gurion] never forgave Golda for what he saw as an act of blatant disloyalty."[46]

This brief examination of the multiple expressions of the Dominant/ Controlling dimensions of Golda's personality reveals a woman who was assertive and outspoken in her convictions, and extremely forceful in their articulation. Cognitively rigid, she had difficulty entertaining nuanced views of the world or ambivalent feelings about people. In her view, Israel had clear-cut security interests and states could be divided into supporters or opponents. In the same vein, she either loved and trusted or hated and distrusted her colleagues and associates. There was never any middle ground. Towards those who displeased her, Golda was capable of aggressive, vengeful behaviour.

SCALE 5B: THE CONTENTIOUS PATTERN

Individuals with a scale elevation of 5 to 9 (the *present* range) of the Contentious pattern are the cynical, headstrong, resolute personalities. Exaggerated Contentious features (scores of 10 to 23, the *prominent* range) occur in complaining, irksome, oppositional personalities.[47] The Contentious pattern (Scale 5A), with an elevation of 17, was the second most important dimension in Golda Meir's personality profile. The oppositional style is an inflated variant of the Contentious pattern and is associated with complaining, irritable, discontented, resistant, and contrarian or ambivalent behaviour.

Even as a young girl, the complaining aspect of Golda's personality profile was in evidence. She hated working in the family grocery store and made no secret of her feelings. However, as she noted, "my mother didn't seem to be moved by my bitter resentment of the shop."[48] As Golda grew older, the confrontational aspects of her personality grew, particularly in her relations with her parents. "That autumn, the autumn of 1912, I defiantly began my first term at Milwaukee's North Division High School and worked in the afternoons and on weekends at a variety of odd jobs, determined never again to ask my parents for money."[49]

In the face of her parents' refusal to countenance her continuing with her education, Golda decided to leave home without even telling her parents. However, after she moved to Denver to live with her sister Sheyna and her husband, she came to resent what she perceived as her sister's overbearing and controlling attitude towards her, and she moved out to live on her own. "I was sometimes as lonely as I was independent, particularly when Morris wasn't around. However, since neither Sheyna nor I were very good at admitting to error or apologizing, it took several months before we finally made up."[50]

In her relationship with her husband, Morris, Golda did not confront him directly when they disagreed but was more likely to behave in a covertly antagonistic and irritated fashion. As she wrote in her autobiography, "it was because of me that Morris had gone to Merhavia in the first place, and now it was because of Morris's 'failure' there that I had to tear myself away from it. Maybe if we had reproached each other openly, it would have been much better for us, but we didn't. Instead, we both felt very much at loose ends and were irritable most of the time."[51]

Golda also exhibited her contentiousness outside the family. After the Germans invaded Russia in 1941, the Hashomer Ha'Tzair (a left-wing youth movement) suggested that the Jews in Palestine send medical help to the Jews in Eastern Europe. When their suggestion was rejected, the group accused Golda and her colleagues of not treating the idea seriously. Golda was infuriated by their charge of "a lack of seriousness" and gave them a thorough tongue-lashing. She would not have minded if they had said that she and her supporters were wrong in their decision, but the charge of "not serious" was enough to inflame her. It was akin to her husband and family members' charge that her activities and attitudes were shallow and superficial. Her reaction was very emotional, since she saw this allegation as a personal attack on her.[52]

At the end of the Second World War, Golda learned that the British authorities were about to use German prisoners-of-war to build military camps in Palestine. The British general secretary, John Shaw, acknowledged the truth of this report but defended the plan on the grounds that there was a shortage of workers. Golda replied angrily that he might want to find workers through the Histadrut. His answer was that it was not possible to trust Jewish workers, since "'things they build tend to explode.' Golda's cynical reaction was: 'The Nazis can be trusted, then?' The plan was abandoned; the British realized that there was a limit as to how much they could provoke the Jews."[53]

When, shortly after Israel celebrated its independence in May 1948, Golda was asked to become the Israeli ambassador to Moscow, she was reluctant to accept the post. She did not want to leave Israel, after working so hard to see it born. "I had a family and dear friends in Israel, and it seemed to me it was grossly unfair to ask me to pack my bags again so soon and take off for such a remote and essentially unknown post. 'Why was it always me'? I thought, in a burst of self-pity ... At least in America I was doing something real, concrete, and practical, but what did I know or care about diplomacy?"[54]

Golda was unhappy and impatient during her stay in Moscow, feeling that her job was pointless since she was isolated from the Jews both in the city and in Russia at large. The diplomatic custom required her to visit other diplomats, at least of those countries that had already recognized the new state of Israel. She found these visits burdensome and they stimulated her contentiousness, as the following exchange attests:

Ambassador: "How did you arrive in Moscow?" [Lou Kadar, Golda's personal assistant, translates this into Hebrew.]
Golda: "What, you don't know how we arrived here?"
Kadar: "I know, he wants to know."
Golda: "Tell him in a plane."
Ambassador: "And where are you staying?" [Again Kadar translates.]
Golda: "Tell him: In the Metropole Hotel."[55]

After this exchange had been repeated several times, Golda lost patience at the banality of the questions that Lou Kadar was translating. "'He wants to know how we arrived in Moscow.' Golda interrupted, 'Tell his excellency, the ambassador, that we arrived riding donkeys.' When afterwards, as expected, he asked: 'Where do you stay?' Golda replied: 'Tell him that we live in a big tent.'"[56]

During her time in Moscow, Golda met with a Russian politician named Zurin, and he mentioned the fact that she had been born in Kiev. "'However, he commented, 'she must not remember a thing from her years as a child there.'" Golda quickly rejoined, "'Right, aside from the preparation for the pogroms.'"[57]

Golda suffered from the fact that her Hebrew vocabulary was extremely limited. On one occasion she heard that one of her colleagues had derisively claimed that she had a vocabulary of about two hundred Hebrew words. When she refused to meet him, and he wondered about her coldness, she explained that "'with such a limited vocabulary as mine, it would be a shame to waste precious words on you.'"[58] A caustic and acerbic tongue is characteristic of the cognitive style of Contentious individuals.[59]

On her return from Moscow after nine months as ambassador, Golda continued to find issues about which to complain. Although she had joined the cabinet as minister of housing and immigration, she continued to be called upon to travel abroad to raise funds. "So, though I begrudged every minute that I was away from Israel, I went on with my fund-raising speeches abroad, traveling often to Europe, the United States, and South America."[60]

Although Golda tried to take care of the immigrants as well as she could in her capacity as minister of housing and immigration, the social gaps in the country were obvious. Nonetheless, she was appalled at the immigrants' lack of appreciation for Israel's efforts on their behalf. "'They are ungrateful,' she used to complain, 'after everything we have done for them.'"[61]

Another hallmark of Golda's contentiousness was her ability to maintain a grudge for an extended period of time, as her long-standing feud with Ben-Gurion attests. Ben-Gurion had decided after the Sinai campaign to replace the older leadership (figures such as Golda Meir, Pinchas Sapir, and Zalman Aranne) with younger people such as Moshe Dayan, Yigal Yadin, and Shimon Peres. Meir opposed this decision, believing that the younger coterie lacked ideological conviction. "I know that the youth should revolt against the old, I revolt against the youths who think that there is no need of ideology." She then added a jab at Ben-Gurion: "And I revolt against the old who defend youths who have no ideology."[62] Ben-Gurion made numerous attempts to mollify Meir, "the raging deity," writing her a warm congratulatory sixtieth birthday letter, but she was not appeased, particularly when she learned that, after the November 1959 elections, Dayan and Yigal Yadin would be appointed as ministers in the new government. She was also furious that Shimon Peres, as the minister of defence, was attempting to subvert her authority as the minister of foreign affairs. She informed Ben-Gurion that she would not be part of the new government, but was persuaded by Eshkol and Sapir to remain.[63] Some said that her jealousy of the special relations between Peres and Ben-Gurion made her loathe Peres from the start. One Mapai politician tried to dispel Meir's detestation of Peres. "He is a very gifted man," the Mapai activist stated. "So was Al Capone!" Golda retorted.[64]

Ben-Gurion's decision to leave Mapai and start a new party, Rafi, with Dayan and Peres and some of the other younger members (following his resignation in 1961 over the Lavon affair) was the last straw for

Meir and cemented her resentment of Ben-Gurion. To her it was inconceivable that Ben-Gurion should break up the glorious party organization of Mapai.[65]

Meir's dislike and resentment of Peres continued even in her retirement. Shimshon Arad, a member of the Israeli diplomatic corps, remembered her critical remark when Peres became chairman of the Labor Party in 1977: "Why did Peres have to call himself chairman when we were all satisfied with being secretary-generals?"[66] Peres himself talks about a significant improvement in relations between him and Meir towards the end of her life when Labor was in opposition. But he acknowledges: "I don't know what she felt in her heart."[67] Arad also had a more direct exposure to Meir's critical disposition. As he recalled, "she was not an easy forgiver." When he was the ambassador to Mexico, they had a falling-out, which he felt was not his fault, and it took him some time to get back into her good graces.[68]

Meir herself was well aware of her Contentious traits. In a conversation with Simcha Dinitz in which she discussed her own unforgiving nature, she commented that "someone I do not like should not have been born."[69] Dr Moshe Yegar also attested to this quality. He knew Meir from the time when he was a relatively junior foreign service officer and recalls her meeting with all the Israeli ambassadors for a full-day session. "She had no sense of humour, did not like wisecracks of any kind, and when someone spoke whom she didn't like, she just would stare at them and they would wilt."[70]

Yegar also remembered a visit Meir made to Rangoon in 1962 as foreign minister when he was the second secretary at the embassy. Her itinerary called for her to speak to the women's club of Rangoon University on the subject of – neither the title nor the idea was hers – the "Contribution of Women to the Establishment of the State of Israel." As someone who disliked feminist slogans and thought men and women should be treated like people, she was clearly upset. "She gave the ambassador a look that could freeze him and said, 'What is that?' He started to explain about the pressure exerted upon him, and another look silenced him. However, she didn't tell him to cancel the talk." On the day of the address, there was a huge reception, attended by a number of men including military attachés. Then she was introduced. "She was modesty itself[,] telling her audience how delighted she was to be there and how proud she was to discuss this important topic of the role of women in Israel … At the end of an hour, she commented, 'So you can see that men and women have contributed equally to the building of Israel.'"[71] In this anecdote, we can see the superficially acquiescent but fundamentally determined and resolute aspects of Meir's Contentious personality.[72]

SCALE 6: THE CONSCIENTIOUS PATTERN

Tied for third place in importance in Golda Meir's personality profile is Conscientiousness, with a score of 12. "Conscientious-style people ... [have] strong moral principle[s] and absolute certainty, and they won't rest until the job is done and done right. They are loyal to their families, their causes, and their superiors. Hard work is a hall-mark of this personality style."[73] Meir's conscientiousness expressed it-self primarily in a sense of extraordinary dutifulness. Throughout her life, her sense of responsibility led her to sacrifice her marriage, time with her children, and her health to what she perceived as a moral ob-ligation to the Jewish state. She was continually torn between her obli-gations and responsibilities to her close loved ones, on the one hand, and her responsibility to the Zionist movement and later the state of Is-rael, on the other. Sometimes her loyalty to friends and family won out, but, for the most part, it was the larger sense of duty to the broader community that triumphed.

When Ben-Gurion visited Milwaukee, Golda, as a young Zionist, longed to meet him, but she knew that Morris, who had invited her to a concert some weeks earlier, would be disappointed if she failed to ac-company him. "I felt duty-bound to go with him, though I can't say I enjoyed the music much that night."[74]

Golda's sense of responsibility also manifested itself in her decision not to join the Labor Zionist movement until she was prepared to com-mit herself to making *aliya*. As she described it: "I was not going to be a parlour Zionist advocating settlement in Palestine for others, and I re-fused to join the Labor Zionist party until I could make a binding deci-sion."[75] However, this decision carried with it a recognition that Morris was disinterested in Zionism and openly opposed to the idea of emi-grating to Palestine. "The idea that I might have to choose between Morris and Palestine made me miserable, and for the most part I kept to myself, working for the Labor Zionists in my free time – making speeches, organizing meetings, raising funds. There was always some-thing that took precedence over my private worries and therefore served to distract me from them – a situation that was not to change much in the course of the next six decades."[76]

As a member of the kibbutz, Golda's sense of duty occasionally took on a compulsive aspect. "I didn't care what I wore every day [on the kibbutz], but it *had* to be ironed. Every night, using a heavy iron heated by coal, I religiously pressed my 'sack,' knowing that the kibbutzniks not only thought I was mad, but also suspected me of not being a true pioneer at heart."[77]

Afterwards, the aging men and women who had been with Golda in Merhavia remembered her as a real *havera*. This means that she had proved equal to the job of a kibbutznik. She had not shirked hard or unpleasant tasks, had not moped about the constant need to subordinate personal moods and desires to the interests of the commune, and had not behaved like a martyr in exercising her responsibilities.[78]

When, following the creation of Israel in 1948, Ben-Gurion informed Golda that she would be the first Israeli ambassador to the Soviet Union, she was in hospital in the United States recuperating from a serious traffic accident that she had incurred while raising funds for the new state. Reluctant to leave Israel to take up a diplomatic posting, she stated: "'At last we have a state. I want to be there. I don't want to go thousands of miles away.'"[79] Moreover, the little Golda knew about Moscow led her to believe that she would be far removed there from any of the important decisions regarding the shape and future of Israel. However, as she observed, "Ben-Gurion was certainly not likely to be swayed by any personal appeals. And then there was the matter of discipline. Who was I to disobey or even demur at a time when each day brought news of fresh casualties? One's duty was one's duty – and it had nothing to do with justice."[80]

Golda's stay in the hospital was shorter than was medically wise and fraught with enormous demands on her time that she felt, in good conscience, she could not refuse. "To begin with, there were the television cameras and the newspapermen ... I suppose I could have refused to be interviewed – and today, of course, that is just what I would do under such circumstances. But at the time I thought it would be good for Israel if we got a lot of publicity, and I felt I mustn't turn down a single request from the press."[81] As much as Golda resented both the posting and the pressure placed upon her, she was too loyal a servant of the state not to obey the government's request.

Later, Meir's appointment as foreign minister upset Moshe Sharett – her predecessor. In his journal, he argued that her cooperation in his dismissal, and her agreement to replace him, raised an important moral question that was not excused by her willingness, which he fully acknowledged, "to jump off the fifth floor" to do Ben-Gurion's bidding. What he was referring to was Golda's sense of duty – her willingness to do anything that was asked of her.[82]

During Meir's tenure as foreign minister, "there was no night and day. Dinitz would be called as late as 10:00 P.M. to come over to Golda's. She was totally dedicated to the task at hand and expected everyone else to be as well."[83] That Meir possessed some ambitious traits is clear; she had a commanding presence and was charismatic. But "for Golda ambition was a dirty word; she preferred to see her drive as part of the ethos of service."[84] And no doubt it was fuelled, to a large extent, by a sense of duty.

A major limitation of the Conscientious personality style is a predilection for "seeing complex matters in black and white, good and bad, or right and wrong terms."[85] Illustrative of this cognitive dimension in Meir's personality profile are the following observations of colleagues and friends. Dayan noted that "she [Golda] is also blessed by the Lord with the capacity to see the world in bold black and stark white, free from the range of twilight shades. If there were a danger of war, then wide-scale mobilization was the answer. And if American help was to be sought, then the United States had to be given foolproof evidence that it was not we who desired war – even if this ruled out pre-emptive action and handicapped us in the military campaign."[86] Based on his observations of Meir while she was foreign minister, David Harmon also described her "as a singularly resolute individual. She would simply shut out people she didn't like, and once she decided she didn't like you, that was it. The world was black and white – no room for greys."[87]

SCALE 5A: THE AGGRIEVED PATTERN

The Aggrieved pattern also received a score of 12 in Golda Meir's personality profile, ranking it, like the Conscientious pattern, in third place; its scale elevation situates it just above the healthy, well-adjusted *present* range (scores of 5 to 9). In this range of the spectrum can be found the humble, unpretentious, deferential personalities. More exaggerated features (the *prominent* category, scores of 10 to 23) occur in self-sacrificing, self-denying personalities. For such individuals, "to live is to serve; to love is to give. These are axioms for individuals who have the Self-Sacrificing personality style. The way they see it, their needs can wait until others' are well served. Knowing that they have given of themselves, they feel comfortable and at peace, secure with their place in the scheme of things."[88]

A self-effacing tendency to downplay personal abilities – characteristic of the Aggrieved personality style – is suggested in Golda's ruminations after her arrival in Palestine as a new emigrant, when she asked herself, "Were we too soft for the country? My sense of uneasiness and guilt about my own failings – to say nothing of my nervousness about Morris's reaction to these unfortunate experiences – lasted throughout our first week in Tel Aviv ... we were hot, tired, and dispirited most of the time."[89]

Because Morris never adjusted to life on the kibbutz, and did not want his children to be raised in a communal setting, Golda, who loved kibbutz life, was prepared to sacrifice her own happiness and moved with Morris to Jerusalem to start a family. Despite her determined efforts, she was desperately unhappy. "All of these hopes and good intentions notwithstanding [for a life as a kibbutznik] instead of the placid domestic life that I now told myself I was ready to accept, the four years that we lived in Jerusalem were the most miserable I ever experienced and when you have lived as long as I have, that's saying a lot!"[90]

Jacob Katzmanthe, national secretary of the youth group of Labor Zionists, remembered how small their offices were and how cramped everyone felt. But "[Golda] made lots of friends right away. She was a very simple, outgoing person who never put on any airs. She was the kind of woman who made other women feel they were her sisters."[91]

In 1946 Golda replaced Moshe Sharett, who had been imprisoned, as head of the Jewish Agency's political department, the chief Jewish liaison with the British. Her associates were surprised at the rapidity with which she learned the ropes. One quality that stood her in good stead was a complete lack of pretence. She was aware of the limitations of her knowledge and knew how to ask for advice and take it.[92]

As noted above, after Golda was appointed ambassador to the Soviet Union, she recognized that Israel needed all the publicity it could get. She was prepared to accept every request from the media for interviews even though she was lying in an American hospital bed, exhausted and in pain. In part, this reflected the Conscientious dimensions of her personality. As well, it tapped into the Aggrieved/self-sacrificing aspects of her character. A belief that to live is to serve is characteristic of this personality pattern.

When Ben-Gurion offered Golda the post of minister of foreign affairs, her predecessor, Moshe Sharett, wrote in his journal that "she knows very well that the position [as foreign minister] is not suitable for her. Through years of experience and familiarity with her, I find she suffers from an inferiority complex, as a result of her limited education. She is very sensitive to her limitations that arise from a lack of general knowledge, her inability to phrase her thoughts in writing, her unfamiliarity with writing a proper speech and her inability to describe accurately the details of state policy."[93] While some of Sharett's analysis could be attributed to "sour grapes," Meir was acutely aware of her limitations and tried to compensate for them.

In her capacity as foreign minister, Meir and Mordechai Gazit, a member of her department, often discussed particular individuals. Gazit would observe that "X" was an awful person, totally untrustworthy, and Meir would reply, "Yes, I agree with you. We have to get rid of him." To which, Gazit would respond, "Now that it's out of your system, you're never going to act." "And, in fact, she didn't."[94] Nor could Golda fire one of her drivers even though she disliked him intensely. As her personal assistant, Lou Kadar, commented to Gazit, Meir was the type of person who had difficulty firing people.[95] In her personal relationships with people, Meir was capable of behaving in a decidedly unassertive and deferential manner, particularly with subordinates. However, on matters of principle, such as the security of the state of Israel, she could be obstinate, strong-willed, and the exact opposite of deferential.

The question has been raised as to why Levi Eshkol was elected to be prime minister in 1963 rather than Meir, who was the most senior member of the Labor Party in the aftermath of Ben-Gurion's resignation two years earlier. It has been suggested that Meir did not feel ready to take on the office of the prime minister, and did not want to be the one to inherit it from Ben-Gurion – to whom she would be compared, and probably not favourably. Her sense of deference also made her feel that, if she succeeded Ben-Gurion, it might be interpreted as the reason behind her opposition to his policies.[96]

Meir was genuinely modest and unassuming. In 1959 Ben-Gurion sent his private secretary, Yitzhak Navon, to tell her that he no longer wanted Moshe Sharett as foreign minister and wished her to take the post: "'Me, she said, do you think I can fill the position? Are you sure that I am up to it?' 'Yes,' he replied, 'trust B.G., he knows you and that is what he has decided. And that was that.'"[97] In 1964, when Pope Paul VI visited Jerusalem, Meir, in her capacity as foreign minister, awaited his arrival in the company of President Zalman Shazar and Teddy Kolleck, the mayor of Jerusalem. As the entourage with the pope approached, Golda leaned over and said to Kolleck in Yiddish, "'If my Mother and Father could see me now.'"[98] When she was appointed to the office of prime minister, her reaction was "'me, the daughter of a carpenter?' When asked why she accepted, she said, 'this is what my friends wanted me to do.' She never said I'm the best person to fill the job."[99]

Ultimately, then, the Aggrieved pattern was significant in Meir's distinguished career and service. Although she had few doubts about her goals or the means necessary to attain them, she was nonetheless tormented throughout her life by feelings of not really being qualified for the many positions she held, a sense that she lacked the necessary education and experience and was intellectually inferior. She exuded an air of strength and authority that seems to have been an effort to repress her feelings of inadequacy and doubts about her suitability for the various positions in government that she occupied.[100]

SCALE 1B: THE DAUNTLESS PATTERN

The scale elevation of the Dauntless pattern, at 11, ranked it within the *prominent* category (scores of 10 to 23). Individuals who score in this range are fearless and daring personalities undaunted by danger. They take clear stands on issues that matter and are not conciliatory or compromising; they often become irritable and aggressive when crossed.

Their self-image is one of independence and autonomy.[101] T. Millon argues that their personal history is often characterized by secondary status in the family. In particular, parents may have given special attention to another sibling who was admired and highly esteemed, at least in the eyes of the "deprived" youngster.[102]

Meir has given us the following illustration of her "secondary status": "One picture is engraved in my memory. When my younger sister, Tzipka, four years my junior, was still a baby, six months or less, my mother was cooking porridge, a great luxury for us in those days. My mother gave me a little, and the rest to my baby sister. She finished eating before me; then mother took a little porridge away from me to give to her. I remember the shock at being deprived of this rare porridge. Even now I can still summon up, almost intact, the picture of myself sitting in tears in the kitchen."[103]

At five, Golda was already feisty, independent, and fearless. According to her aunts, she not only refused to listen to reason but often defied a direct order. Nor would a spanking change her mind – if she was stubbornly set on something. Her mother called her a *kochleffl* – a stirring spoon because she was always shaking things up.[104]

Although schooling in Milwaukee was free, children had to pay for their schoolbooks or, to obtain free ones, plead poverty. Golda felt that it was very humiliating for a child to admit she was too poor to pay for books. At the age of eleven, she appointed herself chairman of a group of friends she called the American Young Sisters Society. Golda persuaded the owner of a hall to donate it for a meeting they planned to hold. The group painted posters and knocked on doors, and, on the evening of the meeting, Golda stood up and addressed a group of adults without a note – a practice she never abandoned. Her message was simple: they needed money for poor children because all children need schoolbooks. The fund-raiser was a great success,[105] a harbinger of things to come.

One of Golda's girlfriends told her about a classmate who threw a penny at her, saying, "'Pick it up!' When she did, he pushed her away, saying sneeringly, 'A dirty Jew will pick up every penny.' Then he ran away with his friends. That evening, Goldie organized a demonstration in front of that boy's house protesting his anti-Semitism."[106] When the issue was one that touched Golda deeply, caution was thrown to the winds and she became a fearless defender for what she believed.

After Golda left home to live with her sister, a quarrel over the late hours Golda kept with various young men caused her to bolt. With no home and no money, Golda, as dauntless as ever, found a tiny room and a job. Miserable and alone, she refused to give in and return either to Milwaukee or to Sheyna's for three years.[107] Later, when she returned to Milwaukee and her parents to pursue her education, her friend Sadie Ottenstein, who lived across the alley and walked with her to school every morning, recalled that "'Goldie was fearless; she was a firebrand with very strong convictions. For her, everything was either right or wrong, with no middle way.'"[108]

A number of classmates also recalled that Golda was an independent thinker. Louise Born, who became a teacher, remembered that Golda always talked about *that* being wrong and *this* being wrong. "'One day I said, "Goldie, if everything's wrong, why don't you start your own country?" And she said, "I might just do that."'"[109]

During her stay in Denver, Golda had become a staunch Zionist, determined to make *aliya*. But, as Ottenstein noted, "'All of us in our crowd dreamed of going to Eretz Yisroel, but Goldie was the one who picked herself up and went, and that was the difference.'"[110] Once in Palestine, Golda showed that she lacked any preconceived notions about desirable and undesirable kinds of work. She did not consider dishwashing humiliating, and kitchen work did not depress her. As a matter of fact, she created something of a sensation at a convention of the cooperatives held in 1922, when she arose and fearlessly asked why women considered kitchen work a disgrace. This speech, one of her earliest public utterances in Palestine, was viewed as heresy by her female comrades.[111]

As part of her self-image of autonomy and resourcefulness, "Golda still had one blouse and skirt which she washed and ironed every day." As Marie Syrkin said, "'she was contemptuous of females like myself who couldn't iron or cook or bake or wash dishes. She used to tell me, 'You intellectuals think it's beneath you.' Once, asked her favorite hobby, she replied smiling, 'washing dishes.'"[112]

After leaving Merhavia for Jerusalem because of Morris's recurring illnesses and his unhappiness living on the kibbutz, Golda stayed home with her young children while Morris tried, unsuccessfully, to find a decently paying job. When a husky young neighbour warned the milkman that he was taking a chance in extending credit to the Meyerson family, Golda, dauntless as ever, caned the meddler in outraged fury. "'No one will take milk from my children.'"[113]

The Dauntless pattern is often reflected in a refusal to consider issues of personal health or safety. Golda suffered from serious acute gallbladder attacks; if they were not severe enough for hospitalization, she would lie completely prostrate on the living-room couch which served as a bed at night. The problem was to get her to agree to stay in bed the following day if the pain had already subsided. But there was always something to get up for: a meeting with the high commissioner in Jerusalem or some other important mission. Although her son, Menachem, and her friend Marie Syrkin would plead with her and explain that she was "killing herself," she would ignore them and go. One of her friends deplored her recklessness and thought she must be motivated by an unconscious death wish.[114]

In 1946 the male leaders of the Yishuv, including Moshe Sharett, were held behind barbed wire in the detention camp in Latrun. Friends of Golda went to her apartment in Tel Aviv and implored her to go into hiding. It was assumed that she too would be arrested. But Golda declined to hide. "'If they want me, they know where I am.'"[115]

UNDERSTANDING GOLDA MEIR'S
PERSONALITY PROFILE

In summary, Golda Meir's primary scale elevation, the Dominant (Scale 1A, score 18), was marginally greater than her second highest elevation, the Contentious (Scale 5B, score 17). However, both scales were appreciably stronger than the next three, the Conscientious (Scale 6, score 12), the Aggrieved (Scale 5A, score 12), and the Dauntless (Scale 1B, score 11). An explanation for these scores follows.

Golda's personality profile was the product of innate constitutional predispositions, familial traits, and life experiences, which included her relationship with her parents and older sister. Golda described her grandfather and grandmother as tough, intransigent individuals, and their daughter, Bluma, Golda's mother, would prove the old adage, "the apple doesn't fall far from the tree." As a child, Golda was told that she bore a striking resemblance to her Bobbe (maternal great-grandmother) Golde, for whom she was named, and who was described as bossy with a will of iron.[116]

Golda's Dominant pattern was also fostered by her relations with her sister and her parents. Although the Mabovitch family was, in Golda's words, "pitifully poor," Golda's older sister, Sheyna, refused to go to work to help out and insisted instead on continuing her studies so she could help to improve the world. Sheyna was a self-professed revolutionary, and her refusal to give up her political work, notwithstanding her mother's pleading, and the danger of being arrested for subversive activity, made a profound impression on young Golda.[117] She identified with her older sister in resisting their mother's demands and in her passionate commitment to Zionism. The message that Sheyna sent and that Golda internalized was clear: first, if one is forceful enough, mothers can be successfully defied; second, there is something very special about the Zionist movement to return the Jews to the land of their forefathers; and third, it is not enough to believe in something, you have to struggle to achieve your goals.

Even as child, it seems as though her sister's and mother's strong convictions spilled over onto Golda; developing her own strong convictions may have been her way of both standing up to her mother and emulating her sister. At the age of eleven, her sense of personal injustice, fostered by the way she was treated by her mother, was projected into the public arena in the form of her strong belief in the inequity of the Milwaukee school system. She not only launched a fund to rectify the injustice and then appointed herself a chairman of the society and hired a hall, but she also sent invitations out to the entire district – all this at the age of eleven. Her mother begged her to write out her speech, but she refused, preferring to say what was in her heart – a pattern that would continue for the next half-century.[118]

At the age of fourteen, Golda finished elementary school. Her marks were good and she was chosen to be class valedictorian. She expected to go on to high school and become a teacher. However, her parents had other plans for her. Her mother "knew exactly what [she] should do." She would work in the shop full time and start thinking seriously about getting married, a status that was forbidden to women teachers by state law. If she insisted on a profession, then she should go to secretarial school and learn to become a short-hand typist. That way, she would not remain an old maid. Nor was Golda's father much help in her battle with her mother. He warned her that "'it doesn't pay to be too clever. Men don't like smart girls.'"[119]

Neither Golda's arguments nor her tears were of any avail. But her sister Sheyna encouraged her in her refusal to bow to her parents' demands. The disputes at home continued when Golda began her first term of high school, supporting herself with part-time jobs, and they intensified with Golda's mother's attempt to find her a husband in the person of a man twice Golda's age. Golda left for Denver to live with Sheyna so that she could continue her schooling.[120] Her assertive Dominant personality trait was constantly stimulated by the differences in values between her and her mother and, to a lesser extent, her father.

Living with Sheyna would shape the strong beliefs, so characteristic of the Dominant personality, that Golda would hold her entire life. Sheyna's small apartment was a centre in Denver for the Jewish immigrants from Russia who had come for treatment at the city's famous Jewish hospital for consumptives. Among the visitors were all manner of anarchists, socialists, and Socialist Zionists. Golda was particularly attracted to the political philosophy of the latter group and their focus on a national home for the Jews. Having witnessed, as a child, Cossack forces terrorizing the Jewish community of Pinsk, she was drawn to the Zionist movement's promise of a safe haven for Jews. But it was the movement's socialist aspects that were particularly appealing. From

Golda's perspective, it was a revolt against the Jewish establishment, given the Zionist belief that only self-labour could truly liberate the Jews from the ghetto and its mentality and make it possible for them to reclaim the land and earn a moral as well as an historic right to it.[121] Golda's subsequent decision to emigrate to Palestine and join a kibbutz was, at least in part, an externalized expression of her opposition to her own personal establishment – her parents and their values – and her internalization of a "good object," her sister and her beliefs.

Both the Contentious and Conscientious patterns in Golda's personality profile were activated after the family's move to Milwaukee. Golda's mother decided, in short order, that her husband's earnings as a carpenter were unlikely to be sufficient to support a family, and she proceeded to open a small grocery store. Golda's father refused to have anything to do with the business, and her mother was forced to rise early every morning to go to the market, shop, and then drag her purchases back to the store. Bluma's enforced absences every morning meant that someone had to tend the store while she was gone. Sheyna, like her father, refused to help. Her socialist principles meant that she could not countenance the idea of becoming a shopkeeper, which in her view was the equivalent of a "social parasite." For months, it was Golda, the youngest in the family, who had to stand behind the counter until her mother returned home – not an easy chore for an eight or nine year old. On the surface, she was superficially acquiescent, but feelings of deep annoyance festered within her. Forced to arrive late to class almost every day, Golda was in tears all the way to school. But Golda's mother seemed unmoved by her bitter resentment. Her anger was exacerbated by her mother's miscarriage, which meant that Golda had to cook and scrub and mind the store, "choking back tears of rage all the time because [she] was forced to miss even more school."[122] Her bottled-up rage would later receive full expression in her refusal to accept her parents' decision to deny her a high school education and her strong-willed decision to leave home over that issue.

In Denver, however, Golda began to chafe under her sister's guardianship and her *contentiousness* boiled over once again. Sheyna objected to the time she was spending with a young man named Morris Meyerson, whom she had met at Sheyna's apartment. Golda was informed that she had come to Denver to study, not to listen to music or read poetry, two of Morris's interests. At the age of sixteen, Golda moved out. Having accepted the invitation of two of Sheyna's friends to live with them, Golda quickly realized that living with two women with advanced tuberculosis was not a long-term solution, and she subsequently got a job to pay for her own room.[123]

Given Golda's obduracy, as well as Sheyna's, a number of months would pass before either of them spoke to the other. After Golda had been on her own for a year (two years after she had left Milwaukee), her father wrote her that if she valued her mother's life, she should return home, which she did on her terms – continuing high school, graduating, and entering a teacher's training college.[124]

Like her Contentious trait, Golda's Conscientious pattern can also be traced backed to her childhood. Although Golda had clearly rebelled against her mother's demands to work in the store, the responsibilities that she was made to shoulder at a very young age seem to have left a lasting imprint, resulting in a strong sense of duty. Despite her rage, as a child Golda seems to have recognized that if she refused to help her mother, no one else would. Thus, she submitted to her dictates, albeit unwillingly. Later in life, she would continue to behave in a dutiful manner, but this behaviour was frequently infused with an underlying resentment, as when she reluctantly decided to leave the kibbutz because of Morris or when she expressed her unhappiness at having been appointed ambassador to the Soviet Union.

Golda, like her sister Sheyna, did not believe that one could be an armchair Zionist. For her, such a commitment necessarily implied an obligation to pick up stakes in the United States and work in Palestine to establish the new Jewish state. But, in her interpersonal relationships, her Conscientiousness went only so far. Although plagued by a strong sense of guilt, she was, nevertheless, prepared to leave her two young children for months at a time to fulfil what she felt were her larger responsibilities to the Yishuv and to the Zionist goal of establishing a Jewish state in Palestine. Israel, as a transcendent goal, inspired Golda to engage in a wide range of Conscientious behaviours, from fundraising activities in the United States to accepting the post of Israeli ambassador to Moscow – a position she most definitely did not want.

Other aspects of Golda's Conscientious pattern can also be traced back to her childhood. From her early life in Russia, she retained a number of difficult memories – including ones of mud and dirt, things that she would hate for the rest of her life. The swamps, the snow in winter, the spring floods, the summer flies were likewise engraved in her soul. She became addicted to cleanliness in an almost obsessive way, and demanded order and cleanliness from others. Some psychologists suggest that this is a clear sign of a lack of love and warmth at home. Even when she served as foreign minister and prime minister, she continued to wash small laundry items and undergarments by hand, and do the dishes in her kitchen after the last guest would leave, even though there was hired help to do the housework. She would rationalize her behaviour by claiming that her most productive thinking would occur as she washed her hair or did the dishes.[125]

Golda also possessed a strain of humility and lack of pretension, which is characteristic of the Aggrieved personality pattern at lower elevation levels. This personality pattern, which received a score of 12, can perhaps be explained by her early commitment to and immersion in the philosophy of Zionist socialism with its emphasis on the group and its needs. A belief in frugality and a non-materialistic way of life were both part and parcel of the ideas of the early kibbutz movement that Golda warmly embraced. As a Russian-born American who emigrated to Israel in her early twenties, Golda was motivated by a desire to serve her people, not by a narcissistic sense of self-importance.

The Dauntless personality trait was also a part of the personality pattern that began in Golda's childhood. Having seen her adored sister Sheyna risk imprisonment and possibly death for her Zionist political activities in Russia, Golda became unafraid of challenges and took risks in her personal life that many more cautious individuals would have eschewed. After her return home from Sheyna's, Golda's attraction to the Labor Zionist movement increased, and she decided to campaign for it on a soapbox outside the neighbourhood synagogue during the high holy days. Her father was mortified and threatened that he would come and pull her by her braid and drag her home. She had no doubt he would do as he said, but she remained undeterred – evidence of the Dauntless component in her personality. He came to get her but was so carried away by his daughter's eloquence that he forgot his threat. The Dauntless and Domineering aspects of Golda's personality had carried the day.

Golda's struggles, with both her parents and her sister, in conjunction with her beliefs, gave her a fearless quality that is characteristic of the Dauntless personality pattern. She left home just before she turned fifteen, moved out of her sister's house at sixteen, made *aliya* when she was twenty-three, and remained undaunted by illness and privation.

Although the Conscientious, Aggrieved, and Dauntless patterns were important parts of Golda's personality profile, the predominance of the Dominant and Contentious traits suggests that she can be characterized primarily as an "abrasive negativist." This pattern was a part of her personality, manifesting itself, particularly, in relationship to her parents, her sister, and those political associates whom she felt condescended to her. An explanation for this behaviour lies in Golda's childhood. Clearly, she did not experience much love or warmth in the Mabovitch household; both parents were too preoccupied with poverty, pogroms, and then making a life in a new country. As well, her parents' experience of five infant deaths – four sons and one daughter – in the nine years between Sheyna's and Golda's births seems to have conditioned them against too great an emotional investment in a child who might not live beyond the age of two. A child who never experiences any sense of being valued or loved for him/herself develops a perspective in which minor frictions with parents are perceived as major confrontations. He or she experiences resentful feelings and angry emotions, engages in power struggles, and often exhibits overtly hostile behaviour. As a child, Golda felt unloved; she was convinced that her mother valued her strictly in terms of an extra pair of hands in the grocery store. Given this mindset, Golda was angry, resentful, and openly hostile.[126]

Labelling Golda an "abrasive negativist" provides for a diagnostic categorization of her personality, but it does not explain the role that her various personality patterns played during her tenure as prime minister. That is the subject of the next chapter.

Golda Meir's Leadership Style

Golda Meir's commitment to the establishment of a Jewish state was unceasing, and her role as a member of the government was significant, but what kind of leader did she prove herself to be as prime minister? This chapter explores the empirical evidence of Golda Meir's leadership style in three broad groupings. In Cluster A, Meir's motivation, her task orientation, and her investment in job performance are examined; Cluster B analyses Meir's management style, both with her cabinet and in the realm of information gathering; and Cluster C studies her interpersonal relations with senior civil servants, her personal staff, the caucus, the party organization outside the Knesset, the opposition, the media, and the public.[1] (See Table 4.)

CLUSTER A: INDIVIDUAL STYLE

Policy Orientation

Let us begin with the four motivating factors – *ideology, pragmatism, power,* and *personal validation* – that shaped Golda Meir's political choices; they are explored, in this section, in order of their importance to her leadership style. Of the 275 relevant items extracted and coded from primary and secondary sources on the topic of policy orientation, 51.6 per cent revealed that Meir was concerned with shaping government policies along *ideological* lines. *Pragmatism* accounted for 34.5 per cent, while the acquisition of power accounted for only 9.8 per cent of all the extracted items. *Personal validation* or popular approval was relatively unimportant to Meir, accounting for only 4 per cent of her behaviour in this area.

IDEOLOGY
Unlike Indira Gandhi, who was motivated primarily by a concern with power, Golda Meir's most important motivation for assuming the office

Table 4
Leadership-style categories: Golda Meir
(Total number of items collected and assessed): 1573

CLUSTER A: Individual Style	
I. MOTIVATION (total evidence in this category: 275)	
a Pragmatism (95)	34.5%
b Personal Validation (11)	4.0%
c Ideology (142)	51.6%
d Power (27)	9.8%
II. TASK ORIENTATION (total evidence in this category: 90)	
a Process (12)	13.4%
b Goal (78)	86.6%
III. INVESTMENT IN JOB PERFORMANCE (total evidence in this category: 215)	
a Circumscribed (19)	8.8%
b Tireless (196)	91.2%

CLUSTER B: Managerial Style	
IV. CABINET MANAGEMENT STRATEGY (total evidence in this category: 280)	
a Uninvolved (13)	4.6%
b Consensus Builder (47)	16.8%
c Arbitrator (40)	14.3%
d Advocate (Authoritative/Peremptory) (180)	64.3%
V. INFORMATION MANAGEMENT STRATEGY (total evidence in this category: 152)	
1. Degree of involvement (89)	
a Low (9)	10.1%
b High (80)	89.9%
2. Sources (63)	
a Ministers/Civil servants (31)	49.2%
b Independent (31)	50.8%

CLUSTER C: Inter-personal Style	
VI. RELATIONS WITH PERSONNEL (total evidence in this category: 19)	
1. Degree of Involvement (6)	
a Low (0)	0%
b High (6)	100%
2. Type of Involvement (13)	
a Collegial/Solicitous – (Egalitarian) (10)	76.9%
b Polite/Formal (1)	7.7%
c Attention-seeking/Seductive (0)	0.0%
d Demanding/Domineering (2)	15.4%
e Manipulative/Exploitative (0)	0%

Table 4
Leadership-style categories: Golda Meir (*Continued*)
(Total number of items collected and assessed): 1573

VII. RELATIONS WITH THE PARTY (total evidence in this category: 84)		
1. Caucus (34)		
a	Uninvolved (0)	0.0%
b	Cooperative/Harmonious (14)	41.1%
c	Competitive/Oppositional (12)	35.2%
d	Controlling/Overbearing (8)	23.5%
2. Extra-Parliamentary Party Organization (50)		
a	Uninvolved (4)	8%
b	Cooperative/Harmonious (20)	40%
c	Competitive/Oppositional (22)	44%
d	Controlling/Overbearing (4)	8%
VIII. RELATIONS WITH OPPOSITION PARTIES (total evidence in this category: 66)		
a	Uninvolved (4)	6.0%
b	Cooperative/Harmonious (23)	34.8%
c	Competitive/Oppositional (34)	51.6%
d	Controlling/Overbearing (5)	7.6%
IX. RELATIONS WITH THE MEDIA (total evidence in this category: 187)		
a	Open (131)	70%
b	Closed (56)	30%
X. RELATIONS WITH THE PUBLIC (total evidence in this category: 205)		
a	Active (200)	97.5%
b	Passive (5)	2.5%

of prime minister was her ideological convictions. She possessed a coherent system of political values that she believed must shape government policy. In this regard, she most resembled Margaret Thatcher, but, whereas Thatcher's ideological views, as will be shown in a subsequent chapter, were firmly anchored in the realm of economic policy and required massive new initiatives, Meir's were heavily invested in foreign policy. More specifically, her primary focus was the security of the state of Israel, which, in her view, required the maintenance of the status quo – no territorial concessions until the Arabs were prepared to negotiate a full and comprehensive peace with Israel.

Central to Meir's ideological convictions was that Jews should no longer tolerate the great powers' partition of their land as they had in 1947. In the aftermath of the 1967 war, any future territorial concessions on the part of Israel should take place only with Arabs who were prepared to negotiate in a cooperative manner. Until such negotiations emerged, which Meir did not seek out or encourage, Israel would remain in the occupied territories, settling them and creating its own de facto partition.[2] Meir's fundamental rationale was Zionist: to settle Jews in non-populated land, extend the Jewish majority, and ensure the safety of the state by expanding the borders. In the case of the West Bank, however, she and Yigal Allon remained loyal to David Ben-Gurion's views – no settlements in the densely Arab-populated areas of Palestine. What Meir hoped for was the eventual restoration of Jordanian sovereignty over the West Bank, in order to maintain Jordanian, rather than Palestinian, political influence in the area. Opposition to an independent Palestinian state stemmed from her unalterable commitment to a dynamic Zionism and Israel's secure frontiers, both of which she saw as threatened by a revanchist Palestinian movement.[3]

Meir's ideological firmness on the Middle East question became evident at the beginning of her tenure. From the time she became prime minister, she told the Knesset that she was determined that Israel would accept nothing less than a "true peace to be reached by the parties to the conflict by means of direct negotiations, which would lead to secure, recognized and agreed borders ... Failing a peace treaty, Israel [would] continue to maintain in full the situation as laid down in the cease-fire agreements."[4] On the same ideological grounds, Meir strongly opposed four-power talks for fear that they would not further the cause of peace in the area but merely provide the Arabs with yet another excuse to oppose direct negotiations with Israel. Her primary concern was that an outside power would try to determine Israel's future and impose a settlement on the country which it could not accept.[5] While she was prepared "to tackle things at the conference table ... we will not forgo Jerusalem, the Golan Heights and some other places. We will not rely on others to protect our shipping rights."[6]

On the surface, the prime minister appeared totally in command, the symbol of strength and authority, but there were times when she appears to have felt herself inadequate for the tasks at hand. Both her age and her poor health contributed to these feelings, as well as her limited educational background, lack of military experience, and a fractious and unstable political coalition. For these lacunae, she compensated with the conviction that she was on the right path and that there was no other. More than ever before, her age caused her to see things in shades of black and white, while her lack of a broad education was covered with a stubborn insistence on certain principles, which may have been fine for an earlier generation but were not really applicable to the seventh decade of the twentieth century.[7] Equally, if not more, important in any explanation of Golda's dogmatism was the importance of the Dominant trait in her personality profile. The cognitive style of those with a Dominant/ Aggressive personality pattern is characterized by the possession of strong, close-minded opinions with regard to beliefs and values. "Once they have a point of view, they will not change it. Hence they tend to be unbending and obstinate in holding to their preconceptions. Of additional interest is the disposition of these personalities to a broad-ranging social intolerance and prejudice, especially toward envied or derogated social groups, ethnic, racial, or otherwise."[8] It is in this context that Meir's dismissal of the Palestinians as a national group can also be partially understood.

Whatever her occasional self-doubts, for Meir, the pre-eminent goal of Israeli security was an idée fixe from which she never deviated. "For her the creation of the state of Israel was part of a historical process of the Jewish people. Although many people saw her as hawkish, such an impression was motivated by her belief that maintaining the security of the state of Israel was essential for the historical continuity of the Jewish people. It was, as it were, their last chance."[9] Golda's hawkish stance was also a function, in part, of her self-image. Dominant personalities see themselves as assertive, energetic, and realistic. Their premise is that we live in a dog-eat-dog world, and, therefore, they must be tough, forthright, and unsentimental.[10] Meir's belief that the Palestinians could never be trusted and talks and negotiations were basically a ruse to weaken Israel was a by-product of this zero-sum-game perspective.

Given the strength and firmness of her ideological views, and the aspects of her personality construct just discussed, it is not surprising that Meir viewed every negotiating attempt as an ordeal by fire, in which the goal of the Arabs was to recover territory lost in the 1967 war without providing Israel with a comprehensive peace settlement or full recognition of its sovereignty. Thus, when, in the aftermath of the War of Attrition, President Sadat of Egypt considered the possibility of arriving at some form of phased Israeli withdrawal in exchange for something far less than a peace treaty – a military agreement, but not a political document – Meir refused to countenance anything less than a full peace for any Israeli withdrawal. Moreover, British sources noted that Meir gave no indication that Israel would retreat from its refusal to take part in peace talks unless and until the Egyptians withdrew their missiles from the Suez Canal cease-fire area.[11]

According to Gideon Rafael, the director general of the Israeli Foreign Ministry at the time, "'Meir was more interested in receiving Phantom jet fighters from Washington than in listening to what Sadat was offering. The Israeli political leadership at the time could not accept the symbolic presence of even a mere token Egyptian police force on the Israeli-occupied east bank of the canal.'"[12] Three years later, however, following the Yom Kippur War, Israel would accept an Egyptian presence much greater than a police force.

As far as the subject of a phased Israeli withdrawal from the Sinai was concerned, on the Israeli side, others in Meir's cabinet, like the defence minister, Moshe Dayan, did consider the possibility. Dayan approached Meir with the idea of a unilateral but only partial withdrawal from Sinai. He felt that, if Egypt agreed to rebuild the canal cities and open the canal (closed since the June 1967 war), this would be the best assurance that its intentions were not to launch another war. If, however, Egypt violated Israel's expectations, the IDF would be able to take care of the situation. Meir strongly disapproved of Dayan's idea and reiterated a firm ideological stance, stating, as we have seen, that "we retreat one inch from the canal ... [we]will in no time land at the international border."[13] Dayan was unable to convince her or their cabinet peers of the merit of his idea.

In fact, the experience acquired during her first two years in office had served to reinforce Meir's convictions and confirm for her that Egyptian leaders could not be trusted while American ones could not be relied upon. First, there was Nasser, who had used the ninety-day cease-fire beginning on 7 August 1970 to construct shelters and move Soviet-made missiles close to the Suez Canal. Second was the United States, which was unable to force Egypt to remove the missiles and which stalled on the supply of Phantom jets to Israel. Then, Nasser's successor, Sadat, also proved himself untrustworthy in Meir's eyes, given what to many in the Israeli establishment seemed bizarre behaviour – signing a Friendship Treaty with Moscow in May 1971, within weeks of consolidating power and jailing a leading pro-Soviet competitor.[14]

Her suspicions about the Arabs notwithstanding, Meir made it clear that her goal was not the permanent retention by Israel of the occupied territories. Ideologically, she was opposed to the notion of Arab labour replacing Jewish labour; several years earlier, she had remarked, "I do not want to find myself regretting the birth of an Arab baby."[15] Her goal was a Jewish Israel, without Arab-populated annexed land but with international Arab neighbours.

That is why she was ready to talk with anyone representing an Arab state but not with a Palestinian political entity as such. In July 1973 Meir declared: "I shall never negotiate with Yasser Arafat. I shall never negotiate with a terrorist organization whose declared policy is to kill the Israelis and destroy the Jewish state."[16] Five months later, at a rally in Jerusalem, the prime minister reiterated that there could be no negotiations with terrorist leaders. While there could be territorial compromises with neighbouring states, the terrorists sought Israel's destruction. "Between life and death there is no compromise," she said.[17]

Meir's ideological fixation concerning the lack of Arab trustworthi-
ness led one Israeli intelligence official to comment that "Golda was
locked in a ghetto-like perception of the world."[18] Years later, in 1977,
when Sadat made it known that he would travel to Israel, Meir did not
believe until the last moment that he would actually come. She even
said to her long-time friend Yisrael Galili, "'Grass will grow in my hand
if he comes to Jerusalem.'"[19]

POLITICAL PRAGMATISM

As ideological as her commitment to Israel's survival was, Meir's early
years in the United States had taught her to value *pragmatism* and involvement in public affairs. These qualities were more important to her
than study for study's sake. She looked upon intellectuals as uncertain,
indecisive, sceptical people. She was not given to long-range planning;
she looked for efficient responses to immediate problems and for the
achievement of well-defined goals.[20]

During her first weeks as prime minister, Meir preferred not to decide
on policy or her own work priorities. She was already exhibiting a work
pattern that would characterize her five years in office – response to external events and few governmental initiatives. From her perspective, new
policies would only stir up problems in her coalition and in the delicate
balance of her party. Since she thought that chances for negotiations with
the Arabs, and Egypt in particular, amounted to zero – the one exception
being Jordan, although King Hussein did not carry much weight in the
pan-Arab arena – she felt it was a waste of time to plant false hopes at
home by making concessions externally. She preferred to deal with tangi-
ble, concrete issues and not toy with a peace philosophy.[21]

As a result, particularly between the autumn of 1970 and the Yom
Kippur War, Meir's leadership style, in terms of motivation, exhibited a
high degree of *pragmatism* in dealings with individuals, groups, and organizations – especially her party and the government – on those domestic issue areas that did not involve matters of security or defence. As
a pragmatist, she also preferred to discuss issues in small circles rather
than in large forums.[22]

POWER

To a large extent, the tough but grandmotherly Golda Meir seems to
capture the idea of servant-leadership described by Robert Greenleaf.
For Greenleaf, the servant-leader "begins with the natural feeling that
one wants to serve, to serve first. Then conscious choice brings one to
aspire to lead. That person is sharply different from one who is leader
first, because of the need to assuage an unusual power drive, or to acquire material possessions. For the latter, it will be a later choice to

serve – after leadership is established."[23] In short, it is the lure of power for its own intrinsic qualities versus the call to exercise it through service. For some, Meir's behaviour exemplifies the first pattern.[24] Richard Nixon, whose time in the White House coincided with Meir's tenure as prime minister, observed that "many leaders drive to the top by the force of personal ambition. They seek power because they want power. Not Golda Meir. All her life she simply set out to do a job, whatever that might be, and poured into it every ounce of energy and dedication she could summon."[25] In a similar vein, Meir herself wrote, "I became Prime Minister because that was how it was, in the same way that my milkman became an officer in command of an outpost on Mount Hermon. Neither of us had any particular relish for the job, but we both did it as well as we could."[26] Notwithstanding these perspectives, there is something of a mythical quality to the belief that Meir was a reluctant candidate for the office of the prime minister. Despite her often cultivated self-effacing behaviour as far as party matters were concerned, "there's little doubt that she wanted the job [of prime minister], that she believed she would do it well, and that this would give her an opportunity to lead the country through difficult times and towards a better future. In addition, she did not want Dayan as prime minister, especially after his comment that Rafi had returned to the Labor party in order to rid it of the old-timers."[27] She would certainly have been considered a member of this latter group.

Although technically at the beginning of her tenure, she was scheduled to be prime minister only until the next general election, approximately a year later. Not only did she want to continue on as prime minister after the general election, but it soon became clear that she could handle the job. She began to enjoy her new role and decided to hold on to it after the elections, especially given her positive role in uniting, or at least providing a degree of discipline to, the Labor Alignment. Within a few weeks, the government of Israel began speaking with one voice, that of Meir's. Differences of opinion did not disappear, they just were not heard in public. Labor ministers in particular did not want to upset the prime minister, especially in a pre-election period, during which Meir would play a central role in choosing the party list for the forthcoming election of the Knesset.[28]

Some scholars argue that Meir was also motivated by considerations of personal *power*, as suggested earlier in her political career – her decision to join Pinchas Sapir and Zalman Aranne to remove Ben-Gurion from power, because he was encouraging younger men to succeed the veterans like herself. Even as far back as 1954, Sharett recorded in his diaries that, when Ben-Gurion retired to Sde Boker, Meir never asked him to take the premiership, likely because she wanted it for herself. Yet there are those who argue that Meir was like Ben-Gurion in that she looked beyond the individual to national issues; she believed that her former mentor was wrecking not only his historic image but also the country's interests by pursuing the Lavon affair, and she preferred to sacrifice Ben-Gurion for the country's sake.[29]

Yet Meir's need for *power* and control can also be inferred from her organizational habits. Given her profound suspicion of intellectual ideas concerning the need for more formal governmental organization and planning for long-term strategy, Meir did neither. She refused to set up a national-security council; therefore, during the 1973 war, a reduced cabinet operated without working papers, without orderly staff work, and without consultation with experts outside the political and military realms. The result, in other words, was what could best be described as an amateurish decision-making process. Even after the traumatic 1973 war, Meir, at age seventy-five, was unable to change her work habits and give up control lest such actions undermine her power.[30]

Indeed, maintaining *power* for the Labor Party, if not for herself, continued to be an important part of Meir's calculus. In the aftermath of the 1973 war, talk of a conference in Geneva under United Nations auspices raised serious concerns in the Labor government. Any discussion about withdrawal or territorial concessions in the midst of an election campaign, especially before all the prisoners-of-war were returned, would have been political suicide. Meir's major concern was to avoid any conference that would complicate further the Labor Party's public standing, prior to the rescheduled December 1973 Knesset parliamentary elections.[31]

PERSONAL VALIDATION

It was only when Golda Meir announced her resignation to the Knesset in April 1974 that the issue of *personal validation* as a motivating factor in her leadership behaviour raised its head. She noted that she could not ignore the public ferment over her government's handling of the Yom Kippur War. In effect, she was taking into account her need to be personally validated as prime minister; in the absence of this validation, she felt she had no choice but to step down. But, in the exercise of her leadership, such personal-validation issues never competed with a motivation that was overwhelmingly ideological, albeit intertwined with pragmatic considerations.

Task Orientation

Like Indira Gandhi and Margaret Thatcher, Golda Meir was concerned more with implementing specific goals than with seeking concurrence from the members of her cabinet or the opposition. Of the 90 relevant items extracted and scored on this topic, 86.6 per cent focused on *goal* implementation and only 13.4 per cent on *process*.

GOAL IMPLEMENTATION

Both in her public appearances and in her speeches, Meir fired up the imagination of Israelis with her results-oriented approach. A typical expression of the growing enthusiasm for her can be found in a letter to his parents sent by Lieutenant-Colonel Yonatan Netanyahu: "'By the way, what do you think about our new Prime Minister? Here in Israel, to our surprise, we've discovered a new star. Even I support her. She's a lot more practical and decisive than the late Eshkol. She's not afraid to take a stand, and she runs things with a much firmer hand than did her predecessor.'"[32] Others closer to her concurred in this assessment. Moshe Dayan assessed Golda's leadership style as "straightforward and direct; [she] did not resort to evasion. Our discussions always ended in a clear decision or understanding, and not in vague formulas or postponement."[33]

Illustrative of the way in which Meir focused on goal implementation was her handling of strikes in the public sector in mid-1971. Faced with a sudden and grave deterioration of services in the public sector, leaders of the Labor Alignment decided, on her initiative, to press for urgent legislative measures which would put an end to wild-cat activities. The bill was designed to make it illegal to strike in defiance of proper union authority, or in breach of a collective agreement, and to render "go-slows" a breach of contract.[34]

PROCESS IMPLEMENTATION

Meir's maiden speech as the new prime minister laid out her view of her essential role and the policy she would follow until elections. She would, she stated, proceed with caution, strive to earn the trust of her ministers, and consolidate Israel's place among nations. What this meant was that she would break no new ground and would refrain from any systematic effort to move in new directions. At this early stage, she even instructed the staff that she had inherited from Eshkol to prepare position papers evaluating new strategies for problem resolution – all in the interest of staying clear of unnecessary disagreements and confrontations with friend and foe alike. "She had no desire to start by splitting the nation, the government and the party, by introducing new ideas into the political arena; that wasn't her style."[35]

At the same time, she made a special effort to get along with her ministers and even managed to neutralize Moshe Dayan, a pivotal figure in the cabinet.[36] Dayan wrote: "When it came for the party to vote on her candidacy for Prime Minister, I abstained ... After a while, my doubts dissipated ... Neither of us forgot the past, but we dealt with the present and thought about the future."[37] After the general election, which confirmed Meir in office as prime minister, she would demonstrate far less concern with process and far more with the implementation of her ideological goals.

Investment in Job Performance

Of the 215 items that were extracted from source materials on this subject, 91.2 per cent demonstrated Meir's *tireless* level of commitment and energy to her job as prime minister. While a small percentage, 8.8 per cent, of the cases, showed instances of *circumscribed* behaviour, most of them involved a situation of overwhelming fatigue or illness that prevented Meir from honouring prior commitments. For the vast majority of the time, Meir refused to place any limits on the amount of effort she expended in what she perceived to be the proper exercise of her responsibilities as prime minister.

TIRELESS

Early on in her tenure as prime minister, Meir travelled to the United States and spent two days in Washington, where she had talks with President Nixon and other top American officials. After the president and the prime minister conferred for about two hours at the White House, there was a lunch given by U.S. Secretary of State William Rogers. Meir and Rogers held a meeting afterwards, which was followed in the evening by a formal dinner hosted by President and Mrs Nixon in Meir's honour. The following day, Meir again held discussions with the president, as well as meeting with Defense Secretary Melvin Laird, the Senate Foreign Relations Committee headed by Senator William Fulbright, and members of the House of Representatives. The prime minister then spent an additional ten days in the United States; her itinerary included visits to Los Angeles – where leading personalities of the movie industry held a "salute to Golda reception" – Chicago, New York, and Milwaukee.[38]

During a visit to Helsinki for a summit of Socialist heads of state, one observer reported that "Premier Meir's display of stamina and energetic drive has left many younger people gasping in a state of utter exhaustion on the sidelines. She arrived late at night at the Marski Hotel in Helsinki, after losing an hour on the time switch from Denmark. While others sought their beds, Mrs. Meir set to work. A stream of delegations moved in and out of her hotel suite on the eighth floor. She worked with political aide Simcha Dinitz on the text of her speech. The PM, as ever enjoying a really good political battle, sometime in the early hours made a surprise appearance at the conference resolutions committee – where the tide had by then turned against the anti-Israeli mood. She personally tabled an amendment which called for 'ensuring the arms power balance.'"[39]

Meir displayed the same energy and commitment at home. In a three-hour tour of Mount Hermon in 1970, Aluf Gur explained to the premier the plans for the new settlements of Ramat Shalom and Ramta, which would be established in two months. "In the army positions she talked with young soldiers, earning their admiration by the physical stamina she showed during the exhausting tour."[40]

CIRCUMSCRIBED

There are virtually no examples of Meir's "taking it easy" on the job. Her commitment was absolute and she pushed herself to the limit. There exists one record of an instance in which she failed to honour a scheduled engagement, but, in the context of the rigorous demands on her time, it translates into yet another indication of her investment of time and energy. One Saturday, "apart from her press conference, she received a Jewish youth delegation and discussed Hebrew education and *aliya* prospects with them. She then received, in turn, a delegation of the association of Swedish-Israeli Friendship, a deputation from the Friends of the Kibbutz youth movement, and a group from 'Action Committee for Mid-East Peace.' Then came a Jewish women's delegation. This endless stream of guests was enough to weary anyone. Israeli journalists were exhausted after the tiring week at Helsinki, yet Meir never seemed to slow down. However, she tried to take things quietly, and a dinner planned at the embassy by Ambassador and Mrs. Varone was called off. Instead, she appeared at an Embassy cocktail party last night."[41]

It is safe to argue that any trace of *circumscribed* behaviour stemmed from advanced age and poor physical health. At the same time, the Yom Kippur War did exact a heavy toll on her energy. In 1974, at the age of seventy-six, Meir, in declining health, was aware that she no longer had the energy necessary for the position of prime minister. As she recounted in her autobiography, "I was beginning to feel the physical and psychological effects of the draining past few months [a reference to the October 1973 war]. I was dead tired and not at all sure that, in this kind of situation, I could ever succeed in forming a government – or even whether I should go on trying to do so. Not only were there problems from without, but there were also difficulties from within the Party."[42] Faced with rumblings in the country about the lack of preparedness for the war, and challenges within the party, Meir decided to tender her resignation as prime minister. Four years later, she would finally succumb to lymphatic cancer, the existence of which she had skilfully concealed for many years.

CLUSTER B: MANAGERIAL STYLE

Cabinet-Management Strategy

As prime minister, Golda Meir employed a mix of strategies to manage her cabinet. Of the 280 relevant items collected and coded on this topic, 64.3 per cent displayed a management-strategy style that involved *advocacy*; in 16.8 per cent of the cases, Meir acted as a *consensus builder*. She served as an *arbiter* 14.3 per cent of the time and was *uninvolved* only 4.6 per cent of the time.

ADVOCATE

Increasingly during her tenure, the main decision-making body in Israel was not the cabinet but what became known as "Golda's kitchen." It focused primarily on national-security policy and the conduct of war. Its origins were in Ben-Gurion's inner circle, a small, informal, and unofficial body. Under Levi Eshkol's tenure (1963–69), the official cabinet played a significant role in determining national-security policy. However, following the formation of the Labor Alignment in 1969, national-security policy went back to being formulated by a small inner circle, composed exclusively of Alignment members, "Golda's kitchen," in which Golda Meir, Moshe Dayan, and Yisrael Galili dominated the proceedings.[43] It generally met Saturday nights in the living room of the prime minister's residence in Jerusalem, with Golda frequently going in and out of her kitchen to bring coffee and sandwiches for those present, in preparation for the weekly cabinet meeting on Sunday.[44] It was a body without a planned agenda, position papers, or preparatory staff work. Minutes were taken and conclusions recorded.

The positive aspects of this arrangement were the small number of participants and the opportunity for them to speak more freely and even disagree with each other, since only Labor Party people were present. The negative aspects were that "Golda's kitchen," with its limited number of participants, enabled Meir both to engage in political manoeuvring against her opponents within the Alignment and to bypass her "second-class" coalition partners. Another questionable aspect of this kitchen cabinet was the involvement of officials and military officers in what was essentially a party body, as well as its "cabal"-like atmosphere. Anyone who opposed Meir's views too openly at the Saturday night meetings was marginalized from her inner circle. Curiously, while she was dictatorial within this inner circle, she respected the Knesset and the opposition – as a parliamentarian, she was clearly a democrat.[45]

While it was understood that the discussions in Meir's kitchen cabinet were simply non-committal consultations aimed at helping the prime minister clarify her position before bringing it to cabinet or committee, it can be argued that they did carry substance and had an important measure of significance in the decision-making process. According to two of its participants, Abba Eban and Mordechai Gazit, "Golda's kitchen" served as a "National Security Council but one with no authority."[46] "There was a tendency of the participants to compete with each other in affirmations of militancy to suit Golda's temperament."[47] Issues were raised and discussed freely, with the prime minister summing up the consensus arrived at, as she understood it. Few disputed her conclusions. She was known for her unusual capacity for arriving at simple conclusions on complex subjects. There was rarely the impression that she was imposing her will on others. "Rather, her leadership style was 'Let's sit down and talk it over,' 'give-and-take,' 'trying to convince.'" If, however, it looked as though a discussion was leading to an undesirable conclusion, she could always hint that this might be dangerous for the country and the movement, leading to war or the rise of the right wing.[48] Golda's willingness to take strong positions in the "kitchen cabinet" was bolstered, no doubt, by the discussions that took place earlier in the "inner kitchen." "Four to six of her closest associates would be called in occasionally to discuss not only policy, but party nominations, and the running of the party. But these meetings were never announced or talked about."[49] Dinitz, Gazit, and, at one time, Dayan tried to convince Meir to set up an advisory body to help her make decisions in a more orderly, institutional way – but nothing came of it. In one case, she asserted that she was "'able to consider things on my own and make a decision without the additional help of a staff.'"[50] Most probably she thought that the staff experts would be academic types who would quickly put her at a disadvantage; she would go by her instincts, and they would come with semi-scientific facts and theories. She would have none of it. It was part of her anti-intellectualism. Conclusions reached by the kitchen cabinet would be brought to the cabinet meeting on Sunday, and the ministers who had not been privy to the earlier discussion knew there was little point in further talk; the prime minister had already made up her mind. She would listen to them patiently, with all due respect. And that was that.[51] Meir's domineering personality, with its dogmatic sense of conviction in her beliefs and values, allowed little room for new ideas to be really heard.

As a result, cabinet meetings were often mere formalities, a means for providing information and getting approval for conclusions that had been arrived at elsewhere. Cabinet approval was required in order to ratify the state budget, various laws, appointments of senior officials and ambassadors, and, of course, particular foreign-policy and defence decisions. Descriptions of cabinet discussions, in a number of ministers'

memoirs, Eban's and Dayan's most notably, were less than complimentary. Meir's ministers would refrain from dissenting on policy, since it
was understood that she intended the cabinet to serve as a vehicle of acceptance for those ideas that had been prepared and discussed elsewhere, that is, in "Golda's kitchen."[52] Those who spoke out publicly in
the cabinet on crucial security issues were more often lower-level ministers who had a weaker grasp of international processes. The cabinet
had another custom: it listened to summaries by ministers of their foreign trips which wasted valuable time and contributed nothing whatsoever to the cabinet's work. On the other hand, staff handling of
budgetary and social issues was generally efficient.[53]

Abba Eban, the Israeli foreign minister, has described the decision-
making process under Prime Minister Meir as amateurish, based on
improvisation and a disinclination to follow a formal structure.[54] Particularly in the foreign-policy arena, she acted largely as an advocate for ideas
that she and her closest colleagues and advisers, her kitchen cabinet, had
agreed upon, and she did not encourage others to bring forward non-
establishment ideas. When Abba Eban did just that in February 1970,
proposing a unilateral cease-fire on Israel's part during the War of Attrition, Meir scolded him unmercifully. The only one who could put unconventional ideas to her was Moshe Dayan.[55]

As far as Golda's ministers are concerned, they were generally loyal
to government policy, not only because of collective responsibility, but
also because of their high regard for her – not to mention their fear that
open criticism would be taken into account on the day of reckoning.
She had direct lines of communication to a number of senior officials,
so she could circumvent ministers at her discretion. The Mossad (Institute for Intelligence and Special Tasks) and the Shabach (National Security Center) reported to her in her capacity as prime minister; and she
had direct contact with her ambassador in Washington, with the heads
of the general staff of the IDF, and with the police.[56]

To a large extent, Meir's *advocacy* role was enhanced by her preference
for secrecy and fear of leaks, although she herself was not averse to having her aides use this tool judiciously. By limiting access to privileged information, the government kept leaks to a minimum; most of those that
did occur came from ministers and senior officials. Therefore, she tended
to trim that group too. The result of this practice was that debate was often stifled or prevented, which left important spheres, most notably foreign affairs and security, not dealt with in an orderly fashion. Alternative
approaches were not brought up for discussion and, where mistakes were
made, suitable conclusions were not always drawn. Meir was insistent
that anything connected with foreign and security matters – a very broad
swath – had to be subject to maximum secrecy and relevant information
had to be released with great discretion.

Under Golda Meir, senior ministers were not privy to secret matters
and were thus unable to participate effectively in foreign and security
discussions. This was most evident on the eve of the Yom Kippur War.
In order to prevent leaks from among her nineteen cabinet ministers,
Meir limited sensitive issues to a ministerial security committee and for-
bade their publication under law.[57] On the evening of 5 October 1973,
only a select few ministers in Meir's government understood definitively
that the Egyptians and Syrians were prepared to attack.[58] Early the next
morning, Meir was told that an attack would take place at 6:00 P.M.
that day. At a cabinet meeting called for 8:00 A.M., Meir, in conjunction with her military advisers and close cabinet ministers in Tel Aviv,
decided not to launch a pre-emptive strike against either the Egyptians
or the Syrians, lest Israel's allies argue that, since Israel had initiated the
conflict, it was not entitled to military assistance.[59]

Meir decided to set up a direct channel of communication between the
White House and Jerusalem, linking Nixon, Kissinger, Rabin, Dinitz, and
herself, and leaving the two respective foreign offices out of the picture.
She also sidelined her foreign minister, Eban, in the same way that Ben-
Gurion had sidelined her when she was foreign minister.

Psychologically, one of the ways in which an individual tries to cope
with a traumatic experience is to identify with the "aggressor" and ad-
minister the same behaviour to others. In this instance, Meir, who was
deeply humiliated by Ben-Gurion's treatment of her, proceeded, perhaps
unconsciously, to behave as he did, and treated Eban with the same disdain to which she had been subjected. It was a move that caused serious
damage to Eban's status and to his ability to function in the complex
realm of U.S.-Israel relations. It was yet another demonstration of Meir's
determination to be the senior spokesperson in the foreign-policy arena.
This realm would now belong almost entirely to the prime minister.[60]

Overall, Meir's method of governing created a system wherein there
were few checks and balances and no alternative evaluations. Her approach to problems was "doctrinaire and inflexible"; she was very
much "the overbearing mother who ruled the roost with an iron hand,"
through an ad hoc system of government known as her "kitchen."[61]
But, once the 1973 war broke out, she proved to be far more inclusive
in her decision-making practices and gave the country the powerful
leadership it required both during the conflict itself and in the involved
post-war political negotiations.

CONSENSUS BUILDER

When she became prime minister, Meir declared "it was my desire to unite
once more, the cabinet which today presents itself to the Knesset, all the
forces represented in the outgoing cabinet, and I am happy to state that all
parties to whom I appealed have accepted my invitation."[62] Hence, she

would try during her tenure to achieve such consensus, or at least project such a picture, both for political and for national-security purposes.

For example, Meir regretted in 1970 that certain Israeli newspapers and, in their wake, international ones had published allegations about differences of opinion within the cabinet over cease-fire policy. "'The entire cabinet without exception is united around our policy, and it desires to preserve the cease-fire on the condition of reciprocity, of course.'"[63]

ARBITRATOR

In the field of domestic affairs, Meir also exhibited the traits of a moderator, guide, and compromiser in dealing with individuals, groups, and organizations – especially within her party and the government.[64] Although she acted as a strong advocate in the field of foreign policy, there were instances of her behaving as an *arbitrator* in this area as well, especially when she was the recipient of conflicting perspectives from her most senior advisers. A prime example occurred when she was faced with growing evidence of an impending Arab attack on the eve of the Yom Kippur War. On the one hand, her chief of staff, David Elazar, pushed for a pre-emptive air strike against, at the least, the Syrians, as well as a general mobilization of Israel's citizen army. On the other hand, Moshe Dayan, the defence minister, wanted only the mobilization of 50,000 troops, and solely for defensive purposes.[65] Meir responded to their policy differences by ordering the mobilization of 100,000 Israelis, a compromise figure taken from the high and low suggestions of the chief of staff and the defence minister, but she refused to authorize a pre-emptive attack.[66]

On many subsequent occasions, Meir also found herself thrust into a position where she had to decide between differing military options proposed by professionals. This she did, "drawing on a large measure of common sense which had stood her in good stead."[67]

Information-Management Strategy

In receiving and processing information, Meir was closely involved in the search for and analysis of policy-relevant data. Of the 152 items that were coded on this topic, 89.9 per cent demonstrated *high* rather than *low* involvement. In only 10.1 per cent of the cases was the prime minister content to allow others to search for or analyse relevant policy data.

DEGREE OF INVOLVEMENT

The degree of involvement that Meir manifested in managing the information necessary to make decisions was very dependent on the nature of the issue. For example, in security policy, foreign affairs, and defence issues, she was heavily involved. But, on a whole range of domestic issues, she was generally content to allow her senior ministers great latitude in shaping the decisions that were reached.

High

In the realm of foreign policy, Meir was deeply involved in the management of incoming information. She read the reports that were prepared for her with great care and detested equivocation. They had to be truthful and have a clear "bottom line."[68] A case in point involves her dealings with the United Nations envoy Gunnar Jarring following the War of Attrition, when it was agreed that the new round of the Jarring talks would be held at the prime-ministerial level. "Mrs. Meir is understood to have studied all the previous documents pertaining to the Jarring mission thoroughly and intends to conduct any important developments in the talks personally."[69]

Low

Prior to the Israeli general elections in 1969, the issues that most occupied Meir were the War of Attrition along the Suez Canal; U.S.-Israel relations, specifically, arms supply and political and economic aid; and terrorism. She left internal social and economic affairs to other ministers, Pinchas Sapir most notably, and foreign relations, except for relations with the United States, to Abba Eban.[70] This pattern was to continue throughout her tenure, if only because a great deal of her time was consumed with pressing international political issues. Still, she tried to stay involved with domestic issues at the later stage of their resolution.

SOURCES OF INFORMATION

Of the 63 relevant items that were extracted and coded, Meir was almost equally likely to rely on ministerial sources for information as she was on independent sources; 50.8 per cent of these were coded as *independent* and 48.2 per cent as *ministerial.*

Independent

Illustrating her reliance on extra-ministerial sources of information and analysis was the case in early 1970 when, faced with serious economic difficulties in Israel, the prime minister met five leading Israeli economists for over four hours at two separate meetings. The economists, led by Professor Don Patinkin of the Hebrew University, had been publicly advocating devaluation as the essential cure for Israel's economic difficulties.[71]

Another case in point was Meir's response to a question about the existence of two foreign-policy teams, one headed by Walter Eytan of the Foreign Ministry, and the other by a "senior Army officer." Meir indicated that, from time to time, teams of experts had been asked to prepare material on various topics. But the experts had not been asked to recommend any particular policies.[72]

Another group on whom the prime minister depended heavily were the senior advisers in her office. Her aides would prepare briefs filtered out from the masses of material which flowed into the prime minister's office from government and other sources, including cables, evaluations, contents of foreign broadcasts – mainly Arab ones – reports on conversations and discussions, letters, and press clippings. Her chief of staff, his assistant, her military adviser, and other officials made the selection. As well, Meir relied on hearsay. She listened to the opinions of a great many different people, such as senior party officials, that were often not presented in writing.[73]

Ministers/Civil Servants

During the meetings of "Golda's kitchen," at which her senior ministers were represented, the discussions were free-flowing and the prime minister used this forum, in part, to seek additional information with which to buttress the arguments she would later make before the full cabinet.[74]

Prior to her departure for Washington after the cease-fire agreement in August 1970, Meir spent the previous weeks before her departure "working overtime with my advisers, in particular with Dayan [the defence minister] and the Chief of Staff, Haim Bar-Lev, on the 'shopping list' that I was going to take to Washington with me."[75]

Following the Yom Kippur War, the idea of direct Egyptian-Israeli talks came from the director general of the Israeli prime minister's office, Mordechai Gazit. Gazit persuaded Meir that there was no reason why Israel should not negotiate directly with Egypt on military matters. As originally conceived, the purpose of the talks was to separate the forces in general. Though U.S. Secretary of State Henry Kissinger was not personally in favour of direct Egyptian-Israeli talks, on 27 October 1973 he conveyed Sadat's unexpected and eager consent to the Israeli negotiating initiative.[76]

CLUSTER C: INTERPERSONAL STYLE

Relations with Senior Civil Servants and Personal Staff

DEGREE OF INVOLVEMENT
High
Meir demonstrated a *high* level of involvement with senior civil servants and her personal staff throughout her tenure as prime minister. Virtually all the relevant items extracted on this subject were coded, accordingly, as high involvement.

TYPE OF INVOLVEMENT

Of the thirteen items that were extracted and coded on the type of involvement that Meir enjoyed with the civil service and her personal staff, 76.9 per cent were coded as *collegial/solicitous* and 15.4 per cent as *demanding/domineering*. Only one item was coded as *polite/formal*.

Collegial/solicitous

Before Simcha Dinitz took the job of Meir's *chef de cabinet*, his predecessor told him that it was an 8-to-5 job. However, he quickly saw that Meir took files home every night from her office to work on, and he offered to help her with them during the evenings. She replied "she knew he had a wife and a young family and she did not want to take him away from them."[77] In this regard, her *solicitous* behaviour towards her subordinates was very similar to that exhibited by Margaret Thatcher, as the chapter on her leadership style will demonstrate.

As a woman who refused to stand on ceremony and who, since her years in the United States and then on the kibbutz, believed in the dignity of labour, Meir was never manipulative or attention-seeking with her personal staff. She genuinely regarded them as her equals. She could, however, be demanding in her dealings with her governmental colleagues.

Specifically, Meir was warm and maternal towards her friends and colleagues, and especially so towards her innermost circle of personal staff that included her driver, housekeeper, bodyguards, duty policemen, and office coffee server. She showed concern for their health and whether their clothes were warm enough for the cold Jerusalem winter. Birthdays, marriages, and other family occasions were not forgotten; she would send small mementos, flowers, and notes – usually a few words on her visiting card. Her staff was expected to respond promptly to the thousands of letters, postcards, and telegrams she received each year. At holiday time, she would send wine and flowers to her friends and subordinates, not for political expediency – she did not need to – but as a human gesture.[78]

Demanding/domineering

As collegial as she was, Meir could also be quite *domineering* in her interpersonal relations. The following incident, recalled by Yitzhak Rabin, who was the ambassador to the United States from 1968 to 1973 (before the Yom Kippur War), illustrates at length what could happen to a target of Meir's wrath. On 4 October 1969 Meir, who was about to return to Israel following a visit to the United States, was approached by Moshe Bitan (head of the Israeli Foreign Ministry's North American division) and told that an American friend had mentioned talk in administration circles about a formula she and Nixon were said to have agreed upon. It was phrased in terms of giving the United States "software" in exchange for which Israel would receive "hardware" – in other words, Israel would agree in writing to the U.S. political outlook on the Middle East, in return for arms and military equipment. Meir was furious. "Summoning me [Rabin], she asked to speak to Kissinger and *ordered* me to listen in and take notes of the conversation ... I listened in as Golda addressed Kissinger in no uncertain terms. "I've been hearing all kinds of things about 'software' for 'hardware.' What is all this? Was any such term mentioned in my presence? And what's all this about a paper that Israel is supposed to provide? Who ever talked to me about such a thing?' Kissinger was clearly embarrassed at the leak, but he agreed that no one had talked to Golda."[79]

Kissinger then tried to discover what portion of the text Israel agreed to and which she opposed. "I [Rabin] phoned Golda back and unfortunately I no longer understood what she was so angry about. Dictate precisely what you want me to tell Kissinger, I begged her. Word for word. I'll tell him exactly what you say. But she dictated nothing and said nothing. Then there were a series of phone calls, from Golda, Allon, Eban, Yosef Tekoa at the United Nations and Chief of Staff Bar-Lev. Thousands of words, many of them enraged. Golda scolded me furiously, but the entanglement remained unresolved."[80]

The prime minister had not finished with the ambassador. Meir thanked Rabin for his report and, a week later, a further cable came notifying him that the proposals that he had discussed with Kissinger were unacceptable to her. She regretted that Rabin had aired them even privately without first requesting permission. Finally, the prime minister told him to notify Kissinger of her sharp reaction, ask him to overlook their private conversation, and tell him to regard his proposals as null and void. "If Kissinger had already notified the president of my proposals, I was to ask him to inform the president of the same."[81]

Many others, like Shimon Peres, also experienced the same type of treatment at Golda's hands. In his memoirs, Peres wrote: "My relations with Golda Meir were always complex and ambivalent and usually unhappy. With Golda, as I learned over the years, there was no such thing as a middle ground: either you were one hundred percent for her, or she was one hundred percent against you. She could not tolerate anything less than adulation. Teddy Kollek once said of her, 'She doesn't so much conduct a foreign policy as maintain a hate list.' On her list were Dag Hammarskjold, the U.N. secretary-general; Christian Herter, the American secretary of state; Kwame Nkrumah, the Ghanaian leader; Michel Debré, the French statesman; our own Abba Eban and myself. She regarded me as someone who failed to appreciate her sufficiently, probably, as she saw it, because of my unswerving loyalty to Ben-Gurion."[82]

Relations with the Party

PARLIAMENTARY CAUCUS

Of the 40 items extracted and coded for Golda Meir's relations with members of the Labor Alignment sitting in the Knesset, 35 per cent were characterized as *cooperative/harmonious*, 30 per cent as *competitive/oppositional*, and 20 per cent as *controlling/overbearing*. She was *uninvolved* 15 per cent of the time.

Cooperative/harmonious

Quite often, Meir would be *cooperative*, helpful, and accommodating. For example, a deepening quarrel over price compensation that threatened to cause a Labor Party rift was settled by the prime minister. She provided a face-saving formula for both Finance Minster Pinchas Sapir and Histadrut Secretary General Yitzhak Ben-Aharon. The six-man subcommittee, set up by the Economic Affairs Committee of the Labor Alignment to produce a solution, unanimously adopted Meir's proposal.[83]

On one occasion, Meir decided to convene the Labor Party Secretariat to discuss the major issues facing Israel. "But as party sources noted, she wishe[d] to avoid any showdown that might endanger the stability of her Government of National Unity and shake party cohesion. That Mrs. Meir seeks to bridge the various differences of opinion inside her party was obvious by the latest decision to put off the Secretariat meeting until May 7."[84]

In the aftermath of the Yom Kippur War, "Prime Minister Meir ... agreed to the Independent Liberals' demand for an advisory National Defence Council, composed of former chiefs of staff and other experts. Independent Liberal Party Knesset whip, Gideon Hausner, and his colleagues were also advised that Mrs. Meir ha[d] agreed to their (and the National Religious Party's) demand to revive the Cabinet Security Committee."[85]

Competitive/oppositional

At the same time, Golda could be fiercely *competitive* in the caucus. It must not be overlooked that she was clearly the "boss of the party." On the question of parliamentary responsibility, which arose during the assessment of the government's conduct of the Yom Kippur War, the prime minister made it crystal clear that under Israeli law, all members of the government were collectively responsible for all its actions, its successes as well as its failures, and there was no separate parliamentary responsibility for each minister.[86] While she could tolerate public criticism, criticism from her party colleagues and their lack of support or collegiality enraged her. She never forgave Yigal Allon, who was deputy prime minister, for simply standing aside and not defending the government's handling of the Yom Kippur War, as Shimon Peres had.[87]

Meir would often get involved emotionally and engage in personal attacks as caucus battles brought out the more aggressive aspects of her Dominant personality. Moshe Dayan claimed that the nomination of Ephraim Katchalski for the presidency was undemocratic, on the grounds that a large number of Labor's Central Committee members had been influenced and even pressured by a telephone campaign. Meir vehemently denied this charge.[88]

In the aftermath of the Yom Kippur War, there were those in the Central Committee of the Labor Party who were clamouring for blood – particularly that of Moshe Dayan, the defence minister. Dayan offered to resign, but Meir, with the full knowledge of the other members of the government, told Dayan that she had full confidence in him.[89]

Controlling/overbearing

At other times, Meir's behaviour could verge on the *overbearing*. Resignations from the cabinet never fazed her. She had used them often herself, and knew their value. Thus, few challenged her views or positions, which, in turn, brought devastating results. Meir's ministers and close advisers accepted her requests and guidelines (she never gave orders) out of habit and fear. During her tenure, there were almost no checks and balances in Israel's governmental system. The expression of reservations about a particular policy or piece of legislation, wrote Abba Eban, "'gave rise to such an angry look from Golda that even the most daring would refrain from expressing an opinion opposite to the PM's.' Even the defense minister took care in her presence; what reservations he had were expressed in private discussions."[90]

At an Alignment caucus meeting in August 1970, Meir turned to the "doves," requesting, "Will all those of you who have been identified with that good little bird please refrain from making declarations for the time being." She knew that the Americans put great store in any sign of dissent, and she would look askance at any such behaviour.[91]

In March 1971 landlords were angered when the government's decision to implement the recommendations of the Raveh Committee (to move towards raising and then decontrolling rents) was overruled by the Labor Alignment. Meir reportedly told the landlords that, if she had been present at the Alignment meeting that discussed the issue, the volte-face would not have occurred. The government then found itself in the "minority" among its own major party and had to withdraw the proposed legislation, although it had already been submitted to the Knesset.[92]

A final example involves the subject of a post-election government, following the Yom Kippur War. Golda made it crystal clear that the party had chosen only one individual as an officeholder in a government. That was the person selected to head its list of candidates, and it was he/she who would form and head the new government, if the election results made that possible. The party had no role to play in choosing the other members of the cabinet. "Golda could not have made herself clearer. If the party wanted her as prime minister, it had to leave her the option of selecting her ministers."[93]

EXTRA-PARLIAMENTARY PARTY ORGANIZATION

Of the 50 items that were extracted and coded on this subject, Golda Meir's relations with the extra-parliamentary party organization were 44 per cent *competitive/oppositional* and 40 per cent *cooperative/harmonious*. The remaining 16 per cent divided equally; 8 per cent were *controlling/overbearing*, and 8 per cent were *uninvolved*.

Competitive/oppositional

Golda's *competitive* spirit demonstrated itself early in her prime-ministerial tenure. For example, during the post-mortem that took place at the Labor Party leadership bureau, she took some responsibility for the party's electoral losses in August 1969. However, she also charged "apparently the Histadrut did not perceive that a new generation had emerged."[94]

In another example, when challenging the government's efforts to maintain good relations with the United States, Deputy Party Secretary General Mordechai Ben-Porat said "the Americans are now conducting a political war of attrition against Israel." In an interview with *The Times,* he alleged that the prime minister had digressed from public policy in her stance on access to Gaza and Sharm-el Sheikh. Meir responded to these charges angrily and a public argument between them ensued.[95]

Similarly, at a Labor Alignment executive meeting, Meir and Yitzhak Ben-Aharon, secretary general of the Histadrut, had a heated exchange during the discussion of the state of labour relations. Meir protested at the report of a significant monthly increase for the construction company Solei Boneh. "We have to start at home and set an example. How could such a thing happen in the labor movement? I did not hear that Solei Boneh or Koor [an industrial holding company] made such big profits," she declared.[96]

Cooperative/harmonious

Meir exhibited both *controlling* and *cooperative* streaks in her dealing with the party. Forty percent of the time, she operated in a *harmonious*, non-combative spirit. Prior to the Knesset elections in August 1969, she left her party colleagues guessing as to how she would compose the next cabinet. Speaking in a more conciliatory tone to ex-Rafi than the other members of the Labor Party leadership bureau, she did not ask Rafi members to dissociate themselves from David Ben-Gurion but instead urged their supporters not to vote for his election list. She reiterated her belief that each of the party's three wings should have the right to choose its candidates for the Knesset and the next cabinet, adding significantly, "I know of no one at this table who would impose a veto on anyone."[97]

Speaking at the party leadership bureau's election post-mortem held to discuss the Labor Party's electoral losses, Meir commented: "'We have been too busy with ourselves for these past ten years and neglected issues to which we should have devoted ourselves and for which our party was established. The public is fed up.'" In an effort to be somewhat conciliatory, she said she trusted that the "'miserable internal situation was at an end [a reference to the squabbling between the groups composing the Labor Alignment] and the party could look forward to a new period.'"[98]

Controlling/overbearing

At times, Meir's *controlling* side got the better of her, as when she refused to attend the Central Committee session of the Labor Party's youth group in Jerusalem. Members of the group planned to ask the prime minister for an early meeting to iron out differences that had arisen between them.[99]

The following is another example of her efforts to control elements of the party organization. After the editors of the Labor Party's house organ, *Ot*, criticized the handling of the Rafah incident in April 1972[100] and called for the dismissal of the senior officer responsible, Meir, supported by Justice Minister Yacov Shimshon Shapiro, expressed particular indignation at the statement that the officer was a danger to democracy, and at the fact that the editor, David Shaham, had set himself up as a judge without knowing all the facts. Responding to their attack, the Labor Party leadership bureau backed down completely and registered support for the manner in which the government had handled the inquiry.[101]

On rare occasions, Meir could be downright *overbearing*. On 3 March 1974 a meeting was called to approve the composition of her cabinet, which included Moshe Dayan as defence minister. The participants included the party faction in the Knesset together with what was called the party's leadership bureau. It was suggested that Yitzhak Rabin replace Dayan as minister of defence. "Most of the speakers were highly critical of the proposed composition of the new government, and all those who favoured it did so with little enthusiasm. Golda stood through it all, very uneasy. When all the speeches were over, and before the proposal on the composition of the new cabinet was put to vote – there was no doubt that it would be approved – Golda took the floor.

After a brief comment on the criticism that had been voiced, she abruptly announced that she was abandoning the task of forming a new cabinet and would so inform the president during the course of the evening. And that was that. A great deal of antagonism had indeed been displayed at the meeting. But Golda's reaction, too, was hardly dignified. This was not her finest hour."[102] It was one more illustration of her inability to tolerate criticism and the *overbearing* quality of her all-or-nothing approach.

Uninvolved

As prime minister in difficult times, Meir did not involve herself very often in the party machinery of decision-making. The following quote attests to her ambivalence. Faced with labour problems in Israel's ports, Meir expressed the hope that the party committee (whose decisions were binding) would produce solutions to the ports' labour problems, so that port services would not again be disrupted. However, her willingness to remain detached was not absolute. In the event of a recurrence of work stoppages, she told her listeners that she could not continue to remain *uninvolved* and the cabinet would reconvene without delay.[103]

Relations with Opposition Parties

The nature of the Israeli electoral system, which gives each political party seats in the Knesset relative to the percentage of votes cast for them (the proportional-representational aspect of Israel's "Basic Law"), ensures that no single political party can form a majority government.[104] Thus, Meir's government, along with those of her successors, would, of necessity, include opposition political parties, thereby requiring the prime minister to demonstrate a cooperative stance with them to ensure their continued participation in and support for the government. In contrast, in an electoral system based on individual constituencies in which the winner of a plurality of votes takes the seat, majority-party governments are much more the rule than the exception, and the prime minister can afford to be less cooperative in dealings with the opposition parties.

With those parties that were members of Meir's coalition government, or potential members, she behaved in a cooperative fashion; with those permanently outside the coalition, she was far more likely to be competitive and oppositional. Of the 66 relevant items extracted and coded, 51.6 per cent were *competitive/oppositional*, 34.8 per cent *cooperative/harmonious*, 7.6 per cent *controlling/overbearing*, and 6 per cent *uninvolved*.

COMPETITIVE/OPPOSITIONAL

For the most part, in her conduct with the opposition, Meir was distinctly *competitive*. In the course of a reply during a foreign-policy debate, shortly after coming to office, the prime minister rebuked speakers who suggested Israel had failed to take action calculated to bring peace closer. They were unrealistic if they said that Israel ever faced a choice between "peace" and "territories." She said she wished that were so, but in fact, Israel's numerous offers to talk peace had not received one single Arab response. Hence, such suggestions were not only pointless, they were harmful and they abetted those who deliberately perverted Israel's stand.[105]

But Meir could be *oppositional* even with coalition members of her government. In 1970 Menachem Begin, the leader of the Herut Party and a member of her government, criticized her for failing to show him the text of a policy statement. Meir reportedly said with some annoyance: "What does Begin want? Does he think I have an obligation to show him every statement before I deliver it?" Yitzhak Klinghoffer, professor of law at the Hebrew University and Knesset member, told the Jerusalem *Post* that this was the first time that Meir had not shown Begin the text of a statement.[106]

Later the same year, after Begin and the Herut Party withdrew their support for Meir's government, debates between them intensified. The prime minister charged Begin with having failed to say a word about what the government ought to do regarding the cease-fire that had been put in place. She noted that three months earlier, when Begin was in the government, the cabinet had unanimously adopted the decision on the cease-fire. It was to have been a reciprocal cease-fire, with a standstill, and "we all said yes." But it was possible only as an integral feature of the whole plan. "Is there a single person here who regrets the cease-fire or its continuation?" she asked. "Are we not all duty bound to think how we can keep the cease-fire going?" To a Herut heckler she riposted: "When you can show us how to have a cease-fire without talks, we'll accept it." Turning to Begin's polemics over the integrity of the land of Israel, Meir said: "I pray for the calling of a debate [by our Arab neighbours] on the territorial terms of the peace. It would imply a proposal for peace," she said.[107]

Meir's opposition challengers came not only from the right but also from the left and she responded to their polemics in kind. The Mapam leadership, which was a part of her government's governing coalition, conveyed to her their party's criticism of government policy on the Ikrit Bir'im issue.[108] This reportedly aroused her ire and led to a sharp exchange, as did the report on details of the new Mapam "peace plan," which provided for a separate Arab municipality in East Jerusalem and abandoned the party's position in favour of the integration of Gaza into Israel.[109]

COOPERATIVE/HARMONIOUS

National-security issues and electoral political necessities, rather than Meir's own predispositions, often required her to seek cooperation across the aisles of the Knesset. After she was selected as prime minister to succeed Levi Eshkol, she held out an olive branch to members of the opposition parties. She declared: "It is my desire to unite once more, in the cabinet which today presents itself to the Knesset, all the forces represented in the outgoing cabinet, and I am happy to state that all parties to whom I appealed have accepted my invitation."[110]

In her attempt to form a government after the 28 October 1969 Knesset elections, Meir took unusual steps. As the Jerusalem *Post* reported, "it is an unprecedented act in Israeli political life for an inner policy-making forum of one party to be addressed by the leader of another, even the Prime Minister. This move, made at Meir's own initiative, as part of her drive to persuade Mapam to join her second government, recalls the time in 1961, when Mrs. Meir, then Foreign Minister, went before the Achdut Ha Avodah Central Committee to persuade them to rejoin the Mapai-led coalition."[111]

CONTROLLING/OVERBEARING

Meir's complex set of attitudes towards the opposition and coalition partners is also illustrated by the incident quoted below. She could be very tough and resolute and at the same time conscientious when it involved the larger picture. Faced with an ongoing strike by medical profession, Health Minister Victor Shemtov and his party, Mapam, had called on the prime minister to delay implementing the cabinet decision to order the doctors back to work until one more attempt was made to reach agreement with them. Meir refused and even signed the order herself after Shemtov declined to do so. Shemtov told a radio interviewer that he saw no contradiction in his representing the government in negotiations with the doctors, on the one hand, and his opposing the government's decision to impose the order, on the other. He said that, while he opposed the decision, he was bound by the majority vote of the cabinet, and to that extent his own opinion was irrelevant.[112] More than thirty years later, Shemtov recalled telling Meir, "'I just can't sign the order. If you want I'll quit the government.' She said, 'Victor, I will sign it on your behalf.'" In his view, although her refusal to countenance a brief extension of negotiations was overbearing, her willingness to sign the back-to-work order demonstrated great collegiality.[113]

UNINVOLVED

Occasionally, the prime minister would choose to remain uninvolved. One example involved her performance in the Knesset. "The Premier's replies to other M.K.'s [members of the Knesset] at question time yesterday were so brief as to be reminiscent of Defence [sic] Minister Dayan's style at the rostrum. Most of her replies were one line or less, and non-committal in the extreme."[114]

Relations with the Media

Of the 187 items that were extracted and coded on the subject of her relations with the mass media, Meir was *open* in 70 per cent of the cases and *closed* 30 per cent of the time.

OPEN/ACCESSIBLE/FRIENDLY

Meir enjoyed excellent relations with the media and a convincing majority of the pertinent items coded revealed her *openness* and willingness to engage journalists and broadcasters both from Israel and from abroad. According to the Jerusalem *Post*, the working press fell in love with the prime minister almost without exception. For example, her 1969 appearance at the National Press Club in Washington was an unqualified triumph. The questions were often provocative, and she fielded them with aplomb. "Would Israel employ nuclear weapons if her survival was in jeopardy?" Reply: "It's such an iffy question, if we had the bomb, if we were in jeopardy, then, I really don't know what to say. But we haven't done so badly with conventional weapons" (laughter and applause). Then came a question about Egyptian Foreign Minister Mahmoud Riad's so-called peace-feelers. Reply: "I hope they fare better than what he had to say last year in Copenhagen" (when Cairo issued a denial, as it had done this time as well). But she reasserted her readiness to meet the Arabs anytime, anywhere (applause). The club president prefaced the final question by saying that he hoped that, even if she was not re-elected, she would feel free to come and address the club again. Then the question: "Her grandson," he said, "says she makes the best gefilte fish in Israel." Would she reveal the recipe to them? Closing her eyes in that familiar squint she had when she laughed, Meir accepted the invitation to come again. She also promised to arrive three days in advance and make the gefilte fish for lunch. "It brought the house down."[115]

Indeed, when she wanted, Meir could be quite playful with reporters. When she left for New York to attend the twenty-fifth anniversary celebrations of the United Nations, she told the attending reporters, "I'll tell you all the news – well, perhaps not all, but most of it, when I come back."[116] She also scored well with the international press, impressing the British media in particular. In an interview published in *The Times*, the prime minister said that she was not prepared to put peace terms to her cabinet and risk breaking it up on a hypothesis. However, she was

prepared to put peace terms to the cabinet when there were real negotiations. "I would risk breaking my cabinet, taking it to the country, if I
thought there were grounds for peace." The influential newspaper editor William Rees-Mogg described Meir as a strong character but with
the "strength of good balance rather than aggressiveness."[117]

On a visit to Scandinavia, the popular respect for Meir deepened into
affection as a result of her frequent television appearances on the various networks. An Israeli reporter for the Jerusalem *Post* claimed that
she had done the best public-relations job ever. "But the trip to Ravio-
meni has topped it all, and our PM is now being referred to affection-
ately as 'the flying grandmother.'"[118]

Meir took care to be particularly accessible to the American media,
which, she believed, could play a valuable role in presenting her government's positions and generating U.S. support for Israel. In a typical visit
to the United States, she travelled from Washington around the country
and finally to New York, where she attended receptions, meetings with
the UN secretary general, the mayor, the governor, a United Jewish Appeal dinner, another for Israel Bonds, a news conference, and meetings
with the editors of some of the more influential newspapers.[119] Every
time she visited the United States, she was flooded with requests for interviews by the press, radio, and television, and she did her best to accept as many as was humanly possible.

Being accessible did not always mean being forthcoming. On occasion, Meir would be available to the press for interviews without necessarily giving them all the answers they wanted. Thus, the ambiguities
surrounding her talks in Washington at the end of 1971 were reflected
in the careful way she avoided giving specific answers to most questions
at her news conference. But she was most definite when asked if she had
attempted to put in perspective for American officials the reported differences within her own government on approaches to a peace settlement. She did not do so, she said, because there were no such
differences.[120] Speaking on the NBC television program "Meet the
Press," Meir again refused to say if she had received concrete assurances on the resumption of deliveries of Phantom fighter planes. But, in
answer to a number of other questions, she indicated general satisfaction with the position of President Nixon.[121]

CLOSED/INACCESSIBLE/UNFRIENDLY

At times, Meir's attitude to the press was less congenial and open. For
example, during a visit to the United States in the fall of 1969, "she was
her own woman all the way." When Israeli newspapermen tried to press
her too hard at the briefing given in Hebrew, she rebuked them: "'If I
told you all about my talk with the President, you should be the first to

let me have it over the head.' What she did have to say referred constantly to her own impressions, her assessment of how the president regarded a particular problem. She never quoted anything President Nixon may have said to her in private on a specific issue."[122]

On another occasion, Meir was deeply distressed by a caustic TV program satirizing her economics minister, Pinchas Sapir. She spoke grimly, and evidently after much reflection, saying that she personally would have no mercy for any minister found guilty of misconduct. But accusations were mounting to a crescendo in the local press as papers tried to outdo each other to satisfy their readership. "'The editors admit this to me,' Meir said. 'All we're short of is People's Courts deciding whom to hang next. It's as if radio and TV were run by the Opposition. I was ashamed of the TV satire about Mr. Pinchas Sapir last Friday night. It was tasteless and it wasn't the first such program.'"[123]

Another telling incident reflecting her partisan attitude towards the press involved the accidental downing of a Libyan airliner by the Israeli air force in February 1973. She cancelled her acceptance of a luncheon invitation from the editorial board of the Washington *Post* after the paper published an editorial strongly critical of Israel over the Libyan plane incident. Meir is said to have felt she could not meet those who had been responsible for the editorial attacks.[124]

Interestingly, it was not until July 1973 that Meir appointed a press spokesman. One of her biographers suggests that she had difficulty accepting the fact that she was the leader of a country in the news and that the arena of communications was an important consideration in governance. He writes that it was as though she had never heard of "spin" and how useful the press could be in presenting the government's side of the story. As a result, he claimed, the press fed on rumours, and the prime minister did little to dispel them. She failed to realize the benefit of good relations with the media because she was so concerned that nothing leak. "Hers was a 'Bolshevik' approach: if you can't control the press, stay clear of it."[125]

An alternative hypothesis explaining the absence of a press spokesman is that Meir initially saw no need for such an individual, since she recognized the need for good relations with the media and was personally available to a supportive press for interviews. However, at the mid-point of her term in office, as the divisions in her cabinet expanded, the number of leaks increased, and the press became less supportive of her policies, she was prepared to appoint a press spokesman to manage the "leaks" and to present her government's position in the best possible light.

In her autobiography, Meir addressed the topic of her negative feelings towards the Israeli press. "The other (though minor) bane of my life during all the time that I was PM – and one that it took me months to accustom myself to, even partially – was the freedom with which various ministers confided in the press, to put it very politely. The constant leaks from cabinet meetings infuriated me, and although I had my own suspicions all along as to the source of sensational revelations by so-called diplomatic correspondents which greeted me so often in the morning papers, I could never prove them – which meant I couldn't do much about them. But my staff very quickly got used to seeing me turn up at the office on the day after a cabinet meeting looking as black as thunder because over breakfast I had read something garbled in the paper that shouldn't have been there at all, garbled or otherwise."[126]

Relations with the Public

When it came to her interactions with the public, of the 205 relevant items that were extracted and coded, Meir behaved in an *active*, engaged manner 97.5 per cent of the time. In only 2.5 per cent of the cases was she *passive* and unengaged.

ACTIVE

Throughout her long public career, Meir had exhibited closeness toward the people she represented, feeling herself to be one of them. While the size of her audience could range from the very large to the very small, the evidence suggests that she displayed the same zeal and energy regardless. During her time in office, she addressed a huge number of groups. Illustrative of her activities are the following ones from 1971 to 1973. She was the convocation speaker at Haifa University on 17 February 1971;[127] she met with a delegation of the House Owners Association, who protested the failure of the government to legislate for rent increases, in March 1971;[128] she agreed to meet the Jerusalem Black Panthers in April 1971;[129] she attended a gala performance of the film version of *Fiddler on the Roof* in Jerusalem in December 1971, telling the packed audience that she thought this was a "great film which would be shown all over the world to Jews and non-Jews alike";[130] she spoke at a rally of Latin American immigrants in December 1972 marking the fifth anniversary of *aliya* from the South American continent;[131] she made an impassioned plea for peace at the annual meeting of the Jewish, Arab, and Druze communities of the Galilee, hosted by Deputy Premier Yigal Allon at his kibbutz, in April 1973;[132] the same month, she addressed 3,000 boys and girls assembled at Binyanei Ha'ooma for the culmination of Jerusalem's Youth Day, held under her auspices;[133] and in September 1973 she met for three hours on a Sunday with a group of Georgian immigrants who wanted "a realistic place" for Rafael Bar-Lavi (Balovashvili), secretary of the Georgian Immigrants' Association, on the Labor Alignment's Knesset list.[134]

Disclaiming any association – past or present – with the feminist movement, Meir cautioned members of the International Women's Seminar to be careful about what they did – "you might just work yourselves into being Prime Minister, and that's a mighty responsible job." On another occasion, addressing a farewell dinner she gave for thirty-eight women from three continents attending the seminar on "The Contribution of Women to Development" at the Tira Batsheva Hotel in Jerusalem, she said that she felt that "perhaps women found a faster way of coming to grips with the essentials – men love to talk."[135]

But nowhere was her active engagement with the public better illustrated than in periods of crisis. "During the War of Attrition, Mrs. Meir visited Belsan after touring the settlements of Yardena, Ashdot Ya'acov and Tirat. She was accompanied by Defense Minister Moshe Dayan, Chief of Staff Rav-Aluf Haim Bar-Lev, and Mordechai Gur, the officer in charge of the Northern Command. After arriving in the area by helicopter, Meir and her party were briefed at the local IDF headquarters. They then drove to Ashdot Ya'acov, where she went down into the shelters to examine conditions. Golda listened gravely as teacher Haim Gut explained that after two and a half years of frontline and shelter life, the kibbutz's young children had begun to show adverse psychological effects."[136]

One of the most touching displays of Meir's openness to the people took place during the period after the Yom Kippur War. She wrote about her many meetings with the parents and wives whose loved ones had not returned. "But how could I say no to parents and wives who thought that if they reached me, I would, magically, have some sort of answer, although I knew that in their hearts, some of them blamed me for the war and for our lack of preparedness. So I saw them all, and for the most part they were very brave indeed ... I spent dozens of hours with those poor parents although all that I could tell them in the beginning was that we were doing whatever we could to find their boys and that we would not agree to any arrangement that did not include the return of prisoners."[137]

PASSIVE

One of the few examples of Meir behaving in a *passive* fashion towards the public occurred during the Yom Kippur War. Her reluctance to appear in public – she preferred to focus on the war and the soldiers during this critical period – created the feeling that she was uncertain and unable to explain what was happening. This image was, of course, wrong, but it stuck. If Meir had any doubts or hesitations, she never gave voice to them, even to those closest to her; she also kept her opinions about certain senior figures to herself.[138]

THE RELATIONSHIP BETWEEN PERSONALITY
PROFILE AND LEADERSHIP STYLE

A fascinating personality who lived in turbulent times, Meir displayed an intriguing leadership style profile that did not totally match the expectations generated by the pre-eminence of her Dominant, Contentious, and Dauntless personality traits. Her leadership style was characterized by a policy orientation that oscillated between ideology, which dominated her motivational calculus, and pragmatism. Because of her ideological commitment, she was strongly goal-oriented and tireless in her efforts. Within the cabinet, she acted as a strong advocate for her beliefs. Evidence suggests that she discriminated in favour of those she liked, who tended to share her ideological beliefs, and against those whom she distrusted and found too "soft." Meir was suspicious of many in her cabinet, and those whom she disliked were well aware of her feelings. She relied quite heavily on her own personal advisers and preferred to use the cabinet as a rubber stamp for what she and her "kitchen cabinet," composed of some senior ministers, party members, and military advisers, had already decided. Again, her behaviour in this regard resembled that of prime ministers Gandhi and Thatcher.

Meir's relations with government personnel were characterized primarily by a collegial and solicitous stance. Her staff found her thoughtful and kind. In contrast, some of her colleagues in government found her tough and incredibly demanding. Meir's relations with the party – both the caucus and the extra-parliamentary party organization – were also characterized by the same split. Half of the time, the parliamentary caucus and the extra-parliamentary party organization were treated in a competitive, controlling fashion, and, in the other half, Meir demonstrated a cooperative or uninvolved stance towards each group.

In her relations with opposition parties, Meir treated them both collegially and competitively. Collegiality was mostly reserved for those parties who formed part of her coalition government or were potential allies; those parties who were neither in the government nor likely to be invited to join were the targets of competition and opposition. Meir was generally accessible to the media; the one exception was the period during the Yom Kippur War where she kept an unusually low profile. In her relations with the public, she was virtually untiring; she was actively engaged in speaking in various public forums and rarely relied on government officials to articulate or defend government policy.

Overall, an empirical analysis of Golda Meir's leadership behaviour in the ten selected categories reveals that, in a majority of them (nine out of sixteen items), the leadership-style patterns matched our theoretical expectations for the Dominant and Contentious personality patterns

– both of which ranked the highest in Meir's personality profile. She was strongly goal-oriented, tireless in the exercise of her job, and a strong advocate within her cabinet. As well, ideology and pragmatism were important motivations – ideology for the Dominant personality type and pragmatism for the Contentious personality type. Meir was heavily involved in the search for information, in relations with personnel, and in dealings with the public. In her relationship with the caucus, as well as with the opposition parties outside her coalition government, she was, as expected for someone with strong Dominant and Contentious traits, also competitive and controlling.

However, on the remaining five items, Meir's leadership behaviour did not support our theoretical expectations for the Dominant and Contentious personality types. Power was not an important motivator, as predicted for both personality patterns. Unlike both Gandhi and Thatcher, who were very focused on acquiring and maintaining power, Meir came to the office of prime minister late in life and was acutely aware that her age and health meant that her tenure would, of necessity, be limited. Rather than relying primarily on independent sources for her information, as predicted for the Dominant, Contentious, and Dauntless character types, Meir – handicapped by a limited knowledge of military matters in a time of serious recurring crises for Israel's security – depended more on her defence minister than might otherwise have been the case. Thus, she relied almost equally on her ministers and her personal advisers. In her relations with her staff, she was very solicitous, contrary to expectations. Given that Margaret Thatcher also behaved in a similar fashion, one could postulate that Dominant personalities are solicitous and collegial to those "beneath them," who are not in a position to challenge their authority and can therefore be considered part of the team or "one of us." However, with those cabinet colleagues whom they dislike but are forced to retain, they will have no difficulty in behaving in the most controlling and overbearing manner. Contrary to expectations, in her dealings with the extra-parliamentary party organization, Meir, like Thatcher, was almost equally likely to be cooperative as competitive and controlling. She had been the party secretary for a period of time and had close ties with many in the organizational wing of the party.

In her relations with the media, too, Meir – like Thatcher – was more open and informative than predicted by her personality traits. As the first woman prime minister of Israel, she was well aware of the foreign and domestic media's interest in her and her views, and she used it to her advantage.

To this point, we have examined the links between Golda Meir's two most prominent personality patterns and her leadership style. It must be remembered, however, that this study explores her most important personality patterns and their links to leadership style. To what extent can the lack of support for the above hypotheses be explained by the impact of the three other patterns, the Conscientious (Scale 6), the Aggrieved (Scale 5A), and the Dauntless (Scale 1B)?

Note that, for the Conscientious personality type, power and pragmatism are expected to be the two prime motivators for policy; for the Aggrieved personality type, pragmatism will dominate; and, for the Dauntless personality type, power and ideology are more pronounced. For three of the five personality patterns – the Conscientious, the Contentious, and the Aggrieved – pragmatism is expected to play a role. This may be a partial explanation for why pragmatism was an important policy motivator for Golda Meir. But it cannot provide the whole explanation since the pursuit of power is also characteristic of the Dominant, Contentious, Conscientious, and Dauntless personality types. Meir was all of those, and yet power was not a significant policy motivator for her. A more salient explanation may be the way Meir came to the office of prime minister. As a compromise candidate, who had never aspired to be prime minister, she was concerned both to maintain the unity of the Labor Alignment and to retain the support of her coalition partners within the cabinet. To those ends, she was forced to be pragmatic, particularly in the domestic arena. In this regard, Meir's situation resembled that of Indira Gandhi's first term in office, when the latter emerged as a compromise candidate. Gandhi was initially unable to challenge the old guard of the party and was thus forced to govern in a decidedly pragmatic fashion until she amassed sufficient power in her own right.

The Aggrieved pattern may also have played a role in Golda's recognition that she was not an authority on military matters. Thus, contrary to theoretical expectations that suggest that Dominant and Contentious personalities will rely on their own independent sources of information, during the War of Attrition and the Yom Kippur War, Meir, as one would expect from an individual with Aggrieved personality traits of deference and diffidence, was more inclined to rely on her defence minister. Her solicitousness with her staff was a by-product both of her genuine humility and of the socialist doctrine of equality that she had lived on the kibbutz. Since Meir largely controlled the extra-parliamentary party organization, she could afford to be more cooperative than might have been expected from someone with her Dominant and Contentious characteristics. Her openness with the press, again contrary to expectations, may have been stimulated by her conscientiousness – it was her duty to be open with the press to try to gain support for her policies and diminish opposition criticism.

While Meir's Dominant and Contentious personality traits had a significant impact on her leadership style in ways that were theoretically expected, there was not a perfect fit. Her age, her background as a member of a kibbutz, and the presence of an Aggrieved personality trait diminished the importance of power as a motivating factor in her behaviour as well as making her more cooperative than expected.

PART THREE

Margaret Thatcher

Margaret Thatcher:
From Grocer's Daughter
to Prime Minister

Margaret Roberts (Thatcher) was born in 1925, the second and last child of Beatrice and Alfred Roberts and the younger sister of Muriel by nearly five years. During her early years, she grew up in the small town of Grantham above her father's grocery store in which all the members of the family helped out. Her mother was a traditional caregiver, and both parents were strict Methodists. As a result, life in the Thatcher household revolved almost exclusively around religion, duty, and hard work. Part of Alfred Roberts's definition of duty was his service to the community in which he lived. He was a local preacher, an independent councillor, and eventually the mayor of Grantham.

Margaret grew up extremely close to her father; it was, in fact, a relationship that would prepare her for the predominantly masculine world she would ultimately come to occupy. She was treated as a first-born in terms of the attention and time her father lavished on her. This dynamic often occurs when there is an age difference of close to five or more years between siblings and the older-born is more independent. Alfred and Margaret would engage in intense political discussions, while Margaret's mother would be occupied in the kitchen. Alfred Roberts was very interested in politics both local and national, and Margaret imbibed his politically conservative ideas and his views on frugality, responsibility, and integrity. In contrast, Muriel seems to have been closer in interests to her mother, and she moved away from home to study physiotherapy when Margaret was only twelve. By the time Margaret was ten, she was already rushing through her homework to listen to her father and his cronies talk politics in the store.[1]

During the 1935 election campaign that returned Stanley Baldwin to Downing Street, Margaret, then ten years old, was a messenger for the local Conservative candidate for Parliament, running between committee room and polling station and checking off the names of voters. When Sir Victor Warrender, the elected Conservative MP, came around to thank the volunteers for their help, she was thrilled and talked about it for days. That was when she first realized that "politics was in my bloodstream."[2]

Because Margaret was a bright, studious, and hard-working student, Alfred was determined that she should have the best possible education. At the age of eleven, she moved from Hunting Tower Elementary to the Kesteven and Grantham Girls School, which was a tuition-paying preparatory school. Alfred could well afford it, but he insisted that she take the scholarship test in case he died and she needed financial help.[3]

Margaret excelled academically, finishing first in her class of thirty-two, except for her last year when she finished second. Her teachers found her to be extremely hard-working, but her classmates thought she was a "grind." She displayed superb powers of concentration and determination, and that filled whatever gap may have existed in her intellectual acumen and creativity. At the age of seventeen, she enrolled in Somerville College, Oxford, where she chose to major in chemistry, because a degree in science seemed to offer more robust job opportunities. However, she set no records academically, graduating as a good second-class chemist. If she was less than enthused with chemistry, she was extremely passionate about politics. She joined the Oxford University Conservative Association and worked for the election of Quintin Hogg, a Tory aristocrat. She spent days door knocking, handing out campaign literature, and enjoying delivering her first political speeches.[4]

After her graduation in 1947, Margaret began working for British Xylonite Plastics (BX). But she hated the job and looked forward to weekends, when she was free to attend various Conservative Party gatherings. In 1948 the local party chief of Dartford was looking for a candidate to run in a safe Labour seat, and Margaret campaigned and won over twenty-six other applicants. Although she lost the Dartford seat in the general election of 1950 and again eighteen months later in the general election of 1951, she accomplished three things: she managed to cut still further into the Labour majority, she developed her political skills, and she received a proposal of marriage from Denis Thatcher, a moderately wealthy businessman.[5]

At twenty-six, Margaret was ready to marry and so was Denis, ten years her senior. Denis was totally smitten with her. "'What caught my eye were the same qualities as now,' he said twenty-five years later when she became party leader. 'She was beautiful, kind and thoughtful. Who could meet Margaret without being completely slain by her personality and intellectual brilliance?'"[6] His money helped make it possible for her to stop working – by then she had left the plastics company for a position with J. Lyons, a food conglomerate – and obtain her law degree; she was then able to write the bar exam shortly after giving birth to twins – a son and a daughter – a year into their marriage.

At this juncture, she decided not to run for office while the children were still young. But, by the time the twins were a year old, she was again restless and determined to find a parliamentary seat. She was refused by six constituency associations; their selection committees told her that, while they were impressed with her qualifications and intelligence, they questioned whether a young wife with two babies would not be better off staying at home. Margaret was furious but undeterred.[7]

Finchley, a safe Tory seat, became available in 1958, and Margaret, one of nearly two hundred individuals who applied to represent it, was chosen as the Conservative candidate. In the 1959 general election that followed, she increased the size of the Tory majority in the constituency by winning 3,500 more votes than her predecessor.[8]

Throughout her early years in Parliament, Thatcher worked tirelessly, doing all her own research and perusing books in the House of Commons library for hours at a time. Two years into her parliamentary career, Prime Minister Harold Macmillan offered her a junior post in the ministry of pensions and national insurance. She would continue in that position until Labour trounced the Conservatives in the election of 1964. Afterwards, Edward Heath, the Conservative Party leader, kept her on as chief opposition spokeswoman on pensions, and in 1965 he gave her the same role with respect to the Department of Housing and Land. Because the Conservatives were in opposition, Margaret had no actual power, but she did acquire knowledge and experience and sharpened her debating skills. When the Conservatives were again defeated in 1966, Heath switched her to the number two spot on the shadow Treasury team, and Thatcher used this new position as a stepping stone to further prominence. She attacked the Labour Party budget, and her spirit and obvious fearlessness won attention.[9] While still in opposition, Heath moved her from Treasury to the Ministry of Fuel and Power and then to Transport; in 1969 she was assigned to shadow the minister of education. Throughout her shuffling from one ministry to the next, Thatcher displayed a consistent right-wing voting pattern in the Commons. She opposed pro-abortion bills and any efforts to reform anti-gay legislation. As well, she spearheaded opposition to an equal-rights motion at the 1968 Tory conference. Her stance infuriated women's activists, but, having been treated as a child with ability rather than as a daughter, she dismissed feminists as women who wanted something given to them that they weren't willing to work for.[10] Her disavowal of the feminist movement and her insistence on disregarding the biased treatment of women was similar to the attitudes and behaviour of both Indira Gandhi and Golda Meir. They had "made it" in a man's world without the need for special treatment and, in their view, so could every other woman.

Following Heath's election defeat of Harold Wilson in June 1970, by a popular-vote margin of 46 per cent to 43 per cent, Thatcher was propelled from opposition spokeswoman on education to secretary of state for education. Suddenly, she was not merely in government but in the cabinet. In that capacity, Thatcher proceeded to adopt two policies that outraged much of the public and created consternation among her colleagues. She opposed changing the traditional grammar and secondary school system as well as the fee-paying "public" (that is, private) schools into a network of larger "comprehensive" schools. Thatcher hated the sheer size of the "comprehensives"; since she had come up through the grammar school system, she knew the benefits of small classes. However, the overall goal of the proposed comprehensive schools was to help break down the existing class barriers in the education system, which resulted in only the highest-scoring 20 per cent, usually from the middle class, going on to academic grammar schools, while the less academically gifted 80 per cent were sent to "secondary modern schools," which were largely vocational in content.[11]

Thatcher then acted on the government's pledge to cut government spending. She did so by ending the $19-million free-milk program for primary schoolchildren aged seven to eleven; poor children, however, would be exempt. She was crucified in the press, and Labour backbenchers routinely cried out "'ditch the bitch.'" But Margaret did learn an important lesson in the proper exercise of political judgment, and the timing of political battles, from the whole ordeal. She also developed a tougher political exterior that would stand her in good stead.

In February 1974, in response to widespread strikes, Prime Minister Heath called a general election. The government was narrowly defeated; although it received fewer votes nationally than the Conservatives, Labour won a four-seat edge over the Tories in the House. As a member of the opposition, Thatcher became shadow environment minister. Seven months later, a frustrated Prime Minister Wilson asked the queen to dissolve Parliament. The second election of 1974 was held on 10 October and gave the Labour Party a forty-three seat advantage over the Tories.

After nine years as party leader, Heath seemed to be coming to the end of his tenure. There was clear dissatisfaction within the cabinet with his leadership style, which was described as autocratic and contemptuous. But there were few challengers prepared to take Heath on and stay the course. Among those who considered running were Keith Joseph and Edward du Cann, but both dropped out.[12] Candidate Thatcher was virtually no one's first choice. With three weeks to go before the leadership balloting, only two of the 276 Tory MPs eligible to vote favoured Thatcher, who had not yet declared herself. She was less than enthusiastic about a seemingly hopeless challenge, feeling that she would be lucky enough to get the post of chancellor of the exchequer. She was, however, leading the opposition's fight against the Labour government's finance bill and doing it extraordinarily well; quite simply, she dominated the parliamentary debate with her commanding grasp of the nuances of the bill as well as the numbers involved. In the absence of any other declared candidates, and in the belief that Heath should not be allowed to continue, Thatcher finally made up her mind to challenge the Conservative leader. In this contest, what would prove to be critically important was the support of Gordon Reece, an ex-journalist and former television producer, who decided to back Thatcher by offering his expertise and knowledge of the media to help in the campaign, as well as that of the Conservative backbencher Airey Neave, who provided campaign strategy and organization and advised her on television technique.[13]

On 3 February, just one day before the first ballot, Thatcher's prospects looked gloomy. Seventy per cent of the rank-and-file members of the Conservative Party throughout the country were said to be in favour of Heath staying on as leader. With the exception of Keith Joseph and one other member who intended to abstain, the entire shadow cabinet was also behind Heath. But the results of the first ballot were stunning: Margaret Thatcher – 130, Edward Heath – 119, Hugh Fraser – 16, and 11 abstentions. Heath submitted his resignation and the second ballot was set for a week later. With his departure, several other high-profile candidates for the leadership emerged: William Whitelaw (former secretary of state for Northern Ireland and party chairman), Geoffrey Howe (the former solicitor general), Jim Prior (a former personal assistant to Ted Heath), and Joe Peyton (the shadow leader of the House). Several people who had supported Heath came over to Thatcher's side, including Norman St John-Stevas. His declaration for Thatcher brought with him a large section of the party's moderate centre, diluting her reputation as a right-wing radical.[14] The outcome of the second ballot would change the face of the Conservative Party. The results were Margaret Thatcher – 146, William Whitelaw – 79, Geoffrey Howe – 19, James Prior – 19, and John Peyton – 11.

In filling the shadow cabinet, Thatcher was aware that she had never held any of the posts in cabinet which are normally considered essential for a potential leader, such as chancellor of the exchequer or home or foreign secretary. Indeed, she had only been a member of the cabinet once, as minister for education, which was considered a relatively minor position. With this in mind, she offered the deputy leadership to William Whitelaw, who was Heath's closest ally, and retained many other of Heath's associates. However, she did appoint some of her own supporters as well; Keith Joseph became number three in the shadow cabinet with a special brief on policy and research, and Airey Neave was appointed to shadow Northern Ireland.[15]

As the newly elected party leader, Margaret attracted awe, alarm, and occasionally detestation among her colleagues. They inevitably compared her with her predecessor, Heath. She did resemble him in industry and application but, in marked contrast, was determined to cultivate the backbenchers in ways he never did. Also, unlike Heath, Thatcher knew almost nothing about foreign affairs. A crash course in world travel was therefore arranged to which she applied herself with customary zeal. Before her first year was out, she had visited France, Germany, Rumania, and Turkey. By the time she became prime minister, she had visited the United States twice, toured the Middle East, made repeated trips all over Europe, and had been to the Far East.

Interestingly, the first of her Far Eastern trips was to India in September 1976. "Here she met one of the few women by whom she has ever allowed herself to be impressed, Indira Gandhi, then in her first eleven year term as prime minister ... An Indian official present at their first encounter later recalled Mrs. Thatcher sitting at Mrs. Gandhi's feet, most earnestly asking her how she did it. How had she made it to the top? How had she stayed there? How had she sustained her domination of her party?"[16] From that point on, in their meetings, their conversations were conducted in an atmosphere of the utmost relaxation. Thatcher seemed to derive strength and comfort from witnessing another woman successfully wielding power. When Gandhi was assassinated in 1984, Thatcher's spontaneous reaction was: "'I shall miss her very much indeed; our friendship had a special quality.'" Indeed, one of her biographers, Hugo Young, suggests that their first meeting in 1976 marked an important step in Margaret Thatcher's journey towards belief in herself as a rising international stateswoman.[17]

In the space of a little more than a year after Thatcher became leader of the Tory Party, Harold Wilson retired as prime minister. He was replaced by James Callaghan, who proved a stronger opponent, and, as a result, the political atmosphere became much more strident. Thatcher's own rhetoric grew in intensity, and she began to sense a greater response in the country. Early in 1977, she told the Zurich Economic Society that she now had reason to believe that "'the tide is beginning to turn against collectivism, socialism, statism, dirigisme, whatever you call it ... It is becoming increasingly obvious to many people who were intellectual socialists that socialism has failed to fulfill its promises, both in its more extreme forms in the Communist world and in its compromise versions.'"[18]

When the Labour government of James Callaghan lost a no-confidence motion by one vote on 30 March 1979, an election was called. In the preceding four years, Margaret Thatcher, as leader of the opposition, had made herself the leader of her party. But many in the shadow cabinet still did not like her, finding her world-view distressingly narrow. It seemed as though the public also shared this perspective. Although Labour was fourteen points behind the Tories when the election campaign began, Callaghan was six points ahead of Thatcher in the personal ratings. "She was seen as untried, unsympathetic, and alarming."[19] To counter this perception, Thatcher the tactician, trumped Thatcher the ideologue, as election tactics dictated a necessary vagueness in the party manifesto. However, the outlines of a distinctively Thatcherite program were there: income-tax cuts, reduced government borrowing, a more strictly controlled money supply, the sale of council houses, and "denationalization" (referring to the selling off of state-owned and operated enterprises). In later years, denationalization would become one of the Thatcher government's central and enduring achievements, but in 1979 the Conservatives were moving cautiously. Only the National Freight Corporation was nominated for return to the private sector.[20] Hence, during the course of the election campaign, Thatcher spent a great deal of time in attacking the Labour government's record and much less in specifying the nature of the changes that the Conservatives would implement. What was most impressive was her display of prodigious energy, as exemplified in walkabouts, factory visits, radio phone-ins, and house visits, as well as the more routine speechmaking.[21]

The 1979 election produced a historic victory for the Conservative Party. But its effect on the leader was still more dramatic. As Young describes it, "it was the beginning of a period which could later be defined as an era, in which an ordinary politician labouring under many disadvantages, grew into an international figure who did some extraordinary things to her country."[22] This election was not a routine political shift but involved a critical mass of popular support behind the Thatcherite appeal for radical change. Not only a Labour government but socialism itself seemed to have been thoroughly defeated.

At the heart of the Conservative platform was a commitment to regenerating the national economy. The first objective was tax cuts, to which Thatcher brought her special proselytizing zeal. The second was "good housekeeping." This idea, with its connotations of thrift, prudence, and balanced budgets, proved to be the guiding star of Thatcher's economic program and exerted a powerful attraction. To some, it seemed a convenient piece of populism, which made economics intelligible, but Thatcher was a firm believer in the homilies of housekeeping.

The third objective involved the control of public spending, which henceforth was not to exceed public revenue. In Thatcher's view, the size of the public budget was a measure of dependence on the state, itself a socially undesirable condition.[23]

Few members of the cabinet, if any, would have dissented from these broad priorities. Rather, it was a question of the balance between them and of the rigour with which they were to be pursued. Even though public-spending cuts were made, these were not enough to offset tax handouts. To bridge the gap, Thatcher and her economic team decided to almost double the value-added tax (VAT) up to a single rate of 15 per cent.

As the first year of her government ended, on the central issue that defined the Thatcher government's purpose, economic and industrial reform, euphoria soon gave way to deep concern and ministers fell to fighting among themselves. Inflation was forecast to reach 18 per cent, the minimum lending rate was at an unprecedented 17 per cent, and business confidence had collapsed since the election, with demand and output weak and investment seriously lagging. Ministers could not agree about what to do with this multifaceted crisis. But Thatcher's response was a tireless repetition of the need to cut public spending, stop printing money, and let interest rates rise.

Parallel with the budgetary shifts in taxes and spending was a second urgent exercise in radicalism: the reform of trade-union law. Jim Prior, who was in charge of this, wanted to pursue a moderate approach to curb violent picketing.[24] But Thatcher wanted tougher action, and in January 1980 a national strike at the British Steel Corporation provided the first set-piece confrontation between the forces of the Thatcher government and the forces of labour. The strike dragged on for thirteen weeks, ending with a 16 per cent pay award, which was at least 4 per cent more than the steel unions would have accepted at the beginning. But the government was more interested in a demonstration effect; the market must rule, no matter how great the social cost, how bloody the factory-gate fighting, or how nonsensical the final price of settlement. Compared with the more intransigent Keith Joseph, Thatcher did not entirely lose sight of the consequences of a long strike, but, in the internal conflict between the pragmatic politician wanting an end to a damaging strike and the doctrinaire economist, the latter eventually won.[25]

Within the Conservative Party, divisions on economic issues could be roughly summarized as a conflict between the moderation, caution, and middle-of-the-road approach of the "wets," most of whom had absorbed their political philosophy under the aegis of Macmillan and then gone on to practise it as ministers in the government of Heath, and the doctrinaire conservatism of the "drys." The "wets" were paternalistic and fearful of extreme measures, such as severe anti-union laws and high unemployment. Their fearfulness was what Thatcher most disliked.

Central to the "wet" position was the belief that a policy combining high inflation, accelerating unemployment, indiscriminate cuts in public spending, all held together by an ideology called monetarism, which few could understand, presaged an electoral disaster. But the "wets" were reluctant to appear to be working against the leadership, nor did they have a position for which they could persuasively argue. Adherents of the "wet" position, Jim Prior, Peter Walker, and Sir Ian Gilmour, supported by Lord Carrington and the leader of the House, St John Stevas, did not believe that what they saw around them – collapsing businesses, high interest rates, devastated jobs – could go on being allowed to happen as a conscious choice of government policy.[26]

They had not, however, reckoned with the immovable and unshakeable "Maggie" Thatcher. In February 1980 she survived a no-confidence motion with a stirring defence of the importance of controlling the money supply. In March she lectured the nation in a party political broadcast in which she made a virtue of the extreme measures the government had been obliged to take; she likened them to an operation following which one feels worse before the convalescence is complete. "'But you do not refuse the operation when you know that, without it, you will not survive.'"[27]

At heart, Margaret Thatcher was an ardent believer and a dedicated missionary to whom beckoning disaster – the steep decline in manufacturing output, a rise in unemployment to 836,000 jobless individuals, the largest number in one year since 1930, and an increase in the exchange rate by 12 per cent, which throttled more businesses to death – was cause only to redouble her faith. It was Thatcher's character, not her wisdom, that both sustained the policy's wavering friends and routed its paralysed enemies.[28] Far from feeling crushed by the economic developments, problems and crises seemed only to expand the sense Thatcher had of fulfilling a personal destiny. Believing, as a matter of ideology, in the limits and not the power of government, she could view without embarrassment the short-term failure of the economy to improve. In fact, she sounded positively serene about the failure of particular firms to survive, or even of particular nationalized industries to make sensible wage settlements. Ultimately, in her mind, that was their own problem. Government's job was to set the context within which economic factors did their business, a task not yet complete.[29]

Unlike almost everyone else in government, of every persuasion, Thatcher found no difficulty in sticking to this policy. In fact, she expressed surprise that anyone could think otherwise. Conviction was in her bones and in her mind: to take any step backwards would be "'absolutely fatal.'"[30] Thus, by January 1981, she felt secure enough to begin to remove those from the cabinet who did not share her ideas. St John Stevas was the first to be let go from office; Francis Pym was moved from the Ministry of Defence to leader of the House, allowing John Nott, a monetarist, to deal more ruthlessly with Defence; and Leon Brittain, a junior minister, was promoted to Treasury.[31]

As the economy continued to weaken, the question facing Thatcher and her chancellor of the exchequer was whether they had the nerve to turn the screw one more time by cutting borrowing and raising taxes, even when the economy was still in a downward spiral. Thatcher's new economic adviser, Sir Alan Walters, argued they had no choice but for government to convince the financial markets, once and for all, that it was a reforming one absolutely determined to bring inflation down. At this juncture, Thatcher was less than certain, but ultimately she was persuaded, and the key budget of the Thatcher years went forward in the face of the impotence of the cabinet "wets."[32]

Although the economic consequences of the budget remained to be seen, its political effect was felt immediately. Greeted with incredulity by her critics, it produced in Margaret Thatcher "a resurgence of almost messianic commitment." The private reservations that she had expressed to her economic adviser, Walters, were eclipsed by her conviction that the budget was correct. Not only did it conform to the economic laws she regarded as axiomatic, but, on a deeper level, Thatcher felt that her position was the only right one. Moreover, she believed that, in being so unequivocally right, she could communicate her own convictions in the matter to a wide audience and persuade them that any discomforts were but minor setbacks on the road to recovery.[33]

Such militant obstinacy was not deployed indiscriminately. In February 1981 the prime minister gave a public exhibition of her capacity for caution. The National Coal Board (NCB), under pressure from the stringent borrowing limits placed on it by government, outlined plans to close twenty-three pits and lose 13,000 jobs. The miners' union called for government intervention to stop the closures, increase the subsidy to the NCB, and block cheap coal coming in from abroad. These demands were a direct challenge to Thatcher's strategy of exposing the nationalized industries to market competition, but in this instance she made a decisive political judgment to climb down, promising to discuss the financial constraints with an open mind.[34]

As it turned out, Thatcher's retreat from confrontation with the miners only hardened her determination to exact a decisive revenge when the time was ripe. In the meantime, having caved in to the miners, an act that appeared to demonstrate the virtues of old-fashioned union militancy rather than the efficacy of new government rigour, the government decided to deal firmly with the civil servants and their demands for a pay raise of 15 per cent. Its response was to offer a 7 per cent pay rise, which was already above the norm it had laid down. As well as curbing pay, however, it was committed to reducing civil service numbers. The dispute dragged on and was finally settled, under the thinnest of face-saving devices, with a 7.5 per cent increase – the very terms against which the leader had staked her position seven weeks earlier. Notwithstanding the £500 million that could have been saved by the earlier settlement – from the seven lost weeks of economic productivity – Thatcher and her allies believed that a demonstration effect had been achieved, namely, that the government meant business.[35] She then showed just how tough she could be in cutting the civil service by 10 per cent over the next four years, one of the more concrete achievements of her first term.[36]

Against a background of mounting national discontent with rising unemployment and outbreaks of civil disorder, Thatcher remained obdurate in the face of growing cabinet concerns, speaking scathingly of those who believed in spending their way out of recession. It convinced her of the need to change the face of the cabinet so that people she could call her own would dominate it. In September 1981 she reshuffled her cabinet to do just that. Capturing the hearts and minds of the nation, however, was to prove more difficult.[37]

An opinion poll published in December 1981 recorded that only 23 per cent of the voters thought Thatcher was doing a good job. Rather than alarming her, she seemed to relish her sense of embattlement. Thatcher's ability to retain power in the absence of any improvement in the economy during that period was largely a function of three major developments: the unpopularity of the Labour Party under the leadership of Michael Foot, which was exacerbated by an internal split in the party's ranks; the growth of the Social Democratic Party (SDP) and the Liberals – a grouping destined merely to be a vote splitter; and the Falklands War.[38]

Compared with unemployment, factory closures, and the future of neighbourhood hospitals, such global crises as the Soviet occupation of Afghanistan or Israel's attack on an Iraqi nuclear installation at Osiraq received only fleeting attention from the parliamentarians. But diplomatic demands on the prime minister were considerable. Though she travelled extensively, she had difficulty adjusting to the norms of diplomatic conduct. Her willingness to engage in abstractions and acknowledge that the diplomatic context must always be fluid was exceedingly limited, and she saw herself as a vehicle to transport the manners and teachings of Downing Street across the globe.[39]

The one foreign-policy arena in which Thatcher scored a notable triumph was in establishing an extraordinarily close relationship with the president of the United States, Ronald Reagan. Throughout the 1980s, the Reagan-Thatcher axis was the most enduring personal alliance in the Western world. "Ronnie," as Margaret called him, saw Thatcher as a heroine of pan-Atlantic conservatism. They shared similar views of the world as a battleground between good and evil – evil being defined as Marxism, socialism, and the Soviet Union, and good being defined as tax cuts, market economics, and individual freedom. The importance of this relationship to Thatcher would be fully realized in the Falklands War.[40]

The Falkland Islands are sovereign British territory off the coast of Argentina; in the early 1980s, 1,800 Britons and hundreds of thousands of sheep inhabited them. All British governments since 1966 had recognized the position of the Falklands as something of an anomaly and indicated their willingness to negotiate a different status with the Argentinian government, which also had historic claims, if the right conditions could be arranged. The major sticking point was that any settlement altering British rule had to be acceptable to the Falkland Islanders. But continuation of British rule was problematic given that the islands could not be defended should the neighbouring mainland power, Argentina, choose to attack. This problem, inherited by Thatcher from Labour in 1979, initially remained a low priority among her government's many foreign-affairs preoccupations.[41]

A junior minister, Nicholas Ridley, who had been put in charge of the Falklands issue in 1979, proposed a transfer of sovereignty to Argentina, with an immediate long-term leaseback to Britain. This was designed to satisfy Argentinian claims while maintaining British protection for the Falkland Islanders' way of life. Though Thatcher was appalled at the thought of giving the Falklands away, whatever the fancy terms, she authorized Ridley to try to sell the plan to the Islanders and to make the case in Parliament. Given the prime minister's ambivalence, however, the government never really organized backbencher support for the proposal, and, within a single half-hour of parliamentary debate, a handful of the Tory right, with support from the Labour and Liberal front benches, was able to render a negotiated change in the status of the Falklands politically impossible.[42]

The logical corollary of rejecting Ridley's plan would have been a strengthening of the Falklands defences in face of a mounting barrage of threats from the military government in Buenos Aires. But since previous Argentinian threats had proved empty, the British government, having formerly decided to lower British capacity outside the NATO area and focus naval power mainly on submarines, announced, in June 1981, that the survey ship HMS *Endurance* would be withdrawn from the South Atlantic. The Foreign Office urged that the vessel's removal be reconsidered, because it would be construed by Argentina as a weakening of British commitment to the Falklands and any meaningful deterrent threat. Notwithstanding the inadvisability of withdrawing the *Endurance* in view of the developing situation, the decision was not rescinded.[43]

As a result, almost until the moment of invasion, the Falkland Islands issue suffered a significant degree of neglect. Lord Franks, who chaired a committee of privy councillors that investigated the conduct of the Falklands War, noted that between January 1981 and 1 April 1982, there was no meeting of the Defence Committee of the cabinet to discuss the Falklands. Nor was there any reference to the Falklands in full cabinet until 25 March 1982. Margaret Thatcher was insufficiently sensitive to the danger in the Falklands until it was too late. "Britain's indifference, indecision, and lack of foresight were accessories before the fact of Argentinian aggression which produced between 2 April and 14 June 1982, the loss of 255 British and over 650 Argentinian lives."44

True, having seen a telegram from the British ambassador in Buenos Aires on 3 March, indicating threats of some unilateral Argentinian action against the islands, Thatcher did write on it, "'We must make some contingency plans,'" but nothing was done. When the head of Argentina's ruling military junta, General Leopoldo Galtieri, escalated the conflict, landing troops on the Falklands dependency of South Georgia on 19 March, the prime minister was kept informed of the mounting debates between the Foreign Office and the Ministry of Defence about what should be done. But it was not until 28 March that Thatcher telephoned Lord Carrington expressing her view that the government should respond effectively to the critical situation in the South Atlantic and the worsening relations with the Argentine government.45

On 1 April 1982 the Argentinians invaded the Falklands; the reaction in British government circles was one of utter disbelief. When Thatcher met the Commons on 3 April, preparations for war were already well advanced with the assembly of a British naval task force. She had met the military and, on advice from the navy that the job could be done, instructed that it should be. "If Phase One [of the conflict] … cast the prime minister as an accomplice in collective negligence, Phase Two, the assembling of a war machine, saw her as the instrument of decisions that were in reality forced upon her. It was after another month had passed, and Phase Three, the fighting itself, was on the brink of starting that the choices were made which really entitled this war to be called Thatcher's War."46

At the outset, the war was in reality Parliament's war. After hearing that the Falklands had been occupied, the House of Commons was outraged. The Conservative right, and not only they, demanded action. The leader of the Falklands lobbyists, Sir Bernard Braine, said there must be no dealing with the "'fascist, corrupt, cruel regime'" in Argentina. The Labour Party, with few exceptions, was almost as militant. Ironically, Thatcher's voice was one of the most moderate in the House. She knew that she would be damned if she did not get the Falklands back but that she would be destroyed if she tried and failed.47

On 2 April, before the decision was made to send the task force, Thatcher held a full cabinet meeting at which each member was asked whether he supported the decision. This bound the government as a whole, making it less easy for her to be a solitary scapegoat. Sending a task force on its way was seen by almost everyone involved in the policy as essentially a negotiating stance. Most Conservatives and the war cabinet continued to believe, for the next month, that the Argentinians would be persuaded not to fight.[48]

During that period, the principal agent of the peace process, American Secretary of State Alexander Haig, submitted at least five variants of a peace proposal. The Haig plan called for an Argentinian withdrawal from the Falklands and the halting of the British task force 1,000 miles north, to be followed by joint control of the Islands under American supervision and a negotiation about sovereignty which safeguarded the wishes of the Islanders for at least five years. But his efforts were to no avail, the plan being badly received in both capitals. Overall, Haig concluded that the Argentinians were the main obstruction. The Galtieri junta was too weak to make concessions, could never agree among themselves, and repeatedly undermined the diplomatic efforts of their civilian foreign minister, Nicanor Costa-Mendez.[49]

Then, on 2 May, Thatcher ordered the British submarine *Conqueror* to sink the Argentinian ship *General Belgrano* in an area outside the designated exclusion zone around the Falklands, and 368 Argentinian sailors were drowned. Subsequent evidence suggested that the *General Belgrano* was actually heading away from, rather than towards, the Falklands. This act hugely escalated a war that, until then, had been almost without incident, save those lost in helicopter accidents. Under instruction from the military, Thatcher had come to see war as a probable necessity in a noble cause. Terence Lewin, the chief of the defence staff, had convinced her that war required decisive action, that a task force far from home could not simply hang around, and that the whole gamble depended upon a calculation that made no provision whatever for delay.[50]

Two days after the *Belgrano* was sunk, HMS *Sheffield* became the first major British casualty of the war. The destroyer was hit by an Exocet missile, with the loss of twenty-one lives and many more sailors grievously injured. Despite her sadness and fear for the safety of the entire British fleet, Thatcher did not wilt. Her fate, she knew, was absolutely bound up with the need for a victory.[51] Until 21 May, when British troop landings finally began, cabinet deliberations took place in an atmosphere of feverish anxiety. The peace process continued, but, as the large troop carriers bore down upon the Falklands, their deployment became ever more inevitable, and no one was sure how a landing could be safely effected. During all this time, Thatcher remained calm and clear-sighted in her belief that the acceptable risks were those of military action, the unacceptable ones those that might flow from any settlement short of a complete Argentinian surrender.[52]

Ultimately, the Falklands War was a seminal event in the life of the Thatcher administration. "Its triumphant end, effacing the many tribulations on the domestic scene, was what guaranteed the Conservatives' political triumph at the next election, and on into the measureless future."[53] If military defeat would have destroyed her, the Falklands victory elevated Thatcher to a new level of public esteem and contributed to a personal conviction of her own rectitude. There was, in her opinion, an important link between the Falklands and everything else the government was attempting. The record, she thought, was made of whole cloth. "'We have ceased to be a nation in retreat. We have instead a new-found confidence, born in the economic battles at home, and tested and found true 8,000 miles away.'"[54] The Conservative victory in the election of June 1983 suggested that Thatcher's views had succeeded in capturing the mood of the country. She was also helped by the disarray within the Labour Party and the beginnings of a short-lived economic recovery that had made itself felt in voters' pockets.

If victory in the Falkland Islands was the defining moment of her first term, the seminal event of Thatcher's second term was unquestionably her handling of the miners' strike of 1984. In March 1984 the National Coal Board announced that twenty uneconomic pits would close over the next twelve months, with the loss of 20,000 jobs. The ensuing strike, led by Arthur Scargill, the president of the National Union of Miners, was a well-anticipated event for which the government was thoroughly prepared, with the heaviest possible stockpiling of coal and the reading of the electricity grid for more oil-fired generation. Scargill's efforts to organize a general strike failed, and, despite considerable violence, the government held firm, Scargill was defeated, and nearly all of the uneconomic pits were closed. The strike demonstrated Thatcher's firmness and her defiant glorying in fierce political combat. But she also revealed an ability to dissimulate – insisting for a month that the government was waiting for management at the National Coal Board to act, and that it was merely a bystander, when in fact it was extremely active in orchestrating the NCB's response.[55]

Hence, after sitting virtually silent for the first ten weeks of the strike, Thatcher began attacking the miners' union with an ever-increasing shrillness. On 19 July 1984 she told the 1922 Committee – consisting of backbench Conservative MPs[56] – that the striking miners and their violence were "'a scar across the face of the country. We had to fight an enemy without in the Falklands. We always have to be aware of the enemy within, which is more difficult to fight and more dangerous to liberty.'"[57]

After months of failed negotiations, miners began coming back to work without an agreement, and the strike was effectively broken. Scargill's extremism was an important accessory to the Tories' continuing political domination. For Labour, it constituted another disaster. Scargill had manipulated Neil Kinnock, the leader of the Labour Party, and the leadership of the trade unions effectively. Unable or unwilling to denounce a major union leader, they became passively associated with every offence he gave to the opinions of middle England.[58] As a result, their popularity fell and Thatcher's rose together with her self-righteousness.

But, if Thatcher's fight against the union was a triumph for her individualistic and anti-socialist views, her dealings with the European Community were less successful. The "Community problem" for Thatcher was the size of the British contribution to Community funds. She was determined that no policy changes should occur until the British overpayment problem was permanently solved. Her refusal to negotiate with the Europeans saw the failure of a number of summit meetings and signalled to France and Germany that her hostility to the continentals was deep-seated and likely to continue.[59]

In another area of foreign policy, the second term saw the British prime minister establish a special relationship with the general secretary of the Soviet Union, Mikhail Gorbachev, as she had with President Reagan in her first term. This relationship enabled her to act as an interlocutor between the superpowers, particularly in the negotiations on arms control, a position that she relished.[60] Apart from engaging in high profile and high-stakes international politics, domestically, Thatcher proceeded with her radical agenda.

As part of its decision to cut taxes and public spending, in 1981 the government had given British universities one month to plan an 18 per cent cut in budgets over three years, and 3,000 posts were eliminated. In the 1983 election, the Tories promised no more cuts, but, within a year, they demanded further cuts of 2 per cent all round. Parsimony was the rule of the day. In a vote of the Oxford dons, Thatcher was refused an honorary doctorate as an expression of their anger at what they felt was her deep and systematic damage to the whole public education system.[61]

The organizational laxity and somewhat chaotic nature of the government's style came forcibly to light with the problem of Westland, Britain's only maker of helicopters, which, facing bankruptcy, had gone to the government for assistance in 1984. In contrast both to Thatcher and to her minister of trade, Leon Brittain, the head of the Ministry of Defence, Michael Heseltine, believed in government intervention to achieve industrial reform. Westland favoured a bid by an American company, Sikorsky, to purchase it, while Heseltine mobilized the Europeans and put together a consortium of continental businesses to buy the company instead. Heseltine's activism on the issue – he warned that, if the sale to Sikorsky went through, Westland would have difficulty selling its products in Europe – went beyond any notion of collective responsibility; yet Thatcher allowed it to continue. Finally, she took a semblance of control by informing Westland that, even if Europe discriminated against the products of the new company, Britain, as a main collaborator in these contracts, would work hard to oppose such unfavourable treatment of the company by the Europeans. Heseltine then raised the ante, stating in a letter to Lloyds Merchant Bank that a Westland-Sikorsky link would render any further involvement by Westland with certain European military projects "incompatible." Not only was this a frontal assault on the prime minister's authority, but also there was no evidence that it held any truth. The opinion of the solicitor general was obtained and leaked to the press, an act that further escalated the controversy by raising the question as to who had leaked the information of a law officer about Heseltine's distortions of the truth.[62]

Whoever leaked the solicitor general's opinion to the press, there is no doubt that Thatcher wanted it done.[63] The prime minister also informed Heseltine that, from then on, all future ministerial statements about Westland would have to be cleared with the cabinet office. Heseltine refused and resigned from the cabinet. He issued a formal statement in which he alleged that meetings had been cancelled, negotiated agreements abrogated, and two ministries allowed to engage in open warfare against each other. He said that the whole affair showed that the prime minister's methods were "'not a proper way to carry on government and ultimately not an approach for which I can share responsibility.'"[64] It was this style of governing that nearly brought about Thatcher's downfall in her second term and that was a major contributor to her eventual ouster as party leader in 1990.

In addition to these developments in the economic sector, Thatcher's second term was also marked by the signing of an Anglo-Irish accord in November 1985, which, for the first time, provided for the joint management by Dublin and London of a mutually troubling issue – that of Northern Ireland. Although Thatcher had initially tried to resolve the problem of Northern Ireland, she quickly recognized the intractable nature of the issue and was thus prepared to allow it to drop far down on her agenda, which had played into Unionist wishes to preserve the status quo. However, given Thatcher's genuine irritation at the sight of unsolved issues, the craving for executive action reasserted itself. It was aided by her warm relationship with Garrett Fitzgerald, the prime minister of Ireland. She admired his ruthless defence of Irish interests against the European Community's assault on milk surpluses on which the Irish economy was heavily dependent.[65] Recognizing a kindred spirit whose assertiveness matched her own, Thatcher was prepared to cooperate with Fitzgerald rather than engage in confrontational behaviour with him.

The Anglo-Irish Accord was a fairly modest document; it began by affirming that there would be no change in the status of Northern Ireland without the consent of the majority of the people there. Even though the Unionists' central demand was acknowledged – there would be no united Ireland – it did allow, for the first time, a consultative role to the government of Ireland in the governance of the North. There would be regular inter-government conferences to discuss security, political, and legal matters, as well as cross-border cooperation and the establishment of a joint secretariat.[66] The Unionists were enraged and felt betrayed by Thatcher, who, until then, had been thought to have a particular sympathy for their perspective. The signing of the accord did not mean that Thatcher was permanently seized with the importance of Ireland or infused with the spirit of Irish comradeship. However, once committed to the agreement, she proved unmovable. Notwithstanding the attacks on the Anglo-Irish Accord, and subsequent evidence that it had solved neither the security problem nor the terrorist threat, it still represented the most durable shift in policy on this most intractable issue by any British prime minister.[67]

Amidst the plethora of often controversial and confrontational policies that were the hallmark of Thatcher's government, fear of losing the next election was a common concern in the Conservative Party throughout her second term in office. In March 1986, in the aftermath of the Westland affair, Thatcher showed that "attack" was still her watchword. She told an interviewer that popular capitalism "has only just got started" in Britain and promised that it would be broadened with far more privatization of state businesses. Radical assaults were also promised on education and housing. In reality, little action was taken on these issues. Having promised to refashion university finance, in the face of displeasure from the middle-class heartland of the Tory Party, the government decided that not even its overwhelming 140-seat majority in the House was sufficient to secure passage of a partial switch from student grants to loans.[68]

Another example of her failure to follow through on boastful and bellicose rhetoric concerned the state earnings-related pensions scheme (SERPS).[69] Under pressure from the Treasury, and also from the obvious losers among future pensioners, Thatcher abandoned her enthusiasm for abolition of SERPS and the program was merely scaled down. This was seen as another cave-in to Tory popular opinion, which only added to the impression of a government that lacked direction.[70] Although Thatcher was often intransigent when it came to economic policy – a subject that engaged her ideological convictions – she was not totally insensitive to electoral considerations. She was prepared to take unpopular positions if she thought she could persuade the electorate of the correctness of her views. However, in the face of evidence to the contrary, she was prepared to abandon her commitments.

But this unimposing record was not, obviously, what determined Thatcher's continuing life as prime minister. Two sets of circumstances were conclusive in propelling her to victory in the 1987 general election. One was the state of the economy. Slow but steady growth had been registered each year since 1981, and inflation stayed at 5 per cent during her second term. In the four years after the 1983 election, average weekly earnings rose by 14 per cent in real terms. By 1987, personal taxation was three-quarters of the way towards its stated target of a 25 per cent standard rate, down from 33 per cent when the Thatcher government first came into office. All employed people felt better off, even if ministers had made a mess of the rest of their program. A second factor was a stock-market boom of unprecedented length.[71] At the same time, although unemployment did not fall below 3.1 million for the whole of the four years, and continued to be placed at the head of most respondents' list of concerns in polling surveys, it generated little impact. One of the successes of the "Thatcherite" enterprise consisted of re-educating the electorate not to be focused on unemployment. The longer unemployment lasted, the more it was accepted as a seemingly unalterable fact of life. In regions like the northeast of England, where the economic situation had worsened, the lack of employment began to be effaced from public consciousness.[72]

Eventually, some signs of discontent surfaced in the year before the elections. During the summer of 1986, Labour inched past the 40 per cent mark in the opinion polls and the Liberal-SDP Alliance, after first slumping, averaged between 25 and 30 per cent in popular support and won significant by-elections. However, both parties again destroyed their own chances. Parties in the Alliance could not fully agree about defence policy and a compromise agreement fell apart. It showed the parties to be inherently split and their leaders, David Owen for the SDP and David Steel for the Liberals, to be incapable of effective leadership. Meanwhile, the Labour leader, Neil Kinnock, was found to have been collecting some of his parliamentary ammunition in the Spycatcher affair[73] from the Australian lawyer acting against the British government. The offence was minor in scale, but it confirmed in the public mind the suspicion that, against the battle-tested and tough Thatcher, Kinnock was naive and inexperienced and lacked the requisite weight to be prime minister.[74]

In retrospect, the results of the 1987 elections were probably a foregone conclusion. Thatcher not only won her third term but, in an election that turned almost completely on her record and iron-will personality, pulled an unexpectedly large majority of 101 seats, 43 fewer than in 1983 but more than double what most Tory analysts had predicted. The scope of the victory certainly reinvigorated her. Fearing defeat, she had been nervous and uncharacteristically hesitant during much of the campaign. But now she was triumphant and determined to move on domestic reforms.[75]

Education was the first area to come under the government's scalpel. The great education reform bill, nicknamed GERBIL, was aimed at reforming the country's public education system. One thousand of England's four thousand secondary schools were deemed unsatisfactory in a 1988 report by the inspectors of schools, and only 14 per cent of British high school students attended college, compared with 59 per cent in the United States. The education bill passed in Parliament gave parents more say in selecting the schools for their children; it also allowed schools to opt out of local supervision and get their funding directly from the central government. A three-Rs curriculum for state-funded schools was instituted, and the funding of higher education was placed under the control of councils appointed by the central government. However, these reforms were less controversial than those aimed at the nation's fifty-two universities. Tenure for university professors appointed after November 1987 was wiped out. As well, Thatcher cut spending for the university sector. In 1978 unconditional grants from the government provided 75 per cent of the university system's funds; a decade later, the figure was 55 per cent.[76]

The impact of Thatcher's crackdown on university funding was quickly felt. By 1988, Oxford had 122 vacant teaching positions and funds to fill only 25 slots. Two of the university's prestigious Regius chairs were unfunded and unfilled in 1989. But Thatcher would not budge. In her view, British universities were suffocating under the weight of countless tenured faculty members who were protected by civil-service salary ladders and allowed to teach irrelevant courses. By 1990, Thatcher wanted 35 per cent more science graduates and 25 per cent more engineers than in 1980. She called for British students to acquire the skills that the country needed to compete in the global economy.[77]

After tackling the educational realm, the prime minister then addressed the national health service (NHS). She explained that her goal was to give hospitals and doctors greater freedom by increasing efficiency and cutting costs. Critics worried that she really wanted to privatize the system, which was true, but there was little public support for such an option. When she tried to introduce private insurance, she was savaged by the opposition and pulled back. But she could not resist fiddling with the system. Some hospitals began to rent, instead of buy, X-ray machines; catering and janitorial services were, in some cases, taken over by private firms; and fees for eye tests and dental exams were introduced, despite polls that showed more than 90 per cent of Britons opposed the charges. No matter how frequently Thatcher explained how she was trying to fix the system, she was accused of trying to destroy it to save money.[78]

Thatcher also proposed to deregulate the legal system. At the heart of the reform was the elimination of the mandatory distinction in the British system between solicitors, who deal directly with clients, and the bewigged barristers who generally have a monopoly on presenting cases in court. To encourage competition and benefit consumers, Thatcher proposed that all lawyers be allowed to deal with clients and argue cases in court after obtaining a certificate of competence. Cases could be accepted on a contingency basis, meaning that fees would be a function of winning. Consumers endorsed the proposals, but the barristers pledged to fight them.[79] In the end, the latter were successful in insisting upon a significant training requirement for solicitors, which in practice prevented them overcoming the division of the profession to any significant extent. Thus, the bill containing these concessions that became law in 1990 had a limited impact; a decade later, the barristers' grip on the higher courts was as strong as ever. "Mrs. Thatcher had once again showed herself readier to take on some vested interests than others."[80] As Simon Jenkins observes, "the lawyers, unlike the miners, had too many friends in high places for a frontal assault."[81]

The arts community also became a target of government parsimony. After appealing directly to the prime minister because they were virtually bankrupt, the chairmen of the National Gallery, the British Museum, the Tate Gallery, the Victoria and Albert Museum, and the Natural Science Museum were told that the government had no money to spare; to deal with their shortfalls, they should either charge admissions, set up fund-raising programs, or sell part of their collections. Thatcher, however, refused to help them by making it more attractive for the private sector to donate works of art in exchange for tax relief.[82]

By the spring of 1988, it had become increasingly apparent that Thatcher was a victim of her own success. With parliamentary majorities of more than a one hundred seats for five years, there were few restraints imposed upon her. Combined with her unrelieved dogmatism and natural belligerence, she had become overbearing and imperious. Her cabinet felt that she was behaving autocratically. She also began to spend less time with her backbenchers, and when she did meet them she did all the talking, leaving them even more disgruntled.[83]

Intra-party criticism took on a sharper edge as Thatcher kept cutting taxes. Nigel Lawson, the chancellor of the exchequer, slashed the top individual tax rates from 60 per cent to 40 per cent, which gave such a large boost to the disposable incomes of the rich that even some of the prime minister's staunchest supporters were embarrassed. It exacerbated anti-government feelings that were already inflamed by a decision to replace local property taxes with a flat-rate poll tax on everyone over the age of eighteen. The lump-sum tax, expected to yield the equivalent of just over $300 per person annually, was designed to fund local government councils. Its real purpose, however, was to limit their expenditures. Thatcher wanted to discourage town councils, elected mainly by non-taxpaying voters, from lavishly spending revenues collected from taxpaying homeowners and businesses. Opponents, who included a number of Tories, argued against a tax that required welfare recipients to pay the same as millionaires. When Parliament voted on the tax in 1988, Tory rebels bolted, and the government's 101-seat majority shrank to the embarrassing margin of only 25. The government subsequently added a "safety net" which called for well-run councils to subsidize higher-spending ones, but this policy managed only to upset the few remaining supporters of the tax plan. [84]

Yet nothing kept Thatcher from hammering at the remaining battlements of the welfare state. Privatization had long been one of the government's most popular policies, but support for it evaporated when water and electric utilities were put on the block. "'The sell off is becoming a turn off,'" trumpeted *The Economist*. Polls showed that 75 per cent of Britons, including many in government, opposed the sale of shares in the nation's water-supply system. It was one thing to sell off state-run companies that operated in competitive markets, but water and electricity were a different story.[85]

At the same time, the British economy was also adversely affected by a sharp mid-term economic slump. The pound, which had hit a high of US$1.85 in late 1988, plunged to US$1.55 in October 1989. The trade deficit had tripled and inflation had doubled since early 1988 to May 1989, making it the highest in Europe. National dissatisfaction with the economy focused attention on the persistent disagreement between the prime minister and her chancellor over what to do about it. Thatcher insisted that market forces maintain the sterling's value, whereas Lawson wanted government intervention to manipulate interest rates as a way of avoiding runaway inflation. The two also differed over whether Britain should join the European Monetary System (EMS), which keeps Western European exchange rates within a narrow band and, therefore, compatible.[86]

Underlying these differences between Thatcher and her ministers was their attitude towards the European Community. Thatcher was totally opposed to British participation in the economic and political integration that the European Community was scheduled to undergo in 1992. More competition, less regulation, free trade with Europe – all that was fine with her. But what she strenuously objected to was both the risk of diminished British sovereignty and the establishment of a giant transnational bureaucracy to run the Community's affairs. While her major constituents, many working-class and lower middle-class Britons, shared Thatcher's distrust of the continent, business leaders, for years her biggest backers, began to worry that her anti-European stance could cost London its primacy as a financial centre.[87]

Intra-party dynamics took a significant turn for the worse in the fall of 1989, when Thatcher reshuffled her cabinet in preparation for the next election. But the dismissal or shift of thirteen out of twenty-two cabinet ministers was badly handled and created bitter feelings within the party. The biggest shock was Thatcher's unceremonious removal of one of her most senior colleagues, Sir Geoffrey Howe, who was then serving as foreign secretary. Howe was replaced by John Major, who had no experience in foreign affairs and who had been in government for only two years as a junior minister. His strongest suit was that he was prepared to allow Thatcher to run British foreign policy without interference.

Three months later, the chancellor, Nigel Lawson, abruptly resigned following an argument over the role of one of Thatcher's private advisers, Sir Alan Walters. Walters and Lawson had been at odds over the latter's persistent urging that Britain join the EMS. When the press published excerpts of a Walters's essay, calling the EMS a "'half-baked concept' and boasting of his own 'considerable influence on economic policy,'" Lawson was enraged. He told Mrs. Thatcher, in effect, that it was "'him or me.'" When Thatcher responded archly that "'advisers advise and ministers decide,'" Lawson found her support insufficient, and he tendered his resignation letter. Thatcher reshuffled her cabinet and, under pressure, fired Walters. Asked in the wake of the Lawson resignation if she intended to change her style, she defiantly responded, "'Certainly not. How can I change Margaret Thatcher?'"[88]

By late 1989, Thatcher's problems had become so acute that there was a brief, ill-fated challenge to her leadership within the Conservative Party – the first since she had taken the party over, nearly fifteen years before. Although it failed to unseat her, the threat from a little-known backbencher, Sir Anthony Meyer, did demonstrate that sixty Conservative MPs were prepared either to vote for him or to abstain. It clearly signified a growing unhappiness with Thatcher.[89]

Dissatisfaction with the prime minister reached its apogee in the late fall of 1990, and on 22 November Thatcher announced a stunning piece of news, unimaginable for a leader with her career success: her resignation as prime minister and leader of the Conservative Party. Five important factors contributed to this monumental development. First was the economic situation and the rate of inflation, which rose from 3 per cent early in 1988 and took a steep climb back up to a level of just under 11 per cent during the fall of 1990. Markets were nervous and homeowners felt the pinch of increased mortgage costs as inflation compounded and exacerbated all of the government's other economic problems – the growing trade deficit, rising unemployment, and recession.[90]

Then there was the question of European integration and the deep disagreement over Britain's future in Europe. After Lawson's resignation as chancellor of the exchequer in October 1989, the issue of Europe had threatened to divide the Conservative Party. Britain became increasingly isolated among members of the European Community as Thatcher railed against the loss of sovereignty. It was her attack on European federalism ("No! No! No!") in late October that was decisive for Sir Geoffrey Howe in his decision to resign from the cabinet on 1 November 1990.[91] Howe accused Thatcher of subverting cabinet policies, declaring "her perceived attitude towards Europe is running serious risks for the future of our nation."[92]

The third variable in the mix was the poll tax – a tax that the Treasury viewed as unjust, unworkable, and insupportably expensive. It was extremely unpopular throughout the country and was the target of a bloody riot in London on 31 March 1990. Thatcher, however, insisted on holding blindly to a commitment dating from 1974, and she was able to enlist the support of enough compliant ministers for the tax to be instituted.[93]

The fourth element in Thatcher's downfall involved the increasingly negative perception of her personal style of leadership. After eleven years of Thatcherism, British voters and the Conservative Party had grown weary of the prime minister's approach to governing and wanted a new leader, one less prone to conflict and controversy and more oriented to consensus, cooperation, and conciliation.[94]

Each of the preceding four ingredients led to the fifth and final component culminating in the end of the Thatcher era – the dimming electoral prospects for the Conservative Party – that its members were determined to reverse. By May 1990, both Thatcher and the Tories appeared headed for certain electoral defeat in any future general election. Conservatives were coming up big losers in virtually every by-election held to fill vacancies in the Commons, even in constituencies that were regarded as "safe" Tory seats. Then, on 18 October, the Tories lost another by-election – a long-time safe Conservative seat on the south coast.[95] Public-opinion polls and by-election defeats indicated that an election was about to be lost and power surrendered to Labour. But the polls also suggested that the Tories would move back into the lead with someone else at the helm.[96]

On 6 November, in agreement with Thatcher, the chairman of the 1922 Committee, Cranley Onslow, announced that the annual process for a party leadership election would be moved up two weeks and any challengers would have to declare themselves by 15 November. This strategy was apparently an attempt to pull the rug out from under any momentum to challenge the leadership, as well as an effort to emphasize the prime minister's prominence as a world leader unconcerned with the internal details of the Conservative Party, since she was scheduled to be in Paris at that time. It was undermined, however, both by the results of the Bradford North by-election on 8 November, in which Labour convincingly retained its seat and the Conservatives were consigned to an embarrassing third-place-finish behind the Liberal-Democrats, and by Sir Geoffrey Howe's resignation speech on 13 November in which he urged his fellow Conservative MPs "'to consider their own response to the tragic conflict of loyalties with which I have myself wrestled for perhaps too long.'"[97]

With the gauntlet thus laid down, one day before the deadline, on 14 November, Michael Heseltine announced that he was standing against the prime minister for party leader and, by extension, head of government. Heseltine promised an immediate and fundamental review of the poll tax under his leadership. He also asserted, "'I am persuaded that I would now have a better prospect than Mrs. Thatcher of leading the Conservatives to a fourth electoral victory.'"[98] Opinion-poll results seemed to support that assertion. All six of them, published on 18 November in the Sunday newspapers, showed that the Conservatives under Thatcher were behind Labour by margins ranging from two to fifteen percentage points but would be ahead under Heseltine's leadership by margins ranging from one to ten points.[99]

The first ballot was scheduled for Tuesday, 20 November, a day when Thatcher would be in Paris for a thirty-five nation Conference on Security and Cooperation in Europe (CSCE). It appears that she totally underestimated the opposition that had built up against her. She did almost no personal campaigning, and the efforts to support her were lacklustre and disorganized. As rival groups within the party exchanged unreliable declarations of loyalty in the lobbies and tearooms of Westminster, her campaign team was mocking the very idea that she would have anything less than an easy victory on the first ballot.[100]

The result of the first ballot vote of Conservative MPs gave Thatcher 204 votes – she had been told by her campaign staff that she could expect a minimum of 238; Heseltine received 152 votes and there were 16 abstentions. The outcome was a clear majority for the prime minister but not sufficient to satisfy the complex rules of her own party.[101] In Paris she stunned many of her senior colleagues by declaring, within minutes of the announcement of the vote, her intention to contest the second ballot. But a clear majority of her cabinet ministers were opposed to her continuing to fight. Thatcher opined that her campaigning had been poor on the first ballot, and that with a better effort she could win on the second. At this stage, no one told her not to stand. Her mood was expressed with a defiant battle cry outside Number 10: "'I fight on, I fight to win.'"[102]

Later that evening, Thatcher interviewed her cabinet ministers individually in her Commons room. She opened each conversation with a short homily on how she had won three elections in a row, how she had overwhelming support in the party throughout the country, how she had not lost a motion of censure or a vote of no confidence, and how she was backed by the majority of MPs on the first ballot. Yet, "'in this funny old world my future as prime minister is cast in doubt. What do you think?'"[103]

One by one, most of the ministers pledged their personal support if she insisted on fighting on, but they also told her that they thought she would be beaten if she did so. The backbenchers and junior ministers conveyed the same disheartening message to the chief whip. Thatcher's most fervent supporters urged her to continue the fight, even though, they too conceded, she would lose. Some of her closest friends informed her that she was putting herself through personal and political torture that could end only in defeat. Her husband, Denis, told his wife, "'Darling, I don't want you to be humiliated.'"[104]

The other consideration was a growing anger among ministers who felt that if she did fight on, she would end up by handing over the mantle of party leadership to an "ideologically opposed corporatist," in the person of Heseltine. If she stood down, he could still be stopped by a "unity candidate," such as Douglas Hurd, the foreign secretary. Sometime during the course of that long evening, Margaret Thatcher decided that the game was over.[105]

Early the next morning, 22 November, Thatcher informed the queen of her decision to resign; a cabinet meeting was scheduled and Thatcher read out her resignation statement. Following her resignation, she addressed Parliament that afternoon, giving a "forceful bravura defence of her administration in the no-confidence debate."[106] The *Guardian* reported in bold headlines: "Dying Swan Gives Commons a Command Performance."[107] Another observer similarly noted that it was characteristic of her that she should face trauma with triumph and choose the moment of her downfall to deliver her greatest parliamentary performance. In this, her last speech as prime minister, she had brushed aside transient adversity, brushed aside even her own resignation to assert herself once again as an iconic world figure of historic importance.[108]

And so the reign of Margaret Thatcher as prime minister – eleven years, six months, and twenty-three days – ended as abruptly and dramatically as it had begun. "The prime minister who had led her party to three successive victories ... [would] leave the field of battle, vanquished not by the opposition party, but by the foes within her own ranks."[109]

As befitted her dominating personality, Thatcher was not tempted "to go gently into the night," notwithstanding her loss of party support. Her designated successor, and victor over Michael Heseltine in the leadership battle, John Major, would find himself continually undermined by her strident opinions on every subject, particularly with regard to British relations with Europe. In fact, some analysts have argued that Thatcher's continued pronouncements, so often at variance with government policy, weakened the Conservative Party, led to Major's defeat at the polls, and assured the continued dominance of the Labour Party under Tony Blair. Her appearances at annual party conferences tended to overshadow both Major and his immediate successor, William Hogue.[110] What finally silenced Thatcher was not any change of heart or modification in her ideas, but ill health. In 2002 she suffered a minor stroke and was forced to abandon her regular public-speaking engagements. In 2005 her daughter Carol alleged that Margaret's health was further adversely affected by the news of her son Mark's unsavoury and illegal role in promoting a coup d'état in the oil-rich African state of Equatorial Guinea. Mark Thatcher was fined the equivalent of US$500,000 (£265,000) and given a four-year suspended jail term.

In the end, Thatcher's record, like that of her confrères Indira Gandhi and Golda Meir, was mixed. On the positive side, she waged a successful struggle against Britain's out-of-control trade unions, which had destroyed three governments in succession; in the course of this battle, she managed to turn the nation's anti-union feeling into a handsome parliamentary majority and a mandate to restrict union privileges by a series of laws that effectively ended Britain's trade-union problem once and for all. "Who governs Britain?" she famously asked as the unions struggled for power. By 1980, everyone knew the answer: Thatcher governs. Once the union citadel had been stormed, Thatcher quickly discovered that every area of the economy was open to judicious reform. Even as the rest of Europe toyed with socialism and state ownership, she set about privatizing the nationalized industries, which had been hitherto sacrosanct no matter how inefficient. It worked. British Airways, an embarrassingly slovenly national carrier that seldom showed a profit, was privatized and transformed into one of the world's best and most profitable airlines. British Steel, which lost more than a billion pounds in its final years as a state concern, became the largest steel company in Europe. In the mid-1980s, privatization was a new term in world government, but by the end of the decade more than fifty countries, on almost every continent, had set in motion privatization programs, floating loss-making public companies on the stock markets and in most cases transforming them into successful private-enterprise firms. Even left-wing-oriented countries that scorned the notion of privatization began to reduce their public sector on the sly. Governments sent administrative and legal teams to Britain to study how it was done.[111] To this day, many credit Thatcher's radical reforms for an economic performance that sets the United Kingdom apart from, and above, its European Union (EU) partners.

But there was a downside to Thatcher's record as well. Politically, she crippled the Conservative Party in the late 1980s and early 1990s and paved the way for Labour's successes. Socially, as a member of the middle class whom she believed to be the backbone of the country, she largely ignored the needs of the poor. Primary, secondary, and tertiary education, health care, and public transportation were all left in a shambles. There was money for road construction, but not for the underground or the railroads, on which the poor were more dependent. She focused her energies on stimulating the private sector, particularly in the south of England; the economy of the north of the country, traditionally the poorest area, languished (as it still does today), with high levels of unemployment and a trans-generational pattern of poverty and the dependency that results from "being on the dole." As well, internationally, her ongoing hostility to meaningful British participation in Europe weakened the EU and contributed to anti-British sentiment on the continent.

Thatcher's legacy, with all its strengths and weaknesses, looms large in the modern political history of Great Britain. No doubt it will continue to do so for some time to come.

The Iron Lady:
The Personality Profile
of Margaret Thatcher

As the longest serving British prime minister in the twentieth century, Margaret Thatcher stimulated a wide range of emotions among her colleagues and the electorate. She was both loved and hated, admired and feared. People responded to her with great intensity – the result of her forceful personality. Unlike either Indira Gandhi or Golda Meir, Thatcher's personality profile was characterized by the strong pre-eminence of a single personality pattern, the Dominant (Scale 1A). Three other patterns emerged as *prominent* (scores from 10 to 23), but at the low end of their respective scales. The analysis of the data for Margaret Thatcher that is presented here includes an MIDC profile, a diagnostic classification of the subject, and a clinical interpretation of significant MIDC scale elevations derived from the diagnostic procedure (see Table 5).

The MIDC profile yielded by the raw scores is displayed in Figure 3.[1] Thatcher's most elevated scale is Scale 1A (Dominant), with a score of 21. The next-highest scale is Scale 5B (Contentious), with a score of 13, followed by Scale 2 (Ambitious) and Scale 6 (Conscientious), with scores of 11 for each. Although all of these scale elevations fall within the prominent (10–23) range, only one of them, the Dominant (Scale 1A), approaches the *mildly dysfunctional* level. The remaining six of the ten basic scales (Scales 1–8) did not reach a level of prominence (10–23) and were thus considered of minor importance for psycho-diagnostic purposes.

SCALE 1A: THE DOMINANT PATTERN

Margaret Thatcher is a classic example of the assertive and strong-willed personality. Even as a five-year-old, she was "bright, studious and serious," quickly developing "a reputation as a know-it-all, constantly shooting up her hand in the air to answer questions."[2] When she was nine, she won a poetry-recital competition. Deputy Headmistress Winifred Wright congratulated her. "You were lucky, Margaret." "I was not lucky," Margaret snapped. "I deserved it."[3]

Table 5
Personality scale scores for Margaret Thatcher

Scale RT%	Personality Pattern	Raw	Ratio
1A	Dominant (Controlling)	21	23.1%
1B	Dauntless (Dissenting)	4	4.4%
2	Ambitious (Asserting)	11	12.1%
3	Outgoing (Extraverted)	4	4.4%
4	Accommodating (Agreeable)	4	4.4%
5A	Aggrieved (Yielding)	6	6.6%
5B	Contentious (Complaining)	13	14.3%
6	Conscientious (Conforming)	11	12.1%
7	Reticent (Hesitating)	8	8.8%
8	Retiring (Introverted)	1	1.1%
	Scales 1–8	83	100.0%
9	Distrusting	8	8.8%
0	Erratic	0	0.0%
	Full scale total	91	110.0%

Note. For the basic Scales 1–8, ratio scores are the raw scores for each scale expressed as a percentage of the sum of raw scores for Scales 1–8 only. For Scales 9 and 0, ratio scores are raw scores expressed as a percentage of the sum of raw scores for all ten MIDC scales (therefore, full-scale ratio totals exceed 100). Scale names in parentheses signify equivalent personality patterns in the Millon Index of Personality Styles.

Margaret observed that, during primary school, she was probably reading more widely than most of her classmates, doubtless through "my father's influence, and it showed on occasion. I can still recall writing an essay about Kipling and burning with childish indignation at being accused of having copied down the word 'nostalgia' from some book, whereas I had used it quite naturally and easily."[4]

From a young age, Margaret had strongly held views. "No matter how many left-wing books I read, or left-wing commentaries I heard, I never doubted where my political loyalties lay. Such an admission is probably unfashionable ... I always knew my mind."[5] When Margaret was thirteen, "someone suggested that at least he [Hitler] had given Germany some self-respect and made the trains run on time. I vigorously argued the opposite, to the astonishment and doubtless irritation of my elders."[6]

"Even at eighteen or nineteen, her political discussions were crushing offensives rather than dialogues. The political jugular was always her goal." A friend at Somerville College, Janet Vaughan, recalled, "'We

Figure 3
The personality profile of Margaret Thatcher

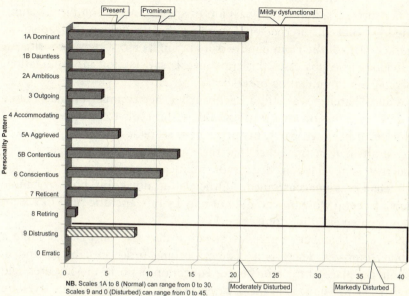
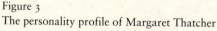

NB. Scales 1A to 8 (Normal) can range from 0 to 30.
Scales 9 and 0 (Disturbed) can range from 0 to 45.

used to argue about politics, but she was so set in steel.'"[7] The nuances
of political concepts failed to engage her. "Obstinacy, resoluteness and
doggedness defined her approach from the outset. She infuriated critics
of conservatism by refusing to acknowledge that any opposing argument
had merit. Her tone was crusading, delivered with the messianic zeal, if
not the rhetorical flourish, of a latter-day television evangelist."[8] More
than anything else in her political make-up, it was Margaret's fierce confidence that she knew right from wrong that marked her out from contemporary politicians. She believed absolutely in her own integrity and
habitually disparaged the motives of those who disagreed with her.[9] Indeed, a dogmatic cognitive style is one of the traits that is characteristic
of the Dominant personality. Such an individual is strongly opinionated
and closed-minded as well as unbending and obstinate in holding to his/
her opinion.[10] With such strong convictions concerning the policies that
Britain should adopt, Margaret's decision to pursue a political career
seemed almost inevitable. The combination of her Dominant personality
in conjunction with her passion for politics – reflecting an identification
with her father – provided the impetus for her subsequent life.

In 1960, when Thatcher was already a member of Parliament, she returned to Kesteven as an honoured guest for an "Old Girls" reunion.
Miss Gillies, the headmistress who had counselled Margaret to wait before applying to Oxford and was, by that time, retired and elderly,
spoke to the gathering. After she misused a Latin phrase in the course of

her address, "Thatcher followed her to the podium and pointedly corrected her old headmistress. Her schoolmates were appalled. Indeed for all her success, spitefulness [was] a trait she had never completely eliminated."[11] Indeed, interpersonal conduct that verges on the sadistic is characteristic of the Dominant personality in its more extreme form. An individual who possesses this trait reveals satisfaction in intimidating, coercing, and humiliating others.[12]

While Thatcher was still a backbencher, her conduct of the "Public Bodies" (Admission to Meetings) Bill – she took on a senior cabinet minister of her own party, his permanent secretary, and the parliamentary draftsmen in the belief that they were either incompetent or obstructive – revealed a degree of political aggressiveness to which Whitehall was unaccustomed. "Officials did not know how to handle such a forceful woman who did not play by bureaucratic rules or accept their departmental wisdom."[13]

Nor did Thatcher's aggressive posture decrease once she became a cabinet minister. There is a distinct pecking order in cabinet, and in Britain the place of the minister for education (a position Margaret held from 1971 to 1974) is in the lower echelons. Ministers at this level are not normally expected to become involved in debate, except by express invitation and on the specific subject of their ministry. Thatcher was either unaware of, or unimpressed by, such convention. She was not afraid to speak up on any subject that engaged her. Although she never spoke unless certain of her facts and figures, "in a very short time she was exceedingly unpopular both with Ted Heath and with the rest of his Cabinet."[14] With juniors and seniors alike, she was always determined to win arguments at whatever costs in bruised egos. If she was losing the main point at issue, she would abruptly change tack to pick up a different point in order to win on that one.[15]

Indicative of the unyielding character of Thatcher's Dominant personality is the following incident. Thatcher's decision to help cut government spending by ending the equivalent of a $19-million free-milk program for primary schoolchildren over the age of six resulted in her being crucified by the press. The criticism was both constant and vicious. Her husband, Denis, noted that she did not have to put up with it and asked her, "Why go on?" Margaret responded, the tears running down her cheeks: "I'll see them in hell first. I will never be driven anywhere against my will."[16]

On another occasion, in 1974, Thatcher found herself debating the proper rate of pay for MPs' secretaries. "This was the last straw. I said that I hadn't come into politics to make decisions like this, and that I would pay my secretary what was necessary to keep her."[17]

In February 1975 Margaret Thatcher was elected the leader of the opposition on a second ballot at the annual Conservative Party conference. When Robert Carr, a Heath loyalist, made it clear to Thatcher that the only post he would accept was that of shadow foreign secretary, she told him in no uncertain terms that she could not promise him that. "Not only was I unwilling to have my hands tied before I had properly considered the shape of the team as a whole; I was not convinced that Robert Carr would have a place in it."[18]

As leader of the opposition, the most important appointment that Thatcher had to make was clearly that of the shadow chancellor. The most obvious man for the job was Keith Joseph, who had invented most of the economic revolution she was proposing. But she was forced to recognize his erratic tendencies and he was left on the sidelines. "'I am not ruthless,' Mrs. Thatcher said, 'but some things have to be done and I know, when they are done, one will be accused of all kinds of things.'"[19]

Welcoming the Helsinki agreement on human rights in a 1975 speech, Thatcher was insistent that "no serious advance towards a stable peace can be made unless some progress at least is seen in the free movement of people and of ideas." She reported that "Reggie Maudling [shadow foreign secretary] came round at once to see me in Flood Street to express both his anger at my delivering such a speech without consulting him and his disagreement with its content. I gave no ground."[20]

Characteristically, during her years as leader of the opposition (1975–79), Thatcher wrote most of her own speeches and always put other people's drafts through several versions. "This was leadership without delegation: one way of asserting command, but not the way the officer class was taught to do it. William Whitelaw [the shadow home secretary] thought these habits very questionable. He didn't like her manner with the shadow cabinet either, which he described as 'governessy.' There was no doubt, he thought, that being a woman, added to being an outsider, imposed on her an irresistible need to assert herself at every opportunity."[21] If she had tended to talk too much in Heath's cabinet, once she was leader she was unstoppable. "'Individually or with a few people,' Whitelaw said, she would 'listen very profoundly. But in a group, where she's determined to get her way, she is inclined not to listen, but to keep hammering her point home.'"[22] For the Dominant personality, "the only way to survive in this world is to dominate and control it."[23]

In January 1976 Thatcher delivered a speech in which she accused the Russians of striving for world dominance. The official Soviet news agency, TASS, called her an "'Iron Lady, the Cold War Warrior,' and embarked upon a campaign to discredit her in Russia. When told that the Russians had called her 'Iron Lady,' she was absolutely delighted. 'That's the greatest compliment they could ever have paid me,' she said, and proceeded to boast about it in public speeches: 'The Russians said I was an Iron Lady,' she said in an election address three years later. 'They were right; Britain needs an Iron Lady.'"[24] It is hardly surprising that the self-image of the Dominant personality is combative. Such an individual is proud to characterize him/herself as assertively competitive, as well as vigorously energetic and militantly hard-headed, and values those aspects of the self that present a pugnacious, domineering, and power-oriented image.[25]

Indeed, there is a plethora of examples of Thatcher's Domineering personality in political life, both in the United Kingdom and abroad. During the mid-1970s, British politics appeared to many observers to be dangerously fragmented, and Thatcher was repeatedly asked whether she would consider forming a coalition with the Liberals. "'Never, but never,' she said, 'would [I] consider a coalition from which could only come irresolute and debilitating government.'"[26]

In late 1977 Thatcher returned to the United States, where she had received much favourable press comment on a visit the previous September. In her first meeting with President Jimmy Carter, she took the opportunity to harangue him in a manner to which he was unaccustomed. According to one of his aides, he said after the meeting that it was "'the first time I've given someone forty-five minutes and only managed to speak for five minutes myself.'"[27]

One of her biographers notes that "the ... more success Margaret experienced abroad, the more convinced she became that her vision for the future was the only way to get Britain back onto its feet ... She was both prophet and warrior; she passionately believed that she was right, and if the British way of life, which she valued above all else, was going to be saved from destruction, then there was need for radical change, and it was her duty to bring that about."[28] On most issues, there was no room in Thatcher's perspective for shades of grey; she saw things in black and white. "What she saw, she spoke about quite bluntly, and what she said, she stuck to."[29] As another commentator observes, "in some ways she never relinquished the simple view of the five-year-old mind. She did see the world in stark black-and-white terms and could not tolerate ambiguity or subtlety." This is a reflection of the dogmatic mindset of the Dominant personality; being strongly opinionated and close-minded inevitably leads to an intolerance for nuance.[30]

In her memoirs, Thatcher repeatedly all but admits so herself. After she spoke out on immigration policy in 1978, suggesting the need for a limitation on numbers of new immigrants from different cultures, the popularity of the Conservative Party rose sharply. This led her to write:

"The whole affair was a demonstration that I must trust my own judgment on crucial matters, rather than necessarily hope to persuade my colleagues in advance; for I could expect that somewhere out in the country there would be a following and perhaps a majority for me."[31]

In the autumn of 1978, there seemed some likelihood of an election, but James Callaghan, the Labour prime minister, announced on television that the problems of the country required a government that would continue to carry out consistent and determined policies. Thatcher was furious; she found opposition horribly frustrating. "'Opposition can only question and exhort,' she stated, 'government can talk and act. I like to get on with things.'"[32]

During the 1979 election campaign, Thatcher observed that, despite the campaign planners' belief "that we should at all cost avoid 'gaffes,' which meant in practice almost nothing controversial – in particular, attacks on trade union power ... in fact, with few concessions, I insisted on doing it my way."[33] In a campaign speech, she asserted, "In politics I've learned something ... if you've got a message, preach it. I am a conviction politician. The Old Testament prophets didn't merely say, 'Brothers, I want consensus.' They said: 'This is my faith and vision. This is what I passionately believe. If you believe it too, then come with me.' Tonight I say to you just that."[34]

As the preponderant element in Margaret Thatcher's personality profile, the Dominant pattern was strongly observed in each of the five domains in which it was measured. Thatcher's *expressive behaviour* was brusque and belligerent, her *interpersonal conduct* intimidating and coercive, her *cognitive style* dogmatic and opinionated, her *mood/temperament* frequently irritable and hostile, and her *self-image* assertive, combative, and tough.

Each of the next three patterns occupies a much less important place in Thatcher's personality profile; however, all are worth examining, since they do occupy a position of *prominence* (scores of 13, 11, and 11 respectively) and clearly help to provide a more complete picture of her personality.

SCALE 5B: THE CONTENTIOUS PATTERN

Individuals who fit the profile of the Contentious pattern are described as cynical, headstrong, and resolute personalities; in a more exaggerated form, they may also exhibit complaining, irksome, and oppositional traits or even caustic, contrary, and negative behaviour patterns.[35]

Thatcher's life is filled with such examples. When she was a student at Kesteven, Margaret was told by Headmistress Gillies that she was too young, at seventeen, to write the entrance exams for Oxford. She "was furious and it was many years before she forgave her old headmistress. Indicative of Margaret's headstrong and resolute behavior was her decision to prepare for the entrance exams on her own."[36]

As a member of the shadow cabinet beginning in 1967, the shadow attorney general found that she talked too much. "How she talked! ... I believe that she honestly did not realize how irritating she was."[37] A hint of this irritation became public when a *Sunday Express* column reported colleagues coming away from meetings complaining that she *never* stopped arguing.[38] Writing in the *Sunday Mirror* on 28 December 1969, Woodrow Wyatt, a Labour MP with a number of Tory friends, described her as "more of a niggler than a debater ... Her air of bossiness, her aptitude for interfering, can be very tiresome and irritating."

In her memoirs, Thatcher recalls that, while serving as a junior minister to three different ministers in the same department, the advice tendered to the ministers by civil servants differed, even though it was on the same topic. "So I complained when both Niall Macpherson and Richard Wood received policy submissions proposing approaches that I knew had not been put to their predecessor, John Boyd-Carpenter ... 'That's not what you advised the previous minister.' They replied that they had known that he would never accept it. I decided then and there that, when I was in charge of a department, I would insist on an absolutely frank assessment of all the options from any civil servants who would report to me."[39]

With her first cabinet appointment, to the Department of Education and Science, Thatcher's hostility to the civil service emerged in sharp focus. Sir William Pile, her permanent secretary, who was reappointed to that post in June 1970, thought that "'she didn't want advice from anyone.' He recalled 'her stubborn refusal to acknowledge some facts and arguments that we put forward.'"[40] They had two "flaming rows" over questions where she wanted to exceed her power. One was the highly publicized case of a left-wing teacher fired by a London school for publishing a book of his pupils' poems. He appealed to the inner London education authority and was reinstated. Thatcher, siding with the governors, wanted to overturn the appeal, but Pile had to tell her that she had no standing in the matter. She found it hard to accept that she did not have the power. In the end, she gave way reluctantly, writing in a note to herself: "'Very well. But I will remember this in my memoirs.'"[41]

Their second run-in was about an official who had made a sensitive decision affecting her constituency without reference to her. Once again she wanted him dismissed. Pile refused. She had difficulty understanding that sacking people was his job not hers. At one point, Thatcher even tried to get rid of Pile himself; she attempted to persuade Heath to move him, alleging that his Russian wife made him a security risk.[42]

Thatcher's resistance and contrariness as well as her clear expression of resentment typify the *expressive* and *interpersonal* behaviour of the Contentious personality type.[43]

Indeed, contrariness and resentment were the twin pillars of her political repertoire. Thatcher observed that "in one respect at least [her role as minister of] the Department of Education and Science (1970–74) was an excellent preparation for the premiership. I came under savage and unremitting attack that was only distantly related to my crimes."[44] To help defuse the hostility between Thatcher and the student population over the government's decision to end the free-milk policy for school-children, Prime Minister Heath appointed Norman St John-Stevas as her number two at the Department of Education. He assumed far more of the public ministerial duties than an undersecretary normally handles in order to take the heat off Thatcher and bridge the increasing differences between her and the educators and the press. "She was so upset for a while that she refused to talk to the press at all, and when she did, treated every question as a trap."[45]

In 1974 there was a lengthy debate in cabinet over existing mortgage rates, and Thatcher, newly appointed as minister of the environment, emerged as "odd woman out." "What mattered to my colleagues was clearly the pledge to abolish the rates, and at Wilton Street, Ted [Heath, the prime minister] insisted on it. I felt bruised and resentful to be bounced again into policies which had not been properly thought out."[46] During the election campaign in September 1974, Thatcher was summoned by Heath to hear the new line on a government of national unity. She was opposed to such a policy for both strategic and tactical reasons. "For myself, I was not going to retreat from the policies which at his [Heath's] insistence I had been advocating. I went away highly disgruntled."[47]

For her challenge to Conservative orthodoxy, Thatcher was targeted with fallacious stories of hoarding food. She felt that this attack played to the snobbery of the Conservative Party, because the "unspoken implication was that this was all that could be expected of a grocer's daughter."[48] "'At the time ... I was bitterly upset by it. Sometimes I was near to tears. Sometimes I was shaking with anger. But as I told Bill Shelton, the MP for Streatham and a friend: 'I saw how they destroyed Keith [Joseph]. Well, they're not going to destroy me.'"[49]

During the 1979 election campaign, Peter Thorneycroft, the chairman of the party, told the deputy chairman, Janet Young, who then spoke to Thatcher, that things were not too good politically and that Ted Heath should appear on the next party election broadcast. In her autobiography, Thatcher describes what happened next: "I exploded. It was about as clear a demonstration of lack of confidence in me [as leader of the party] as could be imagined. If Peter Thorneycroft and the central office had not yet understood that what we were fighting for was a reversal, not just of the Wilson-Callaghan approach, but the Heath Government's approach, they had understood nothing ... To invite [Heath] to deliver a party political for us was tantamount to accepting defeat for the kind of policies I was advancing ... I told [Janet] I would not even hear of it ... still seething, I went to bed."[50] In this instance, there is evidence of a bitter discontent and demanding irritability with friends and relatives. An individual who possesses such a *self-image* effectively sees him/herself as misunderstood, unappreciated, and demeaned by others.[51]

What Thatcher omitted from her account was the extent of her fury at Thorneycroft's suggestion. According to one of her biographers, Penny Junor, "she ... stood up from the table and stormed out of the room, leaving a group of astonished aides who couldn't understand why she should have found the suggestion so offensive. The next morning Denis said, 'I've never seen her so upset, never, ever.' It is an incident that she still refers to at the drop of a hat to berate those who didn't see the harm in appearing with Ted. 'Even you,' she'll say [to Denis], wagging her finger accusingly, 'even you.'"[52] In this vignette, we see evidence not only of Thatcher's Contentiousness but also of her irritability, so characteristic of the Contentious personality. Typical behaviour of this personality type involves the discharge of anger or abuse at the least provocation.[53]

SCALE 2: THE AMBITIOUS PATTERN

At the lower end of the Ambitious pattern (scores of 5–9) are situated the confident, poised, self-assured, ambitious, and persuasive personalities. Exaggerated Ambitious features (scores of 10–23) occur in those individuals characterized by arrogance, a sense of entitlement, and a lack of empathy for others.[54]

Margaret Thatcher's strong drive to be singled out and recognized as special became apparent early in her life. From the outset, she demonstrated a strong streak of self-confidence. When visiting speakers invited questions at the end of their presentations, "it would always be Margaret Roberts that got to her feet. At an age when most of her contemporaries were far too self-conscious to open their mouths in front of so many people, she would ask clear, well-formulated questions, while her friends just looked at each other and raised their eyes to heaven."[55] Margaret managed to set herself apart from the other children one way or another throughout her school years. As a member of the school-debating club, her great confidence in public speaking also distinguished her from her classmates. "Once she got going, Margaret Roberts could be relied to go on and on. She liked nothing more than a captive audience."[56] Later, Margaret's self-confidence in her speaking abilities would manifest itself in her love of debate in the House of Commons and, as prime minister, in the relish with which she engaged her opponents during Question Period.

Margaret's desire to be recognized also expressed itself in a fascination with acting. At Kesteven, she joined the dramatic society and acted in many of the productions. She loved the glamour but mostly the sense of being centre stage and the focus of attention.[57] It fuelled her sense of being special – Daddy's precocious little daughter. School friends recall Margaret at the age of thirteen or fourteen actually declaring that she wanted to be a member of Parliament – long before her contemporaries in Grantham understood what that meant.[58] Her frequent references to "Daddy, the Mayor" and her frank admission about aiming for big things, while failing to endear her to her classmates, revealed both an "ambition [that] was boundless and a candor [that was] guileless."[59]

By the time she was seventeen, Margaret's ambition and self-confidence were in full bloom. As we have seen, when Headmistress Gillies indicated to Margaret that she thought she was too young to attend university, Margaret was barely able to control her anger. She reportedly said, "You're thwarting my ambition," and promptly set about preparing on her own for the Oxford entrance exam, which she successfully passed.[60] Logic and diligence were two of the intellectual qualities most frequently attributed to her by her teachers. "Margaret is ambitious and deserves to do well" was the comment that appeared in her final report.[61]

As Margaret acknowledged, "before I went up to Oxford, I had a less clear idea of what the place would be like than did many of my contemporaries. But I regarded it as quite simply the best, and if I was serious about getting on in life that is what I should always strive for. There was no point in lowering my sights."[62] Those closest to her at Oxford were fellow Methodists, and those with whom she spent the most time were like-minded conservatives. "Politics were her abiding interest, and she would talk about the heights she planned to achieve, without a hint of humility or uncertainty."[63] Margaret joined the Conservative Association and made no secret of her determination to get into Parliament. When asked about her political goals, she responded, "'I ought to be an M.P.'"[64] "She had an intense and, some have said, arrogant certainty that she was right and was never shy about declaring herself."[65]

After her marriage to Denis Thatcher, Margaret went to law school to become a barrister. But her real passion remained the world of politics. In an article she wrote for the *Sunday Graphic* after Elizabeth became the reigning monarch, she made a strenuous plea for the right of women to work both inside and outside the home. "The idea that the family

suffers, is I believe, quite mistaken. Should a woman arise equal to the
task, I say let her have an equal chance with the men for the leading
cabinet posts. Why not a woman Chancellor – or a Foreign Secretary?"
However, she was to be repeatedly hurt and disappointed at the way in
which a number of selection committees in various constituency associations raised the issue of her ability to be wife, mother, and MP. "They
were, after all, an attack on me not just as a candidate, but as a wife
and mother. But I refused to be put off by them. I was confident that I
had something to offer in politics."[66]

When a vacancy for the Finchley seat opened up, the constituency association interviewed Margaret. When asked what she would do if she
were to be nominated, she replied, "I will let the people know what
Conservatism is about and I will lead the troops into battle."[67] Her
statement was strikingly similar to Gandhi's vision of herself as Joan of
Arc leading the Indians against the British. This time the selection committee approved Margaret as their candidate. She herself had no doubt
that she "could cope with even quite abstruse questions of economic or
foreign policy, for I had voraciously read the newspapers and all the
briefings I could obtain. I prepared my speech until it was word perfect,
and I had mastered the technique of speaking without notes."[68]

Margaret won her constituency in the general election in February
1959 and, on the very first day of the new Parliament, notified photog-
raphers in advance when "the youngest MP would be arriving for her
first day at Westminster. A photo of her standing next to the policeman
guarding the MPs' gate made the papers the next day."[69]

Patricia (Paddi) Hornsby-Smith, Thatcher's first parliamentary secretary,
had fully expected that she would have to show the new member around,
teach her the ropes, and ease her in gradually. But such was not the case.
"Mrs Thatcher knew where she was going and what she was doing right
from the start and her only concern was to get down to work."[70] As
Thatcher notes in her autobiography, "a phrase that ... I often used to say
[was] that while the home must always be the centre of one's life, it should
not be the boundary of one's ambitions. Indeed, I needed a career because
quite simply, that was the sort of person I was. And not just any career. I
wanted one which would keep me mentally active and prepare me for the
political future for which I believed I was well-suited."[71]

Thatcher's determination not to allow motherhood to impinge upon her
ambition was evident in the actions she took immediately after the birth of
her twins. From her hospital room, she filled in the bar-examination application, knowing that she might not have the time – or the will – to do it
when immersed in her final year of legal studies and faced with the challenges of organizing "our lives so as to allow me to be both a mother and
a professional woman."[72]

In the summer of 1961, Thatcher became the parliamentary secretary to the minister of pensions and national insurance. A writer who was assigned to profile her noted that "those who know her well detect a strong will, some might say almost a ruthlessness, behind her smiling appearance."[73] Thatcher held the position until the Conservatives were narrowly defeated in 1964. At that time, Alec Douglas-Home, the former Conservative prime minister, stepped down from the leadership and was succeeded by Ted Heath. During the budget debate in 1966, Thatcher listened patiently to the chief secretary to the treasury, John Diamond. Then, very quietly, she rose to her feet and proceeded to pour scorn on Diamond. "'Oh that Gilbert and Sullivan should be living at this hour,' she cried, warming to her theme, 'This is sheer cock-eyed lunacy. I really think the Chancellor needs a woman at the Treasury.'"[74] This was pure rhetoric, "but it did underscore her real ambition in politics at the time – to be the first woman Chancellor of the Exchequer."[75]

When, in October 1967, Heath appointed Thatcher to be the front-bench critic on fuel and power and a member of the shadow cabinet, she observed: "It may be that my House of Commons performances and perhaps Iain Macleod's recommendation overcame a temperamental reluctance on Ted's part."[76] Thatcher then moved to the education portfolio in 1970 and remained there for three and a half years. It was the only cabinet post she held before becoming prime minister. As Hugo Young notes, "it was not for want of trying to escape. Aware that it wasn't a mainline political job, she began to hanker for promotion, or at least a sideways shift into a department closer to the centre after a couple of years in the job. Norman St John-Stevas, her junior minister at the time, retained a clear memory of this impatience."[77]

At the end of May 1974, Thatcher became directly involved with the Centre for Policy Studies (CPS), by then a powerhouse of alternative conservative thinking on economic and social matters, when Keith Joseph invited her to take the post of vice-chairman. Notwithstanding the "fear of provoking the wrath of Ted [Heath, the leader of the Conservative opposition] and the derision of left-wing commentators ... I jumped at the chance to become Keith's [v]ice [c]hairman."[78] Later that year, the failure of the Conservatives under Heath to win the general election prompted continued criticism from the right wing within the party. Keith Joseph, their natural leader, decided that he would not run for the leadership. This was to be Thatcher's golden opportunity. "I heard myself saying: Look, Keith, if you're not going to stand, I will, because someone who represents our viewpoint *has* to stand."[79]

Thatcher explained her decision to stand for the pinnacle of an ambitious politician's career, the leadership, as follows: "Because I'm a true Tory, and I believe that I can rule this country better than anyone else.

And because I saw the Tory Party going too much to the left, and there didn't seem to be anyone who had the thoughts and ideas I had, and it seemed to be absolutely vital for this country that I stood.'"[80]

In the run-up to the Conservative Party conference where the new leader would be chosen, attitudes towards Thatcher's candidacy were tangibly changing. "By this time, as a result of the soundings Airey [Neave, a Conservative MP and Thatcher's campaign manager] had taken, I was actually beginning to feel that I was in with a chance. I said to them [a group of leading national and provincial newspaper journalists] wryly at one point: 'You know, I really think you should begin to take me seriously.' They looked back in amazement, and perhaps some of them soon started to do so. For by the weekend, articles had begun to appear to reappraise my campaign in a different light."[81]

For all her careful outward modesty, Margaret's daughter, Carol, confirms that her mother was not surprised when the Conservative parliamentary caucus voted for her as leader on 11 February 1975. "The outside world may have been surprised … but she had clearly seen herself in a central role … I was reminded of the famous scene in the Robert Redford film, *The Candidate*, where the victorious politician grabs an aide in the loo and barks at him, 'OK, what do we do now?' My mother knew exactly what to do and embraced the leadership as if it had always been her destiny."[82] In the same vein, Junor writes that, on her visit to the United States in 1976, "everywhere she went, she spoke confidently about leading a Conservative government. 'The question is not whether we will win,' she told crowds in New York, 'but how large the majority will be.'"[83]

During the electoral campaign of 1979, Thatcher observed "personally I was conscious that in some strange way I was instinctively speaking and feeling in harmony with the great majority of the population. Such moments are as unforgettable as they are rare. They must be seized to change history."[84] Such was her ambition and self-confidence that, according to her permanent secretary, Sir William Pile, she was impossible to argue with, always wanting to do things that she was not legally permitted to do.[85]

SCALE 6: THE CONSCIENTIOUS PATTERN

Margaret Thatcher also scored in the *prominent* range (10–23) on the Conscientious scale. Not only was she respectful, disciplined, prudent, and orderly – aspects of the Conscientious personality at a lower level – but she also displayed the more exaggerated features such as dutifulness, rigidity, a strong sense of propriety, and dignity. On occasion, too, she could be fastidious and a perfectionist. However, these qualities were never sufficiently strong to reach a level of *mildly dysfunctional* or receive a clinical diagnosis of obsessive-compulsive personality disorder.[86]

Many of her Conscientious traits could be observed from early childhood on. "'She was bright, studious, and serious, even as a five-year-old,' said John Foster, who sat at the next desk. 'She always came top of her class and never needed telling anything twice.' According to a family friend, John Guile, "Alf [Margaret's father] did a good deal to push her in school and in her career and she was quite willing to be pushed. She worked hard at everything, like a diligent adult, with little time to spare."[87]

Margaret started piano lessons at five and her older sister could never keep up with her. "'She was four years younger, but always about three lesson books ahead of me,' Muriel recalled."[88] Despite Margaret's musical gifts, which she seems to have inherited from her mother, she gave up taking piano lessons at the age of fifteen to concentrate on her schoolwork.[89]

Many of her classmates made fun of Margaret, whose behaviour, "so rigid and serious, made her seem so much older than her years ... She knew everyone, but had few friends to invite home after school. She had homework to do anyway, and she wasn't the sort of person to let less diligent classmates copy it."[90] Margaret was the top student at Kesteven every year except her last, when she finished second. Her excellent school record was not a function of her brilliance but rather because "she was an academic grind,"[91] with strong powers of concentration, who excelled as a result of "sheer hard work."[92] Throughout her life, it was her inexhaustible willingness to work longer hours than anyone else, her refusal to go to bed before she had read every last paper that enabled her repeatedly to beat down colleagues and opponents through her sheer mastery of detail.[93]

"Her contemporaries remember her as a model pupil of demure habits and tediously impeccable behaviour. She never put a foot wrong, in the classroom or on the hockey field." The intellectual qualities most frequently attributed to the young Margaret Roberts were "logic and diligence."[94] But she never seemed to quite fit in with her peers, "doubtless because she was always so serious, and gave the impression that she couldn't be bothered with giggly girls who had nothing to say for themselves."[95]

When she arrived at Oxford, Margaret recalled that "there were tight controls over the use of hot water. For example, there must be no more than five inches of water in the bath – and of course I rigidly observed this."[96] During her college years, "Margaret worked hard and was very methodical and neat; she was never late for lectures, never late with her essays, and always appeared to be interested in the subject."[97] Although she put in long hours working for the Oxford University Conservative Association, it was never to the detriment of her work. She would often be up until two or three o'clock in the morning writing her essays. The following morning she would be out of bed at 6:30 or 7:00 for the next round of lectures, lab work, and tutorials.[98]

After her graduation from Oxford with a degree in chemistry, Margaret found employment in the plastics industry. Junor describes her experiences there: "Her rigidity and inability to behave flexibly made her life in industry unnecessarily stressful. She was quite incapable of communicating with the men on the factory floor in any way at all. Where her female colleagues might ask 'Hey Charlie, what about trying this, I think it might work?' and play along with the odd nudge and wink, Margaret would stand rather awkwardly over the man, and in her well-modulated and now perfected true-blue accent, would say, 'Mr. So and So, would you mind trying it this way?' This method, as often as not, elicited the two finger response, and earned Margaret the nickname, 'Duchess,' which stuck throughout her three years at BX Plastics."[99] At the Christmas parties held by the company, her two female colleagues drank and looked as though they were having fun. "Margaret would arrive wearing a long formal dress and sit like a pariah at the feast, obviously hating every minute."[100] Her colleagues remembered her "'as a hardworking, efficient, well-organized' performer in the labs, though not as a particularly brilliant practitioner of academic chemistry."[101]

Although Margaret was always concerned about her appearance, she would never experiment with clothes and always stuck to rather old-fashioned styles and drab colours – a reflection, perhaps, of her religious upbringing, which had little tolerance for personal vanity or female fripperies. She always wore skirts or dresses, never trousers, which were considered radical for a woman. "On her weekends away, she would dash off on Friday afternoons dressed in a smart black suit with a conservative little hat ... 'Minnie Mouse' court shoes, and a handbag tucked under one arm, looking forty-five, if she was a day, and every bit the 'Aunty Margaret' or the 'Duchess' of the factory floor."[102]

After the birth of her twins, Margaret was forced to think about her future. "Talking about combining a career and motherhood was one thing; doing it was another, especially with two babies. But she worried that her mind would turn to mush if she didn't continue her career." She was "'concerned,' she said, 'particularly with two that I would be tempted to spend all my time on the household and looking after them and not continue to read or use my mind or experience.'" She conscientiously filled in the "'entrance form for the final of the law'" as she lay in hospital. She felt that, if she did not do it then, she might never go back to the law. "'But if I did fill in the entrance form now, pride will not let me fail. And so I did. That was really an effort of will.' Five months later she took the bar final and passed."[103] Margaret's decision to complete her law degree was a product of both her Conscientious and Ambitious traits.

When she was offered the Finchley constituency, she committed herself totally. She would sit up working in her room until two or three o'clock in the morning reading and preparing speeches.[104] After she was elected to Parliament, the same pattern continued. Whenever she gave a speech, she would do all the research herself, which frequently involved long hours in the House of Commons library. "Homework was always something she had been good at – what she lacked in original thought she made up for in study – and she never embarked on anything without being properly and thoroughly prepared."[105]

In her first government position as a junior secretary in the Department of Pensions, Thatcher's superior, Boyd-Carpenter [the permanent secretary], recounted that "she very quickly showed a grip on the highly technical matters of social security ... and a capacity for hard work ... which quite startled the civil servants and certainly startled me." Nor was he alone in his judgment. Sir William Pile, the deputy minister of education and science, was very impressed by Thatcher's subsequent performance as minister of the department. "'She worked to all hours of the day and night. She always emptied her box, with blue pencil marks all over the papers. Every single piece of paper was attended to ... She was always a very good trouper, always meticulous about turning up for meetings. If she said she'd be there at two minutes past six, she'd be there at two minutes past six.'"[106]

Her legendary self-discipline was sorely taxed by the assassination in March 1979 of Airey Neave, her great friend and shadow secretary for Northern Ireland (a position to which she had appointed him), at the hands of the Irish Republican Army (IRA). "The shock was colossal, and yet she was able to sit straight down at her desk and draft a tribute to give to the press."[107]

As leader of the opposition, Thatcher "worked formidably hard, sometimes at too many things. One aide said at the time: 'I found her at two o'clock in the morning rewriting a badly drafted letter to some ordinary voter in Sunderland.'"[108] Even though she hated television – she rarely had time to watch it herself and knew that she was not naturally good at projecting herself and her policies – she was, nevertheless, determined to master it.[109]

Thatcher's Conscientious behaviour was also evident outside politics in the realm of the family and the way she related to her children. She never called them by nicknames nor did she play games with them or take them out on a lark, but rather, like her father, she stressed culture, making sure they had music lessons. On occasion, this trait became more intense, reflecting a compulsive quality. Once, when the twins were away at school, and she felt particularly driven, she tore into their toy boxes determined to clean them up. Without hesitation, she threw out long-treasured toys because she was convinced they were no longer used. It never occurred to her to ask the children first if they minded. Nor did it occur to her to ask them to sort through the toys themselves. There was a job to be done, and she decided that it had to be done now. When the twins returned home and discovered the loss of their toys, they were devastated.[110]

In conversation with one of her early biographers, Thatcher discussed what made her so disciplined and dutiful. "'We were Methodists, and Methodist means method.'"[111] "Order, precision and attention to detail are the hallmarks of this kind of piety along with a methodological approach to the differences between right and wrong." As Thatcher described it, "'there were certain things you just didn't do, and that was that. Duty was very, very strongly ingrained into us. Duties to the church, duties to your neighbor and conscientiousness were continually emphasized.'"[112] However, Thatcher's efforts to get rid of members of the civil service who offended her clearly slipped under her ethical radar.

UNDERSTANDING MARGARET THATCHER'S PERSONALITY PROFILE

Thatcher's primary scale elevation, the Dominant (Scale 1A), was significantly greater than her other scores. In fact, the gap between the Dominant pattern and the other personality patterns is sufficiently large that one can virtually characterize Thatcher as a prototypal Dominant personality. Forceful individuals can be identified by an inclination to turn towards the self as the primary source of gratification. However, instead of the Ambitious personality's internalized sense of self-importance, Dominant individuals seem driven to prove their worthiness. They are characterized by an assertive, dominant, and tough-minded personality style. In contrast to their preferred, outwardly powerful appearance, these individuals may feel inwardly insecure and therefore work hard to achieve their goals and excel. In supervisory or leadership positions they usually take charge and see to it that a job gets done. This pattern was exacerbated in Thatcher's case given the role that Conscientiousness (Scale 6) also played in her personality profile. Because such individuals place so many demands upon themselves, they are inclined to demand the same level of performance of their colleagues and subordinates. As we have seen, this description accurately describes Thatcher's behaviour.

Unlike Indira Gandhi but like Golda Meir, Margaret Thatcher's expressive behaviour, interpersonal conduct, cognitive style, moods, and self-image revealed a consistency over time prior to her becoming prime minister. This raises the question of what underlies the particular personality patterns that emerged. More specifically, how can Thatcher's extreme competitiveness, her need to dominate, her aggressiveness, and her need for attention be explained? While genetic predisposition may be a significant factor in the determination of a personality profile,[113] environmental factors such as early parent-child and sibling relations also play an important role.

Thatcher's most recent biographer, J. Campbell, has raised a number of possible explanations for her personality traits, focusing on family dynamics. He suggests that, as the second daughter, the young Margaret may have had to compete with her elder sister to win approval from her busy mother and her demanding father. Such efforts are necessary because the second daughter has to bear the brunt of her parents' disappointment at not having had a son.[114] If Alfred, in particular, had hoped for a son, this may explain why he treated Margaret as his protégé and invested masculine expectations in her that required her to exhibit drive and determination.[115]

Research suggests that fathers who are challenging and somewhat abrasive raise the most socially competent, independent, and intrinsically motivated daughters; in fact, social confidence in girls appears to be inhibited rather than enhanced by unconditional approval and passive acceptance.[116] Muriel's personality, in contrast to that of Margaret's, would have encouraged that process, since "Muriel, like her mother, was quiet and withdrawn, a homebody with no overwhelming passion to better herself."[117] So different were the girls in terms of personality and interests that "throughout their childhood, Margaret and her sister, four-and-a-half years her senior, were never close."[118]

The Roberts home was characterized by a strong sense of practicality, frugality, responsibility, religiosity, and duty. From an early age, Margaret and Muriel were instilled with these values. When Margaret wanted to do something her friends were doing, her father would admonish her, "Never do things just because other people do them."[119] A tough taskmaster, Alfred set high academic and ethical standards for Margaret. Even Margaret's reading was directed – there was no time for such fluff as novels; it was all work, without a moment wasted. All her life she was completely unable to relax for fear she would lose ground, be caught out, and somehow punished for it. It is likely that the pressure she came to internalize was implanted in childhood, largely by her father. Adding to Margaret's insecurity may have been her position in a family that was part of the lower-middle class. Being told constantly

that the family could not afford many of the material goods that neighbours had – including indoor plumbing – may have made Margaret feel
that the "wolf was always at the door" and that poverty was just a
stone's throw away.

Margaret's father was the pre-eminent influence in her childhood and
she looked to him for praise and encouragement. While he doted on her,
sensing her drive and intelligence, he was demanding. But, by hard work
and dedication equal to his own, she became his favourite: a surrogate
son.[120] In turn, she seemed to idealize this handsome, well-built man
who served as town councillor, alderman, and finally mayor of the town
of Grantham. In her autobiography, she recounts their shared passion
for politics and international affairs. "Each week my father would take
two books out of the library, a 'serious' book for himself (and me) and a
novel for my mother. As a result I found myself reading books which
girls of my age would not generally read."[121] Having left school at the
age of thirteen, Alfred was determined that Margaret take advantage of
every educational opportunity. "We would both go to hear 'extension
lectures' from the University of Nottingham about current and international affairs, which were given in Grantham regularly. After the talk
would come a lively question time in which I and many others would
take part."[122] This suggests that Margaret was treated in a special way
by her father, as a function of her intelligence and her interests, and was
encouraged by him to be actively involved in expressing her views. As a
result, both her self-confidence and her ambition were enhanced.

But that is not the whole story; there is a downside. If a child feels
loved only insofar as she lives up to parental expectations, it can produce a deep-seated insecurity. Margaret's extreme combativeness and
driven conscientiousness suggest that she could not take love and acceptance, even from her father, for granted but had to struggle continually
to be the surrogate son he wanted. Yet Margaret's feelings of rebellion
were usually suppressed. "If you were rude or naughty," she once recalled, "you were sent to your room and you stayed there until you
came down and apologized. But this didn't seem to happen all that often."[123] Margaret was obedient, repressing whatever resentment she
may have felt; much later, her rebelliousness burst forth with incredible
energy on the political stage. In fact, her whole career was marked by a
curious tension between conformity and rebellion.[124]

For twenty years, Thatcher accepted the party line, even when she
was violently opposed to many of the decisions she was required to implement. While she was always combative, in the early days she would
generally back down gracefully when she had made her point.[125] However, as prime minister, she presided over the transformation of the Tory
Party and the direction of British public life. It may not be far-fetched to

see her decision to centralize power as, in part, a form of delayed and displaced revenge against her father. Although she paid lip-service to his values, after his death she demonstrated no compunction about eroding the powers of the town councils, notwithstanding Alf's pride at having been both a town councillor and the mayor.

On becoming Britain's first female prime minister, Thatcher paid homage to her father: "He brought me up to believe all the things I do believe and they are the values on which I have fought the election. It is passionately interesting to me that the things I learned in a small town, in a very modest home, are just the things that I believe have won the election. I owe almost everything to my father."[126] Margaret's heavy emphasis on her father's teaching suggests a guilty – perhaps unconscious – compensation for the fact that she was striking at much that he held dear. Her mythologization of Alfred seems to have been almost entirely retrospective. After the age of eighteen, she saw little of him for the remainder of his life. She recalled that he lived long enough to see her in the cabinet, but in fact he did not. This suggests that her father did not share very closely in her triumphs, and that she needed to manufacture such a memory as a way of dealing with her guilty conscience. Alf Roberts had only a graduation photograph of Margaret in his house: nothing more recent, and no pictures of his grandchildren. Mark and Carol were sixteen when Alfred died, yet they appeared to have little memory of their grandfather. "The impression is inescapable that Margaret was very much less devoted to her wonderful father while he was alive, than she became to his sanctified image after he was dead."[127]

But, as a child, Margaret, in an effort to deny the negative feelings she may have felt for the pressure her father placed on her, proceeded to idealize him – his political involvement and his strong convictions. This defence mechanism – a way of warding off the expression of anger – is characteristic of someone with a Conscientious personality trait. Margaret easily embraced the politically conservative views of her father and grew up wanting to be involved in what was then considered a more "masculine" pursuit – politics. "By precept and example, Alfred showed Margaret the way to escape her mother's sphere of stifling domesticity by competing in a man's world. So she blotted out her mother and idealized her father; in due course, she would eerily repeat the pattern by neglecting her own daughter while spoiling her son."[128]

Alf Roberts also instilled in Margaret the habit of hard work, as something both virtuous in itself and the route to self-advancement. Throughout her life, her compulsiveness was evident. She would work longer hours than any one else and refuse to go to bed before she had read every last paper. "As Prime Minister, Mrs Thatcher still prepared for parliamentary questions or international summits like a schoolgirl swotting for an exam."[129] Her conscientiousness enabled her repeatedly to beat down colleagues and opponents by sheer mastery of detail. No matter how much homework they had done, she always expected herself to have done more.[130]

The example of Alfred's tireless community activity bred in Margaret a powerful impulse to public service expressed in terms of Christian duty as well as a shrewd understanding of the rewards to be gained from public life. "Duty" became a euphemism for the ambition that Margaret would manifest and her ability to wrap that ambition in the cloak of duty to the party and the nation. But perhaps the most important legacy that Alfred gave his daughter was an exceptionally powerful moral sense. More than anything else in her political make-up, it was her fierce confidence that she knew what was right which distinguished her from contemporary politicians. Her absolute belief in her own integrity and values allowed her to be exceptionally forceful in disparaging the motives of those who disagreed with her. But the combative and divisive way in which she expressed herself did not come from an identification with her father, who maintained good relations with his opponents in the council chamber.[131]

Margaret's Domineering and Contentious personality traits may have been a function of the early power struggles between herself and her mother.[132] It is worth noting that the major silence in Thatcher's account of her Grantham life surrounds the figure of her mother, Beatrice Roberts. In telling her story, Thatcher constantly deflected attention from Beatrice to focus it on her father. When asked by an interviewer in 1985, "Can I just talk about your mother for a minute?" Thatcher produced the shortest answer of the interview, "Mother was marvellous – yes, go on." Three further questions about her mother yielded answers in which Thatcher referred to her father more than her mother. The memories of her mother that did emerge suggest a woman who saw life in a joyless, stultifying, and repressive way. While this may have been an accurate description, it could also have been a reflection of Margaret's unresolved Oedipal feelings for her father, which invariably involve a disparagement of the mother figure.

When Margaret complained to her mother about her friends having more material possessions, she was repeatedly told, "'Well we're not situated like that.' ... I can still hear my mother, 'well, we're not situated like that.'"[133] When asked if she accepted the injunction that "we're not situated like that," Margaret replied: "One kicked against it. Of course one kicked against it. They [her friends] had more things than we did. Of course one kicked against it.'"[134] But the kicking seems to have been directed primarily at her mother, rather than her father, even though he was at least as frugal as his wife. Indeed, her choice of a generous and affluent husband was, at some level, an expression of her resentment at having been forced to live so economically, when Alfred and Beatrice had the means to provide their family with a higher standard of living.

As a young girl, Margaret recalled going out to buy "new covers for the settee – that was a great event, to have new covers for a settee was a great expenditure and a great event. So you went out to choose them, and you chose something that looked really rather lovely, something light, with flowers on. My mother's comment was 'that's not serviceable.' And how I longed for the time when I could buy things that were not serviceable."[135] Margaret's resentment towards her mother is clearly palpable. It is also unusual. Most daughters, after separating themselves from their mothers, retain a strong instinctive bond with them even when the relationship has been coloured by exasperation and mutual incomprehension.[136] The absence of such a bond suggests that Margaret may have felt deprived of normal motherly love. Indeed, Margaret's extreme competitiveness throughout her life suggests that, as a child, she felt a need to fight for attention; her aggressiveness, on the one hand, and her almost obsessive conscientiousness, on the other, suggests that her childhood was not as rosy as she chose to present it.

What emerged in public was the condescension that Margaret seems to have felt for her mother. In 1975 she told the *Daily Telegraph*: "I loved my mother dearly, but after I was fifteen we had nothing more to say to each other. It wasn't her fault. She was weighed down by the home, always being in the home." Margaret's disdain for and anger with her mother would then find resonance in her relationships with other female authorities. Thus, for example, Thatcher greeted the advice of her headmistress to postpone her application to Oxford because of her relative youth with dismissal and rage, and resolutely set out to prove that she could prepare for the entry examination on her own.

Throughout her life, Thatcher had difficulty with women and deliberately excluded all but one, who filled a minor portfolio, from her cabinet. She also voiced criticism of her over-strict upbringing, which excluded dances, parties, and enjoying herself. One can detect a note of sadness in Thatcher's comment: "'For us it was rather a sin to enjoy yourself by entertainment. Do you see what I mean? Life wasn't to enjoy yourself; life was to work and do things.'"[137] Although Margaret's life became one of work and accomplishment, her choice of husband, Denis Thatcher, seems to have been a riposte to her family. Here was a man who loved life – fast cars, brandy, golf – and who was an Anglican rather than a strict Methodist. Relatively wealthy, he could afford to provide his wife with many of the luxuries she had missed while growing up in her strict and parsimonious household.

Partly because Margaret's father was a grocer and the family lived above the store, everyone was expected to work. As Margaret described it, "in my family we were never idle – partly because idleness was a sin, partly because there was so much work to be done, and partly no doubt because we were just that sort of people."[138] Margaret's legendary self-discipline and willingness to work hard – her conscientiousness – was acquired early in life and was fostered by her father. Rather than rebel overtly against him, Margaret largely buried her resentments and instead idealized her father – accepting some of his values as an integral part of her personality.

In dealing with her ambivalent feelings towards her parents, Margaret seems to have engaged in the psychological defence mechanism known as "splitting," in which the "good" and the "bad" parts of an individual, instead of being integrated, are split off. Thus, she idealized her father as being all "good," while her mother was characterized as the "bad" one. In a state of healthy psychological maturity, individuals can tolerate both the "bad" and the "good" in their loved objects, without the fear that the bad will overwhelm the good and retaliate and punish them.[139]

Overall, the examination of the influence of the Contentious, Ambitious, and Conscientious dimensions of Thatcher's personality profile, in conjunction with the strong impact of the Dominant pattern, provides a multidimensional portrait of her. When Contentious and Dominant features are prominent dimensions in a personality profile, a pattern emerges in which minor frictions tend to develop into major confrontations and power struggles. Some of these "abrasive negativists" may take special joy in spotting inconsistencies in the behaviour and performance of others. They construct arguments that amplify observed contradictions and shove these squarely in the face of their "antagonists" just for the pleasure of undermining their self-confidence and watching them squirm.[140] Such individuals may be given to contemptuous fault-finding and outright insults. During such periods, anyone who crosses them may become an object of scorn and derision. The reader will recall the cruel way in which Thatcher treated her former headmistress and, subsequently, the members of her cabinet.

When the controlling, aggressive aspects of the Dominant personality pattern are associated with the Conscientious pattern, the resulting personality has been described as that of the "enforcing sadist." Such individuals will mask their hostility and aggression under the guise of enforcing the rules for the good of society. They frequently hold positions of power in which the imposition of punishment plays an important role. Cloaked within socially sanctioned roles, they mete out condemnation in the name of justice and their rhetoric is frequently infused with a sense of righteous condemnation for those they deem to have offended their values.[141] The opposition, the trade unions, the civil service, and the universities all became the targets of Thatcher's anger.

If both the Conscientious and Ambitious dimensions of a personality are prominent, the resulting profile has been described as a "bureaucratic compulsive." Such individuals ally themselves with traditional values and established authorities. They flourish in organizational settings, feeling comforted, strengthened, and empowered by clearly defined superior and subordinate relations. "Punctual and meticulous, they adhere to the work ethic like worker ants in a colony, appraising their own and others' tasks with black-and-white efficiency, as done or not done."[142] Thatcher's work ethic was legendary, as were her expectations of similar efforts from her staff. When Dominating and Controlling features also characterize the personality profile, the bureaucratic compulsive will exhibit a rigid adherence to policies and rules that makes them seem officious, high-handed, close-minded, and petty.[143]

Descriptively then, Margaret Thatcher may be depicted as having a Dominant personality pattern with some aspects of the "abrasive negativist," the "bureaucratic compulsive," and the "enforcing sadist." To understand the significance that her personality patterns had for British society and government, the next chapter will examine her leadership style.

Margaret Thatcher's Leadership Style

As we have already done with Indira Gandhi and Gold Meir, this chapter examines and classifies Thatcher's leadership as prime minister within three clusters of the theoretical framework developed for the study of leadership style.[1] Cluster A explores Thatcher's motivation, her task orientation, and her investment in performing her duties as prime minister; Cluster B examines her management style, both with her cabinet and in the realm of information gathering; and Cluster C studies her interpersonal relations with members of the civil service, her personal staff, the caucus, the extra-parliamentary party, the opposition, the media, and the public[2] (See Table 6). In the sections that follow, material drawn from sources like various biographies, Thatcher's own autobiography, and scholarly books and articles on British government are used to illustrate these various aspects of her leadership style.

CLUSTER A: INDIVIDUAL STYLE

Motivation

A convincing 55 per cent of the 695 items extracted and coded on the topic of motivation reveals that Thatcher's shaping of government policies took place along *ideological* lines. Since she was someone who was known for her intensity and commitment to a coherent set of political beliefs, this is to be expected. *Power*, in the sense of dominance and control, accounted for 22.1 per cent of all the extracted items, while *pragmatism* accounted for 20.3 per cent. *Personal validation* or popular approval was singularly unimportant to Thatcher, accounting for only 2.6 per cent of her behaviour in this area.

IDEOLOGY
Evidence of Thatcher's commitment to a doctrinal approach to politics was evident from the beginning of her tenure as prime minister.[3] Her

Table 6
Leadership-style categories: Margaret Thatcher
(Total number of items collected and assessed): 2889

CLUSTER A: Individual Style	
I. MOTIVATION (total evidence in this category: 695)	
a Pragmatism (141)	20.3%
b Personal Validation (18)	2.6%
c Ideology (382)	55.0%
d Power (154)	22.1%
II. TASK ORIENTATION (total evidence in this category: 177)	
a Process (10)	5.6%
b Goal (167)	94.4%
III. INVESTMENT IN JOB PERFORMANCE (total evidence in this category: 219)	
a Circumscribed (6)	2.8%
b Tireless (213)	97.2%

CLUSTER B: Managerial Style	
IV. CABINET MANAGEMENT STRATEGY (total evidence in this category: 324)	
a Uninvolved (5)	1.5%
b Consensus Builder (22)	6.8%
c Arbitrator (23)	7.1%
d Advocate (Authoritative/Peremptory) (274)	84.6%
V. INFORMATION MANAGEMENT STRATEGY (total evidence in this category: 531)	
1. Degree of involvement (260)	
a Low (13)	5%
b High (247)	95%
2. Sources (271)	
a Ministerial (93)	34.3%
b Independent (178)	65.7%

CLUSTER C: Interpersonal Style	
VI. RELATIONS WITH PERSONNEL (total evidence in this category: 207)	
1. Degree of Involvement (80)	
a Low (0)	0%
b High (80)	100%
2. Type of Involvement (127)	
a Collegial/Solicitous – (Egalitarian) (31)	24.4%
b Polite/Formal (25)	19.7%
c Attention-seeking/Seductive (10)	7.8%
d Demanding/Domineering (56)	44.1%
e Manipulative/Exploitative (5)	3.9%

Table 6
Leadership-style categories: Margaret Thatcher (*Continued*)
(Total number of items collected and assessed): 2889

VII. RELATIONS WITH THE PARTY (total evidence in this category: 233)	
1. Caucus (186)	
a Uninvolved (3)	1.6%
b Cooperative/Harmonious (13)	7.0%
c Competitive/Oppositional (150)	80.6%
d Controlling/Overbearing (20)	10.8%
2. Extra-Parliamentary Party Organization (47)	
a Uninvolved (0)	0%
b Cooperative/Harmonious (22)	46.8%
c Competitive/Oppositional (23)	49%
d Controlling/Overbearing (2)	4.2%
VIII. RELATIONS WITH OPPOSITION PARTIES (total evidence in this category: 132)	
a Uninvolved (1)	0.7%
b Cooperative/Harmonious (4)	3.0%
c Competitive/Oppositional (100)	75.8%
d Controlling/Overbearing (27)	20.5%
IX. RELATIONS WITH THE MEDIA (total evidence in this category: 265)	
a Open (209)	78.8%
b Closed (56)	21.2%
X. RELATIONS WITH THE PUBLIC (total evidence in this category: 106)	
a Active (97)	91.5%
b Passive (9)	8.5%

inspiration came, in large measure, from the writings of the economist Friedrich von Hayek, most particularly his work *The Road to Serfdom*. This book offers an important twentieth-century defence of classical liberalism, outlining the philosophical distinction between Western liberal values and German and Soviet totalitarianism. In it, Hayek addresses the basic tenets of socialism or, more accurately, economic planning, arguing that, in a planned economy, people delegate responsibility to a higher body and slowly lose their moral agency and personal freedom. He also asserts that economic planning is inevitably dehumanizing, producing regimes that sacrifice freedom, morality, and truth in pursuit of their conception of the "common good." Thatcher's own long-term goal was nothing less than the elimination of what she called "socialism" from

British politics and the reversal of the whole collectivizing trend of the post-war era. Once in power, her Hayek-inspired philosophy of anti-socialist economics included a number of broad objectives: a cut in public spending and taxes, tight control of the money supply, restraint in detailed intervention in the economy, and trust in the operation of the free market.[4] In public and in private, Thatcher also proved herself to be a relentless and fierce defender and promoter of her political *weltanschauung*. In her view, an important leadership task was to win the battle of ideas, "and this [was] done by frequently expressing basic beliefs and principles."[5] To her it was a matter of principle that "a conviction PM" like herself did not need Whitehall to tell her what to think. "'Don't tell me what,' she had told her advisers in opposition. 'I know what. Tell me how.'"[6]

But, as soon as the new prime minister took office, the impact of an economic recession seemed, according to conventional wisdom, to require something other than Thatcher's new economic approach. A concerted demand developed across the political spectrum that the new government set aside its ideological preconceptions and act in the national interest. Thatcher's hostility to continued subsidies of core British industrial sectors like coal, steel, and transport did not sit well with bureaucratic consensus or popular will. Yet she remained unfazed, determined to do what she felt was right. And the more the defenders of the old consensus demanded she change course, the harder she defied them. Eventually, resisting and standing firm became an end in itself, irrespective of the economic arguments. Thus, the ideological and dogmatic leadership style that would characterize the premiership of Margaret Thatcher was forged very early on in her tenure in office.[7]

It was not only British industry that had to be brought to heel – Thatcher was also intent on implementing reform in trade-union law. In the early days, she enquired whether the independent arbitration service, ACAS, was involved in the efforts to resolve the strike at British Steel, and she reluctantly allowed herself one meeting with the union leaders. She was "torn between the pragmatic, sensible politician wanting to end a damaging strike, and the doctrinaire economist. According to Jim Prior, the secretary of employment, the doctrinaire approach won. The government's greatest triumph, as another minister said at the time, was that 'we didn't settle it with beer and sandwiches at No. 10.'"[8]

In addition, Thatcher's strong ideological commitment to a clearly defined set of economic ideas was accompanied by a powerful sense of moral, almost religious, rectitude that gave her great faith in her own judgment. "'Deep in their instincts, people find what I am saying and doing right, and I know it is because that is the way I was brought up. I

regard myself as a very normal, ordinary person, with all the right, instinctive antennae.'"⁹ Restoring sound money, she told the lord mayor's
banquet in November, was the first objective. "'It is a Herculean task,'
she said. 'But we are not faint-hearted pilgrims. We will not be deflected
by a stony path.'"¹⁰

Such a vigorous leadership style – a natural consequence of her Dominant personality – created the optimum conditions for Thatcher to convert the cabinet, the Conservative Party, and the nation to her way of
thinking. And she used it to her advantage. "I knew that the hardest
battles would be fought on the ground of economic policy. So I made
sure that the key economic ministers would be true believers in our economic strategy. Geoffrey Howe had by now thoroughly established
himself as the Party's chief economic spokesman."¹¹

On the subject of the austere budget she put forward in 1981,
Thatcher, as she went into the Commons to hear the budget speech, commented to Alan Walters, her economic adviser: "'You know Alan ... they
may get rid of me for this.' But, she added, 'it would be in a worthwhile
cause. At least, I shall have gone knowing I did the right thing.'"¹²

Her strong convictions continued to show throughout her tenure.
While campaigning for re-election in 1983, Thatcher underlined what
she saw as the important ideological differences between Labour and
the Conservatives when she told the Scottish Conservative conference,
"'This is an historic election. For the choice facing the nation is between
two totally different ways of life. And what a prize we have to fight for:
no less than the chance to banish from our land the dark, divisive
clouds of Marxist Socialism.'"¹³ This stark, almost apocalyptic language, with its strong religious undertones, characterized her convictions and Manichean perception of the world.

By the beginning of 1985, Chancellor of the Exchequer Nigel Lawson
had been converted to the idea that the time had come for Britain to
join the Exchange Rate Mechanism (ERM) of the European Monetary
System. Thatcher was diametrically opposed to the idea, notwithstanding its support by many of her senior colleagues. Although she articulated her objections in terms of timing and judgment, her opposition
actually rested on ideological grounds. She believed, as part of her free-
market economic philosophy, that exchange rates could not be fixed
and it was folly for governments to try to defy the markets. She was
also opposed to sacrificing any shred of sovereignty over the value of
the pound or the British government's right – illusory though it might
be in practice – to set its own interest rates to try to fix it.¹⁴

But it was quite indicative of Thatcher's unfailing faith and unshakeable commitment to a set of ideas that her philosophy became an "ism"

– Thatcherism. Contributing to her uniqueness as prime minister were her ideological beliefs, in conjunction with her Dominant personality, both of which enabled her to impose a virtual sea change in modern British political and economic life. Illustrative in this regard was her habitual willingness to second-guess her most senior ministers publicly, including the chancellor on anti-inflation policy, the home secretary on measures to combat football violence, and the foreign secretary on a wide range of issues. This was not designed to outmanoeuvre the cabinet for its own sake, as Harold Wilson had done. Rather, it reflected Thatcher's determination to achieve her policy objectives.[15]

As prime minister, Thatcher was so dominant and controlling, displaying such command even of the most minute details of her government, that her close associates worried that she looked too much like a childish know-it-all. She was warned against sounding "too headmistressy," a frequent public criticism.[16] The prime minister was unapologetic. "'I have known some very good headmistresses who have launched their pupils on wonderful careers,' Thatcher told an interviewer. She had no intention of changing." She then went on to say, "'I am what I am. Yes, I do believe in certain things very strongly. Yes, my style is one of vigorous leadership. Yes, I do believe in trying to persuade people that the things I believe in are the things they should follow. I am far too old to change now.' Take me or leave me, she was saying. There was no choice and she knew it."[17]

Throughout her political career, Thatcher remained the quintessential ideologue. Even after ten years in office, she was still preoccupied with making certain that the ideological transformation of Britain that was reflected in the government's radical social and economic reforms – as well as the "remodelling" of Europe on which she had embarked – would be maintained and intensified. It was primarily for these reasons that she was determined not to step down – a decision that was to produce her ultimate defeat within the party.[18]

POWER

A taste for *power* was the second most potent factor shaping Margaret Thatcher's political motivations. She dominated everyone around her as a way of demonstrating her power and control, to the point that her colleagues viewed her as the most assertive, overbearing leader they had ever known. Her command of facts and figures and her reluctance to lose an argument led to an ascendancy over her cabinet that only served to underscore her power, which she was never reticent to use.[19]

Moreover, Thatcher made it clear that, since she was a conviction politician, she had little use for "internal arguments." In her mind, "thrashing things out was a waste of time, because her own convictions took precedence over any need to accommodate other views, or even to listen to them. She no longer deplored the idea of a P.M. saying 'this is what we're going to do,' rather, she suggested that this was exactly the model of Cabinet activity which she favoured. As she remarked ... 'I don't mind how much my ministers talk – as long as they do what I say.'"[20]

Simply put, she did not tolerate challenges to her own power. For example, Thatcher believed that the strength of the civil service posed an unmistakable threat to her political goals, and she was determined to reduce its influence. "As Mrs. Thatcher saw it, her arrival in power posed an irresistible force against an immovable object, and she set to work with quite unusual energy, as an early priority, to establish her personal dominance."[21] By 1983, she was prepared to take on the Foreign Office, "a department which she held in considerably greater contempt than the rest of Whitehall, but which, until June 1983, she had been able to do considerably less about. Now, as well as sacking the foreign secretary, she moved to try and exert over it greater personal control."[22]

Local government also felt Thatcher's interventionist and centralizing tendencies. She saw local authorities, irrespective of party label, as obstacles blocking the implementation of "Thatcherite" policies of privatization, deregulation, and consumer choice. Thus, the thrust of her government's policies was to transfer responsibility away from local authorities to other agencies, private enterprise, and the central government as a way of reducing their power and strengthening her own.[23]

At the same time, Thatcher's drive to acquire and maintain *power* and control of her political-ideological crusade meant that she was determined to extinguish any internal or external rivals. The growing popularity of the Labour Party provided another justification for her increasing preoccupation with issues of power. She observed that the Labour Party had developed a thirst for power, moderated its image, and gained a lead in the opinion polls. To counteract these developments, she felt that "it was important that I should unify the Party around my authority and vision of Conservatism."[24]

In the cabinet, "it was one of her shortcomings as PM that all around her were close to being pygmies. Over nine years she kept only three cabinet members who were there from the start, and none who might constitute a source of countervailing advice, let alone, power, to her own."[25] An increasingly large band of ex-ministers from Thatcher's cabinets told the same familiar story whose narrative had one central theme: "the way in which Mrs. Thatcher dominate[d] government and arrogate[d] power to herself by rejecting notions of collective responsibility and by telling the Cabinet 'what we are going to do.'"[26]

Thatcher's overwhelming insistence on being the active leader of the government – on leading it, as it were, from outside rather than inside – manifested itself in an extremely competitive style; she had a penchant for talking about the government as though she were not a member of it. "The customary pronoun used by prime ministers when speaking about their own government is 'we'; Thatcher's pronoun was usually 'we' but often 'they.' 'They' were making life difficult for her; 'they' had to be persuaded; 'they' were too concerned with defending the interests of their own departments." The language is not typically British. It is more like that used by American presidents when speaking about Congress. The prime minister thought of her own cabinet as being, in effect, another branch of government whose members were not always amenable.[27] She treated them with barely disguised disdain and condescension; the same way she had treated the two most important rivals for her father's respect and affection, her mother and sister. Her sense of security seems to have been contingent on the success of her efforts to diminish the stature of her competitors both within her personal family (her marriage to an older man who was totally supportive and non-competitive appears to have been unconsciously designed to minimize that problem) and in her public family – the cabinet.

As part of her determination to ensure maximum power and control within a democratic framework, historians of the British cabinet have traced the process whereby Thatcher avoided cabinet discussions of many aspects of policy by formulating it in a cabinet committee dominated by her own supporters.[28] But even then, she would not hesitate to go one step further. Case in point was the preparations for the European Council meeting of 1989 in Madrid. At that time, she persisted in trying to exclude her chancellor and foreign secretary from any consultation about the decisions that might be taken at the summit. Instead, she prepared for the meetings by convening a conference of her private advisers – Charles Powell (her secretary), Brian Griffiths, Alan Walters, and Bernard Ingham – with no elected politicians present at all.[29] "This was the kitchen cabinet which had now replaced the formal cabinet as the forum of influence."[30] Although Golda Meir's "kitchen cabinet" also superseded the formal cabinet in its influence, hers, unlike Thatcher's, consisted of her most senior government ministers as well as the heads of the military services, making it more democratic and egalitarian.

PRAGMATISM

Holding firmly to a set of coherent political beliefs and constantly striving for power and control did not mean that Thatcher was incapable of behaving *pragmatically*. Particularly in her first term, when she was still politically insecure, she was willing to take a more cautious approach than her ideological leanings would have preferred whenever prudence or pragmatism seemed to call for it. "She had to a fine degree the political leader's sense of what would play well with the voters, and, very often, when to compromise with her own instincts, in order to secure the greater political good."[31]

However, Thatcher's pragmatism manifested itself primarily in the realm of foreign policy. Unlike her earlier opposition to the Russian way of life on philosophical and ideological grounds, by 1983, her theme had become one of practicality. As one minister who was closely involved at the time recalled, "'she wasn't interested any more in changing the Russians, or recovering Eastern Europe for the Western way of life. She might detest their system but she didn't even want to talk about anything except the strictly practical.'"[32]

Impressed with Gorbachev after they met at Chequers, the prime ministerial retreat, in 1984, Thatcher told the BBC: "'I can do business with Mr. G.'"[33] But she was willing to support him only if she received something in return, such as a palpably reduced threat to the West, an improved human-rights posture, or a better climate for business and trade. Economic considerations were front and centre. Thus, she was willing to back joint business ventures and provide management training if the Soviets wished, for, in the long run, an improved Russian economy could be beneficial for Britain. As well, it could lead to greater openness and erode the Communist system from within. "Something for nothing had never been a Thatcherite philosophy, in life or in a negotiation."[34] At the same time, she was instrumental in stopping Reagan from cutting a deal with Gorbachev on arms control, largely on ideological grounds.

On occasion, Thatcher was capable of modulating even her strongly held views regarding European integration, an issue on which she remained adamantly opposed both throughout her years as prime minister and after she stepped down from office. For example, on the subject of the special meeting of the European Council held at Strasbourg in November 1989, she observed: "I knew that I would be more or less on my own. I decided to be sweetly reasonable throughout, since there was no point in causing gratuitous offence when I could not secure what I really wanted."[35]

Other examples of Thatcher's *pragmatism* in foreign policy involve Commonwealth matters. She strongly opposed the imposition of economic sanctions against South Africa not only because she felt that they would not work but for other purely pragmatic reasons as well: with some $18 billion invested in South Africa and an annual two-way trade worth $3 billion, Britain had more to lose than any other country.[36] Similarly, although her initial instincts were to oppose the transfer of power in Rhodesia (Zimbabwe), she allowed herself to be guided by the Foreign Office and achieved a peaceful settlement – the Lancaster House agreement.[37] It was clear to Thatcher that the most sensitive aspect of the government's approach to the Rhodesia question related to the transitional arrangements. In her view, both for constitutional and for practical reasons, Britain would have to resume direct authority in Rhodesia until the elections were over, though for as short a period as possible. On 15 November 1979 a bill was introduced to provide for the appointment of a governor and for sanctions to be removed as soon as he arrived in Rhodesia. Christopher Soames accepted the post and the sanctions were lifted upon his arrival.[38]

Pragmatism also dictated British foreign policy in its dealings with Hong Kong. Notwithstanding Thatcher's ideological distaste for the Communist regime in Beijing, the government's "negotiating aim was to exchange sovereignty over the island of Hong Kong in return for continued British administration of the entire colony well into the future. This I knew from my many consultations with politicians and business leaders of Hong Kong was the solution which would suit them best."[39]

Overall, then, Thatcher's policy orientation tended to be more ideological in the realm of domestic policy – on economic and social issues – and more pragmatic in the arena of foreign policy, but this reflected the level of control she could exercise over each domain and in each situation. Thus, in her first term, *pragmatic* concerns did overshadow ideological ones in the domestic arena, and, during the Falklands War, she was more strongly motivated by *ideological* considerations. In general, there is strong evidence of an ideological policy orientation being shaped in a pragmatic direction when Thatcher lacked sufficient leverage to forward her agenda.

PERSONAL VALIDATION

Of the three leaders, Thatcher was the least concerned with the need to be popular or well liked. To her, it was more important that she could dominate and control her cabinet, the civil service, and the House of Commons. Where Thatcher sought validation was primarily in terms of her character. It was important for her to be seen as courageous. She set great store by her own fearlessness, a quality that she seemed to cultivate for its own sake, irrespective of the objectives to which it might be directed. "Conspicuous displays of bravery were one way she would distinguish herself from the men around her and the discredited regime they personified. 'I hope that one quality in which I am not lacking is courage,' she told the Commons on 20 November 1979."[40] As Young notes, "this self-regarding tribute, so expressive of her personal scale of values, was to be heard many times."[41]

Task Orientation

The empirical evidence indicates that Margaret Thatcher, like Indira Gandhi and Golda Meir, was predominantly concerned with implementing goals and little interested in seeking concurrence from the members of her cabinet, or the opposition. Of the 114 items extracted and scored on this subject, an overwhelming 94.4 per cent focused on *goal implementation* and only 5.6 per cent on *process*. In marked contrast, Thatcher's successor, John Major, albeit a disciple of hers, would be far more concerned with maintaining cabinet harmony than implementing far-reaching goals.

GOAL IMPLEMENTATION
Margaret Thatcher was probably unique among twentieth-century British prime ministers in having a policy agenda – a set of views and priorities – that was peculiarly her own, not merely her government's or her party's. She had strong feelings about the substance of policy and had policy aims in a number of fields – taxation, public spending, privatization, law and order, the welfare state, relations with the Soviet Union, defence, and the Common Market, among other things.[42] As Thatcher made abundantly clear, "'I am only in politics to do things' and the 'thing' she most wanted to do was to change economic policy. Politics for her was not about process and concurrence seeking but about the implementation of cherished goals."[43] In a speech delivered to the Small Business Bureau on 8 February 1984, Thatcher declared: "'I came to office with one deliberate intent: to change Britain from a dependent to a self-reliant society; from a give-it-to-me to a do-it-yourself nation; a get-up-and-go instead of a sit-back-and-wait Britain.'"[44]

Thoroughly *goal*-driven, with a certain knowledge of the ends she wanted to achieve, Thatcher was interested not in the "what" but in the "how." It was as if political goals were what she decided, and the role of ministers, civil servants, and advisers was to help implement them. As D. Kavanagh notes: "She [was] impatient at what she regarded as generalities in memos from colleagues and civil servants – even when she agree[d] with them. She want[ed] advice about practical measures which [could] achieve objectives."[45]

Hence, although Thatcher correctly described herself as a "conviction politician," she was also a "substance politician" equally concerned with getting things done. Her prime-ministerial style could not have been more different from that of the majority of her predecessors in that "she possessed a clear, and personal, sense of direction in which she wishe[d] to lead the party. She was in politics, as she often said, not 'to be' but 'to do,' not to preside over Britain's economic decline but to try and reverse that decline. She was by temperament and political instinct an activist."[46]

"If she often [sought] to impose her point of view, it is because she actually ha[d] a point of view – and because her point of view matter[ed] more to her than preserving party unity or enjoying a quiet life."[47]

Investment in Job Performance

Of the 219 items that were extracted and classified on this subject, 97.2 per cent of them demonstrated Thatcher's *tireless* level of commitment to her job as prime minister. In only 6 recorded instances, from the large number of sources consulted, was her behaviour found to be *circumscribed*. For the overwhelming majority of the time, Thatcher simply refused to place any limits on the amount of effort she expended in what she perceived to be the proper exercise of her responsibilities as prime minister.

TIRELESS

It was clear from the outset that Prime Minister Margaret Thatcher was going to be very different from her predecessors. From the first hour she made it clear that she wished to see everything and do everything. At the end of the first week, one of her officials recounted, "'She reads every paper she gets and never fails to write a comment on it. 'Nonsense,' 'Needs more briefing.' 'Do this again.' Are what she's constantly writing.'"[48] Anthony Parsons, her foreign-policy adviser, commented on her hands-on style: "'She would go through everything that came over from the foreign office, all the documentation, with a microscope, and examine every single sentence, and test each sentence for the power of its reasoning and the clarity of expression. Nothing sloppy or woolly would escape her.'"[49]

One observer described the prime minister as "conscientious to a fault. She schooled herself in competence. To say that she worked hard would be an understatement. She worked, she has said herself, 'like a Trojan.'"[50] Thatcher's driving energy came to be admired as one of her most obvious qualities. In 1988 she told Brian Walden, television interviewer and former Labour MP, that she "'never let up for the same reason that anyone who has been successful does not lie back ... success has to be earned ... the moment you lie back you are finished.'" As prime minister she permitted herself little rest, rising early, working late into the night, and rarely taking holidays.[51]

The extent of Thatcher's work ethic comes through in an interview with the *Sunday Daily Mail* on 3 February 1985, in which she described the nature of her commitment as prime minister. "'I've never had more than four or five hours' sleep. Anyway, my life is my work. Some people work to live. I live to work.'"[52] As Thatcher wrote in her biography,

"The hours at No.10 are long. I never minded this. There was an intensity about the job of being Prime Minister which made sleep seem a luxury. In any case, over the years I had trained myself to do with about four hours a night. The Private Office too would often be working till 11 o'clock at night. We were so few that there was no possibility of putting work on someone else's desk. This sort of atmosphere helps to produce a remarkably happy team, as well as a formidably efficient one."[53] She dominated the government by sheer physical stamina, as Charles Powell – who matched her energy level – told Junor.[54]

One of her trips abroad demonstrates just how *tireless* Thatcher was. In December 1984, after her first meeting with Mikhail Gorbachev, she flew to China and Hong Kong to sign the agreement turning over the crown colony back to China in 1997. Already halfway around the world, Thatcher decided to return via Washington so she could talk to Reagan about two pet subjects, the Strategic Defense Initiative (SDI) and Gorbachev. Flying from Hong Kong to Hawaii, she landed at Hickham Field at 3 A.M. to refuel, and decided she wanted to see Pearl Harbor. Back on the plane, she did not sleep but still emerged fresh and alert in Washington. At 11 P.M., having been up for two days, the prime minister arrived at the British Embassy on Massachusetts Avenue. "Right, let's have a briefing meeting," she announced as her aides sagged. At midnight, she ended the briefing and asked for the following day's plan. She was to have breakfast with Vice President George Bush at 9 A.M. "Right," she said. "Then, call me at 6 A.M.; my hairdresser can come at 7 A.M., we'll have another briefing meeting at 8 A.M., and we'll go see the Vice President. Until then, I'd best get to my boxes." With that, she strode up the embassy staircase to her room for two more hours of paperwork, followed by four hours' sleep. After breakfast with Bush the next day, she flew by helicopter to Camp David, in Maryland's Catoctin Mountains, for her meeting with Reagan.[55]

Other aspects of the prime minister's responsibilities also elicited the same energy and determination. Once, in a rare gesture to Anglo-French relations, Thatcher was persuaded to deliver the last part of a speech in French. No doubt remembering the way her predecessor, Edward Heath, had mangled the language, she learned the words phonetically, repeating them over and over again until she had the pronunciation correct. Her coach, the French wife of the deputy under-secretary of the Foreign Office, Robin Renwick, recalled, "'I have never met another adult who had such power of concentration, the absolute will of getting it as perfect as she could.'"[56] No aspect of Thatcher's role as prime minister was allowed to escape her extraordinary work ethic, which had been so profoundly shaped by her strict Methodist upbringing and her strong political and economic agenda.

CLUSTER B: MANAGERIAL STYLE

Cabinet Management Strategy

In the area of cabinet management, Margaret Thatcher was a prime minister determined that the cabinet should follow her lead by implementing her policies. Of the 324 items that were extracted and coded on this subject, 84.6 per cent displayed a management strategy style that involved *advocacy*; 7.1 per cent revealed Thatcher in the role of *arbitrator* and 6.8 per cent in the role of *consensus builder*; and, characteristically, in only five recorded instances (1.5 per cent) was she found to be *uninvolved*.

ADVOCATE

Thatcher had a clear view of her role as prime minister; she saw herself as an activist, rather than as an arbiter or a consensus builder, in cabinet disputes. Nor did she expect to act as a spokesman for a collective cabinet view.[57] Again, it is perhaps not unexpected that an individual with a strong Dominant dimension to her personality would take on such an activist role in cabinet. In fact, without exception, all of Thatcher's biographers have written about the extent of her *advocacy* role as prime minister and her refusal to permit her cabinet colleagues to play a meaningful part in shaping policy issues.

From the beginning, the cabinet was marginalized. It was a rare week of her tenure when it assembled more than once (on Thursdays), compared with twice a week under previous administrations, and general discussions were rare. There were also many fewer standing committees of the cabinet, or ad-hoc one-issue committees, than under previous governments. Thatcher made it clear that she wanted not government by committee but government by herself in concert with selected ministers, who were often brought together only semi-formally under her aegis and outside the structures of the conventional system. This system of ad-hoc groups was a way of maintaining the prime minister's control while at the same time bypassing rival centres of power in the cabinet. Nor did she listen silently before exercising the prerogative of summing up. She was less interested in discussion than in stating her opinions. She loved arguing, but it was often on a point that was far from central to the decision. One minister complained that the battles in cabinet or ad-hoc groups were exhausting and unproductive. "'They almost never result in any clarification, mainly because of her habit of going off at a wild tangent and worrying away for half an hour at a minor detail.'"[58]

The various descriptions and accounts of Thatcher's behaviour suggest that "advocate" may be too anodyne a concept to convey fully the way in which she managed her cabinet; "autocrat" captures the essence of her management style more accurately. "Her style was built on domination. None of her colleagues had experienced a more assertive, even overbearing leader. That has always been her way of doing business, and it became much more pronounced when, after having defeated all her male rivals in 1975, she needed to establish a dependable ascendancy over them."[59] Throughout her tenure, her style certainly contributed to the divisions within the cabinet. This was a product of her strong views on most issues and her propensity to express her views boldly at the outset of a cabinet discussion. When combined with a sometimes-dismissive attitude towards opposing colleagues, it tended to charge the atmosphere and polarize cabinet discussions.[60] "An image repeatedly produced since 1982 is one where Mrs. Thatcher is either alone or surrounded by men, whom she dominates, and sometimes annihilates."[61]

Despite Thatcher's repeated declarations that she would have no time for "internal arguments," she nonetheless seemed to relish them. "All who worked with her knew her to be more argumentative than any leader they had ever known. Her style was entirely adversarial. Even trivial conversations had a habit of turning into a verbal contest."[62] But some of her domineering instincts could be quite "nanny-ish." "She has, for example, while seated at the Cabinet table, ordered the Chancellor of the Exchequer, Nigel Lawson, to get his hair cut."[63]

Thatcher also had a preference for ad-hoc committees where she could dominate and control the proceedings. Equally important was her use of the cabinet not as a policy forum to reach decisions but as an instrument to approve policies that had been formulated elsewhere. When issues were discussed in cabinet, Thatcher made it a point of speaking first, in a domineering and authoritative voice, and of expecting her ministers to support her decisions. Those who chose to be recalcitrant, or even independent in their thinking, could expect Thatcher to be confronting, and then to dump them from cabinet at the earliest opportune moment. As Thatcher herself noted, "'Yes, I do drive through things which I believe in passionately – what else do you expect of a Prime Minister. I am not here just to be chairman, I am here because I believe in things.'"[64]

Thatcher also tended to pre-empt meaningful cabinet discussions by publicly expressing her own views on controversial issues. One anonymous Whitehall figure stated, "'Temporarily we don't have cabinet government, we have a form of presidential government in which she operates like a sovereign in her court.'"[65] Besides meeting with cabinet less frequently than her predecessors had, Thatcher saw to it that fewer papers were distributed to its members so they would be less well informed.[66] She relied more on her policy unit and ad-hoc groups and intervened more in departments.[67] Although several colleagues tried to persuade Thatcher to lighten her load by forming some sort of inner cabinet, as most previous prime ministers had done, she refused to do so. "Her most senior colleagues were precisely those whom she most distrusted."[68]

Other politicians were quick to observe her autocratic trait. Upon hearing from Thatcher, during a London meeting, that she was unwavering on the Falklands issue and would proceed with military action, U.S. Secretary of State Alexander Haig cabled Reagan that Thatcher was not going to be dissuaded from the use of force, that she "'had the bit in her mouth.' What struck the whole U.S. team was the strength of her convictions. She was taking a tougher line than anyone in her cabinet. She was not reacting to advice. She was the driving force.'"[69] When the Thatcher government gave American planes the right to use British airspace and bases en route to bombing Libya, the smallest possible group of ministers decided this matter. Then "the second element of a classic Thatcher maneuver came into play: the presentation to the rest of the cabinet of a fait accompli."[70]

However, the unbending determination and single-mindedness that had won Thatcher widespread admiration during the Falklands War and the miners' strike were a serious disadvantage on the Westland issue in 1984. Disagreement over the future of a failing British helicopter company, Westland, led the then minister of defence, Michael Heseltine, to leave the cabinet in protest against Thatcher's attempts to silence him. Thatcher's determination, previously described as hard-headed and single-minded, translated this time into a far less appealing intolerance of dissent. "'She is vulnerable to charges that her style is autocratic and that she likes to govern with a small group of people with whom she is comfortable,' said a senior aide who thoroughly supported her. 'That's not new. She's never been easy.'"[71]

Comparing Thatcher to previous British prime ministers, A. King notes that Thatcher operated in a totally different manner, either stating her views or letting them be known at the outset. She would interrupt ministers with whom she disagreed and insist on defending her position. "Unlike most prime ministers, she [did] not merely chair cabinet discussions; she was an active participant in them. More often than not, she dominated them."[72] Sometimes her participation involved her leading the argument against any minister who was putting a case, very much in the manner of a chief prosecutor interrogating a defendant. Others were not invited to contribute to the discussion unless they too "wanted to have their heads bitten off. Thus, what began as a method for the most expedient conduct of business ended as a means of her getting her own way, irrespective of the merits or political costs."[73]

During the 1970s, the senior figures of the Conservative Party who belonged both to the Carlton Club and to the cabinet were more or less guaranteed access to privileged information and discussion. In the

1980s this changed. The "'One of Us' [Thatcher's inner circle] increasingly acquired a monopoly of privileged information. Those who were not members, including many cabinet ministers, were often kept in ignorance of central aspects of Conservative Party policy. Cabinet ministers sometimes discovered they were about to be sacked through the activities of a prominent member of the 'One of Us.'"[74]

Thatcher's confrontational style of managing the cabinet meant a resistance to change, irrespective of consequences. In his resignation press conference in 1986, Michael Heseltine complained explicitly about Thatcher's style and performance as prime minister, claiming that she had acted unconstitutionally in refusing him permission to discuss the Westland issue in cabinet and in forbidding him to restate views he had publicly expressed in the past.[75] In the aftermath of another resignation, that of Nigel Lawson, in 1989, the *Mail on Sunday* simply took it for granted that cabinet government had been suspended for a decade and that Thatcher had inaugurated a period of "one-woman rule."[76] One disillusioned cabinet member observed, "'She lost all her best supporters by undermining them and never thanking them or congratulating them for anything they did.'"[77] Her leadership style was indistinguishable from her whole being and with it came an ever-increasing deterioration of trust within her cabinet. She fought with colleagues – eventually dismissing or reshuffling more than one hundred – not just over the management of the economy, the poll tax, and Britain's future in Europe but her whole approach to the business of governing. She saw herself as possessing the conscience and the backbone of the party, and she had no difficulty disregarding the views and sensitivities of her cabinet colleagues.[78]

ARBITRATOR

The issues on which Thatcher was prepared to relinquish her advocacy role and act as *arbitrator* between the competing views of cabinet members were very few. One such issue was the dispute over the level of local-authority funding, on which a sharp difference of opinion existed between the Department of the Environment and the Treasury. Thatcher observed "each side had good arguments." She then chose to sum up the discussion at a ministerial meeting "by rejecting both Nick Ridley's and John Major's preferred options and going for something in the middle, which I thought would still give us a tolerable community charge while not validating the large increase in local authority spending in 1980–90."[79] Even in this relatively rare instance of arbitration, then, Thatcher still managed to inject a dose of advocacy into the situation. Still, very unusually for her, she did go around the table counting heads. In fact, throughout the conflict, she introduced a second weekly meeting to keep the full cabinet informed of developments.[80]

More often than not, however, her role as a consensus builder was imposed upon her. In these instances, it was not that she actively sought to build cabinet support for her government's policies, but rather that she was forced to bend her will and accept an emerging consensus. During the Falklands War, for example, there was growing demand both at home and abroad for a cease-fire after the loss of the *Belgrano* and the *Sheffield*. With the exception of Thatcher, Michael Heseltine, and Quintin Hailsham, who favoured a hard line, everyone in the cabinet believed they had no choice but to keep talking with the Argentinians. Thatcher was obliged to announce that the government had made a constructive response to Peruvian proposals to continue negotiations.[81]

On another occasion, in July 1984, there was a full-scale cabinet showdown when Environment Secretary Patrick Jenkins – supported by Housing Minister Ian Gow – resisted Nigel Lawson's demand for a cut of 600 million pounds in the council-house maintenance program. Gow threatened to resign and Jenkins took his case to cabinet and found enough support to force the prime minister and chancellor – following a half-hour adjournment – to back down.[82] In June 1989, similarly, Thatcher was forced to modify her stance on the subject of setting a date to join the Exchange Rate Mechanism partly as a result of the pressure exerted by two of her senior ministers, Geoffrey Howe and Nigel Lawson.[83] Rather than a consensus builder, therefore, it may be more accurate to view Prime Minister Thatcher as someone who was prepared to accept, albeit grudgingly, a strong cabinet consensus.

Information Management Strategy

DEGREE OF INVOLVEMENT

When it came to obtaining and managing information, Margaret Thatcher was intimately involved in the search for and analysis of policy-relevant data. Of the 260 items that were coded on this topic, 95 per cent demonstrated *high* rather than *low* involvement. In only 5 per cent of the cases recorded was the prime minister content to allow others to search for or analyse relevant policy information.

High

Thatcher's involvement in both the search for and the analysis of policy-relevant data reached a level of intensity that few could remember in a prime minister. When he began to work with her in Downing Street, one of her closest official advisers was pleasantly surprised to discover how well informed she was on the details of monetary policy and "how rare it was for her to stumble or miss a trick."[84] For Question Period, the prime minister was backed by the civil servants who briefed her and tried to anticipate supplementary questions. Thatcher took Question Period seriously and went to enormous lengths to prepare for it.[85]

In her autobiography, Thatcher offers numerous illustrations of a staunch determination to master all the available information necessary to produce informed policy. During the Falklands War, when the question concerning the location of Argentinian vessels in the South Atlantic arose, she noted, "Michael Havers [the attorney general] and I had all the relevant charts laid out on the floor in the parlour at Chequers and did the measurements ourselves."[86] In the face of a number of proposals that had been put forth to end the war, Thatcher noted that "a meeting of the War Cabinet had been arranged for that evening and I spent the rest of that day comparing in detail all the different proposals which had been made up to that point in the diplomacy. The closer I looked the clearer it was that our position was being abandoned and the Falklanders betrayed. I asked the Attorney-General to come to No. 10 and go through them with me."[87]

Thatcher was also anxious to be as well informed as possible on the broader issues in foreign policy. For instance, she was concerned with the strategy Britain should pursue towards the Soviet Union over the years ahead. "I had been giving a good deal of thought to this matter and had discussed it with the experts at a Chequers seminar. I began by saying that we had to make the most accurate assessment of the Soviet system and the Soviet leadership – there was plenty of evidence available about both subjects – so as to establish a realistic relationship: whatever we thought of them, we all had to live on the same planet."[88] She had another seminar at Chequers to clarify thinking on tactics towards South Africa. Apart from cabinet ministers Geoffrey Howe, Malcolm Rifkind, and Paul Channon, and Treasury official Ian Stewart, a number of businessmen, academics, and one or two interested and well-informed MPs attended.[89]

Low
There were singularly few examples where Thatcher manifested a low level of involvement, in sharp contrast with the above. She herself cited an instance in which she was prepared to allow the Chancellor of the Exchequer, who, in her view, had the required seniority and experience, to supervise the policy work. "Looking back, this arrangement was successful in one of its aims – that of reducing the burden on me."[90] But the evidence points overwhelmingly to a very high level of involvement on her part, no matter how minute the details concerned.

SOURCES OF INFORMATION
Also characteristic of Thatcher's leadership style was her determination to control policy by ensuring that the information she needed, as well as

the decisions that resulted, were far from exclusively provided by the cabinet but rather flowed primarily through small ad-hoc groups of ministers or her own politically appointed advisers. Twice as much of her documented leadership behaviour – 65.7 per cent of the 271 extracted and coded items – fell into this category, while reliance solely on the cabinet accounted for only one-third of the total amount, 34.3 per cent. Moreover, the vast majority of incidents testifying to Thatcher's reliance on her ministers were drawn from her autobiography, which may include some bias on her part to inflate the extent of her cooperation with cabinet.

Independent

Prime Minister Thatcher strongly preferred to search out information from a variety of sources. These tended to be ad-hoc committees, individual ministers, senior civil servants, and politically appointed advisers. Thatcher's private office became a major source of information for her. It consisted of six fairly senior civil servants who helped with official speeches and parliamentary business and liaised between the prime minister and departmental ministers. In 1970 Thatcher's predecessor, Edward Heath, had established the Central Policy Review Staff (CPRS) to deal with long-term strategy matters and provide briefs for the cabinet as a whole. Thatcher did not approve of this approach and abolished it after her election victory in 1983 – an example of her dislike for so-called professional advice that purported to be above party politics. She decided instead to strengthen the policy unit, which would now consist of eight or nine political advisers, supplemented later by some CPRS members.[91] The unit contributed information and advice on policy, liaised with the party, and helped with speechwriting. Its mandate was to clarify what it was that the government was trying to accomplish, and then to check whether the necessary actions looked likely to work.[92]

Among Thatcher's personal advisers were her press officer and her private parliamentary assistant, as well as an outer circle of unofficial associates who included her speechwriter, Ronald Millar, and her image consultants and publicity gurus, Gordon Reece and Tim Bell. Woodrow Wyatt offered flattery and encouragement; Thatcher valued Wyatt's experience of Fleet Street, the Labour Party, and the trade unions. Other voices, to whom she listened for advice on foreign policy, included Hugh Thomas, the historian of Cuba and the Spanish Civil War; Robert Conquest, the historian of Stalin's purges; and Norman Stone, historian of modern Germany and Eastern Europe. She had a wide range of contacts drawn from different walks of life, from university professors to her hairdresser, whom she encouraged to give her alternative advice. This was one way she tried to avoid becoming the prisoner of Whitehall, and one of the reasons she so often had an advantage over her ministers. She had an extraordinary network of informers who kept her abreast of where she could expect opposition to her policies, and how they were being received among the public. The problem was that her confidants were almost all committed "Thatcherites" who tended, especially as she grew more powerful, to tell her only what she wanted to hear.[93] In view of the range of the prime minister's contacts and her avidity for information, it is understandable that her level of involvement with *independent* sources ranked high.

Given the variety of information available to her, dealing with the prime minister could be quite an exhausting task. "She was always formidably well-briefed from a variety of different sources – the official departmental brief, another from the policy unit, and often a third in her handbag whose origin the unfortunate minister never quite knew, which she would produce triumphantly to catch him out."[94] But the diversity of information sources served political purposes as well. She succeeded in making the position of Nigel Lawson, her chancellor of the exchequer, untenable by openly preferring the advice of her private adviser Alan Walters. She did much the same in foreign policy, listening to Charles Powell, her private secretary, who was a junior diplomat on loan from the Foreign Office to Downing Street, rather than to Geoffrey Howe, her foreign secretary, and the Foreign Office.[95] Indeed, Thatcher's reliance on Powell's non-official foreign-policy advice sometimes had significant policy consequences. Powell drafted a speech that Thatcher delivered in Bruges in September 1988, setting out the government's view of its relations with the European Community. "Its forceful statement of British sovereignty offended many in the Foreign Office, which [was] more communautaire."[96] Moreover, it did little to enhance Thatcher's standing among the members of the European Community.

Thatcher herself provides ample evidence in her autobiography that she often preferred to rely on her own private advisers rather than senior cabinet officials and their respective staffs. She noted, "Percy Cradock (my Special Adviser on security matters), Charles Powell and I drafted and redrafted the arguments I would use with President Reagan. These must be logically coherent, persuasive, crisp, and not too technical."[97] No mention is made of any input from the foreign secretary or the Foreign Office. The same dynamic also operated in Thatcher's conduct of economic policy. She wrote that "tension between myself and Nigel Lawson arose over the independent economic advice that I was receiving from Alan Walters. Alan had returned to No. 10 in May 1989. I have already described his contribution to the 'Madrid conditions' for ERM entry. While the Treasury, thoroughly alarmed by the inflationary effects of Nigel's policy of shadowing the ERM, kept urging ever higher interest rates, Alan now drew my attention to the danger that excessively high interest rates might drive the economy into recession."[98] In the struggle between Lawson, her cabinet appointee, and Walters, her private adviser, for the economic heart and soul of Margaret Thatcher, it was Lawson who would lose out and tender his resignation.

Even a matter as central to her future as her re-election was left largely in the hands of her independent advisers. In 1987 Thatcher ordered her close associate Tim Bell to begin making adjustments to the official campaign, but not to tell anyone. In the meantime, she would start the politicking. This kind of secretiveness was increasingly common in her later years as prime minister. "The stealth stemmed from her private feelings about her ministers and her justifiable concern about where and when certain information was revealed. But setting up what was essentially a clandestine, back-channel political campaign carried furtiveness to a new level."[99]

Ministers/Civil Servants

Examples of Thatcher's reliance upon information from her cabinet in the formulation of policy are drawn largely from her autobiography. In the run-up to the 1983 elections, Thatcher chose to draft the party manifesto. She then proceeded to write to cabinet ministers requesting them to prepare papers on what had been achieved, what was under way, and what still needed to be done. She received most of these papers just before Christmas and spent the holidays reading them.[100] Occasionally, Thatcher even gave credit to her ministers for their assistance. She viewed herself generally as "among the best briefed heads of government on these occasions – partly because I always did my homework and partly because I had a truly superb official team to help me. Perhaps the mainstay of this was David Williamson, who came from the Ministry of Agriculture to the key European policy role in the Cabinet office."[101] Still, overall, Thatcher's management style – be it with respect to the cabinet or to information relevant to her policy formulation – was unmistakably hands-on.

CLUSTER C: INTERPERSONAL STYLE

Relations with Senior Civil Servants and Personal Staff

DEGREE OF INVOLVEMENT

The evidence drawn from biographies of Margaret Thatcher is uniform in its portrayal of her as deeply involved with all levels of government personnel. Indeed, of the 207 items that were extracted and coded on the level of Thatcher's interactions with aides and members of other branches of government with whom she worked, virtually all were characterized by *high* involvement.

High

Unlike most prime ministers, Thatcher was not seen in Whitehall as a remote figure. "Her presence [wa]s all-pervasive ... from the moment she arrived in Number 10, she was determined to interest herself in the selection of top civil servants, to make her own enquiries about candidates for promotion and to be prepared to question, even on occasion to reject, the Senior Appointments Selection Committee recommendations (SASC). She showed a similar interest in appointments to the chairmanships of nationalized industries."[102] However, the prime minister's interest in the structure of government was minimal. What interested her was working with and through individuals. Throughout her years in office, she established close relationships with private secretaries and other officials in her office.[103]

TYPE OF INVOLVEMENT

Of the 127 items extracted and scored on the type of involvement, 44.1 per cent were categorized as *demanding/domineering*, 24.4 per cent as *collegial/solicitous*, 19.7 per cent as *polite/formal*, 7.8 per cent as *attention-seeking/seductive*, and 3.9 per cent as *manipulative/exploitative*.

Demanding/domineering

Even before Thatcher became prime minister, her attitude towards the civil service was apparent. As Sir William Pile, the permanent undersecretary at the Department of Education, noted: "'Within the first ten minutes of her arrival she uncovered two things to us: one, an innate wariness of the civil service, quite possibly even a distrust; and secondly, a page from an exercise book with eighteen things she wanted done that day.'"[104]

In her years as prime minister, Thatcher's relationships with government personnel took on even more of a *demanding, domineering* quality. Given the strength of the Dominant dimension of Thatcher's personality profile as measured in the period before she became prime minister, these findings are not unexpected. As a number of her biographers have attested, her style was built on the twin pillars of domination and the inducement of fear in others, cemented with a cruel wit designed to humiliate.[105] The initiation of fear and humiliation, as well as the tactical use of wit, were important weapons that Thatcher maintained in her arsenal for control and domination purposes. "Carefully controlled displays of anger and disdain, together with her own super-ordinate position as a party leader and prime minister, [were] used to wrong-foot ministers and civil servants, to bully them, on occasion to humiliate them. In this respect ... her leadership style [was] faintly reminiscent of Lyndon Johnson's."[106] In one instance, Thatcher, after consulting with various Swiss bankers, came storming home "to charge the Deputy Governor [of the Bank of England], Eddie George ... with rank incompetence. When Richardson [the governor] returned he got 'a bawling out' ... which left him shaken and furious.'"[107] In the same vein, although she appointed Francis Pym as foreign secretary on the resignation of Lord Carrington, privately, it became well known that she had a poor opinion of him. The more public humiliations came later. During the 1983 election campaign, Thatcher interrupted Pym at a press conference to correct his view that the sovereignty of the Falklands was negotiable. But she did not correct Cecil Parkinson when, introducing those present at another conference, he omitted to acknowledge the presence of the foreign secretary.[108] As well, "her wit ... was often cruel, and she [was] inclined, if not exactly to be overbearing, to make some of her questioners the butts of her jokes and briskness."[109]

Collegial/solicitous

If Thatcher frequently exhibited qualities of abrasiveness, aggression, and self-assertion in her dealings with many of her colleagues whom she had branded as adversaries, she could also exhibit great warmth with those whom she decided were her trusty lieutenants. She demonstrated a most assiduous attention to the details of the lives of those who worked directly for her: "whether they missed a meal, whether their wives had recovered from flu, whether their children had passed exams."[110] With her position as prime minister came police protection. "Margaret quickly won enormous affection from her detectives from the Special Branch, because she was so considerate. In all the years that she ... had protection – and official drivers – not one ... asked for a transfer."[111]

Thatcher's biographers also note this remarkable attention and collegiality to her staff. "Throughout her time as prime minister she took care to establish the strongest bond with each cohort of private secretaries and other officials, as they came forward into her personal service."[112] With cabinet colleagues who found themselves in personal difficulty, she was sometimes amazingly loyal and supportive, even backing those accused of shoplifting and homosexual cruising.[113] After her defeat as party leader, Thatcher had a brief audience with the queen and returned to No. 10 to have a quick drink with members of her staff. "I was suddenly conscious that they too had their futures to think about, and I found myself now and later comforting them almost as much as they sought to comfort me."[114] This pattern of unswerving support and care of those who were "one of us" as opposed to those whom she designated as "one of them" is best explained by her black-white view of the world; colleagues were either all good or all bad. Those who served her loyally and never challenged her were entitled to her unstinting support, those who questioned and opposed her were the

enemy who deserved to be savaged. As already noted, this pattern of
"splitting," in which the good and bad parts of an individual are split
off instead of integrated, was the way in which Thatcher had dealt with
her parents as a child – her father was idealized as the good parent,
while her mother was the bad one.[115]

Polite/formal

Stereotypical perhaps for a British leader, the evidence demonstrates that
Thatcher was almost as *polite* as she was collegial. Illustrative of her politeness and good manners occurred just after she had been chosen prime
minister. She herself recounted that "by about 11 p.m. the list of Cabinet
was complete and had been approved by the Queen. I went upstairs to
thank No. 10 telephonists who had had a busy time arranging all the appointments for the following day. Then I was driven home."[116]

Attention-seeking/seductive

As attentive as she was to her staff, Thatcher believed in reciprocity, especially from men – but only those whom she liked and trusted.
Thatcher liked Cecil Parkinson because he was a committed "Thatcherite," loyal to her, organized, and energetic. He was also good-looking
and raffishly charming. No one in government knew how to handle
Thatcher as well as Parkinson, who, after the death of Airey Neave, became one of her closest political confidants, part of the very select circle
of politicians invited regularly for weekends at Chequers. Parkinson
knew how to jolly and cajole her, get her attention with political detail
or gossip, and flatter her as a woman. Francis Pym acknowledged that,
because she had a man's mind and held a man's job, he had always
treated Thatcher as a man. Pym added that his wife had told him that if
he had treated Thatcher as a woman he would not have lost his job.[117]

But there was another side as well to Thatcher's attention-seeking behaviour – her capacity to allure. Visitors calling on her for the first time
attested to the sex appeal she could project in a private conversation.
"She was thought by her ministers to have a particular weakness for
handsome men of a certain age, who stood up straight and wore well-
cut suits."[118] A newspaper once commented on the "sexy" voice she
had developed on a radio program. In fact, this was the result of a cold.
Shortly afterwards, when Jim Prior was sitting next to her, he said,
"'Margaret, I read in my paper that you have developed a sexy voice.'
Back came her reply: 'What makes you think I wasn't sexy before?'"[119]

Manipulative/exploitative

Not only was Thatcher extremely domineering in her relationships with
senior civil servants, but occasionally her behaviour crossed the line and

became *manipulative* or *exploitive*. "She made a practice of asking officials 'detailed numerical, irrelevant questions,' which seemed to be designed to catch them out; or forked questions, which wrong-footed them whichever way they answered. She had an unsettling way of putting them on the defensive all the time."[120] For example, the local Greater London Council (GLC) councillor for Finchley, Neville Beale, had intended to retire in 1985. But the last thing Thatcher wanted was a by-election in Finchley that would have turned into a media circus and a referendum on her own performance. She summoned Beale to a private lunch and alternatively charmed and bullied him until he promised to stay on.[121]

Relations with the Party

CAUCUS

Of the 186 items coded for Thatcher's relations with the Conservative caucus, 80.6 per cent were characterized as *competitive/oppositional* and 9.2 per cent as *controlling/overbearing*. She behaved in a *cooperative/harmonious* fashion 7.5 per cent of the time and was *uninvolved* only 2.8 per cent of the time.

Competitive/oppositional

During her first administration, Thatcher's personal approval rating slumped to 31 per cent. Her own Tories began to whisper "coup." Thatcher picked up the whispers but held firm. "'I had no second thoughts. None,' she recalled later. 'I never had any doubts that our policies were right.'"[122] The opinions of the members of caucus were irrelevant.

For the prime minister and the cabinet, carrying Parliament meant effectively carrying their party's backbenchers. But Thatcher was not always successful. The prime minister's first government (1979–83) faced significant backbench revolts on the proposed closed-shop amendment in the employment bill in 1980 and on unemployment-benefit cuts in 1981; and, in 1981 as well, it was defeated on proposed changes in immigration rules and had to withdraw a proposal to impose a ceiling on local rates in the face of opposition within the Conservative Party. Dissent increased in the 1983 Parliament, partly because of the Conservatives' larger majority, which enabled rebels to dissent without jeopardizing the government. Thatcher was rebuffed again, largely by her own backbenchers over the choice of speaker in 1983. In July 1985 the government was nearly defeated in the Commons over a vote to reduce the lord chancellor's salary. And in April 1986 the government's closed-shop bill was defeated.

A remarkable example of backbench influence on the prime minister was seen in the resignation of Leon Brittan from Trade and Industry in the aftermath of the Westland affair. Thatcher had rebuffed suggestions that he resign and made it clear that he enjoyed her full confidence. But it was vigorous criticism of him by Tory backbenchers which convinced Brittan and Thatcher that he no longer enjoyed the confidence of the party in Parliament.[123]

While relations between Thatcher and her caucus were clearly *competitive*, then, this did not always translate into her ability to impose her will. The final chapter in her role as prime minister – marked by both the leadership challenge and the lack of caucus support for her bid to retain her job – attests to this fact.

Controlling/overbearing

Thatcher could also be *controlling* and *overbearing* in her relations with caucus. She was interested in beating not only Labour opponents but also senior figures within her own party who had been marked down as "not one of us." All in all, it seems that "her contest was with men generally, not just men on the opposition benches."[124]

The same combative and *overbearing* style was often evident in Thatcher's relations with her cabinet. Her dislike for internal discussions and debate was well known, and when, in her view, there was too much of it, she fired or moved everyone in the cabinet except Francis Pym. She was convinced that she needed a more staunch and dependable inner circle. "Maggie's Monday Massacre" was how the pro-Tory *Sun* headlined the purge that followed the first election.[125] Pym himself was dispatched a day after the second election for suggesting that the prime minister consider a "balanced ticket" – meaning a less hard-line approach.[126] Norman Tebbit, who had been party chairman, returned to private life the day after the third election in 1986, when Thatcher refused to give him a cabinet post.[127] John Biffen, who had been leader of the House of Commons, was also sacked at the same time for repeating Pym's pre-election advice to Thatcher. "'Squashed like flies' was Biffen's description of how cabinet members felt after she was finished with them."[128] He went on to observe: "'What I found extraordinary is how much she resents having to deal with the modest element of opposition that exists.'" Coming from a pre-Thatcher "Thatcherite" who was not a potential rival, Biffen's criticism foreshadowed rising annoyance among Tories with their increasingly autocratic leader, regardless of her electoral successes.[129] In the aftermath of the 1989 election, the defence minister, George Younger, a ten-year cabinet veteran, asked to be dropped, for, as an aide explained, "'he was tired of Mrs. Thatcher's strident, ideology-ridden rigidity.'"[130]

Cooperative/harmonious

While Thatcher displayed predominantly oppositional traits in dealing with her caucus, some evidence of non-adversarial relations also exist, if only towards backbenchers. In her autobiography, Thatcher notes that during the summer and autumn of 1989, there was a growth of political discontent within the Conservative Party, particularly over the economy, high interest rates, and her approach to the European Community. She responded in the following way. "I increased the amount of time set aside in my diary for meeting back-benchers. I made more frequent visits to that fount of gossip, the Commons tea-room. I also began regular meetings with groups of back-benchers, usually recruited according to region, so as to ensure a wide spectrum of views. At these meetings, which usually took place in my room in the House, I would ask everyone around the table to speak their mind and then come in at the end to answer point by point. There was frank speaking on both sides – on one occasion a back-bencher told me it was time for me to go. I may have not complied, but I listened."[131]

Uninvolved

As a domineering, activist leader of her caucus, Thatcher was almost never *uninvolved*. But, by the spring of 1988, she had had parliamentary majorities of more than a hundred seats for five years. No longer feeling she had to court the members of her party, she began to spend less and less time with her backbenchers.[132]

EXTRA-PARLIAMENTARY PARTY ORGANIZATION

Unlike her dealings with the caucus, Thatcher's behaviour vis-à-vis the extra-parliamentary party organization was somewhat more evenly balanced between cooperative and competitive. Of the 47 items that were coded, 49 per cent revealed the prime minister to be *competitive/oppositional* while 46.8 per cent showed her as *cooperative/harmonious* and 4.2 per cent as *controlling/overbearing*. There were no examples of her behaving in an *uninvolved* manner.

Competitive/oppositional

As the evidence suggests, relations between Thatcher and the rank-and-file of the Conservative Party were not always harmonious. Nor were some of her colleagues above attempting to use Conservative Party functions as a platform to challenge her authority. Michael Heseltine routinely managed to rouse the audience at the annual conference to peaks of ecstasy, especially in his opposition to Thatcher's policy for demolishing the power of local government.[133] At the annual conference at Blackpool in 1981, Thatcher later wrote, "I witnessed what seemed to be a concerted attempt to swing the Party against the government's policies both in the conference hall and at the fringe meetings outside."[134] Two of her ministers, Nigel Lawson and Geoffrey Howe, ably rebuffed the backbench "wets" and "strengthened the government's moral authority."[135]

But this ambivalent and frequently antagonistic relationship continued throughout Thatcher's tenure in office. For example, in preparation for the 1987 election campaign, some researchers who had been hired by the party found that the public's opinion of the government was markedly lower than it had been. In their view, this was a problem not so much for conservatism as for the leader of the Conservative Party. Most disturbing from Thatcher's perspective was that the report came with the endorsement of the Conservative central office, which represented the views of the party rank and file.[136]

Cooperative/harmonious

Thatcher's relations with the party's grass roots were also almost equally *cooperative* and *harmonious*. Like many local constituency Conservative Party officers, who were drawn from the professions and small business, Thatcher was self-made and did not come from one of the traditional Tory business interests, land, or a political family. Her open dislike of direct taxation, public spending, and much of the public sector and trade unions, as well as her protective attitude towards homeowners and investors and her sympathy for farmers, small businesses, and the forces of law and order, were all favourite Tory themes, endearing her to Conservatives in general. She was also more willing to allocate political honours to party workers than Heath, who had been particularly niggardly in this regard.[137]

The welcome that Thatcher received from the Scottish Conservative Party conference – an event she always enjoyed – in Perth in May 1982 provides a good example of the *harmonious* relationship that existed between her and the Conservative Party,[138] as does the annual Conservative Party conference in 1983 at Blackpool. On that occasion, former prime minister Heath was sharply critical of Thatcher's economic policies, and he was quietly supported by fourteen of the leading members of the Tory class of 1979. In her speech to the conference, Thatcher indicated that she would not print money to buy illusory jobs at the cost of further inflation. "She ... got her usual rapturous reception. Not for the first or last time, the party faithful at conference backed her against the parliamentary doubters."[139]

But not everyone in the party appreciated the warm reception that Thatcher regularly received from the rank and file. Although William Whitelaw believed that "Thatcherism was ... Conservatism and the party's future was entirely bound up with the lady," a significant point of difference was their attitude towards the Conservative Party conference. For Thatcher, "these were the grass-roots Tories with instincts like hers." Whitelaw, on the other hand, detested them, and mistrusted the adulation the conference regularly gave the leader as fostering a cult of personality.[140] Hence, one can argue that the evidence points to a split picture, of Thatcher being strongly affirmed by the party base and the conservative man and woman on the street while frequently antagonizing members of the caucus.

Controlling/overbearing

Thatcher rarely behaved in a *controlling/overbearing* fashion with the Conservative Party organization, which was the strongest bulwark of her support. However, on a few occasions, she did target members who had been marked down as "not one of us" in an overbearing manner.[141]

Relations with Opposition Parties

Thatcher's relations with the Labour and Liberal-Democratic parties were generally unpleasant, and it is not difficult to see why, given her antagonistic nature. Of the 132 items that were extracted and coded on this subject, 75.8 per cent showed her to be *competitive/oppositional* while 20.5 per cent revealed her as *controlling/overbearing*. Only 3 per cent of her dealings with the opposition were *cooperative/harmonious*.

COMPETITIVE/OPPOSITIONAL

Given the scope of Thatcher's ideological ambitions, it was evident from the start of her tenure that the House of Commons and the political arena in general would be the scene of many battles. As noted earlier, the prime minister was determined to alter the social and economic face of Britain and that meant curbing the power of the trade unions and undermining support for the Labour Party. "If the National Union of Mineworkers was the last enemy, the right of workers to be trade unionists at all was the last sacred cow. Each was sent to the slaughterhouse with a firmness of purpose that owed a lot, and in one case everything, to the adamantine personal opinions of the leader herself."[142] The prime minister's attitude was worse than uncompromising. The general secretary of the Trades Union Congress (TUC) found it "profoundly insulting." In effect, what she told him was that trade-union members could not be trusted with national secrets. Their union membership, in other words, was not compatible with their patriotic duty.[143]

While campaigning for re-election in 1983, "she summoned her people to the colours for battle against not merely the enemy, but the Anti-Christ."[144] For Thatcher, the Labour Party was the devil incarnate. During the campaign, the prime minister covered the government's weakest flank – unemployment – by counter-attacking Labour's record in the 1970s. "'In the end, Labour always runs away,' she jeered in her speech ... They are running away from the need to defend their country ... they are fleeing from the long overdue reform of the trade unions ... above all Labour is running away from the true challenge of unemployment.'"[145]

The prime minister justified the idea of confrontation with trade unionists by noting that, even if the vast majority were decent and hard-working, some were not. She told journalist Jimmy Young, "'Jimmy, some of the unions are confronting the British people. They are confronting the sick, they are confronting the old, they are confronting the children. I am prepared to take on anyone who is confronting those, who is confronting the law of the land, and who is confronting the essential liberties of the country ... If someone is confronting our essential liberties, if someone is inflicting injury, harm or damage on the sick, by God I'll confront them.'"[146]

Understandably, the unions were incensed. "'A major challenge to the existing rights of workers and their unions,' said trades union congress (TUC) General Secretary, Len Murray. But Mrs. Thatcher was ready for a fight. During a heated House of Commons debate, she insisted that 'we have an absolute mandate for these proposals,'" which featured a ban on secondary (or "sympathy") picketing, an effort to break up the closed shop, and encouragement to use secret ballots in union voting. "'They are what the people want ... It is largely because of these proposals that we got more support than ever [in the election of May 1979] from members of trade unions.'"[147]

But the Labour Party and the trade unions were not the only recipients of her fire. The Liberal Party also felt the sting of Thatcher's tongue. In her autobiography, Thatcher states that "the Leader of the Liberal Party, David Steel, accused [her] of 'jingo-ism.' How remote politicians can seem at these times of crisis: neither the audience nor the nation would fall into the same trap of characterizing determination to secure justice and the country's honour in terms like that."[148]

CONTROLLING/OVERBEARING

Frequently, Thatcher's combative style would become an end as well as a means. "In her dealings with the opposition, Mrs. Thatcher was a fighting speaker, who always liked to win, preferably leaving a corpse rather than taking hostages. She did not lose this relish for battle. At difficult times, the little triumphs it made available were a pleasurable distraction. Michael Foot, the Labour leader at this time [1981] gave her opportunities she did not miss."[149]

During a speech, delivered by Thatcher at the Carleton Club in November 1984, she equated the striking miners – and the hard left in general – with Libyan and Palestinian terrorists. "'We must never give in,' she warned, 'to the oldest and least democratic trick of all – the coercion of the many by the ruthless and manipulating few ... The concept of fair play must not be used to allow the minority to overbear the tolerant majority.'"[150]

COOPERATIVE/HARMONIOUS

Given how competitive and dominating Thatcher was with her own party, it is hardly surprising that she exhibited so little *cooperative* behaviour with the opposition. But there was the occasional effort on her part. After she became prime minister in 1979, she hailed her victory as a "watershed election" that marked a decisive rejection of "the all-powerful corporatist state." Yet she was careful not to be provocative in her dealings with the Labour Party, going out of her way to stress that "a strong and responsible trade union movement must play a large part in our economic recovery."[151] After Thatcher, faced with the potential for a massive industrial strike led by the miners' union, backed down on the National Coal Board's plan to close twenty-three pits in 1981, Labour leader Michael Foot crowed over the miners' victory and offered to take the prime minister out to dinner "every time she turns." To this, Thatcher amicably responded in a joking manner: "Doubtless he will not need reminding that on occasion it is a lady's prerogative to say 'No.'"[152]

Relations with the Media

With regard to the press, Thatcher enjoyed a good relationship – significantly more so than with the television networks, especially the BBC. Of the 265 items that were extracted and coded on this subject, she behaved in an *open, accessible,* and *friendly* fashion with reporters and journalists 78.8 per cent of the time. For the remaining 21.2 per cent, she was *closed, inaccessible,* and *unfriendly,* a percentage that reflected her tense relations with the television networks.

OPEN/ACCESSIBLE/FRIENDLY

Notwithstanding her fractious nature, Thatcher always had a good press. It was a feature, interrupted only once, of her entire reign as prime minister, and a blessing that no other British leader in the era of modern communications had enjoyed to the same extent.[153] "A minister who once drew her into a discussion of the press, and remarked on how favourable it had been, told of her reaction. She showed a guileless lack of surprise. 'That's because I've been so kind to them,' she remarked. And this was undoubtedly the case. In the first term, she offered knighthoods to the editors of the *Sun*, the *Sunday Express*, and the *Daily Mail*."[154]

In the aftermath of the Falklands victory, Thatcher was the first prime minister to appear on the cover of a woman's magazine. Both the image and her interview emphasized her softness. In July 1984 she achieved another first, when she appeared as the prime minister on a TV chat show, where she sat next to Barry Manilow, talked to host Michael Aspel about the birth of his twins, and laughed at an impression of her given by Janet Brown.[155] Part attention seeking, part strategic calculation, Thatcher's love affair with the press was pivotal in her conduct of politics.

The press was seen as such a source of support for the Thatcher government that "it was agreed that I would use press interviews as the main platform for me to set out my case. So on Thursday evening (15 November) I was interviewed by Michael Jones of the *Sunday Times* and Charles Moore of the *Sunday Telegraph*. Nor did I back away from the European issue that Geoffrey's speech had reopened. Indeed, I said that a referendum would be necessary before there was any question of our having a single currency."[156] She knew that she would face no hostile questioners.

CLOSED/INACCESSIBLE/UNFRIENDLY

But television was more of a problem than the print media for Thatcher, partly because it did not have owners who could be cultivated. With television, therefore, Conservative tactics were more belligerent than with the press. Some carrots were offered, to be sure, but sticks were more in evidence. "Attacking television programs that offended government sensibilities, while not the exclusive propensity of this Government, was one which it indulged with a growing ruthlessness. Thatcher's direct criticisms may have been relatively infrequent, but there was an undertow of impatience when television failed to see its role as being precisely concordant with government policy, or lapsed from its duties in the ideological struggle."[157]

Thatcher was particularly closed-minded on the topic of what issues should fall under the rubric of national security. Her intolerance was best represented by her fulminations against the BBC for its interviews with Argentinian widows during the Falklands War, its criticism of her for allowing the United States to bomb Libya from British bases, and its interviews with suspected IRA members.[158] She abruptly fired a well-regarded BBC director who had been less than five years in the post. It was a surprising event that seemed to indicate a cruder degree of pressure on the BBC than any previous government had dreamed of. Even the Conservative *Sunday Telegraph* was moved to warn "'the Tory vendetta against the BBC is real and dangerous.'"[159]

Indicative of Thatcher's expectation that the media's role was to be a spokesman for the government was her comment during the Falklands War that "a remark of mine was misinterpreted, sometimes willfully. After Defence Secretary John Nott had made his statement, journalists tried to ask questions. 'What happens next, Mr. Nott? Are we going to declare war on Argentina, Mrs. Thatcher?' It seemed as if they preferred to press us on these issues rather than to report news that would raise the nation's spirits and give the Falklanders new heart. I was irritated and intervened to stop them: 'Just rejoice at that news and congratulate our forces and the marines ... Rejoice.'"[160]

Relations with the Public

All Thatcher's efforts with the media were undertaken to allow her to reach her target audience – the British public. As a politician with a clear agenda that she was determined to sell to the people, the prime minister undeniably preferred to engage directly with the public rather than rely on government officials to articulate or defend government policies. Of the 106 items that were extracted and coded on this subject, 91.5 per cent showed Thatcher to be *active* rather than *passive* in her dealings with the public in its various manifestations.

ACTIVE

When eighteen British soldiers were killed in County Down, Northern Ireland, in August 1979, Thatcher not only condemned the attacks, but went to Northern Ireland to support the troops and visit some of the victims of previous IRA bombs in hospital.[161] During the Falklands War, Thatcher described how she "wrote personally to the families of the soldiers who had died; such letters are not easy to write. There were, alas, to be many more of them during my time in office."[162] Her visits to the troops and her concern for the families of dead soldiers is strikingly similar to the behaviour of both Gandhi and Meir. As mothers of sons, all three women seemed very moved by the loss of young lives. It was also in the late 1980s that Thatcher began to visit the scenes of disasters. Journalists noted her tendency to arrive at such places before members of the royal family.[163] As genuinely sympathetic and concerned as the prime minister was, some element of political calculation may also have been part of the equation.

At the end of March 1981, no fewer than 364 leading economists published a statement that took issue with the government's policy. Thatcher noted that "Samuel Brittan of the *Financial Times* defended us, and so did Professor Patrick Minford from Liverpool University, who wrote to *The Times* answering the 364: I in turn wrote to congratulate him on his brilliant defence of the Government's approach."[164]

On occasion, the vote-getting potential of Thatcher's *active* involvement with the public was openly acknowledged. During a political tour of the English countryside, Thatcher was distressed over the lack of photo opportunities. She proceeded to take matters into her own hands. "That afternoon on our way back from the West Country I had the coach stop at a farm shop, plentifully stocked with bacon, chutney and cream. The following press coaches stopped too and we all piled into the shop. I bought cream and everyone seemed to follow suit. This, I felt, had been my personal contribution to the rural economy; perhaps we might even get some reasonable television film footage at last."[165]

Thatcher proved herself to be particularly effective communicating with the public in her travels abroad. During a G–7 world leaders' summit in Tokyo, Geoffrey Howe recalled: "'There we were, amongst these great established figures – [Valéry] Giscard [d'Estaing], [Helmut] Schmidt, [Jimmy] Carter ... I noticed that the curiosity of the large Japanese audience ... who were amazed to see a woman assuming primacy in male company, was enormous. She spoke last in the statements that they all made to the press conference, and was the only one to do it without notes, achieving a spontaneity and a sparkle that justified the curiosity with which she was first greeted.'"[166] Among Africans who expected to meet a "viperish monstrosity," Thatcher had a quite different effect, "particularly pleas[ing] them by her directness, whether sweeping fearlessly into crowds or describing candidly her intentions."[167] It can be confidently stated that her openness to the public as well as her magnetism did not limit itself to domestic audiences.

PASSIVE

There were a few instances, however, in which Thatcher exhibited a less engaged and enthusiastic stance vis-à-vis the public. She did not enjoy mixing with constituents and "pressing the flesh."[168] During election campaigns, the invariable straggle of demonstrators chanting "Maggie out" meant that she was kept well away from any contact with hostile voters.[169] On a trip to Wales in 1987, she was upset by the angry crowds and exclaimed, "'Oh what dreadful people. We are really wasting our time.'"[170]

THE RELATIONSHIP BETWEEN PERSONALITY
PROFILE AND LEADERSHIP STYLE

In an assessment of Thatcher's leadership style, what emerges as a prominent feature is the sharp dichotomy between those whom she liked and trusted and the "others." Distrusting many in her cabinet, she was controlling, domineering, and sometimes even abusive with them. Individual cabinet ministers whom she favoured received much kinder treatment, but no one was really safe: sooner or later, she would find them unworthy as well and remove them. More often than not, she relied heavily on her own personal advisers and preferred to use the cabinet as a rubber stamp for what she and a small coterie of ministers and advisers had already decided.

Her relations with government personnel also revealed the same pattern. People who worked for Margaret Thatcher in a variety of positions where she was clearly "the boss" found her warm and solicitous; her colleagues, whether in the party or the civil service, found her tough, abrasive, and constantly engaged in one-upmanship. Thatcher's relations with the party were also built on that same fault line. The caucus was treated in a competitive, controlling fashion, as was the non-parliamentary wing of the party about half the time. In the other half of the recorded instances, the non-parliamentary wing was treated with consideration and thoughtfulness since Thatcher viewed it as a counterweight to the caucus. In general, the more distant from formal party machinations and power the Tory members, the fonder Thatcher was of them.

No such love existed between Thatcher and the opposition. The opposition parties were clearly the "enemy" and she related to them as such, while both the print media and the public were courted and treated with collegiality. In these latter two instances, Thatcher felt that she could manipulate both to serve her ends and therefore could afford to be open and available. The one exception was television, and especially the BBC; its critical stance angered the prime minister and she attempted to exert control over it. Thatcher's world-view was clearly one of "us" and "them" and her leadership style in all of its various dimensions reflected that in abundance.

In terms of the relationship between personality and leadership style, an empirical analysis of Margaret Thatcher's leadership behaviour in the ten selected categories reveals that, in seven of them, the leadership-style patterns strongly matched our theoretical expectations for the Ambitious and Dominant personality types.[171] Ample evidence in this chapter has shown that she was strongly goal-oriented, tireless in the exercise of her job, a forceful advocate within her cabinet, and a leader who preferred information from independent sources. As well, Thatcher was strongly motivated by ideology and power, which similarly fitted our theoretical expectations for these personality types. The largely competitive and controlling behaviour that she exhibited with associates, the caucus, and the opposition also fits expectations for the Ambitious, Dominant, and Contentious personality types. All this suggests that a strong case can be made for the predictive power of most of the hypotheses that have been set out in this study.

However, there were three areas in which Margaret Thatcher's leadership behaviour did not meet our theoretical expectations – her relations with personnel, the organizational wing of the Conservative Party, and the media. In all three instances, she behaved in a more conciliatory fashion than expected based on her personality profile. In her dealings with civil servants and her personal staff, she was collegial more than half the time. She was particularly empathic with those who worked directly for her since they lacked an independent power base and were viewed as part of "her team." Similarly, almost 50 per cent of the items extracted on her relations with the organizational wing of the party showed Thatcher to be cooperative and conciliatory – a negation of expectations. Again, these were individuals who were less likely to threaten her agenda. Contrary, as well, to our expectations, Margaret Thatcher behaved in an open, accessible, and friendly manner with the media nearly 80 per cent of the time. It is possible, in this latter case, that the novelty of a female prime minister may have made the media less hostile, which in turn produced a reciprocal response in the prime minister. Or it may well have been the prime minister's use of political favours, such as the granting of peerages that softened potential print-media opposition to her. A third possibility is that the Conscientious dimension in Thatcher's personality may have led her to feel a sense of duty to maintain good relations with the media as a way of promoting her political agenda. Finally, of course, all three factors may have been at play.

Despite the above caveats, it can be plausibly asserted that, overall, Thatcher's personality profile was strongly linked to her leadership style, as convincingly demonstrated in seven of the ten leadership categories, suggesting that knowledge of a leader's personality prior to assumption of office may be a useful predictor of leadership style.

Conclusion

This comprehensive study of the lives and tenures of three female prime ministers has been driven, from the start, by two distinct yet interrelated premises. The first and most fundamental one posits that personality patterns arguably have a discernible impact upon the nature and nuances of political leadership. In order to delimit the relationship between personality and leadership behaviour more precisely, this book adopts a novel approach to the topic: the introduction of an analytical methodology that is both systematic and reproducible. As such, it can be broadly and comparatively applicable to the joint study of prime ministers' personalities and leadership styles, both female and male. The benefits of this methodology are threefold: the adoption and refinement of a rigorous personality diagnostic; the creation of a set of categories to assess leadership style; and the combination of the above in a composite methodological tool that, together with qualitative analysis, can yield meaningful hypotheses about the links between personality and leadership style.

The second premise concerns the selection of the principal subjects for this study. The decision was made to focus on three fascinating female leaders often discussed together but for whom few comparative studies exist: Indira Gandhi, Golda Meir, and Margaret Thatcher. While these three women are often described as "strong" personalities who offered "strong" leadership, few if any studies have delved substantially beyond the surface of this general observation. Hence, another aim of this book was to investigate and describe more precisely their respective personalities and the influence of those personalities on fundamental dimensions of their prime-ministerial leadership.

PERSONALITY PROFILES: A COMPARATIVE EXAMINATION OF PROMINENT TRAITS

The comparative examination of personality profiles conducted in this study from a quantitative and a qualitative perspective yielded some

Table 7
Comparative personality profiles: Gandhi, Meir, and Thatcher

Scale/Pattern	Gandhi	Meir	Thatcher
1A Dominant	19	18	21
1B Dauntless	11	11	4
2A Ambitious	21	9	11
3 Outgoing	8	5	4
4 Accommodating	9	7	4
5A Aggrieved	14	12	6
5B Contentious	20	17	13
6 Conscientious	11	12	11
7 Reticent	21	6	8
8 Retiring	15	1	1
9 Distrusting	8	12	8
0 Erratic	0	0	0
Total	40	40	40

Figure 4
Comparative personality profiles: Gandhi, Meir, and Thatcher

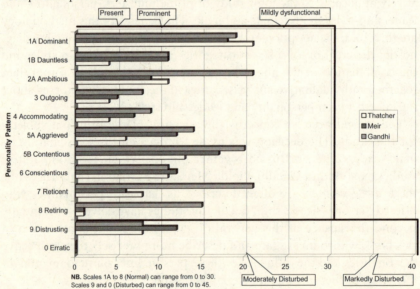

interesting findings. The reader will recall that, according to the diagnostic tool used, scores of 10 to 23 provide evidence of the *prominence* of that personality trait; scores of 15 to 23 provide the base of minimal evidence for a deeply ingrained, inflexible variant of the personality pattern; and scores of 24 to 30 offer a threshold beyond which lies evidence of a personality disorder. Each of the three women had at least one personality pattern above 15, but none had any scores that were above 21. Unlike Meir and Thatcher, Gandhi scored high on four personality dimensions – score values between 19 and 21. Meir had high scores of 18 and 17 on two patterns with the next two tied at 12 and another at 11. Thatcher had a high score of 21 in only one pattern; the remaining three traits, in her case, received scores of 13, with two tied at 11 (See Figure 4).

For all three women, the Dominant trait was found to be very important. Especially for Meir and Thatcher, this pattern proved the most significant in their personality profiles, registering scores of 18 and 21 respectively. Although the Dominant pattern ranked only fourth in importance in Gandhi's personality profile, it still received a high score of 19. Hence, it can be plausibly argued that the Dominant trait was prominent in all three women's personalities and carried through to their political lives. In general, the impact of this pattern on leadership style can be summed up in the following observation about Meir by one of her most astute biographers: "Because of the fact that she had no doubts about the justness of her ways and the means needed to reach them, she became a dogmatic woman characterized by a lack of patience for ideas that did not match her position, and she expressed her views with a sense of self-righteousness that became one of her trademarks in Israel. Anyone who opposed her or her way wasn't 'one of ours.'"[1]

This statement is fully comparable with Gandhi's belief that she, too, understood what was best for India, as reflected, for example, in her decision, made without consultation with her cabinet, to declare a State of Emergency. It is also applicable to Thatcher's own strong convictions about the direction in which Great Britain needed to move in the economic sphere, her self-righteous belief that she knew what was best for the country, and her constant concern about whether this or that colleague was "one of us."[2]

Although strong evidence for such a personality trait is what might be expected from a chief executive officer, leadership-profile studies have demonstrated that, among three successful presidential candidates, Bill Clinton, George W. Bush, and Robert Mugabe, the first two received scores of 7 and 11 respectively on the Dominant/Controlling scale, while the score even for the authoritarian Mugabe was only 14.[3] In none of these cases, then, did the Dominant pattern represent a factor of major importance in their personality profiles. This finding under-scores the need for an explanation of the prominence of the Dominant pattern in all three female leaders.

Three possibilities suggest themselves. One involves the small number of the sample; the findings reported here are limited to our three cases and could, therefore, be unrepresentative of the larger population of fe-male prime ministers. Nor was the choice of our three female prime ministers random. Each was known to be a strong individual, which may have determined that the Dominant pattern would be prominent in all their personalities. Only the investigation of the personality profiles of a much larger number of randomly chosen elected female leaders (as of August 2007, this group numbered seventy-five) would help answer the question as to the ubiquity and importance of the Dominant trait in such individuals.

Let us assume for a moment that a larger study of female prime min-isters did, in fact, demonstrate that the Dominant personality pattern was strong in a significant number of them. A second possible explana-tion for this finding is the role that gender may play. Each woman pro-filed in this study had to fight to assert herself. As a child and a young adult, Indira fought to stand up to her powerful father and assert her independence; Golda resisted her mother and father's views on educa-tion and on a woman's place in the world; Margaret struggled to earn her father's respect and admiration and to disengage herself from her mother and sister's lives and values. Later, all three would be required to fight against strong male opposition within society at large, as well as in their own political parties to achieve political power. As women, competing in an essentially masculine world of politics, having a tough, assertive, strong-willed, and dominating presence seemed to be a sine qua non.

To be taken seriously in the political arena, a place that continues to be a largely male preserve, seems to require a strong, assertive personal-ity (that is, the presence of the Dominant trait at sufficiently high levels to transcend stereotypical notions of what it means to be female, with its traditional connotations of weakness and indecision). In contrast, overly simplified ideas of male-defining traits, with their built-in as-sumptions of strength and power, may mean that men need not demon-strate the same strong Dominant characteristics as women in order to achieve power; thus, their personalities may be marked more by Ambi-tion, Dauntlessness, Outgoingness, or other traits.

To assess the role that gender plays in determining the importance of the Dominant trait, again a larger study in the personality profiling of male and female elected political leaders must be the next logical re-search step. In this way, the differences between them, on this and other personality dimensions, could be assessed, and our preliminary findings evaluated in terms of the accuracy of their ability to be generalized.

If the results of testing a larger sample of female and male leaders do not reveal that the Dominant trait is, in fact, significantly more prevalent in women than in men, the type of political system could be explored as a third possible explanation for our results. In the initial findings presented here, the three female leaders were all heads of parliamentary systems of government. There is an extensive literature on the differences between parliamentary and presidential systems,[4] but the links between the Dominant personality trait and the type of governmental system have not been adequately probed. A pertinent question could be phrased as follows: Given that the leader of the government in a parliamentary system must face weekly question periods in the legislative assembly, and can be replaced by a vote of non-confidence by the legislature and by the membership in her/his own party, does this produce leaders who are significantly more likely to exhibit personality traits of Dominance and Control than their presidential counterparts who enjoy a fixed term of office – save for the rarely successful impeachment process – do not have to respond to weekly public questioning by the members of the legislature, and never face the threat of being unseated in office by the members of their own party? Once more, only a much larger sample of male and female leaders, in both parliamentary and presidential systems of government, can begin to answer this question.

Of course, the impact of gender and political system on personality – be it significant or insignificant – should not obscure the fact that the personality dimensions of every individual are a product both of innate constitutional endowments and of formative life experiences. Differences in gender and political systems may act as intervening variables in terms of explaining the presence or absence of particular traits in particular leaders. This applies as much to the Dominant pattern as to any others.

The Contentious dimension in a personality profile ranked as the second most important for both Meir and Thatcher and the third most significant for Gandhi. The scores for both Gandhi and Meir were fairly high, 19 and 17 respectively, while for Thatcher, it was 13. Why should this be the case? Was it a statistical anomaly – the product of the particular women who were selected for profiling – or would a wider study of female leaders exhibit the same pattern? It is incontestable that girls and young women in an earlier era had to struggle harder to overcome gender-specific challenges and prescribed roles (for example, a typical traditional life as a homemaker). Following on the heels of the feminist movement and the great strides women have made for equality in rights and opportunities around the globe, a new generation of women is no

longer a novelty in the boardrooms of large corporations or in the highest
elected offices in their nations.[5] But women leaders like Gandhi, Meir,
and Thatcher truly paved the way and had to fight hard for their achievements. Their struggles to reach the top in the undeniably male-dominated
political hierarchy may well have amplified their personality-driven cynicism, contrariness, and stubbornness. That said, the Contentiousness of
these women needs to be placed in context: none were seen as the first
choice by their various parties. The Congress Party in India, the Labor
Party in Israel, and the Conservative Party in Great Britain turned to
Gandhi, Meir, and Thatcher, respectively, not enthusiastically – because
they recognized or admired their intrinsic abilities and leadership qualities – but grudgingly, because they saw them as interim or compromise
choices, given the unacceptability of other male candidates who were perceived as divisive or less manageable.

To assess whether gender does play a role in exacerbating the Contentious personality trait in female political leaders, it would be necessary to
examine the significance of this trait in male political leaders. An alternative possibility is that the key factor again is not gender but differences in
parliamentary and presidential systems of government. Surely, it is likely
that parliamentary systems, which are characterized by ongoing public
fights and debates, will attract or favour leaders who manifest a strong element of Contentiousness in their personalities. In contrast, presidential
systems, characterized by a separation of powers and the ability of the
president to remain apart from direct participation in the battles in the
legislature, do not seem to require chief executives to exhibit a high
degree of Contentiousness.

Turning our attention to the Ambitious pattern, the personality profiles
of both Indira Gandhi and Margaret Thatcher also reveal it to be significant. In the case of Gandhi, it was one of the two top dimensions in her
personality, with a score of 21. In Thatcher's case, it just reached prominence with a scale elevation of 11, placing it in a tie for the third most important pattern in her personality profile. However, for Golda Meir, the
Ambitious pattern was not among the five most important in her personality profile, receiving a score of only 9. At the *present* level (scores of 5 to
9), Ambition includes confidence, poise, assertiveness, innovativeness,
and optimism, something that all three women clearly possessed. But at
the *prominent* level (scores of 10 to 23), Ambition is characterized primarily by conceit, immodesty, an inflated sense of self-importance, and
an excessive sense of self-worth. These traits were characteristic of Gandhi and, to a much lesser extent, Thatcher. Only Gandhi approached the
highest scale elevation (scores between 24 and 30), where Ambition is
synonymous with arrogance, indifference to the rights of others, a willingness to be manipulative, and an overweening sense of self.

Given the obstacles, societal pressures, and glass ceilings that women have had to overcome in building the degree of self-confidence and self-esteem required to function at the highest level of politics, it is not surprising that successful female leaders will exhibit more than a minimum level of the personality trait of Ambition. However, both Meir and Thatcher appeared much less narcissistic than Indira Gandhi. It is quite possible that Gandhi's high score on this personality dimension was the product of her privileged background, her father's position as a leading freedom fighter and subsequently prime minister of India, and her role as his daughter and hostess. All of these elements seem to have contributed to give her an inflated sense of self-importance. Unlike Gandhi, who was virtually handed the office of the prime minister on a silver platter, both Meir and Thatcher worked their way up in their respective parties and were not regarded as particularly intelligent or gifted by their colleagues, in the case of Golda, and by both their colleagues and their teachers, in the case of Margaret. In that context, it may have been more difficult for either woman to develop an arrogant and superior sense of self. They were dominating but without a sense of entitlement.

Another finding that differentiates Indira Gandhi from both Golda Meir and Margaret Thatcher was the importance that the Reticent pattern occupied in her personality profile. While it scored at 21 for Gandhi, it received only 6 for Meir and 8 for Thatcher. Given that an individual must be somewhat sociable to become a successful political leader, one would not normally expect Reticence to be an important dimension of a politician's personality profile. But the empirical findings are indisputable. As the only child of parents who spent a great deal of time in prison, Indira's childhood was extremely lonely. That situation, coupled with the disdain with which her father's sister treated her, illuminates some of the reasons why she grew up shy and reticent.[6] Ironically, she was chosen to become prime minister by the Congress Party bosses, in large part, because of this reticence; the presumption was that she would make a good interim leader since she lacked any of her own ambition. Paradoxically, however, although Gandhi scored high on the Reticent pattern, it had little impact on her leadership behaviour. Any combination of the following three factors could be at work here. First, the Reticent components of her personality profile were more evident in early childhood and late adolescence than in adulthood. According to the literature on the psychology of personality, it is not uncommon for personality traits to become more/less pronounced during different developmental stages of one's life. Second, the combined impact of her Ambitious, Contentious, and Dominant traits – which predict certain types of behaviour – seems to have been sufficient to suppress the effects of the Reticent dimension, which anticipates quite different behaviour. Finally, the power inherent in the office of the prime minister to reach the masses and experience their love and devotion could have lessened Gandhi's fear of rejection and thus her reticence.

Turning to the next prominent pattern, the findings again yield an intriguing picture. Unlike Margaret Thatcher's profile, the Aggrieved personality pattern figures prominently in the personality profiles of both Indira Gandhi and Golda Meir. For Thatcher, it only received a score of 6, whereas for Gandhi it was scored at 14 and for Meir at 12. However, in Gandhi's case, the Aggrieved/self-sacrificing dimension of her personality was ranked sixth out of 10, while in Meir's it was tied for third in order of importance, suggesting that it had a greater influence on her leadership behaviour. A lack of pretension, a sense of humility, and a spirit of self-sacrifice may be somewhat more characteristic of female than of male leaders, particularly if they were the primary caregivers for their families, but much more research on both groups of leaders is required to test this hypothesis.

Finally, another significant trait exhibited by the three women – the Conscientious pattern – was scored similarly, at 11 for Indira Gandhi, 12 for Golda Meir, and 11 for Margaret Thatcher. However, its relative importance was very different. For Thatcher and Meir, it tied for third place in their respective personality profiles, while, for Gandhi, it ranked in seventh position in her profile. When Conscientiousness either receives a low score or occupies a position of significantly less importance in a political leader's overall personality profile, there is a greater likelihood that it will have a negative impact on behaviour; thus, a leader whose Conscientious traits either score low in absolute or relative terms may behave in a disrespectful, undisciplined, and imprudent fashion. It comes as no surprise, therefore, that Indira Gandhi, who scored high on Ambition and low on Conscientiousness, behaved in questionable ways – tolerating high levels of corruption and declaring a State of Emergency for dubious reasons.

In general, these findings provide an intriguing, often complex picture of the significance of personality profile traits in our subjects' lives and career trajectories. Perhaps the most interesting of the findings was the apparent potency of various combinations of personality traits for our subjects, a topic that now will be addressed in greater depth.

LEADERSHIP STYLES:
A COMPARATIVE EXAMINATION

In everyday parlance, scholars, biographers, and colleagues variously describe the leadership styles of Gandhi, Meir, and Thatcher as "tough," "controlling," "unsentimental," and "hard-nosed." This study has attempted to "unpack" these popular perceptions and investigate systematically the meanings and dimensions behind them. It has done so by devising and applying a set of categories to explore the multiple facets of leadership behaviour. Overall, after an extensive look at relevant studies and empirical evidence on the exercise of leadership, ten categories were chosen that best capture the most important dimensions of prime-ministerial leadership (See Table 22).

The first category addresses the nature of the motivation for policy choices. A comparative examination of the motives behind policy formulation and action suggests that personal validation was of minimal significance in the motivational calculus of all three leaders. Indira Gandhi was motivated primarily by power and pragmatism, Golda Meir by ideology and pragmatism, and Margaret Thatcher by ideology and power. Ideology played an important role for Meir and Thatcher, as did the quest for power for Gandhi and Thatcher and pragmatism for both Gandhi and Meir. Interestingly, Gandhi emerged as the only non-ideological leader. She was far more concerned with maintaining her power, and only when she was able to defeat her rivals in the Congress Party was she was prepared to behave in a pragmatic fashion. Meir was found to be much less concerned with power than either of the other two women; for her, ideology in national-security affairs – strongly linked to a life-long belief in Israel's right to exist and prosper – and pragmatism on domestic issues shaped her policy choices. Quite like Meir, Thatcher, too, was strongly ideological, but this driving force was manifested largely in the realm of economic policy and, to a lesser extent, foreign policy; also, as with Gandhi, the evidence suggests that Thatcher was motivated by concerns with maintaining political power as well. In terms of other leadership-style categories, in the exercise of their position as prime minister, all three women were found to be strongly goal-oriented and tireless and to have acted primarily as advocates within their cabinets, often dominating them and almost always setting their agendas according to their own preferences. Additionally, the evidence strongly suggests they were heavily involved in the managing of information and in relations with personnel and the public. They differed, however, in the specific nature of those involvements. Indira Gandhi relied significantly on independent sources of information, as did Margaret Thatcher, the most deeply involved in the search for and analysis of data. Golda Meir, on the other hand, used ministerial and independent sources about equally. The nature of their involvement with civil servants and personal staff was also found to differ. Gandhi projected a strongly demanding and manipulative presence, Thatcher was either demanding or manipulative in nearly half of the instances observed in this study and collegial or polite in the other half, and Meir's relations were overwhelmingly collegial.

Figure 5
Comparing leadership styles: Gandhi, Meir, and Thatcher

I. Motivation

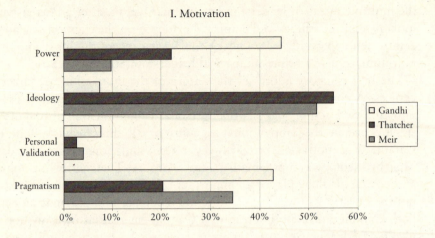

II. Task Orientation

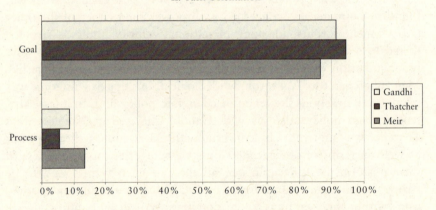

III. Investment in Job Performance

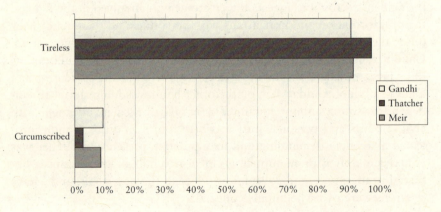

Figure 5 (*Continued*)

IV. Cabinet Management Strategy

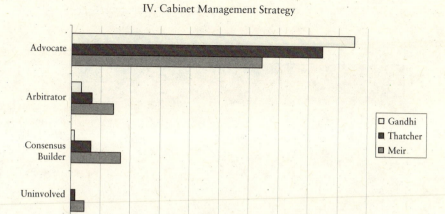

V. (1) Information Management: Degree of Involvement

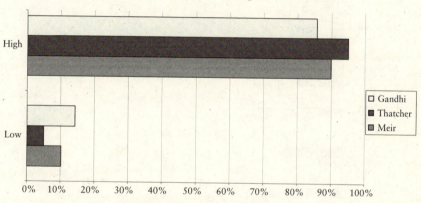

V. (2) Information Management: Sources

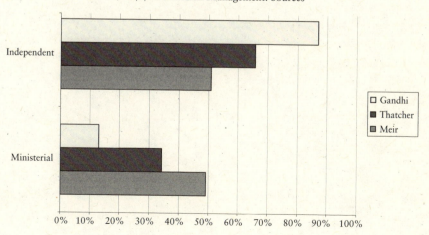

Figure 5 (*Continued*)

VI. (1) Relations w/ Personnel: Degree of Involvement

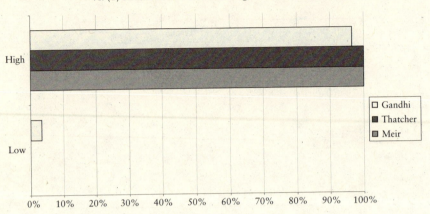

VI. (2) Relations w/ Personnel: Type of Involvement

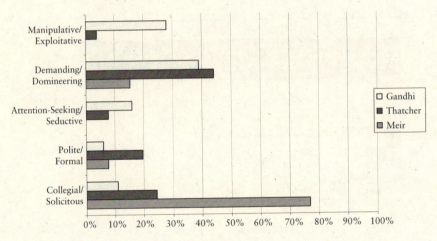

Figure 5 (*Continued*)

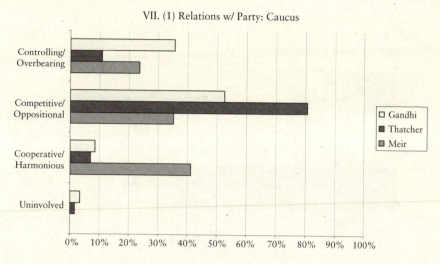

VII. (1) Relations w/ Party: Caucus

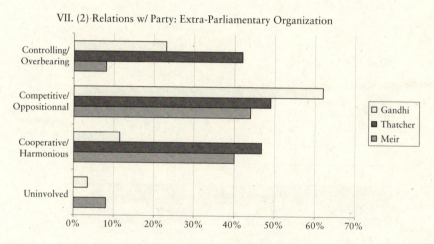

VII. (2) Relations w/ Party: Extra-Parliamentary Organization

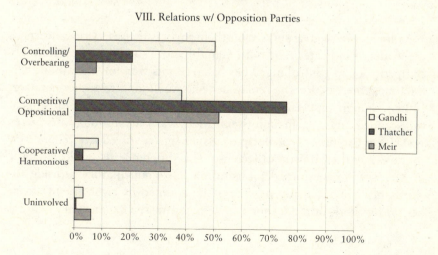

VIII. Relations w/ Opposition Parties

Figure 5 (*Continued*)

IX. Relations w/ The Media

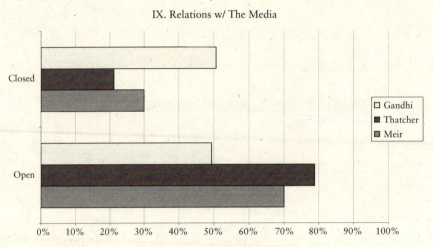

X. Relations w/ The Public

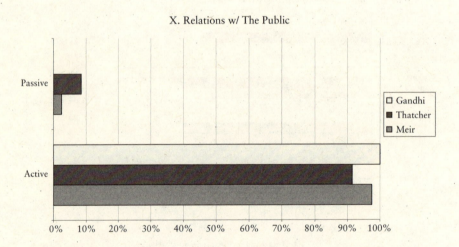

As far as the relationships with their party caucuses were concerned, the evidence indicates that both Gandhi and Thatcher were extremely competitive and controlling; Meir behaved this way for only about half the time, whereas, for the remainder, she was found to be cooperative. Unlike Gandhi and Thatcher, whose popularity and electoral appeal transcended any of their ministers, Meir was only primus inter pares within her cabinet, particularly on issues that involved her reliance on the advice of the Ministry of Defense. This difference also reflected itself in Meir's willingness to demonstrate a more conciliatory attitude towards her caucus, many of whom she counted as close friends from her earlier work in the Labor Party. In contrast, Thatcher and Gandhi created inner circles and internal divisions with their caucuses, taking in-tra-governmental competition to higher levels.

Towards the extra-parliamentary party organization, Gandhi was over-whelmingly competitive and controlling; Thatcher and Meir were almost equally as likely to be cooperative as competitive, albeit for somewhat dif-ferent reasons: Thatcher cultivated the extra-parliamentary party organi-zation as an important source of support against the challenges posed by her caucus, while Meir had developed close ties with the members of the party organization – many of whom had fought alongside her dur-ing the birth of Israel and who had worked closely with her when she was secretary of the Labor Party.

Regarding relations with the various opposition parties, Gandhi's and often Thatcher's styles were overwhelmingly competitive and control-ling; both female leaders even seemed to relish the opportunity to clash with and defeat their political opponents. In contrast, Golda Meir had a somewhat more cooperative relationship with her political adversaries. However, this was a function, in large measure, of the Israeli electoral system, which is based on a country-wide system of proportional repre-sentation – the number of votes that the party list receives determines their proportion of seats in the Israeli parliament, the Knesset. This vir-tually ensures that no Israeli political party is likely to be able to form a majority government, and all Israeli prime ministers have had to exhibit cooperative behaviour towards those opposition parties which could be potential future junior partners in a minority government; Golda Meir was no exception to this customary facet of Israeli electoral politics, of-ten having to be more accommodating to members of opposition par-ties than to those of her own party.

The leaders' styles were also assessed in relation to their interactions with the media. In this dimension of their style, both Thatcher and Meir displayed predominantly accessible and friendly attitudes towards the press, although Meir was not always informative, perhaps because of the sensitive nature of information requested on Israeli security. Nonetheless, both women recognized in the press a venue through which they could reach the public and popularize their ideas; in that sense, they were truly modern politicians attuned to the power and potential of the mass media. However, in Thatcher's case, television – particularly the BBC – was more critical of her and she often responded in kind. While generally accessible to the media, Meir, for her part, was also concerned about government leaks and thus often reluctant to give out too much information. Indira Gandhi was found to be open and accessible to the media about half of the time and closed and inaccessible for the other half. This distribution corresponds temporally to her career trajectory. In the early part of her tenure as prime minister, Gandhi relied on the press to counter the opposition she received from the Congress old guard, but, when the press turned on her after she declared a State of Emergency, she became closed and inaccessible.

A final aspect of their leadership styles involves their interaction with the people. Gandhi, Meir, and Thatcher all recognized the importance of their relations with the public, exhibiting an open and enthusiastic embrace of their constituents that could sometimes give the impression of going beyond simple political expediency and calculation; they seemed to feel very close to the crowds, who, in turn, felt the same way about them. Gandhi, especially, loved large audiences and travelled hundreds of thousands of miles to address people all across India. Meir and Thatcher also enjoyed, and understood the importance of, their relations with the public and used their offices to maintain an open and dynamic relationship with the citizenry. In general, exploring these ten categories in depth provided a rich picture of the styles of these three leaders, allowing us to compare their similarities and identify the unique elements of their leadership.

THE RELATIONSHIP BETWEEN PERSONALITY PROFILES AND LEADERSHIP STYLES

Throughout this book, the personality profiles and leadership styles of three female prime ministers as well as the links between them have been examined individually for each woman. But, inevitably, at the conclusion of such a study, one arrives at the intriguing question suggested throughout its course: Can personalities be predictive of leadership behaviour and, if so, to what extent? The short response is that this issue lies beyond the scope of the present study, the primary purpose of which is not to provide definitive answers but to lay the foundations for future inquiry. Even if one were to imagine, for example, that in contrast to real life, all three of our principal subjects presented only a single personality type, and that personality type demonstrated a perfect empirical match with theoretical expectations for leadership behaviours, the necessarily small number of leaders examined would render any broad generalizations or fixed conclusions untenable. Moreover, in the three selected cases, the potential for definitive prediction was rendered remote by virtue of the fact that each leader's personality was the composite product of a number of different patterns, some with different leadership-style expectations. Sweeping conclusions and generalizations would not only be unscientific but also potentially counterproductive.

However, notwithstanding these unavoidable limitations, I believe that my study provides not only a detailed look into the personalities and leadership styles of three dynamic women but also an appropriate first step for the systematic analysis of this subject. Indeed, a study of this nature can and does reveal a number of suggestive links in support of our preliminary hypotheses. More specifically, as conjectured, those female prime ministers whose personality profiles are characterized by high levels of the Dominant, Ambitious, or Contentious patterns are more likely, as the data suggested, to be goal-oriented, tireless in their jobs, advocates within their cabinets, and intensely involved in the management of information and relations with personnel and the public. Also entirely consistent with our expectations for leaders with Dominant, Ambitious, Conscientious, and Contentious personality traits in their personality profile was the behaviour that Gandhi, Meir, and Thatcher demonstrated towards the public. As hypothesized, all three women leaders were open and available; they sought to talk to the public at large, as a way both to circumvent criticism from their own caucuses, the opposition, and the media and to obtain support for their policies from the electorate. These are important first hints that there may indeed be a close correlation between personality and leadership. At the same time, there were other initial hypotheses that our findings did not fully support. For example, in the area of motivation, the Ambitious pattern was expected to evoke policies driven by a need for self-validation, but there was little empirical evidence in Indira Gandhi's leadership behaviour to support this. Nor was power always a major motivator for those possessing a Dominant pattern in their personality structure. Evidence suggests that Golda Meir, who did score high on this pattern, was motivated primarily by ideology and pragmatism, not power. Similarly, in the case of Margaret Thatcher, for whom the Contentious pattern ranked second in importance, the postulated link to a pragmatic orientation was weak; instead, she was found to be more strongly motivated by power and ideology.

To put the findings in perspective, since the margin in the scores between Thatcher's most prominent personality pattern and the remainder was much larger than in the scores of the other two leaders, it may well be that her leadership style was more strongly affected by her most salient personality pattern – the Dominant one – thus explaining a lack of significant influence for the Contentious pattern. This result suggests that the impact of the most important personality patterns on leadership style will be roughly equal only if the scores on those personality traits are equal, as was virtually the case with Indira Gandhi. Where only one personality pattern receives a very high score, even though there are others that may be diagnostically significant – with a score of 5 or more – it alone may determine the basic features of a specific type of leadership style.

Further, in the category of choice of information sources, theoretical expectations for the Dominant, Ambitious, and Contentious personalities were supported only for Gandhi and Thatcher, who, as expected, relied heavily on independent sources, in contrast to Meir, who depended heavily on a mixture of ministerial and independent contacts. Also, our expectations for relations with personnel were not strongly supported by the results. Dominant, Ambitious, and Contentious personalities are presumed to have largely competitive and controlling relationships, which Indira Gandhi did have; in contrast, however, Margaret Thatcher's relations were also partly collegial while Golda Meir's were predominantly collegial. Gender and class may mitigate the impact of personality in this area. As working mothers, both Thatcher and Meir exhibited motherly concerns with their staff, thus moderating the full force of their Dominant and Contentious personalities. Moreover, the nature and history of modern Israeli politics framed Meir's relations in a spirit of comradeship between fellow pioneers of the state of Israel. Although Gandhi was also a working mother, the non-competitive manner in which she had come to her initial involvement with politics and more generally her status as part of India's "political" royalty may have rendered her distant and unapproachable and thereby allowed her personality patterns to operate unimpeded. Implicit in this discussion is a notion of the role that class and, to some extent, social culture may play in determining some dimensions of leadership style. Thatcher was overly formal and polite, Meir was a former member of a collegial kibbutz, and Gandhi was a product of a rigid and hierarchical caste system.

Consistent with the expectations for their Ambitious and Dominant personality profiles, both Gandhi and Thatcher exhibited competitive and controlling relations with their respective caucuses. In contrast, Meir, who also scored high on Dominance, had a more balanced repertoire of collegial and competitive relations with her party caucus. This difference between Meir, on the one hand, and Gandhi and Thatcher, on the other, may have been a function of the period of time that each woman occupied the office of prime minister, as well as the size of the parliamentary majorities they commanded, which determined the degree of attention expended on backbenchers and on the need for coalition building. Gandhi served a total of fifteen years, and Thatcher's eleven years in office made her the longest-serving British prime minister in the twentieth century. In contrast, Meir served only for five years, leaving politics after the backlash from the Yom Kippur War.

Leaders with Dominant, Ambitious, and Contentious personality patterns are theoretically expected to enjoy competitive and controlling relations with respect to the extra-parliamentary party organization, as well as the opposition parties. According to the findings, however, only Indira Gandhi's leadership behaviour upheld this hypothesis; Thatcher did exhibit competitive and controlling relations with the opposition but also displayed a mixture of competitive and cooperative actions in her dealings with the extra-parliamentary party organization, relying on the latter to balance the power of the caucus. Meir, for her part, demonstrated both competitive and cooperative behaviour in her dealings with both groups. With those members of the extra-parliamentary party organization who were close political allies, she exhibited cooperative behaviour, as she did with those members of opposition parties likely to become members of her governing coalition. In these two cases, situational variables played a limiting role on the impact of personality patterns for both Meir and Thatcher.

Two other areas in which theoretical expectations for Thatcher were not supported by our findings concerned her relations with personnel and the extra-parliamentary party organization. Thatcher was found to be almost equally cooperative as she was competitive, behaving solicitously with those who worked directly under her and cooperating with the extra-parliamentary party organization and her supporters within it to balance the critical forces within her caucus.

As far as similar hypotheses involving personality patterns with respect to the press, these also proved to be unreliable predictors. Dominant, Ambitious, and Contentious leaders were presumed to exhibit a closed, unfriendly stance with the mass media. In reality, two leaders, Thatcher and Meir, were predominantly open, and Gandhi exhibited a mixed pattern of behaviour. Leaders with these personality traits may see themselves as able to manipulate the media to their advantage, using it, in part, as a "bully pulpit" to promote their views and to strengthen their position both within their parties and within their states. It is also possible that the media, in all three countries, enthralled with the novelty of a female political leader, was initially less critical, and the leaders responded in kind by being open and accessible. Once the media's endorsement became less enthusiastic, as it inevitably did, our leaders reverted to theoretical expectations and became less approachable and informative. Nowhere was this better exemplified than in the behaviour of Indira Gandhi, who moved from being totally accessible to the press before the State of Emergency to being completely closed in its aftermath. Gandhi's strong Ambitious pattern, which contained a narcissistic element that caused her to seek attention and exposure, initially inclined her to be open with the press, but after the State of Emergency and her subsequent return to power in 1980, the absence of media support was experienced as a narcissistic wound to which she responded by becoming closed and unfriendly.

Overall, this study's findings and resulting comparisons of the three female leaders' styles point to more general questions. For example, was the intriguing and complex case of Golda Meir an outlier in the weaker association of her personality profile to her leadership style, as compared with that of Indira Gandhi or Margaret Thatcher, or is she more, rather than less, representative of other female leaders? Could there be an association between the length of time a leader serves in office and the extent to which personality has an impact on leadership style? To what extent were the effects of Meir's personality traits held in check because of the relatively shorter time she served as prime minister, as compared to Gandhi and Thatcher? Or do leaders exhibit different facets of their leadership styles in the arenas of domestic and foreign affairs? Answers to these and other questions will become possible only after many more female political leaders have been thoroughly profiled and compared for their personality patterns, leadership styles, and length of time in office.

Nevertheless, although the projected association between personality profiles and leadership styles and the empirical findings was less than perfect, it should be firmly underscored that the personality profiles of Indira Gandhi and Margaret Thatcher were found theoretically, and empirically, to be strongly linked to their leadership behaviour – in nine out of the ten leadership categories in the case of Gandhi, and in seven out of ten for Thatcher. These results provide a promising start that could stimulate further research on this relationship for other female as well as male political leaders. Naturally, one must not overlook the fact that the use of a combined nomothetic approach, "which seeks to establish abstract general laws for indefinitely repeatable events and processes; and an ideographic approach, which aims to understand the unique and nonrecurrent," does pose a number of methodological challenges that have to be carefully considered in designing and executing further research.[7] However, these can be addressed satisfactorily and are further mitigated by the wealth of evidence provided by case studies, when used in conjunction with a systematic set of categories that is itself a product of this composite methodological approach. In this study, examining, in depth, the complex interactions between the personalities and leadership styles of Indira Gandhi, Golda Meir, and Margaret Thatcher also helps enrich our understanding of the nature of the contribution that these three women made to their respective societies. As well, a comparative approach to the examination of the personality profiles of these three women, and the hypotheses developed and tested about their connection to leadership styles, is an attempt to go beyond the simply biographical and to introduce the scientifically systematic. It tries to open the "black box" of concepts of, and links between, personality and leadership to illuminate some of the nuances involved in their interaction. This effort will have been worth it if it manages to offer another way for voters in parliamentary and presidential democracies to think about the projected behaviour of the ever-growing number of female leaders.

APPENDIX

Conceptual Framework and Methodology

This appendix proceeds in four steps: the subject of personality profiles is addressed first; as a second step, a set of categories developed for the purpose of exploring prime-ministerial leadership style is applied to each prime minister; a third step involves a discussion of the expected or hypothesized links between various personality profiles and leadership styles; and, finally, the leadership behaviour that each prime minister exhibited, together with the extent to which the personality profile is predictive of the leadership style, is analysed.

SECTION I: PERSONALITY PROFILES

Background to the Study of Personality

In his 1990 review of the field of personality and politics, Simonton suggested that the dominant paradigm for the psychological examination of leaders had shifted from the earlier preponderance of qualitative, ideographic, psycho-biographical analysis towards quantitative and nomothetic (an approach that seeks to establish abstract general laws for indefinitely repeatable events and processes) methods.[1] For instance, many of the studies of the personalities of political leaders developed by political psychologists were largely impressionistic, based on the psychological insights and categories developed by various authors.[2] The trend towards more quantitative and nomothetic methods of analysis reflects the impact of Hermann's investigation of the influence of personal characteristics on foreign policy,[3] Winter's examination of the role of social motives in leaders' performance,[4] and Suedfeld and Tetlock's work in integrative complexity.[5] Currently, it would be fair to say that the field remains divided between the two approaches.[6]

Conceptually, it can be argued that the only valid way to profile a leader is to subject him/her to direct psychological testing and diagnostic interviews. Since this is clearly impractical, the above profilers devised a content-analytic method[7] from which diagnostic information can be extracted or inferred. However, these are *indirect*, not direct, diagnostic methods, which compounds the problem that the authorship of such source materials may at times be ambiguous or questionable. In addition, the type of psychologically useful information that can be obtained from content analysis about personality traits is limited.

Having been professionally trained as a psychoanalyst as well as a political scientist, I have been surprised to discover that extant approaches to the assessment of political personality bear little resemblance to the tools and techniques of clinical practice. Increasingly, I have become convinced that, both conceptually and methodologically, much of the work ongoing in the area of political personality is psycho-diagnostically peripheral. That is not to say that these studies have no merit; indeed, their political-psychological formulations are frequently insightful and compelling. However, it seems to me that some of these assessment models, particularly those relying on content analysis, do not exactly measure what they purport to measure – personality – raising troubling questions of construct validity.

Why, for example, would anyone want to infer personality indirectly from the content analysis of speeches and published interviews when a wealth of direct observations from multiple sources – commonly referred to as collateral information in the parlance of psycho-diagnostics – already exist in the public record, ready to be mined, extracted, and processed? And why would anyone construct, de novo, political-personality taxonomies – as though politicians comprise a subspecies of Homo sapiens – when classification systems already exist with reference to the general population?

Moreover, there is no logical basis for dismissing the observations of biographers or journalists who are often highly skilled at observing and documenting psychologically meaningful information. In clinical practice, psychologists may rely on collateral information provided by other individuals who have directly observed the subject – family members, associates, co-workers, and supervisors. This is akin to utilizing observations by journalists who interviewed the subject or his/her associates.

In making use of journalist interviews and biographical materials for this study, I was careful to assess the reputation of the writer and to use sufficiently numerous sources to cancel out or at least mitigate the biases of any individual biographer. When the materials extracted and coded from a variety of sources for a given leader were compared, a strong degree of accord among them was found, suggesting a high degree of reliability. Another major approach in the emerging quantitative-nomethetic vein in the study of personality, noted by Simonton, involves the extension of standard personality instruments and techniques to the analysis of biographical material for the indirect assessment of political leaders.[8] Based on the work of Millon[9] and Millon and Everly's detailed analyses of a number of personality disorders,[10] Immelman[11] has developed the notion of personality profiles using biographical materials to analyse the personality patterns. However, despite its promise, thus far Immelman's work has been limited to three tasks: to offer predictions about the future behaviour of aspiring American presidential candidates;[12] to explain the degree of ease or difficulty presidential wives have had in adjusting to their roles in the White House;[13] and to understand the psychological make-up of terrorist leaders and their behaviour.[14] This study extends that reach.

The personality profiles of Indira Gandhi, Golda Meir, and Margaret Thatcher developed in this book are based on the model formulated by Immelman.[15] This model owes its genesis to the conceptual work of Millon,[16] Millon and Davis,[17] Oldham and Morris,[18] and Strack,[19] which offers an empirically validated taxonomy of personality patterns compatible with the syndromes described on Axis II of the fourth edition (1994) of the *Diagnostic and Statistical Manual of Mental Disorders* (*DSM–IV*) of the American Psychiatric Association. A distinguishing attribute of these models is that they provide an integrated view of normality and psychopathology. "No sharp line divides normality from pathological behavior; they are [treated as] relative concepts representing arbitrary points on a continuum or gradient."[20] The advantage of this approach is that personality traits can be understood as traits that everyone possesses; it is the intensity of those traits that enables a distinction to be made between their being either *present, prominent,* or *mildly dysfunctional.*

Method and Sources for Deriving Personality Profiles

Given that Immelman has provided us with a comprehensive review of Millon's model of personality and its applicability to political personality, it is not necessary to recapitulate it here in full. Suffice it to say that the Millon Inventory of Diagnostic Criteria (MIDC), based on Millon's model of personality, is essentially an index; it formally charts and scores twelve personality patterns across eight attribute domains. This assessment tool[21] was compiled and adapted from criteria for normal personality types and pathological variants, such as the Paranoid.[22] Each attribute domain is a distinct facet of human behaviour in which personality traits are manifested (see Table 8).[23] Table 9 spells out the twelve personality scales as well as specific descriptors/diagnostic criteria numbering from "a" to "e" in ascending order of importance of that trait within the specific personality scale.

The scores yielded by the MIDC scales possess the property of rank order but not of equal intervals or absolute magnitude. In interpreting MIDC profiles, it must be borne in mind that the measurement scale is ordinal, intended primarily to classify subjects into a graded sequence of personality classifications or levels, ranging from *present* (scores of 5 to 9) to *prominent* (scores of 10 to 23) and *mildly dysfunctional* (scores of 24 to 40). For individuals exhibiting a Paranoid or Erratic (Border-line) personality pattern, each of which is considered to be a disordered rather than a normal personality type, a score of between 20 and 35 denotes a *moderately disturbed* state, and a score of 36 to 45 a *markedly disturbed* one.[24]

As explained in the MIDC manual, diagnostic significance and cut-off points between normal, prominent, and dysfunctional scale variants are based on rational criteria derived from the specific manner of test construction. As a research instrument, the MIDC is not formulated on some normative "fits all" sample, as is often the case with conventional, commercially produced personality inventories commonly used in clinical practice. Instead, the MIDC diagnostic procedure is more akin to the decision-making process of clinicians when they employ the DSM as a diagnostic tool, and as such it offers a more systematic framework for analysis. This is one of the MIDC's strongest features, and its significant departure from purely qualitative ideographic methods of assessment makes it an attractive tool for the present study.[25]

For the purpose of this study, the MIDC personality inventory was used to code diagnostically relevant information, on the subjects examined, collected from available source materials. Specifically, for Indira Gandhi, Golda Meir, and Margaret Thatcher, this data set included a detailed extraction and coding of material contained in the major biographies and autobiographies available. The final choice of books was based on peer and critical reviews, the richness of the sources on which they were based, and their scholarly contribution to the field. Taken together, these selected texts provided an ample mix of perspectives on and assessments (critical, complimentary, and neutral) of our principal subjects. The wealth of data that they yielded compensated for the fact that none of the leaders under study was accessible for a clinical interview (the traditional, but not exclusive, basis for placement under Millon's taxonomy). Given the large size of the database created, about 30 per cent of the data was extracted and coded independently by two investigators, with agreement on 83.4 per cent of the items, while the remainder was divided in half and coded by one of the two investigators.

In the construction of the personality profiles for each of the three subjects of this study, five of the eight attribute domains – expressive behaviour, interpersonal conduct, cognitive style, mood/temperament, and self-image – were explored for each of twelve personality patterns/scales categorized in Millon's taxonomy.[26] Owing to the absence of sufficient information regarding the remaining three domains – that is, object representations, regulatory mechanisms, and morphological organizations of Gandhi, Meir, and Thatcher – these areas could not be meaningfully examined. In principle, such information is available but only through the process of clinical interviews. Millon has attested that this "narrower scope of [five directly observable] attributes … [is] sufficient to provide a reasonably comprehensive picture" of a person's major characteristics.[27]

Scoring

To assess the relative importance of the twelve personality patterns in the personality profile of the leaders studied here, the presence of the diagnostic criteria associated with each pattern was firstly identified in the research material (biographies, documents, speeches, etc.) Then this presence was measured across the five attribute domains and each letter value from "a" to "e" was given an ascending numerical weight from 1 to 5.[28] The maximum possible score for each of the first ten personality scales was 30. This figure is derived from adding the numerical values assigned to a (1), b (2), and c (3) and then multiplying the result of six by the number of attribute domains. Using the same logic, the maximum possible score for each of the last two personality patterns was 45; this figure was derived from adding the numerical values of d (4) and e (5), for a total of nine, and multiplying it by five – the number of attribute domains. For example, a score of 21 on Indira Gandhi's Ambitious personality pattern was derived from adding the subscores for each of the five domains across which her personality traits were measured. Her expressive behaviour and self-image received a coding of "a," "b," and "c" on the Ambitious scale (1+2+3 x 2), for a numerical count of 12; on the same Ambitious scale, her interpersonal conduct, cognitive style, and mood/temperament were each coded as "a" and "b" (1+2x3), for a numerical count of 9. Together they produced a score of 21. The score sheet graphically depicts the foregoing technical explanation.

Data Analysis

After obtaining an MIDC score, the resulting personality profile of each prime minister was interpreted according to procedures stipulated in the MIDC manual. The principal personality patterns were noted as well

Table 8
Millon's eight attribute domains

Expressive behaviour	The individual's characteristic behaviour; how the individual typically appears to others; what the individual knowingly or unknowingly reveals about him or herself.
Interpersonal conduct	How the individual typically interacts with others; the attitudes that underlie, prompt, and give shape to these actions; the methods by which the individual engages others to meet his or her needs; how the individual copes with social tensions and conflicts.
Cognitive style	How the individual focuses and allocates attention, encodes and processes information, organizes thoughts, makes attributions, and communicates reactions and ideas to others.
Mood/ Temperament	How the individual typically displays emotion; the predominant character of an individual's affect and the intensity and frequency with which he or she expresses it.
Self-image	The individual's perception of self-as-object or the manner in which the individual overtly describes him or herself.
Regulatory mechanisms	The individual's characteristic mechanisms of self-protection, need gratification, and conflict resolution.
Object representations	The residue of significant past experiences, composed of memories, attitudes, and affects that underlie the individual's perceptions of and reactions to ongoing events.
Morphologic organization	The structural strength, interior congruity, and functional efficacy of the personality system.

Source: Millon, *Disorders of Personality: DSM–IV and Beyond* (141–6); *Toward a New Personology: An Evolutionary Model* (chapter 5); and *Personality and Its Disorders: A Biosocial Learning Approach* (32).

as the specific gradation – "a" to "c" (see Table 9) – within the first ten patterns. The two disturbed personality patterns, the Paranoid and the Erratic, were graded as "d" and "e." This procedure serves to identify primary personality designations that are relevant to the accurate classification of the subject in question. The resulting personality patterns (i.e., scale labels) and gradations (i.e., types) are reported in the pattern/gradation format (e.g., a subject can be classified primarily as "Conscientious/respectful").

For Scales 1–8, scores of 5 through 9 signify the *presence* (gradation a) of the personality pattern in question; scores of 10 through 23 indicate robust evidence of a *prominent* (gradation b) variant; scores of 15 through 23 provide minimal evidence of exaggerated features of the basic personality pattern (gradation c); and scores of 24 to 30 indicate robust evidence of these exaggerated variations (gradation c) of the pattern. For Scales 9 and 0, scores of 20 to 35 indicate a *moderately disturbed* syndrome (gradation

Table 9
Millon inventory of diagnostic criteria: Scales and gradations

Scale 1A:	Dominant pattern	
	a.	Assertive
	b.	Controlling
	c.	Aggressive (Sadistic; DSM-III-R, Appendix A)
Scale 1B:	Dauntless pattern	
	a.	Venturesome
	b.	Dissenting
	c.	Aggrandizing (Antisocial; DSM-IV, 301.7)
Scale 2:	Ambitious pattern	
	a.	Confident
	b.	Self-serving
	c.	Exploitative (Narcissistic; DSM-IV 301.81)
Scale 3:	Outgoing pattern	
	a.	Congenial
	b.	Gregarious
	c.	Impulsive (Histrionic; DSM-IV 301.50)
Scale 4:	Accommodating pattern	
	a.	Cooperative
	b.	Agreeable
	c.	Submissive (Dependent; DSM-IV 301.6)
Scale 5A:	Aggrieved pattern	
	a.	Unpresuming
	b.	Self-denying
	c.	Self-defeating (Masochistic; DSM-III-R, Appendix A)
Scale 5B:	Contentious pattern	
	a.	Resolute
	b.	Oppositional
	c.	Negativistic (Passive-aggressive; DSM-III-R, 301.84)
Scale 6:	Conscientious pattern	
	a.	Respectful
	b.	Dutiful
	c.	Compulsive (Obsessive-compulsive; DSM-IV, 301.4)
Scale 7:	Reticent pattern	
	a.	Circumspect
	b.	Inhibited
	c.	Withdrawn (Avoidant; DSM-IV, 301.82)

Table 9 (*Continued*)
Millon inventory of diagnostic criteria: Scales and gradations

Scale 8:		Retiring pattern
	a.	Reserved
	b.	Aloof
	c.	Solitary (Schizoid; DSM-IV, 301.20)
Scale 9:		Distrusting pattern
	d.	Suspicious
	e.	Paranoid (DSM-IV, 301.0)
Scale 0:		Erratic pattern
	d.	Unstable
	e.	Borderline (DSM-IV, 301.83)

d) and scores of 36 to 45 (gradation e) a *markedly disturbed* syndrome. In the course of this study, only those scales that reached the level of *prominent* (gradation b) or higher were explored since they constitute the strongest patterns in the personality profile and were presumed to have the most important influences on leadership style.

To recapitulate, the analysis of the data collected in this study includes the following: a statement of descriptive MIDC numerical values yielded by the scoring procedure; the specific MIDC profiles for Indira Gandhi, Golda Meir, and Margaret Thatcher; diagnostic classifications of the subjects; and, finally, a clinical interpretation of significant MIDC scale elevations derived from the first phases of the diagnostic process.

Personality Profiles: MIDC *Attributes*

Few people exhibit personality patterns in pure or prototypal form. Although the standard diagnostic approach to interpreting MIDC profiles focuses only on the two primary scale elevations for reasons of time and space, personality functioning, in reality, involves the aggregation of several prevailing orientations.[29] This is amply demonstrated in the analysis of the personality profiles of Gandhi, Meir, and Thatcher presented here, where a number of different dimensions of their individual personalities emerged as diagnostically significant. Hence, I have chosen to focus on more than simply two scale elevations. Four personality patterns were discussed in each of the cases of Indira Gandhi and Margaret Thatcher, and five patterns in the case of Golda Meir.

The theoretical foundations for the different personality patterns to be used here are largely drawn from Millon's model of personality,[30] supplemented by the theoretically congruent portraits by Oldham and Morris[31] and Strack.[32] For a detailed description of the core diagnostic features of each of these domains for all twelve personality scales, see Immelman.[33] What follows is a more general description of each of the twelve personality scales that will greatly facilitate the mapping of personality and leadership style.

SCALE 1A: THE DOMINANT PATTERN

The Dominant scale, as with all personality patterns except the Paranoid and Erratic, occurs on a continuum ranging from normal to maladaptive. At the healthy, well-adjusted end (scores of 5 to 9) are assertive, tough, outspoken, and strong-willed personalities. Strack provides the following portrait of the normal prototype of the Forceful (Dominant) personality: "Forceful people seem driven to prove their worthiness. They are characterized by an assertive, dominant and tough-minded personal style. They tend to be strong-willed, ambitious, competitive, and self-determined ... In work settings, these personalities are often driven to excel. They work hard to achieve their goals, are competitive, and do well where they can take control or work independently. In supervisory or leadership positions, these persons usually take charge and see to it that a job gets done."[34]

Exaggerated Dominant features (scores of 10 to 23) occur in those individuals characterized by a controlling, forceful, and overbearing style that can be both intimidating and abrasive. Controlling individuals, though often somewhat disagreeable, tend to be emotionally stable and conscientious. According to Millon, they are generally "tough and unsentimental ... Although many sublimate their power-oriented tendencies in publicly approved roles and vocations, these inclinations become evident in occasional intransigence, stubbornness, and coercive behaviors. Despite these periodic negative expressions, controlling types typically make effective leaders, being talented in supervising and persuading others to work for the achievement of common goals."[35]

In its most deeply ingrained, inflexible form (scores of 24 to 30), the Dominant pattern displays itself in an aggressive, domineering, and belligerent style that is consistent with a clinical diagnosis of the Sadistic personality. Oldham and Morris portray Aggressive (Dominant) personalities as individuals who can undertake huge responsibilities without fear of failure. "They wield power with ease. They never back away from a fight ... When put to the service of the greater good [which often it is not], the Aggressive (Dominant) personality style can inspire a man or woman to great leadership, especially in times of crisis."[36]

SCALE 1B: THE DAUNTLESS PATTERN

Individuals who score within the normal range (scores of 5 to 9) on the Dauntless pattern are the adventurous, enterprising personalities who

Table 10
The Dominant pattern across five attribute domains

Attribute Domains	Present (5–9)	Prominent (10–23)	Mildly Dysfunctional (24–30)
Expressive Behaviour	Assertive: tough; strong-willed; outspoken; argumentative; unsentimental	Forceful: controlling; overbearing; dogmatic	Aggressive: intimidating; domineering; belligerent
Interpersonal Behaviour	Commanding: powerful; authoritative; assertive	Intimidating: abrasive; coercive; fear-inspiring	Belligerent: pugnacious; verbally abusive; derisive; sadistic
Cognitive Style	Opinionated: outspoken; emphatic; adamant; insistent; inflexible	Dogmatic: closed-minded; obstinate	Bigoted: socially intolerant; inherently prejudiced especially towards envied or derogated social groups
Mood/ Temperament	Angry: irritable; cold; unfriendly; excitable; mean-spirited; insensitive	Hostile: aggressive; pugnacious; contentious; belligerent	Malevolent: callous disregard for the rights of others; coarse incivility
Self-image	Assertive: tough; strong-willed; forthright; unsentimental; bold	Competitive: powerful; energetic; hard-headed	Dominant: commanding; combative; values aspects of self that present tough, power-oriented image

Source: Oldham and Morris, *The New Personality Self-Portrait*, 345; Millon and Everly, *Personality and Its Disorders*, 32; and Millon, *Disorders of Personality*, 484–6.

are attracted to calculated risks and challenges and who seek to do things their own way. Exaggerated Dauntless features (scores of 10 to 23) occur in the fearless, daring personalities who are undaunted by danger. In its most deeply ingrained, inflexible form (scores of 24 to 30), the Dauntless pattern displays itself in acts of recklessness, impetuousness, and irresponsibility that transgress established social codes and are consistent with a clinical diagnosis of anti-social personality disorder.

Normal, adaptive variants of the Dauntless pattern (i.e., venturesome and dissenting types) correspond to Oldham and Morris's Adventurous style[37] and Millon's Dissenting pattern.[38] Oldham and Morris suggest that the following eight traits and behaviours are reliable clues to the presence of an Adventurous (Dauntless) style: non-conformity – lives by an internal code of values; challenge – routinely engages in high-risk activities; mutual independence – not overly concerned about others, expects each individual to be responsible for him or herself; persuasiveness – a charmer talented in the art of social influence; wanderlust – likes to keep moving, living by his or her talents, skills, ingenuity, and wits; wild oats – history of childhood and adolescent mischief and hell-raising; true grit – courageous, physically bold, and tough; no regrets – lives in the present, does not feel guilty about the past or anxious about the future.[39] Ultimately, Adventurous types "are fundamentally out for themselves"; they "do not need others to fuel their self-esteem or to provide purpose to their lives, and they don't make sacrifices for other people, at least not easily." Furthermore, they believe in themselves and do not require anyone's approval; they have "a definite sense of what is right or wrong for them, and if something is important to them, they'll do it no matter what anyone thinks." In spite of their self-centredness, adventurous people are capable of advancing a cause in the service of their personal desires or ambition; but fundamentally what matters is the momentary excitement, emotional vitality, or sense of aliveness that they experience, not love of person, country, or cause.[40]

Millon describes the Dissenting (Dauntless) profile as follows: "[It] include[s] *unconventional* persons who seek to do things their own way and are willing to take the consequences for doing so. They act as they see fit regardless of how others judge them. [They are] inclined at times to elaborate on or shade the truth as well as to ride close to the edge of the law ... Most dislike following the same routine day after day and, at times, act *impulsively* and irresponsibly ... Being skeptical about the motives of most people, and refusing to be fettered or coerced, they exhibit a strong need for autonomy and self-determination."[41]

Millon and Davis directly address the relevance of the Dauntless pattern to leadership – specifically at the intermediate range of the continuum, where normality shades into the more aggrandizing, anti-social variant of this pattern. They note that within this range "we find persons [e.g., some very successful industrialists, entrepreneurs, and corporate executives] who have never come into conflict with the law, but only because they are very effective in covering their tracks." They continue: "For many politicians, the deception of doublespeak is a talent necessary for survival. Skirting the edge of deceitfulness, they 'spin' objective events by minimizing negatives and exaggerating positives. When cornered, they focus attention on mitigating circumstances and lie by omission by failing to report the total circumstances and full motives of their actions. Moreover, they deliberately create public policy so complex that any particular aspect might be singled out to impress the special interest of the moment."[42]

In their examination of the developmental background of these so-called "socially sublimated antisocials," Millon and Davis assert that their experiential history is often characterized by secondary status in the family. In particular, parents may have given special attention to another sibling who was admired and highly esteemed, at least in the eyes of the "deprived" youngster.[43]

Table 11
The Dauntless pattern across five attribute domains

Attribute Domains	Present (5–9)	Prominent (10–23)	Mildly Dysfunctional (24–30)
Expressive Behaviour	Adventurous: courageous; physically bold; innovative	Impulsive: daring; fearless; thrill-seeking; risk-taking	Challenging: flouts conventional authority; engages in various illegal activities
Interpersonal Conduct	Selfish: concerned with own needs	Irresponsible: negates marital, parental, financial, and employment obligations	Vindictive: takes satisfaction in humiliating others and engaging in anti-social behaviour, such as swindling, extortion, and fraud
Cognitive Style	Non-conforming: lives by own internal code of values	Contemptuous: disparages conventional ethics and values	Deviant: lacking in empathy
Mood/ Temperament	Unrestrained: irritable; voices feelings without inhibition	Callous: irascible; tendency to vent urges directly	Aggressive: confrontational; pugnacious
Self-image	Unconventional: independent	Self-sufficient: unconstrained by personal attachments	Inviolable: clever; cunning; deviant

Source: Oldham and Morris, The New Personality Self-Portrait, 227–8; Millon and Davis, Personality Disorders in Modern Life, 102–8; and Millon, Disorders of Personality, 442–7.

SCALE 2: THE AMBITIOUS PATTERN

Those who score in the normal range (scores of 5 to 9) on the Ambitious scale are the confident, poised, self-assured, ambitious, and persuasive personalities. Exaggerated Ambitious features (scores between 10 and 23) occur in those individuals characterized by arrogance, a sense of entitlement, and a lack of empathy for others. In its most deeply ingrained, inflexible form (scores of between 24 and 30), the Ambitious pattern displays itself in an exploitative, manipulative style that is consistent with a clinical diagnosis of a narcissistic personality disorder.[44] At the well-adjusted end of the Ambitious scale, "self-confident individuals stand out. They're the leaders, the shining lights, the attention-getters in their public or private spheres. Theirs is a quality born of self-regard, self-respect, and self-certainty – all those words that denote a faith in oneself and a commitment to one's self-styled purpose. Combined with the ambition that marks this style, that ... self-regard can transform idle dreams into real accomplishment ... Self-confident [Ambitious] men and women know what they want, and they get it. Many of them have the charisma to attract plenty of others to their goals. They are extroverted and intensely political. They know how to work the crowd, how to motivate it, and how to lead it."[45]

Strack also provides the following description of the normal (confident) prototype of the Ambitious pattern: "Aloof, calm and *confident*, these personalities tend to be egocentric and self-reliant. They may have a keen sense of their own importance, uniqueness, or entitlement. Confident [Ambitious] individuals enjoy other's attention. But they can be self-centered to a fault and may become so preoccupied with themselves that they lack concern and empathy for others ... Ironically the confident [Ambitious] individual's secure appearance may cover feelings of personal inadequacy and a sensitivity to criticism and rejection. Unfortunately, they usually do not permit others to see their vulnerable side ... In the workplace, confident [Ambitious] persons like to take charge in an emphatic manner, often doing so in a way that instills confidence in others."[46]

Millon summarizes the more exaggerated variants of the Asserting (Ambitious) pattern as follows: "An interpersonal boldness, stemming from a belief in themselves and their talents, characterize(s) those high on the ... Asserting scale. Competitive, ambitious, and self-assured, they naturally assume positions of leadership, act in a decisive and unwavering manner, and expect others to recognize their special qualities and cater to them. Beyond being self-confident, those with an Asserting profile often are audacious, clever, and persuasive, having sufficient charm to win others over to their own causes and purposes. Problematic in this regard may be their lack of social reciprocity and their sense of entitlement – their assumption that what they wish for is their due. On the other hand, their ambitions often succeed, and they typically prove to be effective leaders."[47]

SCALE 3: THE OUTGOING PATTERN

At the normal well-adjusted pole (scores of 5 to 9) of the Outgoing pattern are the congenial, friendly, gregarious, and engaging personalities. Exaggerated Outgoing features (scores of between 10 and 23) occur in those individuals characterized by theatrical, flamboyant, and self-dramatizing personalities. In its most deeply ingrained, inflexible form (scores of between 24 and 30), the Outgoing pattern displays itself in an impulsive, volatile, hedonistic, and excitable style that is consistent with a clinical diagnosis of a histrionic personality disorder. Normal, adaptive variants of the Outgoing pattern (i.e., congenial and gregarious types) correspond to Oldham and Morris's Dramatic style,[48] Strack's Sociable style,[49] and Millon's Outgoing pattern.[50]

Healthy Outgoing individuals "have a need of attention and approval ... They can be quite sensitive to the needs and wants of others,

Table 12
The Ambitious pattern across five attribute domains

Attribute Domains	Present (5–9)	Prominent (10–23)	Mildly Dysfunctional (24–30)
Expressive Behaviour	Confident: self-assured; self-confident; calm	Conceited: self-promoting; haughty; pretentious; self-important; pompous; disdainful	Manipulative: arrogant; imperious; self-righteous; indifferent to the rights of others
Interpersonal Conduct	Self-assured: competitive; persuasive; shrewd; ambitious	Unempathetic: expects favours without assuming reciprocal responsibilities; acts as though entitled	Manipulative: uses others to achieve personal goals or to enhance the self; deceitful; exploitive
Cognitive Style	Imaginative: inventive; innovative; resourceful; belief in their own efficacy	Expansive: unrestrained; fantasies of success in which failure is minimized	Undisciplined: exaggerated; pre-occupied with self-glorifying fantasies of fame
Mood/ Temperament	Unruffled: untroubled; serene; collected; optimistic	Insouciant: imperturbable; nonchalant; sangfroid	Exuberant: ebullient; smug; self-satisfied (however, displays anger when feelings of superiority are punctured)
Self-image	Confident: socially poised; self-assured; self-possessed; secure	Admirable: meritorious; esteemed; valued; enviable	Superior: masterful; unique; entitled to special rights and privileges

Source: Millon, *Millon Clinical Multiaxial Inventory – III*, 32; Oldham and Morris, *The New Personality Self-Portrait*, 79; Strack, "The PACL: Gauging Normal Personality Styles," 489–90; Millon, *MIPS: Millon Index of Personality Styles Manual*, 32; Millon, *Disorders of Personality*, 405; and Millon and Everly, *Personality and Its Disorders: A Bio-Social Learning Approach*, 32, 39.

at least to those aspects that will help them get the attention they seek ... They may have quickly shifting moods and emotions, and may come across as shallow and ungenuine. These persons tend to prefer novelty and excitement and are bored by ordinary or mundane activities ... They often do well interacting with the public, [and] may be skilled and adept at rallying or motivating others."[51]

Millon summarizes the Outgoing pattern as follows: "Gregarious persons go out of their way to be popular with others, have confidence in their social abilities, feel they can readily influence and charm others,

Table 13
The Outgoing pattern across five attribute domains

Attribute Domains	Present (5–9)	Prominent (10–23)	Mildly Dysfunctional (24–30)
Expressive Behaviour	Sociable: friendly; outgoing; lively; animated; gregarious; vivacious; extraverted	Dramatic: flamboyant; theatrical; self-dramatizing	Impulsive: volatile; hedonistic; histrionic; sensation or excitement seeking to prevent boredom or inactivity
Interpersonal Conduct	Demonstrative: displays feelings openly; amiable; gregarious; sociable; desires to be well liked	Attention-seeking: actively solicits reassurance and approval; flirtatious	Seductive: manipulates others to obtain praise or attention; exhibitionistic
Cognitive Style	Unreflective: avoids introspective thought; focuses on external events	Superficial: flighty in thought; speaks and writes in impressionist generalities	Scattered: incoherent; integrates experiences poorly, resulting in scattered learning and thoughtless judgments
Mood/ Temperament	Expressive: lively; spirited; uninhibited	Changeable: frequently displays short-lived and superficial emotions	Impetuous: overly excitable; capricious; exhibits pervasive tendency to be easily enthused and as easily angered or bored
Self-image	Charming: delightful; attractive; social; affable	Gregarious: convivial; stimulating; well-liked	Hedonistic: sensual; self-indulgent; bon vivant; pleasure-seeking; epicurean

Source: Millon, *Disorders of Personality*, 366–9, 371; Millon and Everly, *Personality and Its Disorders*, 33; Millon and Davis, *Personality Disorders in Modern Life*, 236.

and possess a personal style that makes people like them. Most enjoy engaging in social activities, and like meeting new people and learning about their lives. At a more exaggerated level they are talkative, lively, socially clever; often they are dramatic attention getters who thrive on being the center of social events. Many become easily bored, especially when faced with repetitive and mundane tasks ... [Although prone to] intense and shifting moods ... their enthusiasms often prove effective in energizing and motivating others. Inclined to be facile and enterprising, outgoing people may be highly skilled at manipulating others to meet their needs." [52]

SCALE 4: THE ACCOMMODATING PATTERN

Within the normal range (scores of 5 to 9) of the Accommodating pattern are the accepting, uncritical, conciliatory, and placating personalities. Exaggerated Accommodating features (scores of between 10 and
23) occur in those individuals characterized by submissive, reliant, and
docile personalities. In its most deeply ingrained, inflexible form, the
Accommodating pattern displays itself in a dependent, inadequate, and
socially incompetent style that is consistent with a clinical diagnosis of a
dependent personality disorder. Normal adaptive variants of the Accommodating pattern (i.e., cooperative and agreeable types) correspond
to Oldham and Morris's Devoted style, whose characteristics include
caring for others, being very solicitous or protective, and placing others'
welfare above one's own;[53] Strack's Cooperative style;[54] and Millon's
Agreeing pattern.[55]

Individuals who manifest the adaptive variants of the Accommodating pattern "are capable of *empathizing with others*, willingly giving of
themselves and possessing a great capacity for caring and sustained love
for others. They are among the most *trusting* of individuals, communicating unquestioning acceptance of others. They are *modest* and *gentle*
in their demeanor ... Notable is their *uncritical* and *unthreatening*
manner ... Easy to please, they demand little from others, are totally
uncritical, and invariably *gracious*, even to those they may dislike."[56]
"Their congenial *obligingness* is voluntary rather than being coerced or
being a product of self-derogation. Those who fit this pattern are notably *cooperative* and *amicable*."[57] Strack provides the following portrait
of the normal prototype of the Accommodating pattern:

> Cooperative [Accommodating] persons can be identified by a *need
> for approval* and *affection*, and by a willingness to live in accord with
> the desires of others. They usually adapt their behavior to the stan-
> dards of others, but in the process may deny their own needs. Inter-
> personally, these individuals are often *cooperative, reliable,
> considerate of others*, and *deferential*. They may appear even-
> tempered, docile, obliging, self-effacing, ingratiating, or naive. Coop-
> erative individuals often see themselves as being modestly endowed in
> terms of skills and abilities. They are often pleased when they can rely
> on others and may feel insecure when left on their own. Especially
> when faced with difficult or stressful situations, cooperative persons
> seek others to provide authority, leadership, and direction. They often
> prefer group work environments and will typically excel in them if
> given support and guidance. They are usually willing to follow direc-
> tions and cooperate with co-workers in team efforts.[58]

Table 14
The Accommodating pattern across five attribute domains

Attribute Domains	Present (5–9)	Prominent (10–23)	Mildly Dysfunctional (24–30)
Expressive Behaviour	Accommodating: cooperative; adaptable; docile; devoted; compliant; solicitous of others	Submissive: reliant on others; lacks self-assurance; passive; ineffectual; inept	Dependent: inadequate; fearful of responsibilities; acts helpless; socially incompetent
Interpersonal Conduct	Compliant: conciliatory or placating; conflict averse; solicitous; accepting and uncritical	Submissive: devoted; compliant; subordinates own need to stronger, nurturing figures	Clinging: self-sacrificing; helpless; anxiously attached; needs excessive advice and reassurance
Cognitive Style	Unreflective: naive; avoids introspective thought; focuses on external events	Superficial: thoughtless or flighty in reason; speaks and writes in impressionistic generalities	Scattered: rambling; integrates experiences poorly, resulting in scattered learning, and poor judgment
Mood/ Temperament	Serene: mild-mannered; warm-hearted; tender; understanding; empathic	Docile: soft-hearted; uncompetitive; dovish	Timid: avoids social tension; discouraged, and dejected when deprived of social support
Self-image	Considerate: views self as cooperative, thoughtful, and devoted	Inadequate: views self as unassertive or vulnerable	Inept: views self as weak and fragile

Source: Millon, *Disorders of Personality*, 331–4.

Oldham and Morris add the following perspective: "Devoted [Accommodating] types care, and that's what makes their lives worth living. You won't find anyone more *loving*, more *solicitous* of you, more concerned for your needs and feelings, or for those of the group as a whole. At their best, individuals with this style are loyal, considerate, ever-so-helpful players on the team – whether it is the couple, the family, the assembly line, the department, the religious or charitable organization, or the military unit."[59]

SCALE 5A: THE AGGRIEVED PATTERN
Individuals who exhibit an Aggrieved pattern at the normal end of the spectrum (scores of 5 to 9) are humble, unpretentious, and deferential personalities. An exaggerated form of Aggrieved features (scores of 10

to 23) is common in self-sacrificing, self-denying, and self-abasing personalities. In its most deeply ingrained, inflexible form (scores of 24 to 30), the Aggrieved pattern displays itself in masochistic, self-defeating behaviour patterns that are consistent with a clinical diagnosis of a self-defeating or masochistic personality disorder.

Normal, adaptive variants of the Aggrieved pattern (unassuming and self-effacing types) correspond to Oldham and Morris's Self-sacrificing style[60] and Millon's Yielding pattern.[61] The self-defeating, Aggrieved pattern is often a consequence of cultural values and customs as well as unique personal experiences.[62] Unassuming, self-denying individuals live to serve and be helpful to others. "When allowed to give selflessly of themselves, everything is right with the world. Forever putting others above themselves, they have a reputation for being kind, considerate and charitable ... Although they willingly shoulder the burdens of life for those they love, they feel uncomfortable when their good deeds are singled out for praise, honestly believing that no thanks or recognition is necessary."[63]

Oldham and Morris portray the more adaptive variants of this Self-sacrificing (Aggrieved) style as follows: "To live life is to serve: to love life is to give. These are axioms for individuals who exhibit the *Self-sacrificing* personality style. The way they see it, their needs can wait until others are well served. Knowing that they have given of themselves, they feel comfortable and at peace, secure with their place in the scheme of things. At its best and most noble, theirs is the selfless, magnanimous style of which saints and good citizens are made."[64]

Millon focuses on the less adaptive dimensions of the Yielding (Aggrieved) interpersonal trait dimension. "These persons show a disposition to act in a subservient and self-abasing manner ... They are unassertive and deferential, if not servile. Often viewing themselves as their own worst enemies, they behave in an unpresuming, self-effacing, even self-derogating manner, and tend to avoid displaying their talents and aptitudes."[65]

SCALE 5B: THE CONTENTIOUS PATTERN

Individuals who fall within the normal range of the Contentious scale (scores of 5 to 9) typify the cynical, headstrong, resolute personalities. Exaggerated Contentious features (scores of 10 to 23) occur in complaining, irksome, oppositional personalities. In its most deeply ingrained, inflexible form (scores of 24 to 30), the Contentious pattern displays itself in caustic, contrary, and negative behaviour patterns that are consistent with a clinical diagnosis of "negativistic" or passive-aggressive personality disorder.

Normal adaptive variants of the Contentious pattern (i.e., resolute and oppositional types) correspond to Strack's Sensitive style[66] and to Millon's

Table 15
The Aggrieved pattern across five attribute domains

Attribute Domains	Present (5–9)	Prominent (10–23)	Mildly Dysfunctional (24–30)
Expressive Behaviour	Humble: meek; unpretentious; unassertive; chaste	Subservient: un-indulgent; frugal; self-denying; ascetic	Self-denigrating: self-defeating; self-abasing
Interpersonal Conduct	Deferential: yields to expectations of those they follow; distances from those who are supportive	Servile: allows others to exploit, mistreat, or take advantage	Masochistic: renders ineffectual the efforts of others to be helpful; solicits condemnation by accepting undeserved blame and courting unjust criticism
Cognitive Style	Uncertain: unsure; reluctant to express views; diffident	Apologetic: self-effacing in interpreting events	Self-reproachful: self-deprecating; pessimistic in orientation; positive attitudes are voiced without enthusiasm
Mood/ Temperament	Dysphoric: plaintive; wistful; longing; discontented	Forlorn: doleful; unhappy; mournful; miserable	Disconsolate: pathetic; heartbroken; wretched
Self-Image	Inconsequential: unimportant; irrelevant	Unworthy: devoid of value; undeserving of good things such as success or happiness	Contemptible: utterly worthless for their perceived failure to live up to others' expectations

Source: Millon and Davis, Personality Disorders in Modern Life, 496; Oldham and Morris, The New Personality Self-Portrait, 319; Millon, MIPS: Millon Index of Personality Styles Manual, 33; and Millon, Disorders of Personality, 584–9.

Complaining pattern.[67] Strack provides the following portrait of the normal Sensitive [Contentious] pattern: "Sensitive [Contentious] personalities tend to be unconventional and individualistic in their response to the world. They march to the beat of a different drummer and are frequently unhappy with the status quo. They may be quick to challenge rules or authority deemed arbitrary and unjust. They may also harbor resentment without expressing it directly and may revert to passive-aggressive behavior to make their feelings known. Many Sensitive people feel as if they don't fit in, and view themselves as lacking in interpersonal skills ... With their best side forward, sensitive persons can be spontaneous, creative, and willing to speak out for what they believe in."[68]

Table 16
The Contentious pattern across five attribute domains

Attribute Domains	Present (5–9)	Prominent (10–23)	Mildly Dysfunctional (24–30)
Expressive Behaviour	Irritable: cynical; discontented; sullen	Complaining: irksome; resistant	Oppositional: contrary; negativistic
Interpersonal Conduct	Unyielding: superficially acquiescent but fundamentally determined and resolute	Obdurate: recalcitrant; mulish; quarrelsome; disputatious	Oppositional: truculent; obstructive; insolent; chronically complaining; overtly resistant to performance demands
Cognitive Style	Skeptical: cynical; doubting; with an ingrained tendency to question authority	Whining: griping; pessimistic	Negativistic: disdainful; caustic; acerbic
Mood/ Temperament	Moody: fretful; touchy; nettled; impatient	Irritable: obstinate; resentful; critical; petulant; testy	Disgruntled: agitated; irate; peevish; easily annoyed; frustrated, or disappointed by others; likely to induce discomfort or guilt in others
Self-image	Dissatisfied: discontented; critical	Wronged: misunderstood; luckless; unappreciated; demeaned by others	Disillusioned: bitter; disgruntled; envious

Source: Millon, *MIPS: Millon Index of Personality Styles Manual*, 33–4; Strack, "The PACL: Gauging Normal Personality Styles," 490–1; Oldham and Morris, *The New Personality Self-Portrait*, 222; Millon, *Disorders of Personality*, 549–50.

Millon puts it this way: "Those scoring high on the Complaining [Contentious] scale often assert that they have been treated unfairly, that little of what they have done has been appreciated, and that they have been blamed for things that they did not do. Opportunities seem not to have worked out well for them and they 'know that good things don't last.' Often resentful of what they see as unfair demands placed on them, they may be disinclined to carry out responsibilities as well as they could ... When matters go well, they can be productive and constructively independent-minded, willing to speak out to remedy troublesome issues."[69]

Individuals with the most exaggerated elevations on the Contentious pattern (scores of 24 to 30) sometimes referred to as the passive-aggressive personality profile, "raise contrariness to an art form. They stall, complain, oppose, dawdle, forget, scorn those who try to help – and then they feel cheated that life hasn't offered them a better deal. Their inner and outer experience of life is bitter and lacking in pleasure, yet they are unable to see that they themselves routinely close off all avenues of reward."[70]

SCALE 6: THE CONSCIENTIOUS PATTERN

At the normal end of the Conscientious scale (scores of 5 to 9) are found the respectful, disciplined, prudent, and orderly personalities. Exaggerated Conscientious features (scores of 10 to 23) occur in dutiful, rigid, proper, and dignified characters. In its most deeply ingrained inflexible form (scores of 24 to 30), the Conscientious pattern is displayed in perfectionist, meticulous, and fastidious behaviour that is consistent with a clinical diagnosis of obsessive-compulsive personality disorder.

Normal, adaptive variants of the Conscientious pattern (i.e., respectful and dutiful types) correspond to Oldham and Morris's Conscientious style,[71] Millon's Conforming pattern,[72] and Strack's Respectful style.[73] Adaptive variants of this pattern are evident in those individuals who are disciplined and organized, with "an unusual degree of integrity, adhering as firmly as they can to society's ethics and morals."[74] Oldham and Morris describe the personality type this way:

> Most of the key behaviors that identify the *Conscientious* style occur in the area of work. Work is the key domain of functioning for the *Conscientious* style, and it dominates all others. *Conscientious* individuals are competent, organized, good with detail, perfectionistic, thorough, determined and loyal ... They're doers, and doing extends to all hours of the day ... Because they are willing to devote so much time and hard work, individuals with a substantial amount of *Conscientious* style tend to move toward the top of many professions by virtue of good old-fashioned hard work. If the conscientious pattern dominates all other patterns, in the domain of politics, one might expect such individuals to make exceptional seconds in command – the behind the scene individuals who will be best at the implementation of policy. The top managerial positions, however, may require skills that go against the *Conscientious* pattern, such as making quick decisions, setting priorities and delegating responsibility.[75]

Conscientious individuals have also been described as conformists. "Conformers are notably respectful of tradition and authority, and act in a reasonable, proper, and conscientious way. They do their best to uphold conventional rules and standards, following given regulations closely and tend to be judgmental of those who do not. Well-organized and reliable, prudent and restrained, they may appear to be overly self-controlled, formal and inflexible in their relationships, intolerant of deviance, and unbending in their adherence to social proprieties. Diligent about their responsibilities, they dislike having their work pile up, worry about finishing things, and come across to others as highly dependable and industrious."[76]

In his analysis, Strack presents a similar picture:

Responsible, industrious, and respectful of authority[,] these individuals tend to be conforming and work hard to uphold rules and regulations. They have a need for order and are typically conventional in their interests. These individuals can be rule abiding to a fault, however, and may be perfectionistic, inflexible, and judgmental. A formal interpersonal style and notable constriction of affect can make some respectful persons seem cold, aloof, and withholding. Underneath their social propriety there is often a fear of disapproval and rejection, or a sense of guilt over perceived shortcomings. Indecisiveness and an inability to take charge may be evident in some of these persons due to a fear of being wrong. However, among co-workers and friends, respectful [Conscientious] personalities are best known for being well organized, reliable, and diligent. They have a strong sense of duty and loyalty, are cooperative in group efforts, show persistence even in difficult circumstances, and work well under supervision.[77]

SCALE 7: THE RETICENT PATTERN

Those who score within the normal range of the Reticent pattern (scores of 5 to 9) are the circumspect personalities who exhibit cautious behaviour. Exaggerated Reticent personalities (scores of 10 to 23) are guarded, wary, apprehensive, insecure, and inhibited. In its most deeply ingrained, inflexible form (scores of 24 to 30), the Reticent pattern displays itself in a withdrawn style that is consistent with a clinical diagnosis of avoidant personality disorder.

Normal adaptive variants of the Reticent pattern (i.e., circumspect and inhibited types) correspond to Oldham and Morris's Sensitive style,[78] Millon's Hesitating pattern,[79] and Strack's Inhibited style.[80] Oldham and Morris describe normal adaptive Reticent individuals as follows: "When they know the people around them and are sure of their affection and respect, Sensitive [Reticent] types are relieved of their social anxieties and their personalities shine forth. Then, they usually build their lives around a few people around whom they are happy. 'You're always welcome here – you're family,' they will say to their close friends. But they will be slow to establish new ties. Until they begin to trust a new person's feelings for them, they'll seal off their emotions and confidences behind a polite, well-mannered, emotionally distant facade."[81]

Table 17
The Conscientious pattern across five attribute domains

Attribute Domains	Present (5–9)	Prominent (10–23)	Mildly Dysfunctional (24–30)
Expressive Behaviour	Dutiful: well-organized; disciplined; responsible; self-controlled; prudent; punctual; conscientious; moral	Rigid: over-controlled; orderly; stubborn; stingy; possessive; scrupulous in matters of morality and ethics	Perfectionist: pedantic; painfully fastidious; meticulous; excessively devoted to work and productivity
Interpersonal Conduct	Polite: courteous; proper; formal; punctual; dignified; adheres to social conventions; loyal to families, causes, and their superiors	Conforming: exacting; scrupulous in matters of morality; prefers "correct" personal relationships	Uncompromising and demanding with subordinates; ingratiating and obsequious with superiors
Cognitive Style	Circumspect: cautious; deliberate; methodical; wary of new or untested ideas; risk-avoidant	Unimaginative: upset by new ideas; pedestrian; uninspired; routinized	Constricted: mechanical; inflexible; rigid
Mood/Temperament	Restrained: serious; responsible; reasonable; reserved; prudent; dignified	Solemn: unrelaxed; controlled; joyless; uptight	Grave: somber; tense; grim; wooden; heavy
Self-image	Reliable: dependable; responsible; trustworthy; disciplined	Highly conscientious: scrupulous; meticulous; loyal	Righteous: virtuous; filled with moral rectitude; perfectionist

Source: Millon, *Disorders of Personality*, 506–7, 513–5; Oldham and Morris, *The New Personality Self-Portrait*, 64–5; Millon, MIPS: *Millon Index of Personality Styles Manual*, 33; and Strack, "The PACL: Gauging Normal Personality Styles," 490.

Strack also provides the following portrait of the normal prototype of the Reticent pattern:

The inhibited [Reticent] personality is marked by a tendency toward social withdrawal ... this pattern is motivated ... by a fear of negative consequences. Inhibited persons tend to be sensitive to their own feelings and to those of others. They often anticipate that others will be critical or rejecting of them; because of this, they frequently seem shy or skittish in unfamiliar surroundings ... Although inhibited persons tend to get along reasonably well with others, they are often difficult to get to know on a personal level. These individuals usually wish

that they could be at ease with others, but they often are just too uncertain of the consequences of closeness and intimacy to let their
guard down. As a result, they may experience feelings of loneliness,
but be unable or unwilling to do anything about them. Because of
their sensitivity to others, inhibited [Reticent] persons are often described as kind, considerate, and empathic by close acquaintances.[82]

Millon has explored the less adaptive variants of the Hesitating (Reticent) pattern and finds it characterized by

> social inhibition and withdrawal ... [and] has some common ground
> with the self-effacing segment of Leary's [1957] self-effacing-masochistic
> pattern, notable for its tendency to downplay personal abilities, to
> be shy and sensitive, and to experience feelings of anxiety and
> uncertainty ... Those scoring high on the Hesitating [Reticent] scale
> have a tendency to be sensitive to social indifference or rejection, to
> feel unsure of themselves, and to be wary in new situations, especially
> those of a social or interpersonal character. Somewhat ill at ease and
> self-conscious, these individuals anticipate running into difficulties in
> interrelating and fear being embarrassed. They may feel tense when
> they have to deal with persons they do not know, expecting that oth-
> ers will not think well of them. Most prefer to work alone or in small
> groups where they know that people accept them ... Once they feel
> accepted, they can open up, be friendly, be cooperative and partici-
> pate with others productively.[83]

SCALE 8: THE RETIRING PATTERN
Within the normal range of the Retiring pattern (scores of 5 to 9) are
the passive, stolid, unengaged, and unobtrusive personalities. Exaggerated Retiring features (scores of 10 to 23) occur in aloof, detached, socially remote personalities. In its most deeply ingrained form (scores of
24 to 30), the Retiring pattern displays itself in solitary, undemonstra-
tive, lifeless, and asocial behaviour patterns that are consistent with a
clinical diagnosis of schizoid personality disorder.
   Normal adaptive variants of the Retiring pattern (i.e., reserved and
aloof types) are characterized by low levels of sociability and compan-
ionability.[84] They correspond to Oldham and Morris's Solitary style,[85]
Strack's Introversive style,[86] and Millon's Retiring pattern.[87] According
to Oldham and Morris, retiring "solitary-style" individuals are self-
contained people without a need for external guidance, admiration, or
emotional sustenance. They feel no need to share their experiences and
draw their greatest strength and comfort from within themselves. "Solitary men and women need no one but themselves. They are unmoved

Table 18
The Reticent pattern across five attribute domains

Attribute Domains	Present (5–9)	Prominent (10–23)	Mildly Dysfunctional (24–30)
Expressive Behaviour	Watchful: quiet; circumspect; inhibited; hesitant	Guarded: insecure; wary; timorous; uneasy	Avoidant: anxious; avoids social contacts unless certain of being liked
Interpersonal Conduct	Reserved: quiet; private; shy; self-contained	Apprehensive: self-conscious; maintains distance to avoid social rejection or humiliation	Avoidant: reclusive; displays social anxiety and fear of humiliation or derogation
Cognitive Style	Preoccupied: ruminative; immersed in inner thoughts and ideas	Distracted: absent-minded; absorbed; disruptively preoccupied by inner thoughts and ideas	Bewildered: perplexed; irrelevant and intrusive ideation interferes with thought continuity
Mood/ Temperament	Uneasy: anxious; uncomfortable	Anguished: distressed; agitated; emotional experiences marked by confusing feelings of tension, sadness, and anger	Overwrought: tormented; vacillates between desire for affection, fear of rebuff; numbness of feeling
Self-image	Lonely: friendless; isolated but desirous of social acceptance	Alienated: detached; socially isolated; disaffected; empty	Rejected: forsaken; socially inept; inadequate; inferior

Source: Strack, "The PACL: Gauging Normal Personality Styles," 488; Oldham and Morris, *The New Personality Self-Portrait*, 186; Millon, *MIPS: Millon Index of Personality Styles Manual*, 32; Millon, *Disorders of Personality*, 261; Millon and Everly, *Personality and Its Disorders*, 33, 40.

by the madding crowd, liberated from the drive to impress and to please. Solitary people are remarkably free of the emotions and involvements that distract so many others. What they may give up in terms of sentiment and intimacy, however, they may gain in clarity of vision."[88]

Millon summarizes the Retiring pattern as follows: "[Retiring individuals] evince few social or group interests ... Their need to give and receive affection and to show feeling tend to be minimal. They are inclined to have few relationships and interpersonal involvements, and do not develop strong ties to other people ... They tend to work in a slow, quiet, and methodical manner, almost always remaining in the background in an undemanding and unobtrusive way. Comfortable working by themselves, they are not easily distracted or bothered by what goes on around them. Being somewhat deficient in the ability to recognize the needs or feeling others, they may be seen as socially awkward, if not insensitive, as well as lacking in spontaneity and vitality."[89]

Strack has offered the following portrait of the Retiring personality:

> Aloof, introverted, and solitary, these persons usually prefer distant or limited involvement with others and have little interest in social activities, which they find unrewarding. Appearing to others as complacent and untroubled, they are often judged to be easy-going, mild-mannered, quiet and retiring … [In] the workplace these people do well on their own, are typically dependable and reliable, are undemanding, and are seldom bothered by noise or commotion around them … However, these individuals may appear unaware of, or insensitive to, the feelings and thoughts of others. These characteristics are sometimes interpreted by others as signs of indifference or rejection, but reveal a sincere difficulty in being able to sense others' moods and needs. Introversive [Retiring] persons can be slow and methodical in demeanor, lack spontaneity and resonance, and be awkward or timid in social or group situations.[90]

SCALE 9: THE DISTRUSTING PATTERN

According to Millon, there is no normal variant of the Distrusting pattern; "it is hard to conceive [of] normal paranoids. Although a number of these individuals restrain their markedly distorted beliefs and assumptions from public view [exhibiting suspiciousness rather than overt paranoia], at no point does their fundamental paranoid inclination manifest itself in an acceptable, no less successful, personality style."[91] Thus, the Distrusting pattern occurs on a continuum ranging from maladaptive (suspicious) (scores of 20 to 35) to markedly disturbed (paranoid) (scores of 36 to 45). Oldham and Morris describe what is, in effect, the suspicious variant of the Distrusting pattern:

> Nothing escapes the notice of … [people who have a] Vigilant [Distrusting] personality style. These individuals possess an exceptional awareness of their environment … Their sensory antennae, continuously scanning the people and situations around them, alert them immediately to what is awry, out of place, dissonant, or dangerous, especially in their dealings with other people. Vigilant [Distrusting] types have a special kind of hearing. They are immediately aware of mixed messages, the hidden motivations, the evasions, and the subtlest distortions of the truth that elude or delude less gifted observers. With such a focus, Vigilant [Distrusting] individuals naturally assume the roles of social critic, watchdog, ombudsman, and crusader in their private or our public domain, ready to spring upon the improprieties – especially the abuses of power – that poison human affairs.[92]

Table 19
The Retiring pattern across five attribute domains

Attribute Domains	Present (5–9)	Prominent (10–23)	Mildly Dysfunctional (24–30)
Expressive Behaviour	Private: reserved; unsociable; undemonstrative; undiplomatic.	Solitary: indifferent; unresponsive; phlegmatic; stolid; colourless; bland	Impassive: stoical; apathetic; deficient in activation, motor expressiveness, and spontaneity
Interpersonal Conduct	Unobtrusive: private; self-contained; prefers solitary activities	Aloof: indifferent to others; socially disengaged; interpersonally detached	Asocial: reclusive; unresponsive to the emotions and behaviours of others; exhibits minimal interest in the lives of others
Cognitive Style	Vague: fuzzy; unclear; digressive; unfocused	Impoverished: ideas are sparse and meagre and thought processes are obscure	Barren: inarticulate; incomprehensible
Mood/ Temperament	Unemotional: phlegmatic; dispassionate; bland	Flat: impassive; gloomy; apathetic	Bleak: emotionally inert; numb; exhibits a cold, stark quality
Self-image	Bland: placid; satisfied; complacent	Introverted: aloof; somewhat unfeeling; socially unresponsive; insular; ordinary; uninteresting; introverted	Impervious: minimally introspective; unresponsive; indifferent to praise or criticism; somewhat lacking in empathy

Source: Millon, MIPS: Millon Index of Personality Styles Manual, 31; Oldham and Morris, The New Personality Self-Portrait, 275; Strack, "The PACL: Gauging Normal Personality Styles," 488; and Millon, Disorders of Personality, 230–1.

That aspect of Oldham and Morris's description pertaining to hypervigilance ("scanning the people and situations around them") overlaps with the "insecure" variant of the MIDC's Reticent pattern, whereas their reference to the "crusader" role in society incorporates aspects of both the Conscientious and Dominant patterns.

Among the most prominent features of those who exhibit the more extreme form of the distrusting pattern (i.e., a "paranoid style") is their mistrust of others. "They are characteristically *suspicious, guarded*, and *hostile*; tend to misread the actions of others; and respond with anger to what they frequently interpret as deception, deprecation, and betrayal. Their readiness to perceive hidden motives and deceit precipitates innumerable social difficulties, which then confirm and reinforce their expectations. Their need to distance from others, combined with their

Table 20

The Distrusting pattern across five attribute domains

Attribute Domains	Moderately Disturbed (20–34)	Markedly Disturbed (35–40)
Expressive Behaviour	Defensive: distrustful; suspicious; habitually anticipates deception or derogation	Vigilant: scans environment for potential threat; anticipates and is ready to ward off expected derogation
Interpersonal Conduct	Quarrelsome: polemical; disputatious; exasperating and truculent; does not forgive insults and tends to carry grudges	Acrimonious: vexatious; harassing and provocative; precipitates anger by testing loyalties and searching for hidden motives in others
Cognitive Style	Suspicious: highly and unwarrantedly mistrustful of the motives of others	Paranoid: construes innocuous events as signifying hidden or conspiratorial intent; tends to magnify tangential or minor social difficulties into proofs of duplicity, malice, and treachery
Mood/ Temperament	Sullen: humourless; tries to present self as unemotional and objective but is churlish and thin-skinned	Irascible: edgy; envious; jealous; quick to take personal offence and react angrily
Self-image	Formidable: lacks self-doubt; pridefully independent; reluctant to confide in others; highly insular; experiences intense fears of losing identity and status	Inviolable: has persistent ideas of self-importance and self-reference; perceives attacks on self not observable by others; asserts entirely innocuous events as personally derogatory and scurrilous, if not libelous

Source: Millon, Disorders of Personality DSM-IV, 690, 701, 705; and Oldham and Morris, The New Personality Self-Portrait

tendency to magnify minor slights, results in distortions that occasionally cross the bounds of reality."[93] A feature that justifies considering paranoids "among the more structurally defective personalities is the *inelasticity* and *constriction* of their coping skills ... Paranoids display such inflexible controls that they are subject to having their rigid facade shattered."[94]

SCALE O: THE ERRATIC PATTERN

The Erratic pattern, conceptually a decompensated,[95] structurally defective extension of the Accommodating, Outgoing, and Contentious patterns, also has no normal variant. According to Millon, the borderline level of pathology is intrinsically severe or structurally defective.[96] Thus, the Erratic pattern occurs on a continuum ranging from maladaptive to markedly disturbed. At the least maladaptive pole (scores of 20 to 35) are temperamental, capricious, unstable personalities. In its most deeply ingrained, markedly disturbed form (scores of 36 to 45), the Erratic pattern manifests itself in chaotic, self-damaging behaviour patterns that are consistent with a clinical diagnosis of borderline personality disorder.

Oldham and Morris's Mercurial style, though bearing some similarity to the exaggerated (oppositional) and dysfunctional (negativistic) variants of the MIDC's Contentious pattern, is substantially equivalent to the less maladaptive (unstable) variant of the MIDC's Erratic pattern: As they describe these individuals, "life is a roller coaster for those with the Mercurial [Erratic] personality style – and they'll insist that you come along for the ride. From peaks to the valleys, intensity imbues their every breath. Mercurial women and men yearn for experience, and they jump into a new love or a new lifestyle with both feet without even a glance behind. No other style ... is so ardent in its desire to connect with life and with other people. And no other style is quite so capable of enduring the changes in emotional weather that such a fervidly life will bring."[97]

For Millon, it is not only the depth and variability of moods that characterize the Erratic pattern. In its most dysfunctional manifestation, the borderline personality disorder, "borderlines tend to experience extended periods of dejection and disillusionment, interspersed occasionally with brief excursions of euphoria and significantly more frequent episodes of irritability, self-destructive acts, and impulsive anger. These moods are often unpredictable and appear prompted less by external events than by internal factors. Given their divergent background histories, borderlines can be conceptualized as advanced dysfunctional variants of the less structurally defective dependent, histrionic, narcissistic, antisocial and contentious personality patterns."[98]

SECTION II: LEADERSHIP STYLE

Background to the Study of Leadership Style

The examination of political-leadership style has been the focus of many different scholars.[99] This study draws upon a number of these approaches, particularly those that emphasize character and personality as it shapes leadership style. It uses the personality profile system developed by Millon,[100] with modifications by Immelman.[101]

But what exactly do we understand by the concept of leadership style? A brief look at the literature reveals that, while every scholar seems to have his or her own vocabulary, the underlying concepts appear quite similar in many instances. For some, like Renshon, leadership style is defined

Table 21
The Erratic pattern across five attribute domains

Attribute Domains	Moderately Disturbed (20–34)	Markedly Disturbed (35–40)
Expressive Behaviour	Precipitous: displays abrupt or unpredictable shifts in position or mood; rash	Chaotic: displays a desultory energy level with sudden, unexpected, and impulsive emotional outbursts
Interpersonal Conduct	Capricious: although needing attention and affection, is unpredictably contrary, manipulative, and volatile, frequently eliciting rejection rather than support	Paradoxical: frantically reacts to fears of abandonment and isolation, but often in angry, mercurial, and self-damaging ways; threatens suicide as an instrument of punishment
Cognitive Style	Inconsistent: experiences erratic perceptions and thoughts	Capricious: experiences rapidly changing, fluctuating and antithetical thoughts and conflicting emotions towards self and others, notably, love, rage, and guilt
Mood/ Temperament	Temperamental: excitable; moody; rapid, unstable shifts in mood; volatile	Labile: has either marked shifts from normality to depression to excitement or extended periods of dejection and apathy
Self-image	Uncertain: experiences a confused, nebulous, or wavering sense of identity; troubled	Conflicted: immature sense of identity; underlying feelings of emptiness; seeks to redeem rash and impulsive actions with expressions of contrition and self-punitive behaviours

Source: Millon, Disorders of Personality, 646, 661–2, 703; and Oldham and Morris, The New Personality Self-Portrait, 293.

as a leader's approach to dealing with the responsibilities of his or her office, that is, how he or she approaches and carries out his or her responsibilities. For others, like Kaarbo, it connotes "the leaders' work habits, how they relate to those around them, how they like to receive information, and how they make up their minds."[102]

Many scholars have noted important single variables for leadership style, including the degree of partisan responsiveness,[103] the degree of active involvement and experience in different issue areas,[104] and preferred strategies for coping with uncertainty.[105] In a more ad hominem approach, both Greenstein[106] and Renshon[107] start with the man – in their studies, it is President Bill Clinton. Then, they isolate clusters of leadership-style observations, including such variables as interest in policy matters and politics, verbal facility and proclivity, dynamism and ebullience, lack of discipline, insensitivity to organization, personal charm, resilience, action and initiative, delight in campaigning, and a willingness to shade meaning.

Other researchers have developed a more formal typology of leadership style. Johnson[108] suggests a formalistic style stressing the importance of order and analysis, a competitive style focusing on involvement and controversy, and a collegial style emphasizing teamwork. George[109] adapts these styles and argues that three variables – cognitive style, sense of efficacy, and orientation towards political conflict – underlie this typology. Earlier, Barber[110] had proposed a categorization of leadership styles along two dimensions – activity (active/passive) and outlook (positive/negative). These are two classic dimensions of temperament.

In their analysis of advisory systems, Hermann and Preston[111] review the various studies of presidential-leadership style and distil four common variables – involvement in the policy-making process, willingness to tolerate conflict, motivation for leading, and preferred strategies for resolving conflict. To these variables, Kaarbo[112] adds two more drawn from the literature on organizational-leadership style – relations with members of the cabinet and task orientation.

The present study includes five of these variables: motivation for leading, task orientation, cabinet-management strategy, information-management strategy, and relations with the party. It proposes an additional four variables that best capture and examine prime-ministerial relations with civil servants and personal staff, opposition parties, the media, and the public, and a fifth one focusing on investment in job performance. These have been grouped into three clusters that reveal important aspects of leadership behaviour in three nested spheres of activity: cluster one, the leader – (I) motivation, (II) task orientation, and (III) investment in job performance; cluster two, the leader and the executive – (IV) cabinet and (V) information-management strategies; and cluster three, the leader and relations with (VI) other personnel, (VII) the party, (VIII) the opposition, (IX) the media, and (X) the public. (See Table 22.)

Let us now proceed by examining the variables in each of the three clusters a little more closely. The first leadership-style variable centres on the question of a prime minister's motivation for leading. A survey of the literature suggests that a variety of needs and incentives induce individuals into assuming leadership positions in politics.[113] A leader may be motivated by duty and pragmatism, a belief that he or she has an obligation to the party to take on a leadership role and to shape government policies along incremental lines; by personal validation, the

Table 22
Leadership-style categories

CLUSTER A: Individual Style

I.   MOTIVATION (What shapes broad political choices)

     a Pragmatism
     (shaping government policies along incremental lines with the view of system maintenance)

     b Personal Validation
     (popular approval/acceptance/narcissistic issues)

     c Ideology
     (a coherent system of political beliefs that shapes government policies with an agenda for significant change)

     d Power
     (dominance and control)

II.   TASK ORIENTATION

     a Process
     (concurrence building – the group and the hierarchy of relations with them – means)

     b Goal
     (task accomplishment/issues, ends)

III.   JOB PERFORMANCE

     a Circumscribed
     (limits placed on amount of energy and commitment)

     b Tireless
     (High level of commitment and energy)

CLUSTER B: Managerial Style

IV.   CABINET–MANAGEMENT STRATEGY
(How PM organizes composition of and manages the decision-making process within the cabinet)

     a Uninvolved

     b Consensus Builder

     c Arbitrator

     d Advocate (Authoritative/Peremptory)

V.   INFORMATION–MANAGEMENT STRATEGY

     1. Degree of involvement

         a Low
         (use of filters to minimize direct involvement in search for, and analysis of, policy-relevant data)

         b High
         (PM more directly involved)

     2. Sources

         a Ministers/Civil Servants

         b Independent (Variety of sources)

Table 22
Leadership-style categories (*Continued*)

CLUSTER C: Interpersonal Style

VI. RELATIONS WITH SENIOR CIVIL SERVANTS AND PERSONAL STAFF
(How leader interacts with aides and members of the senior civil service)
1. Degree of Involvement
    a Low
    b High
2. Type of Involvement
    a Collegial/Egalitarian/Solicitous
    b Polite/Formal
    c Attention-seeking/Seductive
    d Demanding/Domineering/Antagonistic/Competitive
    e Manipulative/Exploitative

VII. RELATIONS WITH THE PARTY
(Relationship between leader, caucus and extra-parliamentary organization)
1. Caucus
    a Uninvolved
    b Cooperative/Harmonious
    c Competitive/Oppositional
    d Controlling/Combative/Overbearing/Manipulative/Exploitative
2. Extra-Parliamentary Party Organization
    a Uninvolved
    b Cooperative/Harmonious
    c Competitive/Oppositional
    d Controlling/Combative/Overbearing/Manipulative/Exploitative

VIII. RELATIONS WITH OPPOSITION PARTIES
    a Uninvolved
    b Cooperative
    c Competitive/Oppositional
    d Controlling/Combative/Overbearing/Manipulative/Exploitative

IX. RELATIONS WITH THE MEDIA
    a Open
    (accessible, informative, friendly)
    b Closed
    (inaccessible, uninformative, unfriendly)

X.   RELATIONS WITH THE PUBLIC
    a Active
    (prefers direct engagement with the public)
    b Passive
    (little direct engagement with the public and/or preference for government
    officials to articulate and defend government policy)

wish to be popular and to be accepted; by an ideological agenda, a coherent system of political beliefs that will shape government policy; or
by the drive for power, dominance, and control. Motives shape the way
in which the leader will define his or her responsibilities and manage the
cabinet and the party – in short his/her task orientation.

Research on groups and organizations[114] suggests that leaders serve
primarily two functions and often emphasize or focus on one or the
other. These goals are best summarized as organizational survival and
policy achievement. The prime minister whose involvement centres
around policy achievement is more interested in solving policy problems in an effective manner, with positive results; the problem-solving
competencies and skills of those around him or her are as important as
the quality of the product. On the other hand, the prime minister whose
involvement is more focused on the policy process sees the cabinet as a
community of interlocking parts with shared interests in containing
conflict and disagreement and in enhancing common values and beliefs.
It is important for this type of leader to empower others and to increase
the interdependence and loyalty among members of the cabinet.

The amount of investment of energy and time that a prime minister
brings to his/her role is another variable of leadership style.[115] Whether the
leader places limits on the energy and commitment that is invested in the
office of the prime minister or, alternatively, tirelessly demonstrates a high
level of energy and commitment is an important and telling characteristic of
that person's leadership style. Another critical facet of leadership style is the
way in which the prime minister organizes the composition of and manages
the decision-making process within the cabinet. How does he or she resolve
policy dilemmas? To what extent is he or she involved in the policy process? Who else becomes involved – as well as how and how much – becomes part of the locus of decision making and is also something that the
prime minister decides. All or most members of the cabinet can be included
in various aspects of the foreign or domestic policy-making process, or the
prime minister can single out particular people or subgroups.[116] Again, this
is an important variable revealing of the leader's style. Since prime ministers
are often dealing in the cabinet with factions within their own party and/or
with members of other parties, whom they interact with and how they do
so can reflect their general strategy regarding party relations. In the cabinet
context, party matters shape and constrain what the government can do.
Prime ministers can try to balance the various groups and see their role as
building consensus across factional and party lines. They can also reward
their own faction or party by including them in policy making and remaining aloof from the others, or they can reward those parties and factions that
are perceived as having views closer to their own.[117] In these activities, the
prime minister's style may run the gamut from largely uninvolved to consensus builder, to arbitrator, and to strong advocate.

The second variable in the leader-executive relations cluster involves the management of the nature and sources of information. Although information in a cabinet setting is usually channelled through the various ministries, prime ministers will differ as to how they choose to review such information and how they relate to their close advisers. They may want all the basic facts about the problem or situation and do the interpretation themselves, or they may be interested only in reviewing summaries and policy options. Of interest here is the amount of input the prime minister wants in the way problems and issues are framed and added to the agenda. As Giddings has observed, "the process by which prime ministers prepare themselves for meetings may be more significant in determining the decision-making outcome than the meeting itself."[118]

An additional issue in the management of the flow of information is whether the prime minister uses a network of individuals on whom he/ she relies to filter information and minimize direct involvement in the search for and analysis of policy-relevant data, or whether he/she is more likely to be directly involved in the process. Closely related is the question regarding the prime minister's preferred source of information. Does he/she prefer to receive policy-relevant data from the cabinet and senior civil servants or does he/she rely on alternative sources? This is an issue that reveals the degree of the leader's confidence and trust in his/her own abilities as well those of his/her colleagues.

The final cluster of leadership-style variables focuses on the prime minister's interpersonal relations with those with whom he or she works (i.e., state-level governmental officials, members of the judiciary, etc.), with his or her own party, and with the opposition, the media, and the public. The prime minister interacts with a number of individuals on a daily basis. The extent of the involvement may be high or low; stylistically it may encompass patterns ranging from solicitousness to politeness, to a demanding manner, or even to exploitation. With both the caucus and the extra-parliamentary party organization, the prime minister may behave cooperatively or be competitive, combative, and overbearing. Since conflict is a pervasive element in cabinet life, both in highly factional single-party cabinets and in coalition cabinets,[119] the management style of party relations by a prime minister is quite significant. As Weller notes, prime ministers are party leaders; they almost always hold the former position as long as they hold the latter.[120] In the cabinet context, then, dealing with party factions is not just a party matter; it is a government matter as well and often affects the policy-making process.[121]

For example, the leader may consider factions within the prime minister's party but outside his/her own particular group of loyalists as competitors for power. In such a case, the prime minister's strategy for dealing with such factions may be competitive, and the prime minister may use policy making to gain ground against this internal opposition; he or she may act as an advocate and impose his or her own personal position, thus playing a more forceful role in the proceedings than prime ministers who choose a cooperative strategy and prefer to arbitrate conflict or seek consensus.[122] Alternatively, a prime minister who chooses a cooperative strategy will need to take a more facilitative role and broker a decision through bargaining and negotiation. Or he/she can also decide not to become involved in intra-parliamentary party conflict and remain above the fray.[123] Of course, the same range of options exists for the prime minister's relations with opposition parties. Next, as far as his/her relations with the media are concerned, the prime minister may be accessible and informative or inaccessible and hostile.

Prime ministers who focus on implementing significant policy changes are more likely to generate greater opposition, which, in turn, will be reflected particularly in that section of the media that opposes government policy. Those leaders who are more concerned with maintaining the political process through incremental changes are less likely to face this animosity. In the face of hostility on the part of the media, the prime minister is more likely to become less accessible and more hostile.

Analysts also focus on "how the leader carries out or implements decisions," based on the way in which the leader mobilizes, orchestrates, and consolidates support for his or her policy decisions.[124] Hence, the importance of this final variable, "relations with the public." Does the prime minister attempt to sell his/her policies by going beyond the party and Parliament to appeal to the public at large? Does he/she try to educate or manipulate the public or does the leader exhibit little direct engagement with the public, preferring government officials to articulate and defend government policy? Those prime ministers who focus on policy achievements are more likely to use the prime ministership as a "bully pulpit," while those who stress the policy process will be less inclined to try to generate additional support among the public.

Method and Sources for Assessing Leadership Styles

SOURCES OF DATA

For this book, information sources concerning a prime minister's leadership style were multiple, including primary (speeches, autobiographies, letters) and secondary (biographies, political accounts and analyses) material. In the study of Indira Gandhi, many of the same biographical sources were employed for the data both on personality profile and on leadership style. And, for all three prime ministers – Gandhi, Meir, and Thatcher – care was taken to ensure that data for leadership style was extracted only from the period in which each served as prime minister, and that materials on their personality profiles were drawn from earlier time periods. For the study of Margaret Thatcher, biographical material was supplemented with scholarly analyses of her role as prime minister, while, in the examination of Golda Meir's leadership style as prime minister, the paucity of both biographical information and scholarly analyses led to a greater reliance on journalistic reports and on interviews with major figures, with whom she was close, conducted by the author.

LEADERSHIP-STYLE INVENTORY

As noted, the assessment framework[125] consists of ten categories (I–X) and a number of subcategories that qualitatively assess the dynamics of leadership style. The ten leadership-style domains tap three major clusters of leadership behaviour. The first cluster examines motivation, task orientation, and investment in job performance; the second cluster looks at cabinet- and information-management strategies; and the final cluster focuses on interpersonal relations with senior civil servants, personal staff, the party, opposition, media, and public. Table 22 displays the full taxonomy.

SCORING

The goal was to produce a picture that captures the quantitative proportion of each of the qualitative measures within each category. Tallying the coded instances of the presence of each measure and then simply calculating the percentage of each over the total of observed/coded entries for each of these dimensions best achieved this. Thus, for example, in the category of motivation for leadership, four qualitatively different reasons were examined: pragmatism, personal validation, ideology, and power. Then, the proportion of each of these four variables was calculated so that the strength of each, as a percentage of the total, could be assessed. To illustrate: of a total of 100 observations, 50 were coded as pragmatism, 30 as personal validation, and 10 each for ideology and power. This was done for each of the remaining nine categories and subcategories (categories V, VI, and VII each have a set of subcategories), with a view to producing a distinct leadership-style profile for each of the three prime ministers studied.

SECTION III: THEORETICAL LINKS BETWEEN PERSONALITY PATTERNS AND LEADERSHIP-STYLE BEHAVIOUR

Although human beings tend to exhibit more than one significant or predominant personality pattern, it is perhaps most useful to begin a discussion on the theoretical links between personality patterns and leadership style with an examination of each pattern individually. Given the scope of the research and the limits of this book, I have chosen to focus on the four most important personality patterns for each prime minister, all of which reached a level of prominence (scores of 10 and above). In the case of Golda Meir, I examined a fifth personality pattern because the scores between patterns ranking fourth and fifth differed by only one point.

For Gandhi, Meir, and Thatcher, six different personality patterns fit the above criterion: the Dominant, the Ambitious, the Contentious, the Dauntless, the Conscientious, and the Reticent. Thus, the theoretical links between such personality patterns as the Outgoing, the Accommodating, the Retiring, the Paranoid, and the Erratic and their concomitant leadership styles are not included in this analysis; instead, only the theoretical links between the six most significant personality patterns and leadership styles are discussed. This theorizing is important, for, once we can speculate about the contribution of each of these six personality patterns to leadership style, then we are in a position to examine each woman's actual leadership style and to explore the ways in which a combination of these personality patterns affected it.

Dominant Leaders

Leaders whose personality patterns reflect the Dominant pattern at a level of 10 and above (i.e., those individuals characterized by controlling, forceful, and overbearing traits whose cognitive styles are highly opinionated) are conjectured to be more likely to be primarily concerned with issues of *power* and *ideology*; at the same time, they are expected to be significantly less occupied with *pragmatic* or *self-validation* issues. To assert control over one's environment in the face of opposition requires the acquisition of power; as well, such individuals, given their strong opinions and ideas, might be expected to have an ideological bent. Since they are not interested in maintaining a version of the status quo, they are less likely to be pragmatic in their outlook. Nor are they primarily concerned with being liked, and hence they display a relative disinterest in issues of self-validation.

Dominant leaders are more likely to be *goal-* rather than *process-*oriented. Motivated by *power* and *ideology*, the assumption is that they are less likely to be interested in maintaining good relations among their colleagues than in accomplishing ideological goals. For these reasons, their investment in job performance is also more likely to be *tireless* than *circumscribed* – not for them, the relaxed, casual, laissez-faire approach.

These types of prime ministers are also expected to be more likely to act as *advocates* within their cabinets than as *consensus builders* or *arbitrators*. Given their personalities, which stress domination, toughness, and strong beliefs, as well as the nature of their goals and the energy they bring to bear on their implementation, they are also more likely to exhibit a *high* degree of involvement in managing information. Additionally, their competitiveness leads them to prefer to obtain their information from a variety of *independent* sources, rather than relying merely on the *cabinet* and the *civil service*.

In the area of personnel management, Dominant leaders can be expected to be both *highly interactive* with aides, assistants, and staff and, given their concern with power as a means to exercise control, to treat their subordinates in an extremely *demanding, domineering*, and perhaps even *exploitative* fashion. In their dealings with members of their caucus, the extra-parliamentary party organization, and the opposition, Dominant leaders are unlikely to remain *uninvolved* or to behave in a *cooperative/harmonious* fashion. Given their competitive natures, they probably view all these constituencies as potential sources of challenge to their leadership, and thus their leadership behaviour is more likely to be *oppositional, competitive*, and even *controlling* and *overbearing*.

Outside the parliamentary arena, Dominant prime ministers are equally unlikely to enjoy harmonious relations with the media; rather, they will want to dominate and control it. As a result, their relationship with the media is more likely to be characterized as *hostile* and *uncooperative* in a competition for control over the image and agenda projected. In their dealings with the public, Dominant leaders can be expected to be *active* rather than *passive*. Given their *strong-willed, outspoken* personalities, such leaders are likely to prefer to articulate and defend their policies themselves.

Dauntless Leaders

Leaders with significant Dauntless personality traits are likely to be motivated by *power* and, to some extent, *ideology*. As daring, risk-taking individuals, with a strong streak of non-conformity, they are unlikely to be motivated by issues of *self-validation* or *pragmatism*. They are also more likely to be *goal*-oriented than *process*-oriented, given their adventurous and innovative approach to policy matters and their relative lack of interest in the machinery of government or the maintenance of harmonious relations with the members of their cabinet. For these reasons, their investment in job performance is also more likely to be *tireless* than *circumscribed*.

These types of prime ministers are also expected to be more likely to act as *advocates* within their cabinets than as *consensus builders* or *arbitrators*. Because their personalities stress competition, risk-taking, and adventurousness, they are also more likely to exhibit a *high* degree of involvement in managing information. As well, their competitiveness leads them to prefer to obtain their information from a variety of independent sources, rather than relying merely on the cabinet and the civil service.

In the area of personnel management, Dauntless leaders can be expected to be only reasonably *interactive* with civil servants and personal staff, given their tendency to act in a notably autonomous fashion and their disinclination to adhere to conventional standards. They will tend to treat their subordinates in a jovial and convivial fashion; however, when obstructed or crossed, they may become confrontational and difficult. In their dealings with members of their caucus, the extra-parliamentary party organization, and the opposition, Dauntless leaders are more likely to remain *uninvolved* and to behave in a *cooperative/harmonious* fashion when things go well and to become *demanding* and *difficult* when problems of control arise.

Outside the parliamentary arena, Dauntless prime ministers are unlikely to enjoy harmonious relations with the media; since they often act hastily, failing to plan ahead or heed consequences, they are likely to be the target of media attacks. As a result, their relationship with the media is more likely to be characterized as *hostile* and *uncooperative*. In their dealings with the public, Dauntless leaders can be expected to be *active* rather than *passive*. Since their personalities are *self-confident* and *outspoken*, such leaders are likely to prefer to articulate and defend their policies themselves.

Ambitious Leaders

Leaders with prominent Ambitious personality traits are likely to be motivated by all four factors – *power, pragmatism, ideology,* and *self-validation* – in descending order of importance. As extremely confidant, often-arrogant individuals with a strong belief in their talents and their leadership ability, *power* is an obvious motivator for their leadership behaviour. Their ambition, which is largely in the service of their own personal needs, may also dictate a policy of *pragmatism*, as a way of ensuring their continued success. At the same time, given that their personality patterns demonstrate cognitive expansiveness, that is, they display extraordinary confidence in their own ideas and potential for success, they may be motivated by *ideology* and the wish to transform their societies. Those ranking very high on the Ambitious scale have a strong narcissistic component to their personalities and need affirmation of their self-esteem; thus, they are likely to be motivated by the need for *personal validation*.

Prime ministers who rank high on the Ambitious personality scale are more likely to be *goal-* than *process-*oriented. Motivated as they are by factors that involve their own advancement and success, their interest in maintaining good relations with their colleagues is much less important than their ability to achieve their *goals*. Their wish to prove themselves means that they are more likely to be *tireless* in the amount of effort they will expend in their jobs.

Ambitious leaders are also more likely to act as *advocates* within their cabinets than as *consensus builders* or *arbitrators*. Given that their personalities stress self-promotion, persuasiveness, and a high degree of arrogance and entitlement, they are less likely to take on a constrained role for themselves. These characteristics also mean that they are more likely to exhibit a *high* degree of involvement in managing information and to prefer to obtain their information from a variety of *independent sources* so that they can make up their own minds.

In the arena of personnel management, Ambitious prime ministers are likely to be *highly interactive* with civil servants and personal staff and to treat their subordinates in an *arrogant, manipulative*, and *exploitive* fashion. They are also more likely to engage in *attention-seeking* behaviour than most other personality types except for the Outgoing personality, since they require a good deal of self-validation to maintain their somewhat fragile self-esteem. In their dealings with members of their caucus, the extra-parliamentary party organization, and the opposition, Ambitious personalities are likely to be *involved* and to exhibit a range of behaviours. When it appears that behaving in a *cooperative* or *harmonious* way will further their interests, they will do so for instrumental reasons. But their self-absorbed manner will more frequently produce behaviour that is *competitive, oppositional, controlling,* and even *overbearing*. That said, because Ambitious personality types are more likely than their Dominant counterparts to exhibit both *cooperative* and *competitive* types of behaviour with their staff, the expectation is that the latter will demonstrate a greater degree of *controlling* and *overbearing* behaviour in this area.

Outside the parliamentary arena, Ambitious prime ministers may enjoy some degree of *harmonious* relations with the press, if they feel the press can be manipulated. However, the combination of a critical press and the sensitivity of the Ambitious personality to narcissistic wounding means that their relationship is more likely to be characterized by a *lack of cooperation* and even outright *hostility*. In their relations with the public, Ambitious leaders can be expected to be more *active* than *passive*. Given their self-confidence and their certitude about themselves and their persuasiveness, such leaders will more probably prefer to articulate and defend their policies themselves rather than relying on others.

Aggrieved Leaders

Those leaders demonstrating a high elevation on the Aggrieved personality profile are humble, unassuming, and unpretentious and avoid

displaying their talents and aptitudes. They conduct themselves in a deferential manner and are likely to behave in a yielding manner – adhering to the expectations of those they follow. Individuals who score high
on this personality scale are unlikely to be motivated by either *power*,
ideology, or *personal validation* – all of which require a more active
stance. Issues of *pragmatism* are likely to be the highest on their motivational calculus. Such figures can be expected to serve either as caretaker
or as interim prime ministers.

Aggrieved prime ministers, with their uncertain and diffident personalities, are more likely to be *process-* than *goal*-oriented, given that the
latter requires a much greater willingness to engage actively in the political arena. Their general lack of certainty, their diffidence, and their
self-sacrificing qualities also make them more likely to invest a considerable amount of effort in their jobs, as a way of trying to diminish their
overall sense of inadequacy.

Because Aggrieved leaders are unsure of themselves, they are less
likely to take on the role of *advocates* or *arbitrators* within their cabinets; they are far more likely to be relatively *uninvolved* or to act as
consensus builders.

In the management of information, the humble and unpretentious
Aggrieved prime minister is more likely to manifest a *low* degree of involvement and to prefer to rely on his/her ministers for information on
the assumption that they rather than he/she are in a better position to
make judgments based on an independent search for information. Relations with personnel, aides, assistants, and staff are likely to follow the
same pattern. As befits the uncertain, self-effacing Aggrieved personality, the extent of the involvement will be *low* and most likely characterized by a *polite/formal* and *collegial/harmonious* manner.

In their various party relations – with their caucuses, the extra-parliamentary party organization, and the opposition – Aggrieved personality
leaders are more likely to be either *uninvolved* or *cooperative* – again a
reflection of their uncertainty and humility. Finally, as self-effacing,
somewhat pessimistic individuals, who do not see themselves as very
important, Aggrieved prime ministers are more likely to be *closed* than
open with the media, and more *passive* than *active* in their dealings
with the public, preferring their aides to speak on their behalf.

Contentious Leaders

The core diagnostic feature of Contentious leaders is non-conformity.
They are outspoken, unconventional, and frequently unhappy with the
status quo. Since they are quick to challenge rules and authority, they
are more comfortable when they themselves constitute the authority.

They are therefore more likely to be motivated by *power*. *Pragmatism*, the art of the possible, is also likely to be a relatively important motive in their leadership behaviour, since they lack the requisite belief that major changes of an ideological nature are feasible. As consistent sceptics about human nature, they do not generally look for *personal validation*; nor, given their negative outlook, is a preoccupation with *ideology* and the possibility for significant change likely to be an important source of motivation.

In view of their individualistic, independent, and caustic natures, Contentious leaders are unlikely to evince much concern with or interest in the machinery of government or to care about consensus building. Rather, they are more likely to be *goal-* than *process*-oriented. Unlike Dominant and Ambitious leaders, Contentious leaders will be more likely to invest only a *circumscribed* amount of energy and effort into their jobs since they frequently feel put upon and behave in a *complaining*, *obstructive*, and *recalcitrant* fashion.

Contentious prime ministers will be more likely to act as *advocates* in their relationships with their cabinets, since they are determined, resolute, and even wilful personalities. As such leaders are also sceptical, doubting, and critical, they are more likely to prefer *direct involvement* in the search for and analysis of policy-relevant data as well as the use of a *variety of sources* to assuage their doubts about the accuracy of the data or the reports they receive.

In the area of personnel management, Contentious leaders are less likely to be intensely interactive with senior civil servants and personal staff. Their involvement, a function of their feelings of being misunderstood and unappreciated by others, is most probably *low*. As a result of their embittered, disgruntled view of life, the type of involvement is most likely to be of a *demanding/domineering* nature.

In view of their complaining and irritable traits, Contentious leaders are more likely to exhibit *competitive/oppositional* than *cooperative* behaviour in their relations with their party caucus, the extra-parliamentary party organization, and opposition parties. Lacking trust and being sceptical, such leaders are unlikely to be *open* and thus are more inclined to be *uninformative* and *unfriendly* with the media. Lastly, their dealings with the public are more likely to be *passive* than *active*, since they are more disposed to resent the demands on their time and to feel pessimistic about the impact they might have on the public.

Conscientious Leaders

Leaders whose personality pattern is dominated by the trait of Conscientiousness are less likely to be motivated by *ideology* or *personal validation* and more likely to be motivated by *power* and *pragmatism*. As overly controlling, rigid, and perfectionist individuals, they are likely to try to concentrate power in themselves as a way of preventing matters from spinning out of control. Since this personality type tends to be characterized by a lack of imagination and a structured pedestrian form of cognition, they eschew new or untested ideas; ideological notions tend to be an anathema and they are more comfortable with a *pragmatic* approach to political problems.

Conscientious leaders are inclined to be interested both in accomplishing their *goals* (demonstrating their hard-work ethic) and in the *process* itself (keeping the machinery of government oiled). They are notably respectful of tradition and authority and unbending in their adherence to social proprieties. This translates into a leadership style that pivots on the need for productivity in the form of policy implementation and in the proper types of relationships among members of the government and the civil service.

Prime ministers whose Conscientious patterns predominate are more likely to act as *advocates* within their cabinets and less likely to be *consensus builders* or *arbitrators*. Having displayed due deference to their superiors when they were junior ministers and ministers, they now expect to be treated in the same way by their cabinet colleagues and are inclined to be unbending in their relations with them. Since such leaders tend to lack imagination and to be somewhat rigid, policy choices will often take on the colouration of black and white – a situation in which the building of *consensus* plays a secondary role to the implementation of the morally "correct" or the most efficient policy. Given their penchant for over-control, orderliness, and perfectionism, they are likely to exhibit a *high* degree of involvement in managing information, as a way of protecting themselves from possible error. At the same time, however, their respect for order and hierarchy is likely to make Conscientious prime ministers prefer to obtain that information from *cabinet* and the *civil service* rather than from *independent sources*.

In terms of relations with personnel, Conscientious leaders are expected to be *highly interactive* with aides, assistants, and staff, lest something important escape their notice. And their treatment of their subordinates is likely to be mixed. At the lower end of the *prominent* range, they are likely to treat them in a polite and courteous fashion; at the higher end of that range and beyond, their perfectionist tendencies are more in evidence, leading to uncompromising and demanding behaviour. They are less likely to engage in *attention-seeking* behaviour with their aides, since duty, not vanity, is their modus operandum.

In their dealings with members of their caucus and the extra-parliamentary party organization, the same patterns of behaviour are expected. They will treat those whom they consider as subordinates in either a *cooperative/harmonious* or a *competitive/oppositional*, even *domineering*, fashion depending on the intensity of their Conscientious trait. By the same token, if they view members of their caucus or the opposition party or parties as equals, they will behave in a more *cooperative* manner.

In their relations with the media, Conscientious leaders are also likely to behave in a *polite/formal* but reasonably *cooperative* manner. With the public, the behaviour of Conscientious leaders can be expected to be somewhat mixed. They are likely to be more *active* than *passive* in view of their strong sense of duty and responsibility; however, given their rigid, perfectionist personalities, they are unlikely to enjoy this aspect of governing and may be prepared to allow their senior colleagues some role in articulating and defending the government's policies.

Reticent Leaders

Those leaders who demonstrate a high elevation on the Reticent personality profile have a leadership style that differs markedly from those of the Dominant, Ambitious, and Contentious personality types. Since Reticent individuals are characterized primarily by social inhibition and withdrawal, leaders who score high on this personality scale are unlikely to be motivated by either *power, ideology,* or *personal validation*, all of which require a more active stance. Issues of *pragmatism* are significantly more likely to be higher on their motivational calculus.

Reticent prime ministers, with their circumspect and inhibited personalities, are more likely to be *process-* than *goal*-oriented, given that the latter requires a much greater willingness to involve oneself actively in the political arena. Their Reticence also makes them more likely to prefer investing only a *circumscribed* amount of effort in their jobs, thus leaving more time for private concerns.

Because Reticent leaders are predominantly insecure and ill at ease, they are less likely to take on the role of *advocates, arbitrators,* or *consensus builders* within their cabinets; instead, they are far more likely to be relatively *uninvolved*. In the domain of information management, Reticent prime ministers are more likely to manifest a *low* degree of involvement and a preference for relying on the cabinet and the civil service for information. Relations with civil servants and aides are likely to follow a similar pattern. As befits the ill-at-ease Reticent personality, the extent of interpersonal interaction is expected to be *low* and most likely characterized by a *polite/formal* manner.

In their various party relations – with their caucus, the extra-parliamentary party organization, and the opposition – Reticent leaders are more likely to be *uninvolved*; this is a reflection of their tendency to try to limit the extent of their social involvement, even if that occurs in a

political setting. Finally, as withdrawn individuals, Reticent prime ministers are quite evidently more likely to be *closed* than *open* with the media and more *passive* than *active* in their dealings with the public,
preferring their aides to speak on their behalf.

ASSESSING THE IMPACT OF PERSONALITY PATTERNS ON LEADERSHIP STYLES

Far beyond the clinical and scholarly typologies, few leaders in real life exhibit a personality profile where a single pattern predominates. Had that
been the case, this study's exploration of the links between personality and
leadership style would have been much simpler than it was. When a leader
exhibits a personality profile in which three or four patterns can be found
to exist with significant scale values, analysis of the impact of each of these
patterns on leadership style is rendered difficult. While one may be able to
theorize about the leadership style of a leader with only one or two important personality patterns that largely predict similar behaviour (i.e., like
the Dominant/Ambitious or the Reticent/Retiring personality profiles), hy-
pothesizing about leadership behaviour when faced with a leader with a
number of salient personality patterns that predict very different kinds of
leadership behaviour is a more complicated undertaking.

One solution is to measure the combined weight of the most important personality patterns that are theoretically linked to similar kinds of
leadership behaviour. If, for example, three of the four most important
personality patterns seem to be empirically linked to certain hypothesized leadership behaviours, then there is a greater likelihood that the
combination of these three patterns will have a greater weight in determining leadership style than the fourth one. To illustrate this point, consider a situation in which the Dominant, Ambitious, Contentious, and
Reticent patterns all are strongly elevated in an individual's personality
profile. The first three patterns all theoretically predict, *grosso modo*,
similar leadership styles, while the fourth postulates very different kinds
of behaviour. If one finds little or no empirical evidence of the behaviour
predicted by the Reticent pattern, this may simply mean that the combination of the other three patterns – the Dominant, Ambitious, and Contentious – was sufficient to overpower the Reticent pattern. Such may
explain, in part, the case of Indira Gandhi.

Alternatively, if there is a sizeable gap between the score of one personality pattern and the remainder, a case could be made for examining
only the impact of that pattern on leadership style. Similarly, if the largest gap is between the two highest scoring patterns and the last two, then
the last two could be set aside as less relevant in their expected impact on
leadership style.

Notes

INTRODUCTION

1 See Genovese, ed., *Women National Leaders*; Brunstetter, *Women in Power*.
2 Blondel, *World Leaders*, 116.
3 See Zarate's "Political Collections" for a brief profile of each of these elected female leaders. Available at www.terra.es/personal 2 monolith.
4 See Steinberg, "The Making of Female Presidents and Prime Ministers."
5 For an examination of the impact of dynastic inheritance on female political leaders, see Richter, "Exploring Theories of Female Leadership in South and South-east Asia."
6 Bumiller, *May You Be the Mother of a Hundred Sons*, 164; Manushi Collective, *Our Alarming Silence*, 2–5.
7 Quoted in the London *Times*, 10 May 1978.
8 Thompson, "Golda Meir: A Very Public Life," 156.
9 Everett, "Indira Gandhi and the Exercise of Power," 127.
10 Stoessinger, *Why Nations Go to War*, 135–6.
11 Genovese, "Margaret Thatcher and the Politics of Conviction Leadership," 206.
12 Thompson, "Golda Meir: A Very Public Life," 157.
13 Genovese and Thompson, "Women as Chief Executives: Does Gender Matter?" 7.
14 Manushi Collective, *Our Alarming Silence*, 3.
15 Everett, "Indira Gandhi and the Exercise of Power," 128.
16 Young, *The Iron Lady*, 306–12.
17 *Daily Mirror*, 1 March 1980.
18 Genovese, "Margaret Thatcher and the Politics of Conviction Leadership," 207.
19 For a more complete explanation see appendix, section I.
20 Additional details are available in the appendix, section II.
21 The specific links are spelled out in the appendix, in section III.

CHAPTER ONE

1 *The Hindu*, 5 November 2001.

2 I. Gandhi, *My Truth*, 12.

3 Ibid.

4 Fallaci, *Interview with History*, 173.

5 I. Gandhi, *My Truth*, 16.

6 Ibid., 17.

7 Malhotra, *Indira Gandhi*, 37.

8 Everett, "Indira Gandhi and the Exercise of Power," 107–8.

9 Malhotra, *Indira Gandhi*, 41–2.

10 Gupte, *Mother India*, 182.

11 Malhotra, *Indira Gandhi*, 43–4.

12 Ibid., 44.

13 Moraes, *Mrs. Gandhi*, 75–6.

14 Michaelis, "An Interview with Indira Gandhi."

15 Saygal, *Indira Gandhi*, 19.

16 Ibid., 201–3.

17 I. Gandhi, *My Truth*, 69.

18 Malhotra, *Indira Gandhi*, 60.

19 Masani, *Indira Gandhi*, 90.

20 Frank, *Indira*, 214.

21 Moraes, *Mrs Gandhi*, 99.

22 Frank, *Indira*, 235–6.

23 Malhotra, *Indira Gandhi*, 61.

24 Ibid., 61.

25 Norman, *Indira Gandhi*.

26 Gupte, *Mother India*, 231–2.

27 Frank, *Indira*, 252–3.

28 Ibid.

29 Masani, *Indira Gandhi*, 117.

30 Frank, *Indira*, 261–6; Masani, *Indira Gandhi*, 120.

31 Masani, *Indira Gandhi*, 124–5.

32 Malhotra, *Indira Gandhi*, 79.

33 Masani, *Indira Gandhi*, 128.

34 Malhotra, *Indira Gandhi*, 79.

35 Vasudev, *Indira Gandhi*, 258.

36 Bhatia, *Indira*, 169.

37 Masani, *Indira Gandhi*, 131–2.

38 Malhotra, *Indira Gandhi*, 86–7.

39 Masani, *Indira Gandhi*, 137.

40 Ibid., 138.

41 Ibid.

42 Ibid., 144–5.

43 Gupte, *Mother India*, 285–7.

44 Masani, *Indira Gandhi*, 152–4.

45 Frank, *Indira*, 296.

46 Gupte, *Mother India*, 291.

47 Malhotra, *Indira Gandhi*, 78–9.

48 Gupte, *Mother India*, 295–6.

49 Malhotra, *Indira Gandhi*, 100.

50 Ibid., 100–1.

51 Malhotra, *Indira Gandhi*, 103.

52 Bhatia, *Indira*, 197–8.

53 Ibid., 198.

54 Ibid., 199–200.

55 The president would be elected by an electoral college of central and state legislators, in which the Congress had a narrow majority of 2 per cent.

56 Masani, *Indira Gandhi*, 182.

57 Ibid., 182–3.

58 Ibid., 183.

59 Ibid., 184–7.

60 Ibid., 187–8.

61 Malhotra, *Indira Gandhi*, 118–19.

62 Ibid., 119–20.

63 Bhatia, *Indira Gandhi*, 228.

64 Malhotra, *Indira Gandhi*, 116–17.

65 Placing an untouchable in Rashtrapati Bhavan, the presidential palace and the former residence of the British viceroy, would have also been a fulfillment of Gandhi's long-standing dream (Malhotra, *Indira Gandhi*, 117–18).

66 Ibid., 116.

67 Frank, *Indira*, 319.

68 Malhotra, *Indira Gandhi*, 122.

69 Frank, *Indira*, 316.

70 Ibid., 317.

71 Masani, *Indira Gandhi*, 211.

72 Frank, *Indira*, 319.

73 Ibid., 323.

74 Malhotra, *Indira Gandhi*, 128.

75 Frankel, *India's Green Revolution*, 460.

76 Bhatia, *Indira Gandhi*, 234.

77 Masani, *Indira Gandhi*, 235.

78 Ibid., 239.

79 Mohammed Ali Jinnah articulated the political argument that Muslims would never be safe in a Hindu-dominated India and therefore needed their own state. This was in sharp contrast to the views espoused by Mahatma Gandhi and the other leaders of the Indian National Congress Party, who opposed the territorial division of India based on religious lines in the belief that Muslims and Hindus could live harmoniously side by side.

80 Ibid., 236.

81 Malhotra, *Indira Gandhi*, 133–4.

82 Ibid., 134.

83 Frank, *Indira*, 333.

84 Ibid., 334.

85 Ibid.

86 Ibid., 336–7.

87 Sisson and Rose, *War and Succession*, 213–14.

88 Nayar, *India after Nehru*, 208.

89 Frank, *Indira*, 348.

90 Ibid.

91 Ibid., 349.

92 Ibid., 349–50.

93 Ibid., 359–60.

94 Gupte, *Mother India*, 435–6.

95 Moraes, *Mrs Gandhi*, 220.

96 Gupte, *Mother India*, 436.

97 Frank, *Indira*, 375.

98 Gupte, *Mother India*, 437–8.

99 Wolpert, *A New History of India*, 399.

100 Moraes, *Mrs. Gandhi*, 222.

101 Malhotra, *Indira Gandhi*, 178.

102 Ibid., 173.

103 Shah Commission *Report*, 1978.

104 Malhotra, *Indira Gandhi*, 169.

105 See Carras, *Indira Gandhi*, especially chapters 2 and 3.

106 For a perceptive account of Indira and Sanjay's relationship, see Frank, *Indira*, especially chapter 17.

107 Malhotra, *Indira Gandhi*, 193.

108 Jayakar, *J. Krishnamurthi*, 347–8.

109 Malhotra, *Indira Gandhi*, 192.

110 Frank, *Indira*, 410.

111 Ibid., 409–10.

112 Ibid., 411–13.

113 Ibid., 414–33.

114 Malhotra, *Indira Gandhi*, 211.

115 Ibid., 212–13.
116 Frank, *Indira*, 440.
117 Manor, *Nehru to the Nineties*, 8.
118 Frank, *Indira*, 448.
119 Malhotra, *Indira Gandhi*, 228.
120 In addition to communal riots in Kashmir, the Punjab, and Assam, there was also tribal violence in the latter state. The indigenous tribal peoples of Assam rose up against high-caste Assamese domination and demanded that "unauthorized occupants" be thrown out of their tribal areas. For more details, see Frank, *Indira*, chapters 19 and 20, and Malhotra, *Indira Gandhi*, chapters 16 and 17.
121 Frank, *Indira*, 452–60.
122 Ibid., 454.
123 Malhotra, *Indira Gandhi*, 257–8.
124 Frank, *Indira*, 471–2.
125 Malhotra, *Indira Gandhi*, 261–2.
126 Ibid., 288.
127 Frank, *Indira*, 483.
128 S. Gandhi, *Rajiv*, 8.
129 Malhotra, *Indira Gandhi*, 303.
130 Ibid., 18–19.
131 Tully and Satish, *Amritsar*, 9.
132 Frank, *Indira*, 499.

CHAPTER TWO

1 For more details concerning the conceptual framework and methodology, see appendix, section I.
2 Millon, *Millon Clinical Multiaxial Inventory–III*, 32.
3 See appendix, section 1, Scale 2: The Ambitious Pattern, for more details.
4 Malhotra, *Indira Gandhi*, 37.
5 Vasudev, *Indira Gandhi*, 30.
6 Hutheesing, *Dear to Behold*, 44.
7 Mohan, *Indira Gandhi*, 187.
8 Vasudev, *Indira Gandhi*, 59.
9 Fallaci, *Interview with History*, 172–3
10 Ibid., 60.
11 I. Gandhi, *Anand Bhawan Memories*, 31.
12 Frank, *Indira*, 159.
13 Ibid., 160–2.
14 Frank, *Indira*, 190.
15 Ibid., 237–9.
16 Ibid., 236–7.

17 Hangen, *After Nehru, Who?* 162.

18 Malhotra, *Indira Gandhi*, 81.

19 Ibid.

20 Ibid., 83.

21 Ibid., 83–4.

22 Ibid., 84.

23 Frank, *Indira*, 106.

24 Malhotra, *Indira Gandhi*, 84.

25 Ibid., 85.

26 Ibid., 85–6.

27 Ibid., 87.

28 Ibid., 88.

29 See appendix, section I, Scale 7: The Reticent Pattern, for additional details.

30 Malhotra, *Indira Gandhi*, 35.

31 Ibid., 36–7.

32 Carras, *Indira Gandhi*, 6.

33 Frank, *Indira*, 28–9.

34 Ibid., 29–32.

35 Ibid., 39.

36 Ibid., 39–40.

37 Carras, *Indira Gandhi*, 7.

38 Vasudev, *Indira Gandhi*, 136.

39 S. Gandhi, ed., *Freedom's Daughter*, 389–90.

40 Vasudev, *Indira Gandhi*, 79.

41 Millon, *Disorders of Personality*, 265.

42 Vasudev, *Indira Gandhi*, 79.

43 Frank, *Indira*, 84.

44 Ibid., 125.

45 Ibid., 129.

46 Ibid., 123.

47 Carras, *Indira Gandhi*, 6.

48 Masani, *Indira Gandhi*, 40.

49 Frank, *Indira*, 150.

50 Malhotra, *Indira Gandhi*, 46.

51 I. Gandhi, *My Truth*, 115.

52 Ibid.

53 Frank, *Indira*, 249.

54 I. Gandhi, *My Truth*, 115.

55 Frank, *Indira*, 249.

56 I. Gandhi, *My Truth*, 115.

57 Frank, *Indira*, 249.

58 I. Gandhi, *My Truth*, 115.

59 Frank, *Indira*, 249.

60 I. Gandhi, *My Truth*, 115.

61 Ibid.

62 Frank, *Indira*, 249.

63 Ibid., 279–80.

64 Sahgal, *Indira Gandhi*, 7–8.

65 For more details about the Contentious Pattern, see the appendix, section I, Scale 5B.

66 Carras, *Indira Gandhi*, 37.

67 Ibid., 37–8.

68 Frank, *Indira*, 51–2.

69 Ibid., 69.

70 Mohan, *Indira Gandhi*, 120.

71 Ibid.

72 Frank, *Indira*, 109.

73 S. Gandhi, ed., *Freedom's Daughter*, 336.

74 Ibid., 359.

75 Ibid., 136–44.

76 Ibid., 156–7.

77 S. Gandhi, ed., *Two Alone, Two Together*, 29.

78 Ibid., 43–4.

79 Frank, *Indira*, 217.

80 Ibid.

81 Ibid., 217–24.

82 Carras, *Indira Gandhi*, 91.

83 Ibid., 90.

84 Norman, ed., *Indira Gandhi*, 63.

85 Ibid., 96–7.

86 Malhotra, *Indira Gandhi*, 83.

87 Ibid., 85.

88 For further details on the Dominant Pattern, see appendix, section I.

89 Vasudev, *Indira Gandhi*, 33.

90 Malhotra, *Indira Gandhi*, 41.

91 Masani, *Indira Gandhi*, 28–30.

92 Vasudev, *Indira Gandhi*, 21–2.

93 Bhatia, *Indira Gandhi*, 41–2.

94 Masani, *Indira Gandhi*, 8.

95 Bhatia, *Indira Gandhi*, 41.

96 Frank, *Indira*, 93.

97 S. Gandhi, ed., *Freedom's Daughter*, 369–90.

98 Frank, *Indira*, 132.

99 Ibid., 392.

100 S. Gandhi, ed., *Freedom's Daughter*, 395.

101 Frank, *Indira*, 132.

102 Ibid., 138.
103 Malhotra, *Indira Gandhi*, 49.
104 Frank, *Indira*, 173.
105 Vasudev, *Indira Gandhi*, 276.
106 Frank, *Indira*, 253.
107 Ibid.
108 Ibid.
109 Bhatia, *Indira Gandhi*, 159.
110 Malhotra, *Indira Gandhi*, 83.
111 Ibid., 68–9.
112 Ibid.
113 Masani, *Indira Gandhi*, 99.
114 Ibid., 126.
115 Carras, *Indira Gandhi*, 38.
116 Malhotra, *Indira Gandhi*, 378.
117 Bhatia, *Indira Gandhi*, 197–8.
118 See Millon, *Disorders of Personality*, 411–12, and Millon and Davis, *Personality Disorders*, 278–9.
119 Ibid., 556 and 476.

CHAPTER THREE

1 For a description of the conceptual framework and methodology for assessing leadership styles, see appendix, section II.
2 Gupte, *Mother India*, 287.
3 Frank, *Indira*, 311.
4 Malhotra, *Indira Gandhi*, 116.
5 Frank, *Indira*, 311.
6 Gupte, *Mother India*, 375.
7 Sahgal, *Indira Gandhi*, 53.
8 Frank, *Indira*, 319; Malhotra, *Indira Gandhi*, 147.
9 Gupte, *Mother India*, 381.
10 Frank, *Indira*, 375.
11 Ibid., 386–7.
12 Malhotra, *Indira Gandhi*, 235.
13 Gupte, *Mother India*, 367.
14 Frank, *Indira*, 456.
15 Ibid., 471.
16 Vasudev, *Indira Gandhi*, 354.
17 Malhotra, *Indira Gandhi*, 94.
18 Vasudev, *Indira Gandhi*, 357.
19 Masani, *Indira Gandhi*, 155.

20 Frank, *Indira*, 311.

21 Masani, *Indira Gandhi*, 224.

22 Malhotra, *Indira Gandhi*, 100.

23 Frank, *Indira*, 327.

24 Malhotra, *Indira Gandhi*, 150.

25 Vasudev, *Indira Gandhi*, 371.

26 Malhotra, *Indira Gandhi*, 95.

27 Ibid., 142–3.

28 Gupte, *Mother India*, 492.

29 Carras, *Indira Gandhi*, 10.

30 Drieberg, *Indira Gandhi*, 71.

31 Lucas, "She Stands Remarkably Alone." In an interview with Oriana Fallaci in 1972, after she became prime minister, she made essentially the same points, arguing that, for her, socialism meant justice and "trying to work in a more egalitarian society." *Interview with History*, 166–7.

32 Masani, *Indira Gandhi*, 98.

33 Frank, *Indira*, 312.

34 Masani, *Indira Gandhi*, 211.

35 Frank, *Indira*, 318.

36 Ibid., 320.

37 Moraes, *Mrs Gandhi*, 220.

38 Gupte, *Mother India*, 436.

39 Carras, *Indira Gandhi*, 210.

40 Frank, *Indira*, 410.

41 Ibid.

42 Ibid., 261.

43 Ibid., 308.

44 Masani, *Indira Gandhi*, 161.

45 Carras, *Indira Gandhi*, 169.

46 Gupte, *Mother India*, 401.

47 Ibid., 413.

48 Malhotra, *Indira Gandhi*, 160.

49 Carras, *Indira Gandhi*, 151–2.

50 Ibid., 237.

51 Vasudev, *Indira Gandhi*, 361.

52 Frank, *Indira*, 304.

53 Malhotra, *Indira Gandhi*, 103.

54 Vasudev, *Indira Gandhi*, 410.

55 Masani, *Indira Gandhi*, 230.

56 Frank, *Indira*, 356.

57 Gupte, *Mother India*, 457.

58 Ibid., 500.

59 Vasudev, *Indira Gandhi*, 370.

60 Sahgal, *Indira Gandhi*, 42.

61 Gupte, *Mother India*, 360.

62 Ibid., 376.

63 Vasudev, *Indira Gandhi*, 373.

64 Frank, *Indira*, 342.

65 Masani, *Indira Gandhi*, 238–9.

66 Dhar, *Indira Gandhi*, 210.

67 Malhotra, *Indira Gandhi*, 126.

68 Ibid., 360.

69 Ibid., 379.

70 Carras, *Indira Gandhi*, 233.

71 Ibid., 221.

72 Frank, *Indira*, 410.

73 Gupte, *Mother India*, 457–8.

74 Ibid., 235.

75 Ibid., 246.

76 Gupte, *Mother India*, 295–6.

77 Malhotra, *Indira Gandhi*, 125.

78 Gupte, *Mother India*, 409.

79 Malhotra, *Indira Gandhi*, 140.

80 Frank, *Indira*, 294.

81 Ibid., 313–14.

82 Carras, *Indira Gandhi*, 169–70.

83 Frank, *Indira*, 407.

84 Ibid., 409.

85 Malhotra, *Indira Gandhi*, 192.

86 Frank, *Indira*, 443.

87 Ibid., 479.

88 Ibid., 294.

89 Ibid., 323.

90 Gupte, *Mother India*, 286.

91 Frank, *Indira*, 294.

92 Ibid., 376–7.

93 Carras, *Indira Gandhi*, 210.

94 Gupte, *Mother India*, 286.

95 Ibid., 376.

96 Frank, *Indira*, 353.

97 Gupte, *Mother India*, 327.

98 Malhotra, *Indira Gandhi*, 297.

99 Ibid., 147–8; Frank, *Indira*, 319.

100 Gupte, *Mother India*, 365.

101 Ibid., 352–3.

102 Ibid., 438.

103 Malhotra, *Indira Gandhi*, 287–8.

104 Masani, *Indira Gandhi*, 242.

105 Ibid., 264.

106 Ibid., 277.

107 Ibid., 249.

108 Vasudev, *Indira Gandhi*, 382.

109 Carras, *Indira Gandhi*, 301.

110 Masani, *Indira Gandhi*, 252.

111 Frank, *Indira*, 354.

112 Gupte, *Mother India*, 353.

113 Frank, *Indira*, 305.

114 Masani, *Indira Gandhi*, 205–6, 208.

115 Frank, *Indira*, 411.

116 Gupte, *Mother India*, 362.

117 Ibid., 362–3.

118 Malhotra, *Indira Gandhi*, 118.

119 Ibid.

120 Gupte, *Indira Gandhi*, 360.

121 Malhotra, *Indira Gandhi*, 163–6.

122 Frank, *Indira*, 382.

123 Vasudev, *Indira Gandhi*, 364.

124 Ibid., 448–9.

125 Ibid., 162.

126 Ibid., 93.

127 Gupte, *Mother India*, 310.

128 Masani, *Indira Gandhi*, 175.

129 Frank, *Indira*, 316.

130 Masani, *Indira Gandhi*, 197.

131 Vasudev, *Indira Gandhi*, 504.

132 Masani, *Indira Gandhi*, 211.

133 Malhotra, *Indira Gandhi*, 129.

134 Gupte, *Mother India*, 374.

135 Carras, *Indira Gandhi*, 208.

136 Malhotra, *Indira Gandhi*, 122.

137 Vasudev, *Indira Gandhi*, 501.

138 Carras, *Indira Gandhi*, 140.

139 Malhotra, *Indira Gandhi*, 128–9.

140 Frank, *Indira*, 349.

141 Ibid., 360.

142 Malhotra, *Indira Gandhi*, 147.

143 Sahgal, *Her Road to Power*, 176–7.

144 Malhotra, *Indira Gandhi*, 246.

145 Vasudev, *Indira Gandhi*, 511.

146 Malhotra, *Indira Gandhi*, 116.

147 Frank, *Indira*, 349.

148 Ibid., 358.

149 Ibid., 360; Gupte, *Mother India*, 433.

150 Frank, *Indira*, 379.

151 Ibid., 382; Gupte, *Mother India*, 438–9.

152 Carras, *Indira Gandhi*, 253.

153 Gupte, *Mother India*, 439.

154 Frank, *Indira*, 401; Malhotra, *Indira Gandhi*, 178.

155 Malhotra, *Indira Gandhi*, 178.

156 Gupte, *Mother India*, 455.

157 Frank, *Indira*, 386.

158 Malhotra, *Indira Gandhi*, 235.

159 Frank, *Indira*, 469.

160 Malhotra, *Indira Gandhi*, 290.

161 Frank, *Indira*, 485.

162 Malhotra, *Indira Gandhi*, 103.

163 Vasudev, *Indira Gandhi*, 409.

164 Ibid., 411.

165 Malhotra, *Indira Gandhi*, 128.

166 Frank, *Indira*, 359.

167 Malhotra, *Indira Gandhi*, 162.

168 Frank, *Indira*, 367.

169 Ibid., 368.

170 Malhotra, *Indira Gandhi*, 259.

171 Gupte, *Mother India*, 367–8.

172 Vasudev, *Indira Gandhi*, 364.

173 Gupte, *Mother India*, 353.

174 Malhotra, *Indira Gandhi*, 138.

175 Gupte, *Mother India*, 285.

176 Malhotra, *Indira Gandhi*, 289.

177 Vasudev, *Indira Gandhi*, 407.

178 Ibid., 487.

179 Gupte, *Mother India*, 301.

180 Frank, *Indira*, 324.

181 Ibid., 482.

182 Malhotra, *Indira Gandhi*, 295.

183 Sahgal, *Indira Gandhi*, 39; Gupte, *Mother India*, 329.

184 Frank, *Indira*, 378.

185 Ibid., 380.

186 Carras, *Indira Gandhi*, 242.

187 Frank, *Indira*, 387.

188 Malhotra, *Indira Gandhi*, 274.

189 Frank, *Indira*, 300.

190 Gupte, *Mother India*, 284.

191 Ibid., 331–3.

192 Ibid., 454.

193 Vasudev, *Indira Gandhi*, 67.

194 Frank, *Indira*, 302.

195 Ibid., 326.

196 Ibid., 388.

197 Ibid., 384.

198 Gupte, *Mother India*, 450.

199 Ibid., 457; Frank, *Indira*, 441.

200 Masani, *Indira Gandhi*, 265.

201 Malhotra, *Indira Gandhi*, 307.

202 For these hypotheses, see appendix, section III.

203 Ibid.

204 Ibid.

205 Ibid.

CHAPTER FOUR

1 Meir, *My Life*, 16.

2 Ibid., 15.

3 Ibid., 27–9; Fallaci, *Interview with History*, chapter 4, Golda Meir, 110.

4 Syrkin, *Golda Meir*, 19–22.

5 Thompson, "Golda Meir," 137.

6 Ibid.

7 Syrkin, *Golda Meir*, 37–47.

8 Ibid., 35–6.

9 Noble, *Israel's Golda Meir*, 17.

10 Ibid., 17–19.

11 Ibid., 20.

12 Ibid., 21.

13 Thompson, "Golda Meir," 138.

14 Ibid., 139.

15 Meir, *My Life*, 67.

16 Ibid., 81.

17 Noble, *Israel's Golda Meir*, 31.

18 Meir, *My Life*, 87–8.

19 Thompson, "Golda Meir," 140.

20 Meir, *My Life*, 90.

21 Ibid., 94.

22 Ibid., 93.

23 Syrkin, *Golda Meir*, 82.

24 Noble, *Israel's Golda Meir*, 35–6.

25 Meir, *My Life*, 102.

26 Ibid., 103.

27 The Histadrut was the general organization for labour created by the Zionist movement in Palestine. It was (and still is) far more than a labour union, serving as both owner of enterprises and representative of workers' interests.

28 Thompson, "Golda Meir," 141.

29 Martin, *Golda Meir*, 155.

30 Ibid., 197–8.

31 Ibid., 162.

32 Ibid., 227–8.

33 Ibid., 256–7.

34 Noble, *Israel's Golda Meir*, 39–40.

35 Meir, *My Life*, 148.

36 Ibid., 36.

37 M. Meir, *My Mother*, 36.

38 Noble, *Israel's Golda Meir*, 50–1.

39 The Jewish Agency was the quasi-state organization that coordinated the various groups and movements involved in Jewish life in Palestine under the British mandate. It was, and understood itself to be, a government in training.

40 Golda was clearly disappointed to be ignored by the British. There are two possible reasons why she was not included on the list of those to be arrested: her official responsibilities were only indirectly related to the military dimension of the struggle for independence; and the authorities likely did not believe that a woman could be much of a danger. See Thompson, "Golda Meir," 159n.9, and Syrkin, *Golda Meir*, 114–17.

41 Syrkin, *Golda Meir*, 149–68.

42 Meir, *My Life*, 91.

43 Syrkin, *Golda Meir*, 172.

44 Ibid., 184.

45 Ibid., 191.

46 Ibid., 195–6.

47 Ibid., 197.

48 Ibid., 197–8.

49 Sachar, *A History of Israel*, vol. 1, 323.

50 Syrkin, *Golda Meir*, 201–2.

51 Medzini, *The Proud Jewess*, 153.

52 Ibid., 154.

53 Ibid., 156–7.

54 Ibid., 165.

55 Ibid., 212–16.

56 Medzini, *The Proud Jewess*, 191–2.

57 Meir, *My Life*, 245–54.

58 Thompson, "Golda Meir," 145.

59 Meir, *My Life*, 281.

60 Ibid., 284–7.

61 Viorst, *Sands of Sorrow*, 115.

62 Sharett, Journal, 13 June 1956, cited in Bar-Zohar, *Shimon Peres*, 128.

63 Eban, *Personal Witness*, 336–7.

64 For the details concerning her negotiations with the French leaders, see Bar Zohar, *Ben Gurion*, 230–1.

65 Ibid., 236–58.

66 Viorst, *Sands of Sorrow*, 86–7.

67 Syrkin, *Golda Meir*, 280–5.

68 Ibid., 287.

69 Ibid.

70 Fallaci, *Interview with History*, 104.

71 Syrkin, *Golda Meir*, 289.

72 Ibid., 290–6.

73 Ibid., 296.

74 Ibid., 297–303.

75 Bar-Zohar, *Ben-Gurion*, 286, and *Shimon Peres*, 201–5.

76 Syrkin, *Golda Meir*, 303–4.

77 In 1954, Pinchas Lavon had resigned because of a disastrous intelligence mishap in his Ministry of Defense. Subsequently, he came upon what he alleged to be new evidence that would prove his innocence and demonstrate that he had not given the fatal instruction to activate an intelligence unit that had been captured, with the resultant hanging of two of its members by order of an Egyptian court. A seven-member cabinet committee had subsequently investigated the matter and concluded that Lavon had indeed been blameless. Ben-Gurion argued that the acquittal of Lavon implied that Colonel Benjamin Gibli, who had been director of military intelligence at the time of the affair, had given the disastrous order. The prime minister argued that an acquittal of one citizen with a consequent condemnation of another was a matter for legal action, not political appraisal. He presented the action of the cabinet committee as a major corruption of the democratic process and of juridical integrity. Ben-Gurion's critics, among them Levi Eshkol and Golda Meir, thought he was exaggerating the importance of a formalistic and debatable issue, upsetting the national priorities, and preventing the nation from getting on with its vital work. See Eban, *Personal Witness*, 315.

78 Ibid., 327.

79 Meir, *My Life*, 289–91.

80 Thompson, "Golda Meir," 146.

81 Ibid., 147.

82 Sachar, *A History of Israel*, vol. 1, 627.

83 Thompson, "Golda Meir," 147.

84 Meir, *My Life*, 374.

85 Eban, *Abba Eban*, 461.

86 Author's interview with Shimshon Arad (Israeli ambassador to Mexico and the Netherlands), 20 November 2004, Jerusalem, Israel.

87 Meir, *My Life*, 376–8.

88 Thompson, "Golda Meir," 148.

89 Stein, *Heroic Diplomacy*, 18.

90 Israel State Archives (ISA) 106/1993/1P, 18 April 1969, cited in Gorenberg, *The Accidental Empire*, 190.

91 Interview with Gideon Rafael (director general of the Israeli Foreign Ministry, April 1967-December 1971), 25 March 1992, Jerusalem, Israel, cited in Stein, *Heroic Diplomacy*, 18.

92 Eban, *Personal Witness*, 477–8.

93 Sachar, *A History of Israel*, vol. 1, 711–12.

94 Eban, *Personal Witness*, 482–4.

95 Stein, *Heroic Diplomacy*, 57.

96 Eban, *Personal Witness*, 485.

97 Ibid., 489.

98 Ibid.

99 Stein, *Heroic Diplomacy*, 58.

100 Interview with Gideon Rafael, cited in Stein, *Heroic Diplomacy*, 59.

101 Gazit, "Egypt and Israel," 97–101.

102 Eban, *Personal Witness*, 499.

103 Ibid., 500.

104 Ibid., 500–1.

105 Sachar, *A History of Israel*, vol. 2, 4.

106 Stein, *Heroic Diplomacy*, 61–2.

107 Eban, *Personal Witness*, 515–16.

108 Meir, *My Life*, 336.

109 Stein, *Heroic Diplomacy*, 63.

110 Syrkin, *Golda Meir*, 335–6. Nor did she change her views after she became prime minister. Interviewed by Oriana Fallaci in 1972, she argued that "to the east and west of the Jordan you find the same people. I've already explained that once they were called Palestinians and later were called Jordanians [after Churchill partitioned Palestine in 1922, the territory west of the Jordan became Cisjordania and the territory east of the Jordan became Transjordania]. Two names for the same people. If they want to call themselves Palestinians or Jordanians I couldn't care less. It's none of my business. But it's my business that they don't set up another Arab state between Israel and what is now called Jordan. In the stretch

of land between the Mediterranean and the borders of Iraq there's room for only two countries, one Arab and one Jewish." Fallaci, *Interview with History*, 105.

111 Syrkin, *Golda Meir*, 355–6.
112 Meir, *My Life*, 421.
113 Rabinovitch, *The Yom Kippur War*, 50.
114 Remarks by Mordechai Gazit at the Conference on the October War, the Middle East Institute, Washington, D.C., 9 October 1998, cited in Stein, *Heroic Diplomacy*, 70.
115 Meir, *My Life*, 423–4.
116 Stein, *Heroic Diplomacy*, 70.
117 Safran, *Israel: The Embattled Ally*, 285–6.
118 Interview with Golda Meir, 26 December, 1978, Tel Aviv, Israel, cited in ibid.
119 Rabinovitch, *The Yom Kippur War*, 94.
120 Meir, *My Life*, 426.
121 Ibid., 424–5.
122 Eban, *Personal Witness*, 529.
123 Dayan did not seem to be talking about total surrender but rather a surrender of some territory. Rabinovitch, *The Yom Kippur War*, 220.
124 Ibid.
125 Hersh, *The Samson Option*, 225–31.
126 Eban, *Personal Witness*, 532–9.
127 Sachar, *A History of Israel*, vol. 2, 3.
128 Eban, *Personal Witness*, 554.
129 Meir, *My Life*, 455.
130 Eban, *Personal Witness*, 561–2.
131 Meir, *My Life*, 455–6.
132 Sachar, *A History of Israel*, vol. 2, 3.
133 Eban, *Personal Witness*, 563–4.
134 Meir, *My Life*, 458.

CHAPTER FIVE

1 See Table 9 for scale names. Solid horizontal lines on the profile form signify cut-off scores between adjacent scale gradations. For Scales 1–8, scores of 5 through 9 signify the *presence* (gradation a) of the personality pattern in question; scores of 10 through 23 indicate a *prominent* (gradation b) variant; and scores of 24 to 30 provide strong evidence of a *mildly dysfunctional* (gradation c) variation of the pattern. For Scales 9 and 0, scores of 20 through 35 indicate *a moderately disturbed* syndrome (gradation d) and scores of 36 through 45 (gradation e) a *markedly disturbed* syndrome.

2 For more details, see appendix, section I.

3 Syrkin, *Golda Meir*, 18.

4 Medzini, *The Proud Jewess*, 23.

5 Meir, *My Life*, 25.

6 Ibid., 41.

7 Martin, *Golda Meir*, 37–8.

8 Meir, *My Life*, 42.

9 Ibid., 43.

10 Ibid., 50.

11 Ibid., 47.

12 Ibid., 64.

13 Ibid., 58–68.

14 Ibid., 75.

15 Ibid., 84–5.

16 Ibid., 87.

17 Medzini, *The Proud Jewess*, 94.

18 Ibid., 107.

19 Ibid., 116.

20 Medzini, *The Proud Jewess*, 117.

21 Meir, *My Life*, 211–12.

22 Medzini, *The Proud Jewess*, 169.

23 Meir, *My Life*, 264.

24 Ibid., 198.

25 Medzini, *The Proud Jewess*, 202.

26 Meir, *My Life*, 279.

27 Ibid., 281–2.

28 Medzini, *The Proud Jewess*, 273–4.

29 Ibid., 262–3.

30 Ibid., 14–16.

31 Ibid., 18.

32 Author interview with Shimon Peres, 16 November 2004, New York City. Peres was prime minister of Israel on three occasions and was elected president in 2007.

33 Meir, *My Life*, 327.

34 Ibid., 336.

35 Eban, *Personal Witness*, 337.

36 Author interview with Meron Medzini, 14 October 2004, Jerusalem.

37 Author interview with Michael Harish, 14 October 2004, Jerusalem. Harish worked for Meir when she was foreign minister and the international secretary of the Labor Party. He later became minister of industry and trade and secretary general of the Labor Party.

38 Ibid.

39 Eban, *Personal Witness*, 336–7.

40 Telephone interview with Shimshon Arad, 20 November 2004. Arad was a member of the Israeli diplomatic corps: ambassador-at-large, 1960–64; ambassador to Mexico, 1964–68; and ambassador to the Netherlands, 1968–72.

41 Telephone interview with Simcha Dinitz, 13 February 2003. Dinitz was ambassador to Washington from 1973 to 1979.

42 Eban, *Personal Witness*, 476–7.

43 Dayan, *Story of My Life*, 77.

44 Medzini, *The Proud Jewess*, 350.

45 Telephone interview with former President of Israel, Yitzhak Navon, 9 November 2004.

46 Ibid.

47 For more details see appendix, section I.

48 Meir, *My Life*, 19.

49 Ibid., 26.

50 Ibid., 52.

51 Ibid., 98.

52 Medzini, *The Proud Jewess*, 96–7.

53 Ibid., 113.

54 Meir, *My Life*, 236.

55 Medzini, *The Proud Jewess*, 180.

56 Ibid.

57 Ibid.

58 Ibid., 14–16.

59 See Millon, *Disorders of Personality*, 551–2.

60 Meir, *My Life*, 268.

61 Medzini, *The Proud Jewess*, 210.

62 Labor Party Archives (LPA), Golda Meir, speech at Mapai's Secretariat, 6 December 1958, cited in Bar-Zohar, *Shimon Peres*, 200.

63 Medzini, *The Proud Jewess*, 305–8.

64 Meir Barely (1974), *From a Movement to an Apparatus* (Tel Aviv: Elilev), 168–9. The Mapai activist was Yitzhak Bareli, Meir's father. Cited in Bar-Zohar, *Shimon Peres*, 139.

65 Medzini, *The Proud Jewess*, 323.

66 Telephone interview with Shimshon Arad, 20 November 2004.

67 Author interview with Shimon Peres, 16 November, 2004, New York City.

68 Telephone interview with Shimshon Arad, 20 November, 2004.

69 Telephone interview with Simcha Dinitz, 13 February 2003.

70 Author interview with Moshe Yegar, 7 October, 2004, Jerusalem. Yegar was ambassador to Sweden (1988–90) and the Czech Republic (1993–95).

71 Ibid.

72 See also Millon, *Disorders of Personality DSM–IV*, 550–1.

73 Oldham and Morris, *The New Personality Self-Portrait*, 62.

74 Meir, *My Life*, 58.

75 Ibid.

76 Ibid., 64–5.

77 Ibid., 90.

78 Syrkin, *Golda Meir*, 80.

79 Ibid., 211.

80 Ibid., 236–7.

81 Ibid., 238.

82 Bar-Zohar, *Armed Prophet*, 1189.

83 Telephone interview with David Harmon, 10 February 2004. Harmon was a professor of education at the Hebrew University who lived in the Foreign Ministry as a youngster for six years during the period when his father was ambassador to the United States.

84 Telephone interview with Shimshon Arad, 20 November 2004.

85 Millon, *Disorders of Personality DSM–IV*, 519.

86 Dayan, *Story of My Life*, 377.

87 Telephone interview with David Harmon, 10 February 2004.

88 Oldham and Morris, *The New Personality Self-Portrait*, 319. For more details see appendix, section I.

89 Meir, *My Life*, 78.

90 Ibid., 100.

91 Martin, *Golda Meir*, 183.

92 Syrkin, *Golda Meir*, 154.

93 Bar-Zohar, *Armed Prophet*, 1192.

94 Telephone interview with Mordechai Gazit, 20 February 2004.

95 Ibid.

96 Medzini, *The Proud Jewess*, 317.

97 Telephone interview with Yitzhak Navon, 9 November 2004.

98 Telephone interview with David Harmon, 10 February 2004.

99 Author interview with Moshe Yegar, 7 October, 2004, Jerusalem.

100 Medzini, *The Proud Jewess*, 14–15.

101 For additional details, see appendix, section I.

102 Millon, *Disorders of Personality, DSM–IV*, 462.

103 Israel Shenker, "Golda Meir, 80, Dies in Jerusalem."

104 Martin, *Golda Meir*, 11, 32.

105 Syrkin, *Golda Meir*, 25.

106 Interview with Regina Hamburger Medzini, cited in Martin, *Golda Meir*, 35.

107 Martin, *Golda Meir*, 47.

108 Interview with Sadie Ottenstein, cited in Martin, *Golda Meir*, 55.

109 Interview with Louise Born, cited in ibid., 65.

110 Interview with Sadie Ottenstein, cited in ibid.

111 Ibid., 78.

112 Interview with Marie Syrkin, cited in ibid., 254.

113 Ibid., 85.

114 Syrkin, *Golda Meir*, 136.

115 Ibid., 150.
116 Meir, *My Life*, 17–18.
117 Ibid., 21–2.
118 Ibid., 38–9.
119 Ibid., 40–1.
120 Ibid., 42-4.
121 Ibid., 45–8.
122 Ibid., 33–8.
123 Ibid., 50–1.
124 Ibid., 60–1.
125 Medzini, *The Proud Jewess*, 24.
126 For additional details, see Millon, *Disorders of Personality, DSM–IV*, 556.

CHAPTER SIX

1 For an analysis of the conceptual framework and methodology used in the assessment of the various dimensions of leadership style, see appendix, section II.
2 Perlmutter, *Israel: The Partitioned State*, 206.
3 Ibid., 207–8.
4 Speech to the Knesset, 16 December 1969.
5 Jerusalem *Post*, 20 March 1969.
6 Ibid., 20 April 1969.
7 Medzini, *The Proud Jewess*, 356.
8 Millon, *Disorders of Personality*, 485.
9 Telephone interview with Simcha Dinitz, 13 February 2000.
10 Millon, *Disorders of Personality*, 485.
11 Jerusalem *Post*, 5 November 1970.
12 Interviews with Gideon Rafael, 25 March 1992, Jerusalem, and Nicholas A. Veliotes, 7 September 1995, Washington, D.C., quoted in Stein, *Heroic Diplomacy*, 60.
13 Interview with Gideon Rafael, 25 March 1992, cited in ibid.
14 Stein, *Heroic Diplomacy*, 8.
15 Jerusalem *Post*, 4 August 1972.
16 Ibid., 1 July 1973.
17 Ibid., 14 December 1973.
18 Interview with Alouf Hareven, 2 August 1992, Jerusalem, quoted in Stein, *Heroic Diplomacy*, 64.
19 Interview with Mordechai Gazit, 22 March 1992, Jerusalem, quoted in Stein, *Heroic Diplomacy*, 64.
20 Medzini, *The Proud Jewess*, 387.
21 Ibid., 359.
22 Ibid., 379.
23 Greenleaf, "Servant Leadership," 22.

24 See Provizer, "In the Shadow of Washington."

25 Nixon, *Leaders*, 285–6.

26 Ibid., 286.

27 Ibid., 355.

28 Ibid., 358.

29 Jerusalem *Post*, 5 May 1978.

30 Medzini, *The Proud Jewess*, 451.

31 Stein, *Heroic Diplomacy*, 121.

32 Netanyahu and Netanyahu, *Self-portrait of a Hero*, 185.

33 Dayan, *Story of My Life*, 361.

34 Jerusalem *Post*, 21 July 1971.

35 Medzini, *The Proud Jewess*, 357.

36 Ibid., 359.

37 Dayan, *Story of My Life*, 553.

38 Jerusalem *Post*, 24 September 1969.

39 Ibid., 26 May 1971.

40 Ibid., 8 May 1970.

41 Ibid., 31 May 1971.

42 Meir, *My Life*, 455.

43 Perlmutter, *Israel*, 211–14.

44 For more information on "Golda's Kitchen," see Ben-Meir, "Decision Making," 130–3; Ben-Porat, "Decision Making," 92–6, 215–16.

45 Author interview with Arie Lova Eliav, 7 October 2004, Jerusalem. Eliav was a member of the Knesset (1965–75) and secretary general of the Labor Party during this period.

46 Medzini, *The Proud Jewess*, 382.

47 Eban, *Personal Witness*, 468.

48 Medzini, *The Proud Jewess*, 382.

49 Author interview with Shimon Peres, 16 November, 2004, New York City. Peres also stated that he was not a participant in the "inner kitchen."

50 Ben-Meir, "Decision-Making," 133.

51 Medzini, *The Proud Jewess*, 382.

52 Telephone interview with Simcha Dinitz, 13 February 2000.

53 Medzini, *The Proud Jewess*, 380.

54 Eban, *Personal Witness*, 468–555.

55 Medzini, *The Proud Jewess*, 365.

56 Ibid., 379.

57 Ibid.

58 Herzog, *The War of Atonement*, 51.

59 Interview with Golda Meir, 26 December 1978, Tel Aviv, quoted in Stein, *Heroic Diplomacy*, 71.

60 Medzini, *The Proud Jewess*, 367.

61 Herzog, *The War of Atonement*, 281–2.

62 Jerusalem *Post*, 18 March 1969.

63 Ibid., 18 February 1970.

64 Ibid., 379.

65 Herzog, *The War of Atonement*, 52.

66 Stein, *Heroic Diplomacy*, 71.

67 Ibid.

68 Telephone interview with Simcha Dinitz, 13 February 2003.

69 Jerusalem *Post*, 10 January 1971.

70 Medzini, *The Proud Jewess*, 359.

71 Jerusalem *Post*, 11 March 1970, 8 June 1970.

72 Ibid., 20 May 1971.

73 Medzini, *The Proud Jewess*, 383.

74 Ibid., 382.

75 Meir, *My Life*, 387.

76 Stein, *Heroic Diplomacy*, 98.

77 Telephone interview with Simcha Dinitz, 13 February 2003.

78 Medzini, *The Proud Jewess*, 385.

79 Rabin, *The Rabin Memoirs*, 155–6.

80 Ibid., 182.

81 Ibid., 203.

82 Peres, *Battling for Peace*, 98.

83 Jerusalem *Post*, 12 November 1970.

84 Ibid., 26 April, 1970.

85 Ibid., 16 January 1974.

86 Dayan, *Story of My Life*, 443; telephone interview with Simcha Dinitz, 13 February 2003.

87 Telephone interview with Simcha Dinitz, 13 February 2003.

88 Jerusalem *Post*, 1 April 1973.

89 Dayan, *Story of My Life*, 443.

90 Medzini, *The Proud Jewess*, 382.

91 Jerusalem *Post*, 21 August 1970.

92 Ibid., 2 March 1971.

93 Dayan, *Story of My Life*, 443.

94 Jerusalem *Post*, 7 September 1969.

95 Ibid., 18 March 1971.

96 Ibid., 21 July 1971.

97 Ibid., 12 August 1969.

98 Ibid., 7 September 1969.

99 Ibid., 23 March 1971.

100 Press reports appearing during March 1972 indicated that an area in Rafah (southern part of the Gaza strip) had been fenced off by the military authorities. This incident gave rise to some controversy which led to a debate in the Knesset. On 28 March 1972 the Jerusalem *Post* reported

that Minister Yisrael Galili had stated in a speech in the Knesset that "the Gaza Strip would not again be separated from Israel." The minister was further quoted as stating that "there are political reasons for accelerating settlement in the Gaza Strip ... and [he] revealed that 'some time' this year an army outpost, Nahal Sinai, would become a civilian settlement. Press reports also indicated that the incident surrounding the fencing off of the land in the Rafah area was the subject of an investigation by the chief of staff, whose forces were responsible for carrying out the fencing. These same reports stated that the results of this investigation were not disclosed to the government but that three senior army officers had been reprimanded and one of them transferred from his post. Another report on 28 March 1972 in the *Post* added that the fencing off of land had involved "the unauthorized transfer of some 6,000 Bedouin from the Pithat Rafah area, the destruction of some 24 buildings, water holes and the fencing in of 20,000 dunams of land [approximately 5,000 acres]." Other reports indicated that compensation was being offered to the evicted persons and that it was planned to resettle them in alternative accommodation.

101 Ibid., 27 April 1972.
102 Dayan, *Story of My Life*, 499.
103 Jerusalem *Post*, 20 October 1969.
104 Since 1996, some structural changes have been made to the Israeli electoral system. For details, see Mahler, "Israel's New Electoral System."
105 Jerusalem *Post*, 16 December 1969.
106 Ibid., 28 May 1970.
107 Ibid., 17 November 1970.
108 The Ikrit Bir'im issue had to do with the former Arab residents of the villages Ikrit and Bir'im who had been residing legally in Israel since their villages were evacuated during the 1948 war. During the summer of 1972, a group of former Bir'im residents took refuge in a church in the village and refused to leave unless allowed to return to their homes. They were subsequently removed by the police.

Deputy Premier Yigal Allon opposed Meir's stance, as did many opposition members. Concern was also voiced within Mapam circles that the policy had been designed and decided upon without them. Meeting with the Israeli authorities, Joseph Raya, the Greek Catholic archbishop of Israel, protested the government's decision not to allow the villagers to return, particularly in light of Meir's earlier promise to reconsider their request. Meir stated that her government was working on the rehabilitation of those villagers who so desired "by means of cash indemnification, allocation of alternative land and aid in building new homes." Dissatisfied with the Government's response, Raya ordered that no masses were to be held for a Sunday (or two) in a show of mourning and protest. At the same time, he stated he would not "wash laundry in public" (i.e., seek the Vatican's help to deal with domestic Israeli matters). See Jerusalem *Post*, 13 July, 2 August, 9 August, 11 August 1972.

109 Ibid., 11 August 1972.
110 Ibid., 18 March 1969.
111 Ibid., 1 December 1969.
112 Ibid., 11 August 1971.
113 Author interview with Victor Shemtov, 7 October 2004, Jerusalem.
114 Jerusalem *Post*, 13 August 1970.
115 Ibid., 3 October 1969.
116 Ibid., 19 October 1970.
117 Ibid., 19 February 1970.
118 Ibid., 1 June 1971.
119 Medzini, *The Proud Jewess*, 368.
120 Jerusalem *Post*, 5 December 1971.
121 Ibid., 6 December 1971.
122 Ibid., 3 October 1969.
123 Ibid., 23/25 December 1971.
124 Ibid., 28 February 1973.
125 Medzini, *The Proud Jewess*, 379.
126 Meir, *My Life*, 386.
127 Jerusalem *Post*, 18 February 1971.
128 Ibid., 2 March 1971.
129 Ibid., 11 April 1971.
130 Ibid., 13 December 1971.
131 Ibid., 18 February 1972.
132 Ibid., 27 April 1973.
133 Ibid., 2 April 1973.
134 Ibid., 18 September 1973.
135 Ibid., 5 June 1970.
136 Ibid., 22 January 1970.
137 Meir, *My Life*, 435–6.
138 Medzini, *The Proud Jewess*, 443–4.

CHAPTER SEVEN

1 Ogden, *Maggie*, 40.
2 Ibid.
3 Ibid.
4 Ibid., 40–51.
5 Ibid., 53–60.
6 *The Times*, 5 October 1970, cited in McFadyean and Renn, *Thatcher's Reign*, 120.

7 Ogden, *Maggie*, 73.

8 Ibid., 74.

9 Ibid., 102.

10 Ibid., 104.

11 Ibid., 108–9.

12 Ibid., 115–20.

13 Ibid., 119–22.

14 Junor, *Margaret Thatcher*, 91–2.

15 Ibid., 94–8.

16 Young, *The Iron Lady*, 120.

17 Ibid.

18 Ibid., 121.

19 Ibid., 128.

20 Ibid., 129.

21 Ibid., 130.

22 Ibid., 135.

23 Ibid., 140–7.

24 Ibid., 190–4.

25 Ibid., 197.

26 Ibid., 200–1.

27 Ibid., 202.

28 Ibid., 206–7.

29 Ibid., 207.

30 Ibid.

31 Ibid., 209–16.

32 Ibid., 212–14.

33 Ibid., 216.

34 Ibid., 225–6.

35 Ibid., 226–8.

36 Ibid., 336.

37 Ibid., 228–32.

38 Ibid., 241–2.

39 Ibid., 247.

40 See Smith, *Reagan and Thatcher*, especially 76–93, for an examination of Britain-U.S. relations during the Falklands crisis.

41 Young, *The Iron Lady*, 259.

42 Lebow, "Miscalculation in the South Atlantic," 105–6.

43 Young, *The Iron Lady*, 260–1; for extensive details on this case, see the *Franks Committee Report*.

44 Ibid., 258, 262.

45 Ibid., 263.

46 Ibid., 263–4.

47 Ibid., 264–5.

48 Ibid., 268.

49 Haig, *Caveat*, 261–302.

50 Young, *The Iron Lady*, 276.

51 Ibid., 278.

52 Ibid., 277–9.

53 Ibid., 279.

54 Ibid., 281.

55 Ibid., 355–70.

56 The committee was formed following the 1922 general election; hence its
    name.

57 Ibid., 371.

58 Ibid., 371–7.

59 Ibid., 382–8.

60 Smith, *Thatcher and Reagan*, 146–76.

61 Young, *The Iron Lady*, 400–14.

62 Ibid., 431–58.

63 Ibid., 443–4.

64 Ibid., 447.

65 Ibid., 464–72.

66 Ibid., 472.

67 Ibid., 473.

68 Ibid., 498–9.

69 For additional details, see Deakin, *The Politics of Welfare*, a well-informed
    account of the evolution of social policy under the Thatcher government.

70 Young, *The Iron Lady*, 499.

71 Ibid., 501–2.

72 Ibid., 502.

73 This involved the Thatcher government's efforts to block publication of the
    memoirs of a retired MI5 officer, Peter Wright. There is no question that
    Wright's *Spycatcher* was a serious breach of the confidentiality expected of
    secret-service personnel; the government was thoroughly entitled to ban it,
    as it had done with many less sensational books before. The problem was
    that Wright was living in Australia, and he published his book there, as well
    as in Ireland and the United States, with extracts even appearing in the Brit-
    ish press. Trying to stop its publication was a classic case of shutting the
    barn door after the horse had bolted. See Campbell, *The Iron Lady*, 387.

74 Young, *The Iron Lady*, 505–8.

75 Ogden, *Maggie*, 300–3.

76 Ibid., 305–8. A parenthetical note: it was not until 1988 that Oxford Uni-
    versity even bothered to solicit funds from its 116,000 living graduates,
    some of them the most successful and richest men and women in the world.

77 Ibid., 308.

78 Ibid., 309.

79 Ibid., 309–10.

80 Campbell, *The Iron Lady*, 576.

81 S. Jenkins, *Accountable to None*, 195.

82 Ogden, *Maggie*, 310–11.

83 Ibid., 313.

84 Ibid., 311–12.

85 Ibid., 314–15.

86 Ibid., 315–17.

87 Ibid., 315–16.

88 Ibid., 320–2.

89 Ibid., 324.

90 John, "The Fall of the Iron Lady, 1990," 126–7.

91 Ibid., 127.

92 *Hansard*, Geoffrey Howe, resignation statement in the House of Commons, 13 November 1990.

93 John, "The Fall of the Iron Lady, 1990," 127.

94 Geelhoed, *Margaret Thatcher*, 173–4.

95 Ibid., 178.

96 John, "The Fall of the Iron Lady, 1990," 127–8.

97 Ibid., 132.

98 Baldwin, "The Demise of the Prime Minister," 135.

99 Watkins, *A Conservative Coup*, 182.

100 John, "The Fall of the Iron Lady, 1990," 134.

101 The candidate with an absolute majority wins on the second ballot, but not necessarily on the first. A surplus majority of 15 per cent of the total electorate, 56 votes of the 372 Conservative MPs at the time, was also necessary. Thatcher's margin over Heseltine was only 52, four short of the necessary 15 per cent (John, "The Fall of the Iron Lady, 1990," 135).

102 Ibid., 135.

103 *The Economist*, "Pulled Down," November 1990, 30.

104 *Sunday Times*, 25 November 1990.

105 John, "The Fall of the Iron Lady, 1990," 136.

106 Ibid., 137.

107 23 November 1990, 1.

108 Anderson, *John Major*, 156.

109 Geelhoed, *Margaret Thatcher*, 185.

110 William Hogue's successors as Conservative Party leader were Ian Duncan Smith, Michael Howard, and David Cameron.

111 Johnson, "Leaders and Revolutionaries: Margaret Thatcher."

CHAPTER EIGHT

1 See Table 9 for scale names. Solid horizontal lines on the profile form signify cut-off scores between adjacent scale gradations. For Scales 1–8, scores of 5 through 9 signify the *presence* (gradation a) of the personality pattern in question; scores of 10 through 23 indicate a *prominent* (gradation b) variant; and scores of 24 to 30 indicate an exaggerated, *mildly dysfunctional* (gradation c) variation of the pattern. For Scales 9 and 0, scores of 20 through 35 indicate a *moderately disturbed* (gradation d) syndrome and scores of 36 through 45 a *markedly disturbed* (gradation e) syndrome.

2 Ogden, *Maggie*, 4.

3 Ibid., 36.

4 Thatcher, *The Path to Power*, 17.

5 Ibid., 28.

6 Ibid., 36.

7 Ogden, *Maggie*, 48–9.

8 Ibid.

9 Campbell, *The Grocer's Daughter*, 31.

10 Millon, *Disorders of Personality*, 484.

11 Ogden, *Maggie*, 45.

12 Millon, *Disorders of Personality*, 484.

13 Campbell, *The Grocer's Daughter*, 133. The Public Bodies (Admission to Meetings) Act, 1960 gave the press and the public a right of access to the meetings of local councils. Ostensibly a measure directed towards more open government, it was a curious choice for Thatcher to choose to support it as a private members' bill given that it was neither close to her heart nor one that the Conservatives on the local council in Finchley supported. She did so for two reasons: first, the Conservative Party had committed itself to some such measure in the 1959 election manifesto and she took it over as a favour to the whips' office; second, and more important, Thatcher was determined to weaken trade-union power. During the newspaper strike of 1958, certain Labour councils had voted to support the strikers by excluding from council meetings reporters who worked for papers being produced with strike-breaking labour. The 1960 act put an end to that behaviour (Young, *The Iron Lady*, 44–6).

14 Junor, *Margaret Thatcher*, 68–9.

15 Campbell, *The Grocer's Daughter*, 218.

16 Ogden, *Maggie*, 112.

17 Thatcher, *The Path to Power*, 228.

18 Ibid., 284.

19 Young, *The Iron Lady*, 104–5.

20 Thatcher, *The Path to Power*, 352–3. Maudling would be removed as shadow foreign minister in 1977 for his lack of agreement with Thatcher on economic and foreign affairs. See ibid., 319.

21 Young, *The Iron Lady*, 118.

22 Murray, *Margaret Thatcher*, 118.

23 Millon, *Disorders of Personality*, 485.

24 Junor, *Margaret Thatcher*, 110.

25 Millon, *Disorders of Personality*, 484.

26 Campbell, *The Grocer's Daughter*, 362.

27 Young, *The Iron Lady*, 121.

28 Junor, *Margaret Thatcher*, 114.

29 Ibid., 115.

30 Gardner, *Leading Minds*, 237.

31 Thatcher, *The Path to Power*, 411.

32 Junor, *Margaret Thatcher*, 119.

33 Thatcher, *The Path to Power*, 440.

34 Ibid., 451.

35 For a more complete description of the Contentious pattern, see appendix, section I.

36 Junor, *Margaret Thatcher*, 14.

37 Rawlinson, *A Price Too High*, 274.

38 *Sunday Express*, 30 June 1968.

39 Thatcher, *The Path to Power*, 123.

40 Young, *The Iron Lady*, 72.

41 Campbell, *The Grocer's Daughter*, 216.

42 Ibid.

43 See Millon, *Disorders of Personality*, 549–50.

44 Thatcher, *The Path to Power*, 170.

45 Junor, *Margaret Thatcher*, 74.

46 Thatcher, *The Path to Power*, 248.

47 Ibid., 260.

48 Ibid., 268.

49 Ibid., 269.

50 Ibid., 456.

51 Millon, *Disorders of Personality*, 560.

52 Junor, *Margaret Thatcher*, 126.

53 Millon, *Disorders of Personality*, 553.

54 For a more detailed description of the Ambitious pattern, see appendix, section I.

55 Junor, *Margaret Thatcher*, 11.

56 Ibid.

57 Ogden, *Maggie*, 41.

58 Junor, *Margaret Thatcher*, 25.

59 Ogden, *Maggie*, 46.
60 Junor, *Margaret Thatcher*, 17–18.
61 Young, *The Iron Lady*, 110.
62 Thatcher, *The Path to Power*, 36.
63 Junor, *Margaret Thatcher*, 17–18.
64 Ogden, *Maggie*, 52.
65 Junor, *Margaret Thatcher*, 21.
66 Thatcher, *The Path to Power*, 94.
67 Ogden, *Maggie*, 74.
68 Thatcher, *The Path to Power*, 96.
69 Ogden, *Maggie*, 86–7.
70 Junor, *Margaret Thatcher*, 42.
71 Thatcher, *The Path to Power*, 80–1.
72 Ibid., 81.
73 *The Times*, 11 October 1961.
74 Junor, *Margaret Thatcher*, 60.
75 Ibid., 62.
76 Thatcher, *The Path to Power*, 142.
77 Young, *The Iron Lady*, 67.
78 Thatcher, *The Path to Power*, 252.
79 Ibid., 266.
80 Junor, *Margaret Thatcher*, 85.
81 Thatcher, *The Path to Power*, 273.
82 C. Thatcher, *Below the Parapet*, 11–12.
83 Junor, *Margaret Thatcher*, 114.
84 Thatcher, *The Path to Power*, 430.
85 Campbell, *The Grocer's Daughter*, 216.
86 See Millon, *Disorders of Personality*, 515–19. For more details on the Conscientious pattern, see appendix, section I.
87 Ogden, *Maggie*, 36.
88 Ibid.
89 Junor, *Margaret Thatcher*, 8.
90 Ogden, *Maggie*, 39.
91 Ibid., 49.
92 Junor, *Margaret Thatcher*, 9.
93 Campbell, *The Grocer's Daughter*, 30.
94 Young, *The Iron Lady*, 11.
95 Junor, *Margaret Thatcher*, 10.
96 Thatcher, *The Path to Power*, 36.
97 Ogden, *Maggie*, 22.
98 Junor, *Margaret Thatcher*, 19.
99 Ibid., 26.
100 Ibid., 27.

101 Young, *The Iron Lady*, 15.

102 Junor, *Margaret Thatcher*, 28.

103 Ogden, *Margaret Thatcher*, 71.

104 Ibid., 31.

105 Ibid., 50–1.

106 Young, *The Iron Lady*, 72.

107 Junor, *Margaret Thatcher*, 123.

108 Young, *The Iron Lady*, 118.

109 Campbell, *The Grocer's Daughter*, 402.

110 Junor, *Margaret Thatcher*, 49.

111 Murray, *Margaret Thatcher*, 42.

112 Young, *The Iron Lady*, 6.

113 See, for example, Steven Pinker, *The Blank Slate*.

114 See Kammeyer, "Sibling Position and the Feminine Role."

115 Campbell, *The Grocer's Daughter*, 31.

116 See Baumrind, "Reciprocal Rights and Responsibilities in Parent-Child Relations."

117 Ogden, *Maggie*, 36.

118 Ibid.

119 Thatcher, *The Path to Power*, 6.

120 Campbell, *The Grocer's Daughter*, 21.

121 Thatcher, *The Path to Power*, 28.

122 Ibid., 19.

123 *Sunday Express*, 20 July 1975.

124 Campbell, *The Grocer's Daughter*, 32–3.

125 Ibid., 123.

126 Ibid., 446–7.

127 Ibid., 33.

128 Ibid., 21.

129 Ibid., 30.

130 Ibid.

131 Ibid., 30–1.

132 See Abse, *Margaret, the Daughter of Beatrice*.

133 Webster, *Not a Man to Match Her*, 15.

134 Ibid.

135 Ibid.

136 Campbell, *The Grocer's Daughter*, 20.

137 Ibid., 24.

138 Thatcher, *The Path to Power*, 11.

139 For more information on the psychological defence mechanism of "splitting," see Laplanche and Pontalis, *The Language of Psychoanalysis*; Klein, *Envy and Gratitude*.

140 Millon, *Disorders of Personality*, 556.

141 Ibid., 490–1.
142 Ibid., 179.
143 Ibid., 521–2.

CHAPTER NINE

1 For a thorough description of the conceptual framework and methodology for the analysis of leadership style, see appendix, section II.
2 For a description of the conceptual framework and methodology for assessing leadership styles, see ibid.
3 Young, *The Iron Lady*, 21–2.
4 Campbell, *The Iron Lady*, 5.
5 Kavanagh, *Thatcherism and British Politics*, 246.
6 Campbell, *The Iron Lady*, 41.
7 Ibid., 7.
8 Young, *The Iron Lady*, 197.
9 Ibid., 140.
10 Ibid., 192.
11 Thatcher, *The Path to Power*, 26.
12 Young, *The Iron Lady*, 215.
13 Ibid., 323.
14 Campbell, *The Iron Lady*, 227.
15 Kavanagh, *Thatcherism and British Politics*, 263.
16 Ogden, *Maggie*, 196.
17 Ibid., 196–7.
18 Campbell, *The Iron Lady*, 675.
19 Young, *The Iron Lady*, 137.
20 Webster, *Not a Man to Match Her*, 143.
21 Young, *The Iron Lady*, 153.
22 Ibid., 379.
23 Campbell, *The Iron Lady*, 373–4.
24 Thatcher, *The Downing Street Years*, 560.
25 Young, *The Iron Lady*, 543.
26 Webster, *Not A Man to Match Her*, 144.
27 King, *The British Prime Minister*, 117–18.
28 Ibid.
29 Campbell, *The Iron Lady*, 612.
30 Young, *The Iron Lady*, 353.
31 Ibid., 544–5.
32 Ibid., 391.
33 Interview with the BBC, 17 December 1984, in the Margaret Thatcher Foundation Archives, at http://www.margaretthatcher.org
34 Ogden, *Maggie*, 278.

35 Thatcher, *The Downing Street Years*, 760.

36 Ogden, *Maggie*, 265.

37 Campbell, *The Iron Lady*, 314–15.

38 Thatcher, *The Downing Street Years*, 77.

39 Ibid., 259.

40 Young, *The Iron Lady*, 198.

41 Ibid.

42 King, *The British Prime Minister*, 98.

43 Young, *The Iron Lady*, 148–9.

44 Ogden, *Maggie*, 342.

45 Kavanagh, *Thatcherism and British Politics*, 247.

46 King, *The British Prime Minister*, 116.

47 Ibid., 98.

48 Young, *The Iron Lady*, 158.

49 Ibid., 381.

50 Webster, *Not a Man to Match Her*, 127.

51 Ibid., 96.

52 Ogden, *Maggie*, 344.

53 Thatcher, *The Downing Street Years*, 20.

54 Campbell, *The Iron Lady*, 289.

55 Ogden, *Maggie*, 239.

56 Campbell, *The Iron Lady*, 313.

57 Kavanagh, *Thatcherism and British Politics*, 250.

58 Ibid., 430–1.

59 Ibid., 137.

60 Ibid., 257.

61 Webster, *Not a Man To Match Her*, 73.

62 Young, *The Iron Lady*, 149.

63 Ogden, *Maggie*, 176.

64 Panorama BBC TV interview, 25 January 1988, cited in Kavanagh, *Thatcherism and British Politics*, 250–1.

65 Young, *The Iron Lady*, 430.

66 Campbell, *The Iron Lady*, 443.

67 Kavanagh, *Thatcherism and British Politics*, 254.

68 Campbell, *The Iron Lady*, 444.

69 Ogden, *Maggie*, 185–6.

70 Young, *The Iron Lady*, 476.

71 Ogden, *Maggie*, 250.

72 King, *The British Prime Minister*, 117.

73 Campbell, *The Iron Lady*, 444.

74 Webster, *Not a Man to Match Her*, 139.

75 Kavanagh, *Thatcherism and British Politics*, 262–3.

76 Webster, *Not a Man to Match Her*, 144.

77 Interview with Lord Jenkin, quoted in Campbell, *The Iron Lady*, 447.

78 John, "The Fall of the Iron Lady, 1990," 127.

79 Thatcher, *The Downing Street Years*, 655.

80 Campbell, *The Iron Lady*, 136.

81 Ibid., 147.

82 Ibid., 235.

83 Ibid., 613.

84 Young, *The Iron Lady*, 146.

85 Kavanagh, *Thatcherism and British Politics*, 264.

86 Thatcher, *The Downing Street Years*, 229.

87 Ibid., 206.

88 Ibid., 323.

89 Ibid., 515.

90 Ibid., 281.

91 Kavanagh, *Thatcherism and British Politics*, 252.

92 Ibid.

93 Campbell, *The Iron Lady*, 33–5.

94 Ibid., 445.

95 Ogden, *Maggie*, 319.

96 Kavanagh, *Thatcherism and British Politics*, 253.

97 Thatcher, *The Downing Street Years*, 473.

98 Ibid., 713.

99 Ogden, *Maggie*, 295.

100 Ibid., 279.

101 Ibid., 729.

102 King, *The British Prime Minister*, 126.

103 Young, *The Iron Lady*, 159.

104 Young and Sloman, *The Thatcher Phenomenon*, 24.

105 Ibid., 137.

106 King, *The British Prime Minister*, 131. After Johnson chose Hubert Humphrey as his running mate, Humphrey gave a speech in November 1964, two months before taking office, on the subject of education. Carried away by his enthusiasm, he departed from his text and incurred the president's wrath. Johnson was furious at Humphrey for giving the impression that he would be the architect of the administration's education policies; this was Johnson's terrain and Humphrey was informed about that in no uncertain terms. To humiliate Humphrey further, Johnson called in the White House reporters who were with him at his ranch and told them, "'Boys, I've just reminded Hubert that I've got his balls in my pocket.'" Steinberg, *Shame and Humiliation*, 75.

107 Campbell, *The Iron Lady*, 82.

108 Webster, *Not A Man to Match Her*, 152.

109 Cosgrove, *Margaret Thatcher*, 16.

110 Junor, *Margaret Thatcher*, 101.

111 Ibid.

112 Young, *The Iron Lady*, 159.

113 Ogden, *Maggie*, 203.

114 Thatcher, *The Downing Street Years*, 858.

115 See chapter 8.

116 Thatcher, *The Downing Street Years*, 29.

117 Ogden, *Maggie*, 202.

118 Young, *The Iron Lady*, 310.

119 Ibid.

120 Interviews with Sir Michael Partridge and Sir Douglas Wass, cited in Campbell, *The Iron Lady*, 19.

121 Interview with Neville Beale, cited in ibid., 382.

122 Ogden, *Maggie*, 171.

123 Kavanagh, *Thatcherism and British Politics*, 265.

124 Webster, *Not a Man to Match Her*, 136.

125 Ogden, *Maggie*, 176.

126 Ibid., 303.

127 Ibid.

128 Ibid., 304.

129 Ibid.

130 Ibid., 318–20.

131 Thatcher, *The Downing Street Years*, 830.

132 Ogden, Maggie, 313.

133 Young, *The Iron Lady*, 434.

134 Thatcher, *The Downing Street Years*, 154.

135 Ibid.

136 Young, *The Iron Lady*, 509.

137 Kavanagh, *Thatcherism and British Politics*, 267.

138 Thatcher, *The Downing Street Years*, 221.

139 Campbell, *The Iron Lady*, 123.

140 Young, *The Iron Lady*, 236.

141 Webster, *Not A Man to Match Her*, 136.

142 Young, *The Iron Lady*, 354.

143 Ibid., 357.

144 Ibid., 323.

145 Campbell, *The Iron Lady*, 196.

146 Webster, *Not a Man to Match Her*, 155.

147 Ogden, *Maggie*, 166.

148 Thatcher, *The Downing Street Years*, 222.

149 Young, *The Iron Lady*, 242.

150 Campbell, *The Iron Lady*, 363.

151 Ibid., 47.

152 Young, *The Iron Lady*, 226.

153 Ibid., 510.

154 Ibid.

155 Webster, *Not a Man to Match Her*, 85.

156 Thatcher, *The Downing Street Years*, 840.

157 Young, *The Iron Lady*, 511.

158 Ogden, *Maggie*, 334.

159 Campbell, *The Iron Lady*, 406.

160 Thatcher, *The Downing Street Years*, 208.

161 Campbell, *The Iron Lady*, 75.

162 Ibid., 57.

163 Webster, *Not a Man to Match Her*, 107.

164 Thatcher, *The Downing Street Years*, 138.

165 Ibid., 581.

166 Young, *The Iron Lady*, 174.

167 Ibid., 179.

168 Ogden, *Maggie*, 206.

169 Campbell, *The Iron Lady*, 517.

170 Ibid.

171 For an analysis of the hypotheses that were developed to predict the relationship between personality profiles and leadership styles, see appendix, section III.

CONCLUSION

1 Medzini, *The Proud Jewess*, 18.

2 Young, *The Iron Lady*, 329–546.

3 See Immelman, "The Political Personalities of 1996 U.S. Presidential Candidates Bill Clinton and Bob Dole" and "The Political Personality of U.S. Presidential Candidate George W. Bush"; and Immelman and Beatty, "The Political Personality of Zimbabwean President Robert Mugabe."

4 See, for example, Lipset, "The Social Requisites of Democracy Revisited," 1–22.

5 See Dowd, *Are Men Necessary?* for a discussion as to how much must still be done for the playing field for women to be truly level.

6 There is growing research evidence that traits of shyness and reticence may be largely part of one's constitutional endowment. See, for example, *Communication Education*, 49: 1 (January 2000), and *Genome News Network*, 21 April 2000.

7 See Nagel, *The Structure of Science*, 547.

APPENDIX

1 Simonton, "Personality and Politics," 670–92.

2 See, for example, George and George, *Woodrow Wilson and Colonel House*; Greenstein, "The Two Leadership Styles of William Jefferson Clinton"; Post, "Saddam Hussein of Iraq"; Renshon, *High Hopes* and *The Psychological Assessment of Presidential Candidates*; Steinberg, *Shame and Humiliation*; and Volkan and Itzkowitz, *The Immortal Ataturk*.

3 Hermann, "Leader Personality and Foreign Policy Behavior"; "Effects of Personal Characteristics of Political Leaders on Foreign Policy"; "Explaining Foreign Policy Behavior Using the Personal Characteristics of Political Leaders"; "Personality and Foreign Policy Decision Making"; and "Assessing the Foreign Policy Role Orientations of Sub-Saharan African Leaders."

4 Winter, "An Exploratory Study of the Motives of Southern African Political Leaders Measured at a Distance"; and "Leader Appeal, Leader Performance, and the Motive Profiles of Leaders and Followers."

5 Suedfeld and Tetlock, "Integrative Complexity of Communications in International Crises"; Tetlock, "Integrative Complexity of American and Soviet Foreign Policy Rhetoric."

6 For a selection of articles that treat these two approaches, see Post, *The Psychological Assessment of Political Leaders*.

7 Content analysis is a standard methodology in the social sciences for studying the content of communication. The method of content analysis enables the researcher to include large amounts of textual information and, by detecting the more important structures of its communication content, systematically identify its properties. Such amounts of textual information must be categorized according to a certain theoretical framework, which will inform the data analysis and provide a meaningful reading of content under scrutiny.

8 Simonton, "Personality and Politics"; see also Kowert, "Where Does the Buck Stop? Assessing the Impact of Presidential Personality"; Milburn, "The Q-sort and the Study of Political Personality"; Simonton, "Presidential Personality"; and Rubenzer and Faschingbauer, *Personality, Character, and Leadership in the White House*.

9 Millon, "A Theoretical Derivation of Pathological Personalities"; "Personality Prototypes and Their Diagnostic Criteria"; *Toward a New Personology*; "Normality: What May We Learn from Evolutionary Theory?"; MIPS: *Millon Index of Personality Styles Manual*; *Millon Clinical Multiaxial Inventory–III*; and *Disorders of Personality*. Also, Millon and Davis, *Personality Disorders in Modern Life*.

10 Millon and Everly, *Personality and Its Disorders*.

11 See Immelman, "The Assessment of Political Personality"; *Millon Inventory of Diagnostic Criteria Manual II–Revised;* "The Political Personalities of 1996 U.S. Presidential Candidates Bill Clinton and Bob Dole"; "The

Political Personality of U.S. Vice President Al Gore"; "The Political Personality of U.S. President George W. Bush"; "The Political Personality of
Zimbabwean President Robert Mugabe"; "The Political Personality of
2004 U.S. Presidential Candidate John Kerry"; "The Personality Profile
of September 11 Hijack Ringleader Mohammed Atta"; "The Personality
Profile of Al-Qaida Leader Osama Bin Laden"; and "'Bin Laden's Brain':
The Abrasively Negativistic Personality of Dr. Ayman Al-Zawahiri."

12 Immelman, "The Political Personalities of 1996 U.S. Presidential Candidates Bill Clinton and Bob Dole"; "The Political Personality of U.S. Vice
President Al Gore"; "The Political Personality of U.S. Presidential Candidate George W. Bush."

13 Immelman and Hagel, "A Comparison of the Personalities of Eleanor
Roosevelt and Hillary Rodham Clinton."

14 Immelman, "The Personality Profile of September 11 Hijack Ringleader
Mohammed Atta"; "The Personality Profile of Al-Qaida Leader Osama
Bin Laden"; and "'Bin Laden's Brain': The Abrasively Negativistic Person-
ality of Dr. Ayman Al-Zawahiri."

15 Immelman, "The Assessment of Political Personality."

16 *Disorders of Personality.*

17 *Personality Disorders in Modern Life.*

18 *The Personality Self-Portrait; The New Personality Self-Portrait.*

19 Strack, "The PACL: Gauging Normal Personality Styles."

20 Millon, *Millon Clinical Multiaxial Inventory–III*, 283.

21 See Immelman and Steinberg, *Millon Inventory of Diagnostic Criteria*, 2nd
ed., unpublished research scale.

22 See Millon, *Disorders of Personality.*

23 Table 8 provides a description of the attribute domains across which personality can be measured.

24 *Scales 1–8*:
   Score of 5 points: Evidence for Level I (*present*) personality pattern. Justification: identification of a criterion at the first level (scored 1 point) in all
   five attribute domains of a given personality type.
   Score of 8 points: Minimal evidence for Level II (*prominent*) personality
   pattern. Justification: identification of a criterion at the second level (scored
   2 points) in four of five attribute domains of a given personality type.
   Score of 10 points: Strong evidence for Level II (*prominent*) personality pattern. Justification: identification of a criterion at the second level (scored
   2 points) in all five attribute domains of a given personality type.
   Score of 15 points: Minimal evidence for Level III (Mildly Dysfunctional)
   personality pattern. Justification: identification of a criterion at the third level
   (scored 3 points) in all five attribute domains of a given personality type.
   Score of 24 points: Strong evidence for Level III (Mildly Dysfunctional) personality pattern. Justification: identification of a criterion at the third level

(scored 3 points) in all five attribute domains of a given personality type
(i.e., 25 points) or identification of a criterion in any four of five attribute
domains at all three levels (scored 1, 2, and 3 points) of a given personality
pattern.

Scales 9 and 0:

Score of 16 points: Minimal evidence for Level IV (Moderately Disturbed)
personality type, with potential for personality impairment. Justification:
identification of a criterion at the fourth level (scored 4 points) in any four
of the five attribute domains of the Distrusting or Erratic pattern.

Score of 20 points. Strong evidence for Level IV (Moderately Disturbed)
personality type, with potential for personality impairment. Justification:
identification of a criterion at the fourth level (scored 4 points) in all five
attribute domains of the Distrusting or Erratic pattern.

Score of 25 points. Minimal evidence for Level V (Markedly Disturbed)
personality type, with potential for markedly disturbed personality functioning. Justification: identification of fourth level (scored 5 points) in all
five attribute domains of the Distrusting or Erratic pattern.

Score of 36 points. Strong evidence for Level V (Markedly Disturbed) personality type with some degree of personality de-compensation. Justification: identification of a criterion at the fourth level (scored 4 points) in all
five attribute domains of the Distrusting or Erratic pattern, plus identification of a criterion at the fourth level (scored 4 points) in three of the five attribute domains of these patterns (i.e., 37 points) or identification of a
criterion at both the fourth (scored 4 points) and fifth (scored 5 points) levels in four of the five attribute domains of these patterns (i.e., 36 points).

25 Detailed information concerning the construction, administration, scoring,
and interpretation of the MIDC provided in the MIDC manual is available
upon request from the author (Immelman) or on the Internet at http:
//www.csbsju.edu/uspp/Research/Research-Instruments.html

26 Millon, *Clinical Multiaxial Inventory – III*, 292.

27 Millon, *Toward a New Personology: An Evolutionary Model*, 160.

28 See Immelman, *Millon Inventory of Diagnostic Criteria Manual II–Revised*.
Unpublished manuscript, available from the author or on the Internet (see
n.25).

29 Ibid., 18. See n.23.

30 Millon, *MIPS: Millon Index of Personality Styles Manual*; Millon, *Millon
Clinical Multiaxial Inventory–III*; and Millon and Davis, *Disorders of Personality*.

31 *The Personality Self-Portrait* and *The New Personality Self-Portrait*.

32 Strack, "The PACL: Gauging Normal Personality Styles."

33 *Millon Inventory of Diagnostic Criteria Manual II – Revised*.

34 Strack, "The PACL: Gauging Normal Personality Styles," 490.

35 *MIPS: Millon Index of Personality Styles Manual*, 34.

36 *The New Personality Self-Portrait*, 345.
37 Oldham and Morris, *The New Personality Self-Portrait*, 227–8.
38 MIPS: *Millon Index of Personality Styles Manual*.
39 Oldham and Morris, *The New Personality Self-Portrait*, 227–8.
40 Ibid., 228–9.
41 MIPS: *Millon Index of Personality Styles Manual*, 33.
42 Millon and Davis, *Personality Disorders in Modern Life*, 107.
43 Ibid.
44 Millon, *Millon Clinical Multiaxial Inventory – III*, 32.
45 Oldham and Morris, *The New Personality Self-Portrait*, 79.
46 Strack, "The PACL: Gauging Normal Personality Styles," 489–90.
47 Millon, MIPS: *Millon Index of Personality Styles Manual*, 32.
48 Oldham and Morris, *The New Personality Self-Portrait*, 85–6.
49 Strack, "The PACL: Gauging Normal Personality Styles."
50 Millon, MIPS: *Millon Index of Personality Styles Manual*.
51 Strack, "The PACL: Gauging Normal Personality Styles," 489.
52 Millon, MIPS: *Millon Index of Personality Styles Manual*, 31–2.
53 Oldham and Morris, *The New Personality Self-Portrait*, 108–9.
54 Strack, "The PACL: Gauging Normal Personality Styles."
55 Millon, MIPS: *Millon Index of Personality Styles Manual*.
56 Millon, *Millon Clinical Multiaxial Inventory – III*, 335.
57 Millon, MIPS: *Millon Index of Personality Styles Manual*.
58 Strack, "The PACL: Gauging Normal Personality Styles," 489.
59 Oldham and Morris, *The New Personality Self-Portrait*, 108.
60 Ibid.
61 Millon, MIPS: *Millon Index of Personality Styles Manual*.
62 Millon, *Disorders of Personality*, 589.
63 Millon and Davis, *Personality Disorders in Modern Life*, 496.
64 Oldham and Morris, *The New Personality Self-Portrait*, 319.
65 Millon, MIPS: *Millon Index of Personality Styles Manual*, 33.
66 Strack, "The PACL: Gauging Normal Personality Styles."
67 Millon, MIPS: *Millon Index of Personality Styles Manual*.
68 Strack, "The PACL: Gauging Normal Personality Styles," 490–1.
69 Millon, MIPS: *Millon Index of Personality Styles Manual*, 34.
70 Oldham and Morris, *The New Personality Self-Portrait*, 222.
71 Ibid.
72 Millon, MIPS: *Millon Index of Personality Styles Manual*.
73 Strack, "The PACL: Gauging Normal Personality Styles."
74 Millon, *Disorders of Personality*, 506–7.
75 Oldham and Morris, *The New Personality Self-Portrait*, 64–5.
76 Millon, MIPS: *Millon Index of Personality Styles Manual*, 33.
77 Strack, "The PACL: Gauging Normal Personality Styles," 490.
78 Oldham and Morris, *The New Personality Self-Portrait*, 180–1.

79 Millon, *MIPS: Millon Index of Personality Styles Manual*.
80 Strack, "The PACL: Gauging Normal Personality Styles."
81 Oldham and Morris, *The New Personality Self-Portrait*, 186.
82 Strack, "The PACL: Gauging Normal Personality Styles," 488.
83 Millon, *MIPS: Millon Index of Personality Styles Manual*, 32.
84 Ibid., 31.
85 Oldham and Morris, *The New Personality Self-Portrait*, 275–6 .
86 Strack, "The PACL: Gauging Normal Personality Styles."
87 Millon, *MIPS: Millon Index of Personality Styles Manual*, 31.
88 Oldham and Morris, *The New Personality Self-Portrait*, 275.
89 Millon, *MIPS: Millon Index of Personality Styles Manual*, 31.
90 Strack, "The PACL: Gauging Normal Personality Styles," 488.
91 Millon, *Disorders of Personality*, 705.
92 Oldham and Morris, *The New Personality Self-Portrait*, 157.
93 Millon, *Disorders of Personality*, 690.
94 Ibid.
95 The inability to maintain defence mechanisms in response to stress, resulting in personality disturbance or psychological imbalance.
96 Ibid., 666.
97 Oldham and Morris, *The New Personality Self-Portrait*, 293.
98 Millon, *Disorders of Personality*, 646.
99 See, for example, on the American presidency: Etheredge, "Hard-ball Politics: A Model"; Etheredge et al., *Personality and Political Leadership*; Greenstein, *Leadership in the Modern Presidency* and *The Presidential Difference*; Renshon, "A Preliminary Assessment of the Clinton Presidency," *The Clinton Presidency, High Hopes*, and *The Psychological Assessment of Presidential Candidates*; Barber, *The Presidential Character*; Hermann, *The Psychological Examination of Political Leaders*, "Presidential Leadership Style, Advisory Systems and Policy Making," "Advice and Advisers in the Clinton Presidency," and "Assessing Leadership Style"; Hermann and Preston, "Presidents, Advisers, and Foreign Policy"; George, *Presidential Decision Making in Foreign Policy*; George and George, *Presidential Personality and Performance*; and George and Stern, "Presidential Style, Management and Models." On prime-ministerial leadership in various European countries, see Kaarbo, "Prime Minister Leadership Styles in Foreign Policy Decision-Making," and Kaarbo and Hermann, "Leadership Styles of Prime Ministers."

    In addition, attempts have been made to link particular types of leadership style with such antecedents as motives and needs. See Winter, *The Power Motive*, "The Power Motive in Women – and Men," "Personality and Foreign Policy," and "Presidential Psychology and Governing Styles"; Walker and Falkowski, "The Operational Codes of U.S. Presidents and Secretaries of State"; Barber, *The Presidential Character*; George and

George, *Woodrow Wilson and Colonel House* and *Presidential Personality and Performance*; Hermann, *The Psychological Examination of Political Leaders*; Renshon, *The Clinton Presidency, High Hopes*, and *The Psychological Assessment of Presidential Candidates*; George, "The 'Operational Code'"; Holsti, "The 'Operational Code'"; Walker, "The Interface between Beliefs and Behavior," "The Motivational Foundations of Political Belief Systems," and "The Evolution of Operational Code Analysis"; Walker et al., "Profiling the Operational Codes of Political Leaders"; Immelman, "The Assessment of Political Personality" and "Personality in Political Psychology"; Simonton, "Presidential Style"; and Winter, "Presidential Psychology and Governing Styles."

100 *MIPS: Millon Index of Personality Styles Manual*; *Millon Inventory of Diagnostic Criteria Manual II – Revised*; *Millon Clinical Multiaxial Inventory– III*; *Disorders of Personality.*

101 "The Assessment of Political Personality"; *Millon Inventory of Diagnostic Criteria Manual II – Revised*; and "Personality in Political Psychology."

102 Kaarbo, "Prime Minister Leadership Styles in Foreign Policy Decision-Making," 553.

103 Campbell, *Managing the Presidency.*

104 Crabb and Mulcahy, *Presidents and Foreign Policy Making.*

105 Hermann, "Assessing the Foreign Policy Role Orientations of Sub-Saharan African Leaders."

106 "Presidential Leadership Style of Bill Clinton"; "The Two Leadership Styles of William Jefferson Clinton"; and "Political Style and Political Leadership."

107 "A Preliminary Assessment of the Clinton Presidency."

108 *Managing the White House.*

109 "Presidential Management Styles and Models."

110 *The Presidential Character: Predicting Performance in the White House.*

111 "Presidents, Advisers, and Foreign Policy."

112 "Prime Minister Leadership Styles in Foreign Policy Decision-Making."

113 See Kaarbo and Hermann, "Leadership Styles of Prime Ministers," 251–2.

114 See, for example, George, *Presidential Decision Making in Foreign Policy*; Bass, *Stogdill's Handbook of Leadership*; and Burke and Greenstein, *How Presidents Test Reality.*

115 See Barber, *The Presidential Character*, 4th ed.

116 Hanreider and Auton, *The Foreign Policies of West Germany, France, and Britain.*

117 Kaarbo and Hermann, "Leadership Styles of Prime Ministers," 247–8.

118 "Prime Minister and Cabinet," 46.

119 See t'Hart, *Groupthink in Government.*

120 *First among Equals.*

121 Kaarbo and Hermann, "Advice and Advisers in the Clinton Presidency."

122 See Muller, Phillip, and Gerlich, "Prime Ministers and Cabinet Decision-Making Processes"; and Hermann, "Assessing the Foreign Policy Role Orientations of Sub-Saharan African Leaders."

123 Kaarbo and Hermann, "Leadership Styles of Prime Ministers."

124 Renshon, *High Hopes* and *The Psychological Assessment of Presidential Candidates*.

125 Steinberg, Kotsovilis, and Osweiler, "Leadership Style Inventory," Table 22.

Bibliography

Abse, L. (1989). *Margaret, Daughter of Beatrice: A Politician's Psycho-biography of Margaret Thatcher*. London: Jonathan Cape.

American Psychiatric Association. (1994). *Diagnostic and Statistical Manual of Mental Disorders*. 4th ed. Washington, D.C.: Author.

Anderson, B. (1991). *John Major: The Making of the Prime Minister*. London: Fourth Estate.

Baldwin, N.D.J. (1991). "The Demise of the Prime Minister." *British Politics Group Newsletter*, no. 64 (spring): 5.

Barber, J.D. (1992). *The Presidential Character: Predicting Performance in the White House*. 4th ed. Englewood Cliffs, N.J.: Prentice-Hall.

Bar-Zohar, M. (1977). *Armed Prophet: The Life of David Ben-Gurion*. Israel: Magal Books.

– (2003). *Ben-Gurion: A Biography*. Israel: Magal Books.

– (2007). *Shimon Peres: The Biography*. New York: Random House.

Bass, B.M. (1981). *Stogdill's Handbook of Leadership: A Survey of Theory and Research*. Englewood Cliffs, N.J.: Prentice-Hall.

Baumrind, D. (1978). "Reciprocal Rights and Responsibilities in Parent-Child Relations." *Journal of Social Issues*, 34: 179–89.

Ben Meir, Y. (1987). *Decision Making – Issues in National Defense – The Israeli Perspective*. Tel Aviv: Tel Aviv University.

Ben-Porat, Y. (1981). *Conversations*. Jerusalem: Hotsa'at 'Idanim.

Bhatia, K. (1974). *Indira Gandhi: A Biography of a Prime Minister*. London: Angus Wilson.

Blondel, J. (1980). *World Leaders: Heads of Government in the Post-War World*. Beverly Hills, Calif.: Sage.

Bowlby, J. (1969–80). *Attachment and Loss*. 3 vols. London: Hogarth Press.

Brunstetter, M.P. (1989). "Women in Power: Meir, Thatcher, and Aquino." Paper presented at the annual meeting of the American Political Science Association, Atlanta, Georgia, 31 August–3 September.

Bumiller, E. (1990). *May You Be the Mother of a Hundred Sons*. New York: Fawcett Colombine.

Burke, J.P., and F.I. Greenstein. (1991). *How Presidents Test Reality: Decisions on Vietnam, 1954 and 1965*. New York: Russell Sage Foundation.

Campbell, C. (1986). *Managing the Presidency: Carter, Reagan and the Search for Executive Harmony*. Pittsburgh: University of Pittsburgh Press.

Campbell, J. (2000). *Margaret Thatcher. Vol. 1: The Grocer's Daughter*. London: Jonathan Cape.

– (2003). *Margaret Thatcher. Vol. 2: The Iron Lady*. London: Jonathan Cape.

Carras, M.C. (1979). *Indira Gandhi: In the Crucible of Leadership*. Boston: Beacon Press.

Communication Education. (2000). 49, no. 1 (January).

Cosgrove, P. (1978). *Margaret Thatcher: A Tory and Her Party*. London: Hutchison.

Crabb, C.V., and K.V. Mulcahy. (1988). *Presidents and Foreign Policy Making*. Baton Rouge, La.: Louisiana State University.

Daily Mirror (London). 1 March 1980.

Dayan, M. (1976). *Story of My Life*. London: Weidenfeld and Nicolson.

Deakin, N. (1987). *The Politics of Welfare*. London: Methuen.

Dhar, P.N. (2000). *Indira Gandhi: The Emergency and Indian Democracy*. New Delhi: Oxford University Press.

Dowd, M. (2005). *Are Men Necessary?* New York: G.P. Putnam's Sons.

Eban, Abba. (1977). *Abba Eban: An Autobiography*. New York: Random House.

– (1992). *Personal Witness: Israel through My Eyes*. New York: G.P. Putnam's Sons.

Etheredge, L. (1979). "Hard-ball politics: A Model." *Political Psychology*, 1: 3–26.

– and J.D. Barber, D.G. Winter, P.M. Sniderman, and G. Cocks. (1993). "Personality and Political Leadership." In Neil J. Kressel, ed., *Political Psychology: Classic and Contemporary Readings*. 108–54. New York: Paragon House.

Everett, J. (1993). "Indira Gandhi and the Exercise of Power," In Michael Genovese, ed., *Women as National Leaders*. 103–34. Newbury Park, Calif.: Sage Publications.

Fallaci, O. (1976). *Interview with History*. New York: Liveright Publishing.

Frank, K. (2001). *Indira: The Life of Indira Nehru Gandhi*. London: Harper Collins.

Frankel, F.R. (1971). *India's Green Revolution: Economic Gains and Political Costs*. Princeton, N.J.: Princeton University Press.

Freud, A. (1965). *Normality and Pathology in Childhood*. New York: International Universities Press.

Freud, S. (1933). "New Introductory Lectures on Psychoanalysis." In *The Standard Edition of the Complete Psychological Works of Sigmund Freud*, 22: 3–182. London: Hogarth Press.

Gandhi, I. (1971–86). *Selected Speeches and Writings of Indira Gandhi*, vols. I–V. New Delhi: Publications Division, Ministry of Information and Broadcasting.

– (1980). *My Truth*. New York: Grove Press.

– (1989). *Anand Bhawan Memories and Other Personal Essays*. [Delhi]: Indira Memorial Trust.

Gandhi, S., ed. (1989). *Freedom's Daughter: Letters between Indira Gandhi and Jawaharlal Nehru 1922–39*. London: Hodder.

– (1992). *Rajiv*. Delhi: Viking/Penguin.

Gardner, H. (1995). In collaboration with E. Laskin. *Leading Minds: An Anatomy of Leadership*. New York: Basic Books.

Gazit, M. (2002). "Egypt and Israel," In M. Gazit, *Israeli Diplomacy and the Middle East Peace Process*. London: Routledge.

Geelhoed, B. (1992). With the assistance of J.F. Hobbs. *Margaret Thatcher: In Victory and Downfall 1987–1990*. New York: Praeger.

Genome News Network. (2000). 21 April.

Genovese, M. (1993). "Margaret Thatcher and the Politics of Conviction Leadership." In Genovese, ed., *Women as National Leaders*. 177–210. Newbury Park, Calif.: Sage Publications.

– and S. Thompson. (1993). "Women as Chief Executives: Does Gender Matter?" In Genovese, ed., *Women as National Leaders*. 1–13. Newbury Park, Calif.: Sage Publications.

George, A.L. (1979). "The Causal Nexus between Cognitive Beliefs and Decision-Making Behavior: The 'Operational Code.'" In L. Falkowski, ed., *Psychological Models in International Politics*. 697–718. Boulder, Colo.: Westview Press.

– (1980). *Presidential Decision Making in Foreign Policy: The Effective Use of Information and Advice*. Boulder, Colo.: Westview Press.

– (1988). "Presidential Management Styles and Models." In C.W. Kegley, Jr, and E.R. Wittkopf, eds. *The Domestic Sources of American Foreign Policy: Insights and Evidence*. 107–26. New York: St Martin's Press.

– (1998). *Presidential Personality and Performance*. Boulder, Colo.: Westview Press.

– and E. Stern. (1998). "Presidential Style, Management and Models." In A.L. George and J.L. George, eds. *Presidential Personality and Performance*. 199–280. Boulder, Colo.: Westview Press.

– and J.L. George. (1964). *Woodrow Wilson and Colonel House: A Personality Study*. New York: Dover Publications.

Giddings, P. (1995). "Prime Minister and Cabinet." In D. Shell and R. Hodder-Williams, eds., *Churchill to Major*. 30–70. Armonk, N.Y.: M.E. Sharpe.

Gorenberg, G. (2006). *The Accidental Empire: Israel and the Birth of the Settlements, 1967–1977*. New York: Henry Holt.

Greenleaf, R. (1995). "Servant Leadership." in J. Wren, ed., *The Leaders Companion*. New York: Free Press.

Greenspan, S.I., and G.H. Pollock, eds., (1990). *The Course of Life: Psychoanalytic Contributions toward Understanding Personality Development*. Rockville, Md.: National Institutes of Mental Health.

Greenstein, F. (1993–94). "Presidential Leadership Style of Bill Clinton: An Early Appraisal." *Political Science Quarterly*, 108: 589–601.

– (1994). "The Two Leadership Styles of William Jefferson Clinton." *Political Psychology*, 15: 351–61.

– (1995). "Political Style and Political Leadership: The Case of Bill Clinton." In S.A. Renshon, ed., *The Clinton Presidency: Campaigning, Governing, and the Psychology of Leadership*. 137–47. Boulder, Colo.: Westview Press.

Gupte, P. (1992). *Mother India*. New York: Charles Scribner's Sons.

Haig, A. (1984). *Caveat: Realism, Reagan and Foreign Policy*: New York: Macmillan.

Hangen, W. *After Nehru, Who?* (1963). London: Rupert Hart-Davis.

Hanreider, W.F., and G.P. Auton. (1957). *The Foreign Policies of West Germany, France, and Britain*. Englewood Cliffs, N.J.: Prentice-Hall.

Harris, K. (1989). *Thatcher*. London: Fontana.

Hart, H.C. (1976). "Indira Gandhi: Determined Not to Be Hurt." In H.C. Hart, ed., *Indira Gandhi's India: A Political System Reappraised*. 241–73. Boulder, Colo.: Westview Press.

t'Hart, P. (1994). *Group Think in Government*. Baltimore: Johns Hopkins University Press.

Hayek, F.A. (1944). *The Road to Serfdom*. Chicago: University of Chicago Press.

Hermann, M.G. (1974). "Leader Personality and Foreign Policy Behavior." In J.N. Rosenau, ed., *Comparing Foreign Policies: Theories, Findings, and Methods*. 201–34. New York: Wiley.

– ed. (1977). *The Psychological Examination of Political Leaders*. 131–44. New York: Free Press.

– (1978). "Effects of Personal Characteristics of Political Leaders on Foreign Policy." In M.A. East, S.A. Salmore, and C.F. Hermann, eds., *Why Nations Act: Theoretical Perspectives for Comparative Foreign Policy Studies*. 49–68. Beverly Hills, Calif./London: Sage.

– (1980). "Explaining Foreign Policy Behavior Using the Personal Characteristics of Political Leaders." *International Studies Quarterly*, 24: 7–46.

– (1984). "Personality and Foreign Policy Decision Making: A Study of 53 Heads of Government." In D.A. Sylvan and S. Chan, eds., *Foreign Policy Decision Making: Perception, Cognition, and Artificial Intelligence*. 53–80. New York: Praeger.

– (1987). "Assessing the Foreign Policy Role Orientations of Sub-Saharan African Leaders." In S.G. Walker, ed., *Role Theory and Foreign Policy Analysis*. 161–98. Durham, N.C.: Duke University Press.

– (1994). "Presidential Leadership Style, Advisory Systems and Policy Making: Bill Clinton's Administration After Seven Months." *Political Psychology*, 15: 363–74.

– (1995). "Advice and Advisers in the Clinton Presidency: The Impact of Leadership Style." In S.A. Renshon, ed., *The Clinton Presidency: Campaigning,*

Governing and the Psychology of Leadership. 149–64. Boulder, Colo.: Westview Press.

– and J.T. Preston. (1995). "Presidents, Advisers, and Foreign Policy: The Effects of Leadership Style on Executive Arrangements." *Political Psychology*, 15: 75–96.

Hersh, S. (1991). *The Samson Option: Israel's Nuclear Arsenal and American Foreign Policy*. New York: Random House.

Herzog, C. (1975). *The War of Atonement: October 1973*. Boston: Little Brown.

Holsti, O. (1970). "The 'Operational Code' Approach to the Study of Political Leaders: John Foster Dulles' Philosophical and Instrumental Beliefs." *Canadian Journal of Political Science*, 3, no. 1: 123–57.

Hutheesing, K. (1969). *Dear to Behold: An Intimate Portrait of Indira Gandhi*. New York: Macmillan.

Immelman, A. (1993). "The Assessment of Political Personality: A Psychodiagnostically Relevant Conceptualization and Methodology." *Political Psychology*, 14: 725–41.

– (1998). "The Political Personalities of 1996 U.S. Presidential Candidates Bill Clinton and Bob Dole." *Leadership Quarterly*, 9, no. 3: 335–66.

– (2000). "The Political Personality of U.S. Vice President Al Gore." Paper presented at the twenty-third annual scientific meeting of the International Society of Political Psychology, Seattle, Washington, 16–19 July.

– (2002). "The Personality Profile of Al-Qaida Leader Osama Bin Laden." Paper presented at the twenty-fifth annual scientific meeting of the International Society of Political Psychology, Berlin, 16–19 July.

– (2002). "The Personality Profile of September 11 Hijack Ringleader Mohammed Atta." Paper presented at the twenty-fifth annual scientific meeting of the International Society of Political Psychology, Berlin, 16–19 July.

– (2002). "The Political Personality of U.S. President George W. Bush." In L.O. Valenty and O. Feldman, eds., *Political Leadership for the New Century: Lessons from the Study of Personality and Behavior among American Leaders*. 81–103. Westport, Conn.: Greenwood Press.

– (2003). "Millon Inventory of Diagnostic Criteria Manual II – Revised." Unpublished manuscript, available from the author, Department of Psychology, St John's University, Collegeville, Minn., 56321–3000, or on the Internet at http://www.csbsju.edu/uspp

– (2003). "Personality in Political Psychology." In I.B. Weiner (series ed.) and T. Millon and M.J. Lerner (vol. eds.), *Handbook of Psychology: Vol. 5. Personality and Social Psychology*. 599–625. New York: Wiley.

– (2005). "Political Psychology and Personality." In S. Strack, ed., *Handbook of Personology and Psychopathology*. 128–225. Hoboken, N.J.: Wiley.

– and B. Steinberg (compilers). (1999). "Millon Inventory of Diagnostic Criteria" (2nd ed.). Unpublished research scale, available from Immelman,

St John's University, Collegeville, Minn., 56321–3000, or on the Internet at
http://www.csbsju.edu/uspp

– and J. Hagel. (1998). "A Comparison of the Personalities of Eleanor
Roosevelt and Hillary Rodham Clinton." Paper presented at the twenty-first
annual scientific meeting of the International Society of Political Psychology,
Montreal, Quebec, 12–15 July.

– and K. Kuhlmann. (2003). "'Bin-Laden's Brain': The Abrasively Negativistic
Personality of Dr. Ayman Al-Zawahiri." Paper presented at the twenty-fifth
annual scientific meeting of the International Society of Political Psychology,
Boston, 6–9 July.

Jayakar, P. (1986). *J. Krishnamurthi: A Biography*. Delhi: Penguin Books.

Jenkins, P. (1988). *Mrs. Thatcher's Revolution*. Cambridge, Mass.: Harvard
University Press.

Jenkins, S. (1995). *Accountable to None: The Tory Privatisation of Britain*.
London: Hamish Hamilton.

John, L.G. (1994). "The Fall of the Iron Lady, 1990." In J.S. Thompson and
W.C. Thompson, eds., *Thatcher: Prime Minister Indomitable*. 125–41. Boulder, Colo.: Westview Press.

Johnson, P. (2005). "Leaders and Revolutionaries: Margaret Thatcher." *Time
Magazine 100*, Special Edition.

Johnson, R.T. (1974). *Managing the White House: An Intimate Study of the
Presidency*. New York: Harper Row.

Junor, Penny. (1983). *Margaret Thatcher*. London: Sidgwick and Jackson.

Kaarbo, J. (1997). "Prime Minister Leadership Styles in Foreign Policy Decision-making: A Framework for Research." *Political Psychology*, 18: 553–81.

– and M. Hermann. (1998). "Leadership Styles of Prime Ministers: How Individual Differences Affect the Foreign Policymaking Process." *Leadership
Quarterly*, 9: 131–52.

Kammeyer, K. (1967). "Sibling Position and the Feminine Role." *Journal of
Marriage and the Family*, 20: 494–9.

Kavanagh, D. (1990). *Thatcherism and British Politics: The End of Consensus*.
London: Oxford University Press.

Klein, M. (1975). *Envy and Gratitude and Other Works 1946–1963*. London:
Hogarth Press.

Kidwai, A. (1996). *Indira Gandhi: Charisma and Crisis*. New Delhi: Siddhi
Books.

King, A., ed. (1986). *The British Prime Minister*. London: Macmillan.

Kowert, P.A. (1996). "Where *Does* the Buck Stop? Assessing the Impact of
Presidential Personality." *Political Psychology*, 17: 421–52.

Laplante J., and J.B. Pontalis. (1973). *The Language of Psychoanalysis*. New
York: W.W. Norton.

Lebow, N. (1985). "Miscalculation in the South Atlantic: The Origins of the
Falkland War." In R. Jervis, R.N. Lebow, and J. Stein, eds. *Psychology and
Deterrence*. 89–124. Baltimore: Johns Hopkins University Press.

Lipset, S.M. (1994). "The Social Requisites of Democracy Revisited." *American Sociological Review*, 59: 1–22.

Little, G. (1988). *Strong Leadership: Thatcher, Reagan and an Eminent Person.* Melbourne: Oxford University Press.

Lucas, A.J. (1966). "She Stands Remarkably Alone." *New York Times Magazine*, 27 March.

Mahler, G. (1997). "Israel's New Electoral System: Effects on Policy and Politics." *Middle East Review of International Affairs*, 1, no. 2. Available online at http://meria.idc.ac.il/journal/1997/issue2/jv1n2a2.html

Mahler, M.S. (1972). "On the First Three Phases of the Separation-Individuation Process." *International Journal of Psychoanalysis*, 53: 333–8.

Malhotra, I. (1989). *Indira Gandhi: A Personal and Political Biography.* London: Hodder and Stoughton.

Manor, J., ed. (1994). *Nehru to the Nineties.* London: Hurst.

Manushi Collective. (1979–1980). "Our Alarming Silence: Women, Politics and the Recent Elections." *Manushi*, 4: 2–6, 76.

Martin, R.G. (1988). *Golda Meir: The Romantic Years.* New York: Charles Scribner's Sons.

Masani, Z. (1975). *Indira Gandhi.* New York: Thomas Y. Crowell.

McFadyean, M., and M. Renn. (1984). *Thatcher's Reign.* London: Chatto and Windus: Hogarth Press.

Medzini, M. (1990). *The Proud Jewess.* (In Hebrew.) Jerusalem: Edanim.

Meir, G. (1975). *My Life.* New York: G.P. Putnam's Sons.

Meir, M. (1983). *My Mother, Golda Meir.* New York: Arbor House.

Millburn, T.W. (1977). "The Q-sort and the Study of Political Personality." In M.G. Hermann, *The Psychological Examination of Political Leaders.* 131–46. New York: Free Press.

Millon, T. (1969). *Modern Psychopathology: A Biosocial Approach to Maladaptive Learning and Functioning.* Philadelphia: W.B. Saunders. (Reprinted 1985 by Waveland Press, Prospect Heights, Ill.)

– (1986). "Personality Prototypes and their Diagnostic Criteria." In T. Millon and G.L. Klerman, eds. *Contemporary Directions in Psychopathology: Toward the DSM–IV.* 671–712. New York: Guilford.

– (1986). "A Theoretical Derivation of Pathological Personalities." In T. Millon and G. L. Klerman, eds. *Contemporary Directions in Psychopathology: Toward the DSM–IV.* 639–69. New York: Guilford.

– (1990). *Toward a New Personology: An Evolutionary Model.* New York: Wiley.

– (1991). "Normality: What May We Learn From Evolutionary Theory?" In D. Offer and M. Sabshin, eds., *Diversity of Normal Behavior: Further Contributions to Normatology.* 356–404. New York: Basic Books.

– with C. Millon and R.D. Davis. (1994). *Millon Clinical Multiaxial Inventory – III.* Minneapolis: National Computer Systems.

– and G.S. Everly, Jr. (1985). *Personality and its Disorders: A Biosocial Learning Approach.* New York: Wiley.

– with L.G. Weiss, C.M. Millon, and R.D. Davis. (1994). *MIPS: Millon Index of Personality Styles Manual.* San Antonio, Tex: Psychological Corporation.

– with R.D. Davis. (1996). *Disorders of Personality: DSM – IV and Beyond.* New York: Wiley.

– and R.D. Davis. (2000). *Personality Disorders in Modern Life.* New York: Wiley.

Mohan, A. (1967). *Indira Gandhi.* New York: Hawthorne Books.

Moraes, D. (1980). *Mrs Gandhi.* Delhi: Vikas Publishing House.

Muller, W.C., W. Philipp, and P. Gerlich. (1993). "Prime Ministers and Cabinet Decision-Making Processes." In J. Blondel and F. Muller-Rommel, eds. *Governing Together.* 223–56. New York: St Martin's Press.

Murray, P. (1980). *Margaret Thatcher.* London: W.H. Allen.

Nagel, E. (1961). *The Structure of Science: Problems in the Logic of Scientific Explanation.* London: Routledge and Kegan Paul.

Nayar, K. (1975). *India After Nehru.* Delhi: Vidas.

Netanyahu, Binyamin and Iddo, eds. (1980). *Self-Portrait of a Hero: The Letters of Jonathan Netanyahu (1963–1976).* New York: Random House.

Nixon, R. (1983). *Leaders.* New York: Warner Books.

Noble, Iris. (1972). *Israel's Golda Meir: Pioneer to Prime Minister.* New York: Julian Messner.

Norman, D., ed. (1985). *Indira Gandhi: Letters to an American Friend 1950–1984.* London: Weidenfeld and Nicolson.

Ogden, C. (1990). *Maggie.* New York: Simon and Schuster.

Oldham, J.M., and L.B. Morris. (1990). *The Personality Self-Portrait.* New York: Bantam Books.

– (1995). *The New Personality Self-Portrait.* New York: Bantam Books.

Peres, S. (1995). *Battling for Peace: A Memoir.* New York: Random House.

Perlmutter, A. (1985). *Israel: The Partitioned State.* New York: Charles Scribner's Sons.

Pinker, S. (2002). *The Blank Slate: The Modern Denial of Human Nature.* New York: Viking.

Post, J. (1991). "Saddam Hussein of Iraq: A Political Psychology Profile." *Political Psychology,* 12: 279–90.

– ed. (2005). *The Psychological Assessment of Political Leaders.* Ann Arbor: University of Michigan Press.

Provizer, N. (2001). "In the Shadow of Washington: Golda Meir, Duty and the Call to Power." In Kevin Cope, ed. *George Washington in and as Culture.* New York: AMS Press.

Rabin, Y. (1979). *The Rabin Memoirs.* London: Weidenfeld and Nicholson.

Rabinovitch, A. (2004). *The Yom Kippur War: The Epic Encounter That Transformed the Middle East.* New York: Schocken Books.

Rawlinson, P. (1989). *A Price Too High.* London: Weidenfeld and Nicolson.

Renshon, S.A. (1994). "A Preliminary Assessment of the Clinton Presidency: Character, Leadership and Performance." *Political Psychology,* 15: 375–93.

– ed. (1995). *The Clinton Presidency: Campaigning, Governing and the Psychology of Leadership*. Boulder, Colo.: Westview Press.

– (1996). *High Hopes: The Clinton Presidency and the Politics of Ambition*. New York: New York University Press.

– (1996). *The Psychological Assessment of Presidential Candidates*. New York: New York University Press.

Richter, L. (1991). "Explaining Theories of Female Leadership in South and South-east Asia." *Pacific Affairs*, 63: 524–40.

Rubenzer, S., and T. Faschingbauer. (2004). *Personality, Character, and Leadership in the White House: Psychologists Assess the Presidents*. Washington, Potomac Books.

Sachar, H.M. (1976). *A History of Israel, Vol. I: From the Rise of Zionism to Our Time*. New York: Alfred A. Knopf.

– (1987). *A History of Israel, Vol. II: From the Aftermath of the Yom Kippur War*. New York: Oxford University Press.

Safran, N. (1978). *Israel: The Embattled Ally*. Cambridge: Belknap Press of Harvard University Press.

Sahgal, N. (1978). *Indira Gandhi: Her Road to Power*. New York: Frederick Ungar.

Shah Commission of Inquiry: Interim Report I, II. Third and Final Report, Vols. I–III. (1978). Ministry of Information and Broadcasting, New Delhi.

Simonton, D.K. (1986). "Presidential Personality: Biographical Use of Gough Adjective Check List." *Journal of Personality and Social Psychology*, 51:149–60.

– (1988). "Presidential Style: Biography, Personality and Performance." *Journal of Personality and Social Psychology*, 55: 928–36.

– (1990). "Personality and Politics." In L.A. Pervin, ed. *Handbook of Personality: Theory and Research*, 670–92. New York: Guilford.

Sisson, R., and L.E. Rose. (1990). *War and Succession: Pakistan, India, and the Creation of Pakistan*. Berkeley: University of California Press.

Smith, G. (1991). *Reagan and Thatcher*. New York: W.W. Norton.

Stein, K.W. (1999). *Heroic Diplomacy: Sadat, Kissinger, Carter, Begin and the Quest for Arab-Israeli Peace*. New York: Routledge.

Steinberg, B. (1996). *Shame and Humiliation: Presidential Decision Making in Vietnam*. Montreal and Pittsburgh: McGill-Queen's University Press and Pittsburgh University Press.

– (2001). "The Making of Female Presidents and Prime Ministers: The Impact of Birth Order, Sex of Siblings and Father-Daughter Dynamics." *Political Psychology*, 22, no. 1: 89–110.

– (2005). "Indira Gandhi: The Relationship between Personality Profile and Leadership Style." *Political Psychology*, 26, no. 5: 755–89.

– and S. Kotsovilis and J. Osweiler. (2005). "Leadership Style Inventory." In Steinberg, "Indira Gandhi: The Relationship between Personality Profile and Leadership Style." *Political Psychology*, 26, no. 5: 755–89.

Stern, D.N. (1985). *The Interpersonal World of the Infant: A View from Psychoanalysis and Developmental Psychology*. New York: Basic Books.

Stoessinger, J. (1990). *Why Nations Go to War*. New York: St Martin's.

Strack, S. (1997). "The PACL: Gauging Normal Personality Styles." In T. Millon, ed. *The Millon Inventories: Clinical and Personality Assessment*. 477–97. New York: Guilford.

Suedfeld, P., and P.E. Tetlock. (1977). "Integrative Complexity of Communications in International Crises." *Journal of Conflict Resolution*, 21: 169–84.

Syrkin, M. (1969). *Golda Meir: Israel's Leader*. New York: G.P. Putnam's Sons.

Tetlock, P.E. (1985). "Integrative Complexity of American and Soviet Foreign Policy Rhetoric: A Time-Series Analysis." *Journal of Personality and Social Psychology*, 49: 1565–85.

Thatcher, C. (1996). *Below the Parapet: The Biography of Denis Thatcher*. London: HarperCollins.

Thatcher, M. (1993). *The Path to Power*. London: HarperCollins.

– (1995). *The Downing Street Years*. London: HarperCollins.

Thatcher Foundation. http://www.MargaretThatcher.org

Thompson, S. (1993). "Golda Meir: A Very Public Life." In M. Genovese, ed. *Women as National Leaders*. 135–60. Newbury Park, Calif.: Sage Publications.

The *Times*. 10 May 1978.

Vasudev, U. (1974). *Indira Gandhi: Revolution in Restraint*. Delhi: Vikas Publishing House.

Viorst, M. (1987). *The Sands of Sorrow: Israel's Journey from Independence*. New York: Harper and Row.

Volkan, V., and N. Itzkowitz. (1984). *The Immortal Ataturk: A Psychobiography*. Chicago: University of Chicago Press.

Walker, S.G. (1977). "The Interface between Beliefs and Behavior: Henry Kissinger's Operational Code and the Vietnam War. *Journal of Conflict Resolution*, 21: 120–68.

– (1983). "The Motivational Foundations of Political Belief Systems: A Reanalysis of the Operational Code Construct." *International Studies Quarterly*, 27: 179–202.

– and L. Falkowski. (1984). "The Operational Codes of U.S. Presidents and Secretaries of State: Motivational Foundations and Behavioral Consequences." *Political Psychology*, 5: 237–65.

– and M. Schafer and M.D. Young. (2003). "Profiling the Operational Codes of Political Leaders." In Jerold Post, ed., *The Psychological Assessment of Political Leaders: With Profiles of Saddam Hussein and Bill Clinton*. 215–45. Ann Arbor: University of Michigan Press.

Watkins, A. (1991). *A Conservative Coup: The Fall of Margaret Thatcher*. London: Duckworth.

Webster, W. (1990). *Not a Man to Match Her: The Marketing of a Prime Minister*. London: Women's Press.

Weller, P. (1985). *First among Equals.* Sydney: George Allen and Unwin.

Winnicott, D.W. (1957). *Mother and Child. A Primer of First Relationships.* New York: Basic Books.

– (1965). *The Maturational Process and the Facilitating Environment.* New York: International Universities Press.

Winter, D. (1973). *The Power Motive.* New York: Free Press.

– (1980). "An Exploratory Study of the Motives of Southern African Political Leaders Measured at a Distance." *Psychology,* 2: 75–85.

– (1987). "Leader Appeal, Leader Performance, and the Motive Profiles of Leaders and Followers: A Study of American Presidents and Elections." *Journal of Personality and Social Psychology,* 52: 196–202.

– (1988). "The Power Motive in Women – and Men." *Journal of Personality and Social Psychology,* 54: 510–19.

– (1992). "Personality and Foreign Policy: Historical Overview of Research." In E. Singer and V. Hudson, eds., *Political Psychology and Foreign Policy.* Boulder, Colo.: Westview Press.

– (1995). "Presidential Psychology and Governing Styles: A Comparative Psychological Analysis of the 1992 Presidential Candidates." In S.A. Renshon, ed. *The Clinton Presidency: Campaigning, Governing and the Psychology of Leadership.* 113–34. Boulder, Colo.: Westview Press.

– and A.J. Stewart. (1995). "Commentary: Tending the Garden of Personality." *Journal of Personality,* 63: 711–27.

– and N.B. Barenbaum. (1985). "Responsibility and the Power Motive in Women and Men." *Journal of Personality,* 53: 335–55.

Wolpert, S. (1977). *A New History of India.* New York: Oxford University Press.

Young, H. (1990). *The Iron Lady: A Biography of Margaret Thatcher.* New York: Noonday Press, Farrar, Straus and Giroux.

– and A. Sloman. (1986). *The Thatcher Phenomenon.* London: British Broadcasting Corporation.

Index

DATE			